高等学校"十一五"规划教材·科技英语系列

新编科技英语阅读教程

主 编 范莹芳

副主编 杨 琪 杨振华

哈尔滨工业大学出版社

内 容 简 介

本书主要是为大学本科高年级学生及研究生编写的,是与《科技英语翻译教程》和《科技英语写作教程》相配套的教材。本书侧重于提高读者的英语语言能力,内容丰富,信息前沿,语言地道。本书所选文章分精读和泛读两类,难度适中,实用性较强。每个单元均设计了练习题,针对性较强。本书可作为理工科本科高年级学生及研究生教材,也可供英语爱好者作为英语科普读物使用。

图书在版编目(CIP)数据

新编科技英语阅读教程/范莹芳主编. —哈尔滨:哈尔滨工业大学出版社,2011.10
全国高等学校"十一五"规划教材·科技英语系列
ISBN 978-7-5603-3005-1

Ⅰ.①新… Ⅱ.①范… Ⅲ.①科学技术-英语-阅读教学-高等学校-教材 Ⅳ.①H319.4

中国版本图书馆 CIP 数据核字(2010)第 066453 号

责任编辑	郝庆多
封面设计	张孝东
出版发行	哈尔滨工业大学出版社
社　　址	哈尔滨市南岗区复华四道街10号 邮编150006
传　　真	0451-86414749
网　　址	http://hitpress.hit.edu.cn
印　　刷	哈尔滨工业大学印刷厂
开　　本	787mm×960mm 1/16 印张18 字数417.6千字
版　　次	2011年10月第1版 2011年10月第1次印刷
书　　号	ISBN 978-7-5603-3005-1
定　　价	30.00元

(如因印装质量问题影响阅读,我社负责调换)

前　言

科技英语作为一种实用英语文体形式，用于定义现象、阐释理论、描述过程等。为了准确客观地传递信息，科技文献往往要运用结构复杂、修饰繁多，甚至有些晦涩难懂的长句来表达事理现象的逻辑关系，这给读者的阅读和理解带来诸多困难。

根据多年对本科生和研究生的教学反馈情况，针对阅读障碍问题，我们结合多年的教学与研究实践，收集和整理了32篇不同类型的科普文章，从不同的侧面反映了当今科技发展的现状和趋势，同时展现了科技英语自身的语言特点。

本书所选内容丰富，难易兼顾，共分16个单元，内容均选自互联网上的科普文章，涉及能源、环境保护、互联网、生物、计算机、农业、基因工程、气候、地理等领域。每个单元包含两个内容相关联的篇章，每个篇章后设有一般词汇与科技术语解释以及与课文相关的练习等，并在全书的最后提供了练习的参考答案，以便读者使用。

本书具有以下特点：

题材新颖，时代性强：收录了热门科技领域的最新报道。

难度适中：每单元收录A、B两篇文章，分别适合精读和泛读，方便老师和学生根据实际教学情况灵活选用。

练习形式多样：包括阅读理解、简答、选词填空以及语义解释等，帮助学生了解科普文章的特点和相关知识。

读、译相结合：每个单元后都选取了同本单元主题一致或相近的篇章、长句练习以帮助学生提高翻译技能，并更好地熟悉和掌握科技文体的英汉转化过程。

本书编写中吸收了最新的科技研究成果，参考和引用了有关论著、文章及其他文字资料，文中未能一一注明，在此向有关作者表示感谢。由于编写时间较为仓促，如有遗漏或不当之处，敬请同行专家及广大读者随时提出宝贵意见。

编　者
2010年5月

目 录

Unit 1　Cybersecurity ·· 1

　　Text A　BioVault Locks Up Biometrics ·· 1
　　Text B　New Chip Brings Military Security to Commercial Processors [Abridged] ········· 9

Unit 2　Science Mystery ··· 17

　　Text A　The Great Ketchup Mystery ·· 17
　　Text B　The Mystery of the Bermuda Triangle ··· 26

Unit 3　Biometrics ·· 32

　　Text A　How will Increasingly Sophisticated Biometric Technologies Affect You? ········ 32
　　Text B　Financial Institutions Evaluate Biometrics ···································· 39

Unit 4　Psychology ··· 46

　　Text A　Gene plus Stress Equals Depression Debate ·································· 46
　　Text B　Work: Kindness and Corporation ··· 54

Unit 5　Energy ·· 60

　　Text A　Nuclear Fusion: Energy for the Future? ······································ 60
　　Text B　Energy Independence and Climate Change: Linked But Separate ········ 69

Unit 6　Ecology ··· 76

　　Text A　Extinction Crisis Looms in Oceania ·· 76
　　Text B　Bio-Invaders ··· 86

Unit 7　Agriculture ··· 96

　　Text A　Optimistic Future for Agriculture Predicted ·································· 96
　　Text B　Sustainable Agriculture: Perennial Plants Produce More; Landscape Diversity
　　　　　　Creates Habitat for Pest Enemies ··· 106

Unit 8　Arctic and Antarctic ·· 112

　　Text A　The Last Unexplored Place on Earth(Extracted) ························· 112
　　Text B　Arctic Land Grabs could cause Eco-Disaster ······························ 122

Unit 9	**Endangered Species**	130
Text A	Willdife Conservation 2.0	130
Text B	10 Studies that Revealed the Great Global Amphibian Die-Off-and Some Possible Solutions	140

Unit 10	**Genetic Engineering**	147
Text A	Evolution by Intelligent Design	147
Text B	Building Better Humans	156

Unit 11	**Disease and Treatment**	164
Text A	Mosquito and Cucumber Salad Anyone?	164
Text B	Is Hypnosis Moving Closer to Mainstream Medicine?	174

Unit 12	**Nuclear Power**	180
Text A	Oil Is Out; Is Nuclear In?	180
Text B	The Necessity of Nuclear Power	190

Unit 13	**Material Science**	196
Text A	The Kilogram Isn't What It Used to Be—It's Lighter	196
Text B	How to Build an Invisibility Cloak	207

Unit 14	**Mars**	214
Text A	Terraforming Mars	214
Text B	The Truth about Water on Mars: 5 New Findings	225

Unit 15	**Space Travel**	231
Text A	Russia's Dark Horse Plan to Get to Mars	231
Text B	Solar Sailing	241

Unit 16	**Mind and Brain**	248
Text A	The Big Similarities and Quirky Differences between Our Left and Right Brains	248
Text B	Is Patriotism a Subconscious Way for Humans to Avoid Disease?	258

Keys to Exercises 266

Unit 1   Cybersecurity

Text A

BioVault Locks Up Biometrics

1. If a user, a web customer say, wishes to send a message or other data to another user, an online shop, over an unsecured network, the message must be encrypted to avoid interception of sensitive information such as passwords and credit card information.

2. Encryption relies on authentication being symmetric to work. In other words, the user's password or PIN must match the password or PIN stored by the online shop to lock and unlock the data. This is because encryption systems use the password or PIN to produce, or seed, a random number that is used as the cipher for encrypting the data. If the passwords do not match exactly then the seed will be incorrect, the random number different and the decryption will fail.

3. One way to avoid users having to remember endless, complicated passwords is to use biometrics, including fingerprints, iris pattern, face recognition. However, biometrics is not a symmetric process. The initial recording of biometric data samples only a limited amount of the information, the pigment pattern in one's iris, for instance. The unlocking process then compares the iris pattern, or other biometric "token", being presented for access with the sample stored in the database. If the match is close enough, the user can gain entry.

4. The reason for this asymmetry is that any biometric system takes only a digital sample of data from the fingerprint or iris, for instance. Moreover, even the legitimate user will not be able to present exactly the same biometric data repeatedly. The close enough aspect of biometrics does not make biometrics insecure, provided that the closeness is very precise, but it does mean that biometric tokens cannot be used to create a secret key for an encryption algorithm.

5. Bobby Tait and Basie von Solms of the University of Johannesburg, Gauteng, South Africa, explain how biometrics can nevertheless be used to make a consistent secret key for encryption.

6. In conventional encryption, if Alice wishes to send a secret message to Bill, then she must encrypt the message, whether it is an email or credit card details transmitted from her computer to the online shop. In order for the encryption algorithm to provide cipher text that is random, a secret key must be

provided. Alice and Bill must share exact copies of their secret key for this to work.

7. Aside from the asymmetry in biometrics, this approach will not work because Alice and Bill cannot provide the same biometric token to encrypt and decrypt the message. Now, Tait and von Solms have used the so-called BioVault infrastructure to provide a safe and secure way for Alice and Bill to share biometric tokens and so use their fingerprints, iris pattern, or other biometric to encrypt and decrypt their data without their biometrics being intercepted.

8. The BioVault encryption system works as follows:

9. In phase 1, Alice identifies herself to the authentication server, and indicates that she wants to send an encrypted message to Bill and requests Bill's biometric key from the server.

10. In phase 2, the server retrieves a random biometric key from Bill's stored biometric keys.

11. In phase 3, Alice uses the biometric key to encrypt her message and sends it to Bill.

12. In phase 4, Bill receives the message sent by Alice, and decrypts the message by testing the biometric keys in his database against the received cipher text.

13. The fact that each biometric key (data) is unique means that the BioVault system can irrevocably identify and authenticate users through their biometric keys (data) and detect fraudulent use of biometric keys.

14. Tait adds that the same approach could also be used to digitally sign electronic documents, files, or software executables using biometrics. He will be presenting the team's results on this aspect of their work in the UK at the beginning of September. "If passwords or tokens are used for authentication, only the password or token is proven as authentic—not the user that supplied the token or password," he explains. "Biometrics authenticates the user directly—this was one of the drivers behind the BioVault development."

(http://www.sciencedaily.com/releases/2009/07/090731085817.htm)

Glossary

biometrics [baiəu'metriks] a branch of biology that studies biological phenomena and observations by means of statistical analysis *n*. 生物测定学

encrypt [in'kript] convert ordinary language into code *v*. 加密

interception [intə(:)'sepʃən] the act of intercepting; preventing something from proceeding or arriving *n*. 截击,截取,截住,截断,拦截,窃听

authentication [ɔ:θenti'keiʃən] validating the authenticity of something or someone *n*. 证明,鉴定

symmetric [si'metrik] having similarity in size, shape, and relative position of corresponding parts *adj*. 对称的

cipher ['saifə] a message written in a secret code *n*. 暗号

iris ['aiəris] muscular diaphragm that controls the size of the pupil; it forms the colored portion of the eye *n*. 虹膜

token ['təukən] an individual instance of a type of symbol *n*. 表征,记号

asymmetry [æ'simətri] a lack of symmetry *n*. 不对称

insecure [insi'kjuə] lacking in security or safety *adj*. 不安全的

algorithm ['ælgəriðəm] a precise rule (or set of rules) specifying how to solve some problems *n*. 算法

decrypt [di:'kript] convert code into ordinary language *v*. 译,解释

infrastructure ['infrə'strʌktʃə] the basic structure or features of a system or organization *n*. 基础结构,基础设施

retrieve [ri'tri:v] get or find back; recover the use of *v*. 取回

irrevocably [i'revəkəbli] in a way incapable of being retracted or revoked *adv*. 不能取消地

fraudulent ['frɔ:djulənt] intended to deceive *adj*. 欺诈的,不正的,不诚实的

Exercises

A. Fill in each blank with one of the given words in its correct form.

| retrieve | identify | legitimate | consistent | token |
| insecure | fraudulent | irrevocable | decrypt | infrastructure |

1. In the wild, New Caledonian crows use a range of tool types for extracting invertebrate prey from holes and crevices, and in captivity, they have been shown to make, or select, tools to _____ food rewards.

2. The result is that the resource, whether it is a website, an email server, or a database, cannot respond to _____ traffic in a timely manner and so essentially becomes unavailable to users.

3. The study, authored by a professor at the Rotman School of Management at the University of Toronto and his collaborator at Northwestern University, calls such individuals "_____ contributors", people who contribute all the time, regardless of others' choices.

4. At any given time, as many as 18 percent of those surveyed felt _____ about their jobs. But only about 5 percent of respondents in the first survey and 3 percent of respondents in the second survey reported feeling anxious about their jobs both times they were interviewed.

5. The agencies are also advising operators of offending web sites that they must take prompt action to correct and/or remove promotions of these _____ products or face enforcement action.

6. A number of prominent politicians, including Sen. Edward Kennedy, who wrote a foreword for her earlier book on school _____, strongly support efforts to fund much-needed school repairs, remodeling and rebuilding.

7. For instance, during a concert, when the sound of the crowd mixes with several instruments, our brain

can still _____ the specific notes played by the trumpet, the violin or any other instrument in the orchestra.
8. In one study, a control group asked to do a favor without compensation was significantly more willing to help move a sofa than those offered a _____ payment.
9. Cancer is primarily caused by _____ alterations to genes, called mutations.
10. Modern cryptography relies on the use of digital "keys" to encrypt data before sending it over a network, and to _____ it at the other end.

B. Skim the text and then answer the following questions.
1. What is BioVault?
2. Why must message be encrypted if a person wants to send message to another over an unsecured network?
3. Why is biometric system asymmetric?
4. Is it possible for two persons to share biometric tokens to encrypt and decrypt their data without their biometrics being intercepted?
5. What can be used to ensure cybersecurity?

C. Read the text and choose the correct answer to each of the following questions.
1. Which feature of authentication does encryption rely on? _____.
   A. The user's PIN matching that stored to lock or unlock data
   B. The user's PIN changing dynamically
   C. The authentication being asymmetric to work
   D. The user's PIN matching the password of the computer
2. One way to avoid users having to remember endless, complicated passwords is to use the following except _____.
   A. fingerprints   B. iris pattern   C. hand recognition   D. face recognition
3. In order for the encryption algorithm to provide cipher text that is random, _____ must be provided.
   A. a secret key   B. biometric token   C. a secret message   D. a password
4. The fact that each biometric key (data) is unique means that the BioVault system can _____.
   A. revocably identify users   B. irrevocably authenticate users
   C. detect fraudulent use of passwords   D. detect biometric keys
5. Biometrics cannot help people to _____.
   A. use fingerprints to encrypt and decrypt data
   B. digitally sign electronic documents
   C. log in with incorrect password

D. authenticate users directly

D. Explain the underlined parts.

1. If a user, a web customer say, wishes to send a message or other data to another user, an online shop, <u>over an unsecured network, the message must be encrypted to avoid interception of sensitive information</u> such as passwords and credit card information.
2. Encryption relies on <u>authentication being symmetric</u> to work.
3. However, biometrics is not a symmetric process. <u>The initial recording of biometric data samples only a limited amount of the information,</u> the pigment patter in one's iris, for instance.
4. The close enough aspect of biometrics does not make biometrics insecure, <u>provided that the closeness is very precise, but it does mean that biometric tokens cannot be used to create a secret key for an encryption algorithm.</u>
5. Bobby Tait and Basie von Solms of the University of Johannesburg, Gauteng, South Africa, <u>explain how biometrics can nevertheless be used to make a consistent secret key for encryption.</u>
6. <u>Aside from the asymmetry in biometrics,</u> this approach will not work because Alice and Bill cannot provide the same biometric token to encrypt and decrypt the message.
7. The fact that each biometric key (data) is unique means that the BioVault system can <u>irrevocably identify and authenticate users through their biometric keys (data) and detect fraudulent use of biometric keys.</u>
8. Alice <u>identifies herself to the authentication server,</u> and indicates that she wants to send an encrypted message to Bill and <u>requests Bill's biometric key from the server.</u>
9. Bill receives the message sent by Alice, and <u>decrypts the message by testing the biometric keys in his database against the received cipher text.</u>
10. "Biometrics authenticates the user directly—<u>this was one of the drivers behind the BioVault development.</u>"

E. Read the passages in this section and decide whether each of the following statements is true or false.

Passage One

Ethical hacking is a white hat technique, wherein the hacker breaches the security of a computer system or the network, to expose the security systems vulnerability. A career in ethical hacking, as a consultant, has bright prospects considering the dependence of the entire world on computer technology, and easy access to world wide web.

What is Ethical Hacking?

In ethical hacking, the hacker identifies the weakness in the system, but instead of taking advantage of the situation, alerts the owner, so that the later can fix the problem and make his system secured. The ethical hacker can convey the message to the owner by various means ranging from a simple phone call to leaving an electronic card in the system, as an obvious signal that the system was breached. Ethical hackers use the same tools as hackers do, but they are not a threat to the system. Some people do ethical hacking as a hobby, while some pursue it as their career.

Basic Requirements to Become an Ethical Hacker

The ethical hacker has to posses excellent programming and networking skills, as well as good working knowledge of various operating systems. All these skills should be backed up with the knowledge of necessary hardware and software. More importantly a certified ethical hacking or cyber security course is the basic requirement to become an ethical hacker. Ethical hacking is not a process which can be executed with a snap of the finger, being patient is the important key, especially in ethical hacking for beginners. In some cases, you may have to monitor the system for days or weeks to get a single opportunity to hit the jackpot.

(http://www.buzzle.com/articles/ethical-hacking-for-beginners.html)

_____ 1. In ethical hacking, the hacker identifies the weakness in the system, and takes advantage of the situation.

_____ 2. Ethical hackers and hackers use different tools.

_____ 3. Ethical hacking is not an easy process, and being patient is the important key, especially in ethical hacking for beginners.

Passage Two

We live in an Internet age. Socializing is extremely easy today. Communicating to people around the world is a matter of a few clicks on the Internet. The Internet has facilitated an easy access to information across the globe, thus making life easy. However, if you look at this Internet age from a different point of view, you will realize that it has in fact bred many illegal and unethical practices. While some use the Internet for gaining information, others use it for destruction of sensitive data. While some use the web as a communication platform, others derive pleasure from intruding in the Internet privacy of individuals and seek enjoyment from breaching Internet security. Cyber-bullying is one such activity that this section of Internet users indulge in. Let us find more about this unethical Internet practice, cyber bullying.

Cyber Bullying—An Introduction

Cyber bullying is the act of threatening, harassing or humiliating a person through use of Internet or any other digital interactive media. Targeting a person by means of emails, text messages or online postings is also referred to as cyber bullying. Teens are often seen falling prey to online bullying practices. Some of them might indulge in practices like sending online messages to cell phones with intention to hurt or embarrass the receiver.

Cyber bullying is not just associated with children and youngsters. It is also observed in adults and is referred to as cyberharassment. Cyber bullying practices range from simple activities like continuously bombarding someone with emails right up to sexual abuse by means of the Internet. Passing abusive remarks about someone, making him/her a subject of ridicule in online forums and spreading gossip or rumors about him/her are also classified under the category of cyber bullying practices.

Cyber bullying is of two types, namely direct or through a proxy. Direct attacks often involve the use of instant messengers and emails to humiliate individuals. Sending vulgar photographs through emails or uploading them on blogs and social networking sites is a form cyber bullying through direct attacks. Sending junk mails or spams and spreading malicious code by means of emails are some other examples of direct cyber bullying. When cyber bullying practices take place without the knowledge of the person being used as a bully, it is said to take place through a proxy. At times, warnings and "click here" messages can be deceptive. They may be programmed to send wrong information to the Internet service providers, thereby resulting in a legal action against the user clicking on these warnings or messages. In cyber bullying through a proxy, the cyber bullies victimize benign users by committing Internet crimes in their name.

(www.buzzle.com/articles/cyber-bullying.html)

_____ 4. Cyber-bullying is an activity in which people can derive pleasure from intruding in the Internet privacy of individuals and seek enjoyment from breaching Internet security.

_____ 5. Targeting a person by means of emails, text messages or online postings is not cyber-bullying.

_____ 6. Sending vulgar photographs through emails or uploading them on blogs and social networking sites is a direct form of cyber bullying.

Passage Three

Spyware is a hidden software program. It is often used to monitor the browsing and shopping habits of computer users. Spyware can also be a remote control program that steals confidential banking and personal information.

Spyware has quickly become the most prominent internet security problem. According to the National Cyber Security Alliance, spyware infects more than 90% of home PCs. Recent survey shows that spyware is also sneaking into the network of corporate computers.

Spyware is often coupled with free downloads, such as free music, game and software downloads. Spyware may slow down computer, hijack homepage and create uncontrolled pop-up advertisements. Some spyware programs can remain unnoticed, secretly gathering information from the computer. Once installed, spyware is difficult to remove without the help of dedicated antispyware software.

Due to the rise of spyware activity, antispyware software are in great demand these days. But are these spyware removal tools the same? Do they provide what the security consumers need?

There are many reports that some antispyware programs installed their own spyware and adware to the computer. One consumer was quoted saying: "It's a rip-off. I downloaded the free trial of an antispyware program, only to find out that it added its own adware to my computer." Other consumers have complained that the antispyware program they use cannot detect all spyware programs. Some even slow down the computer and create pop-up advertisements.

There are a few good antispyware programs in the market today. On the other hand, dozens of spyware removal programs are blacklisted by consumers. Beware of spyware removal tools that are heavily promoted by e-mail campaigns. Never run any free downloads and free scans from unknown software publishers. Their programs may as well be spyware programs themselves. Read independent product reviews from renowned computer magazines or reputable sources. Spending some extra time in research can save you a lot of hassles in the long run.

(http://www.buzzle.com/editorials/6-1-2006-97948.asp)

_____ 7. According to the National Cyber Security Alliance, spyware infects 90% of home PCs.

_____ 8. Download free music or free game may create uncontrolled pop-up advertisements.

_____ 9. Antispyware does not introduce adware or slow down the computer.

_____ 10. Dozens of spyware removal programs are blacklisted by organizations.

F. Cloze. Fill in each blank with one suitable word.

Hackers have developed increasingly __1__ means of tampering with the Web, including __2__ or pirating critical software applications in both public and private sectors of business. Traditional security measures have protected software only by using __3__ activities such as encrypting files or hiding programs behind firewalls and security perimeters. The problem with passive approaches is that they provide just a single defense layer that experienced hackers can __4__ of quickly, leaving applications with no protection once that security level is __5__.

The Internet obviously has opened up new markets and business opportunities, but it has also provided for the rapid dissemination of malware, different types of viruses, and compromised applications that can bring business to a __6__. With companies increasing global distributions and online sales, and increasing numbers of businesses conducting operations online, the risk to transactions and software is growing __7__. __8__ the perimeter of a network, application, or system is no longer sufficient in today's distributed computing environment. To safeguard their __9__ property, companies need to adopt new approaches that __10__ security directly into software and data.

1. A. sophisticated   B. complex   C. compound   D. delicate
2. A. defecting   B. infecting   C. affecting   D. effecting
3. A. passive   B. active   C. positive   D. negative
4. A. remove   B. displace   C. dispose   D. destroy

5. A. broken   B. exceeded   C. retained   D. breached
6. A. halt   B. stop   C. termination   D. setback
7. A. slightly   B. gradually   C. exponentially D. suddenly
8. A. Securing   B. Sustaining   C. Overcoming   D. Maintaining
9. A. intellect   B. intellectual C. intelligent   D. intellective
10. A. involve   B. engage   C. integrate   D. unite

G. Translate the following passages into Chinese/English.

1. SearchWiki is a tough sell because most of us are already trained to surf the Web quickly, skipping ahead and back through links without taking the time to rank those results or comment on them. And it only works with Google searches. If you like the idea of more personalized Web searches but would like to use other search engines or don't want to do extra work, you might like Surf Canyon. Once downloaded, this tool displays bull's-eyes beside certain results to show that Surf Canyon has found additional related hits. Clicking on this bull's-eye reveals those suggested links, pulled from deeper down in the search results, and these links might have bull's-eyes of their own. This cascade of data goes on and on as an algorithm studies which of the returned results you do or don't choose.

2. Surf Canyon 最近针对那些希望长期享受个性化服务的用户推出了一款软件包,在 my. surfcanyon.com 上可以查到。借助它,用户可以挑选出一些喜欢的网站并从中接收新闻、购物、研究或体育和娱乐搜索结果。用户还可以在这个网页的可用网址名单上加入没有列入其中的自己喜欢的网址;同样也可以将不喜欢的网址加入黑名单,这样就不会有来自此类网站的搜索结果了。跟谷歌不同,Surf Canyon 不会保存你的历史记录或搜索偏好。如果你没有使用上述提及的那个链接建立起个人偏好记录,它就会完全依据你的即时操作——比如当你优先选择了某个而不是另一个链接时——作出反应。

Text B

New Chip Brings Military Security to Commercial Processors [Abridged]

1. Last week, a spot check of electric grid systems revealed that hackers had infiltrated the U.S. electric grid. The government inspections, motivated by a 2007 Idaho National Laboratory demonstration of the vulnerabilities of the U.S. grid, revealed more than the inspectors had bargained for: The invaders had left behind potentially disruptive malware. The increasing threat from better-financed hackers, the growing need to build security into a chip at the start of the chip-design process (rather than as an afterthought), and the blurring line between military and civilian targets have been at the center of many

U.S. Department of Defense concerns. The mounting hysteria has led the government to pour millions into the problem, and on 1 April, Congress introduced a bill that would let the president declare a "cybersecurity emergency", shutting down Web traffic to compromised infrastructure such as the power grid.

2. But the answer could be found in something decidedly less grandiose: Last month, Pleasanton, Calif. based CPU Tech introduced into the commercial market a secure processor that had previously been available only for military systems. The Acalis CPU872 is the first microprocessor born of new methods the Pentagon learned from its hunt for secret kill switches in the commercial chips the agency buys. But beyond just defense contractors, CPU Tech is targeting commercial users of PowerPC processors at big firms and agencies including those responsible for securing public infrastructure, such as electric power generators and subway systems.

3. CPU Tech vice president Pat Hays says the Acalis CPU872 has three features that other secure processors don't: First, instead of being integrated on the same board with the processor or functioning as a coprocessor like a graphics-processing unit, the Acalis puts the security muscle in the same chip with the processor. Second, each chip is manufactured at a trusted foundry certified by the U.S. Department of Defense. Finally, the security key —the "secret handshake" that secure chips create to make sure trusted sources can gain access and other sources can't—is generated on the chip in a way that thwarts two of the most common attacks on secure systems.

4. "We made sure a chip would be protected from people like us," says Hays, referring to CPU Tech's other business—reverse-engineering chips for military contractors. As a subcontractor on Trust in Integrated Circuits, a program of the Defense Advanced Research Projects Agency (DARPA), CPU Tech gleaned knowledge that it applied to the design of the CPU872 processor. "Our work, in fact, laid the groundwork for TIIC," says CPU Tech founder Ed King.

5. By necessity, the U.S. military uses many commercial off-the-shelf chips manufactured outside the United States because of a shifting integrated-circuits industry. Security experts have written extensively about the risk this creates for the country's national security, as malicious hardware and software modifications can theoretically be introduced during the manufacturing process. But the line between military and civilian targets has blurred significantly in the United States as well as in other Western countries. Hacking into civilian infrastructure could lay the groundwork for organized, government-coordinated warfare. This goes beyond conspiracy theory: A September 2008 Idaho National Laboratory report found a link between the Russian attack on Georgia and a preceding wave of malicious cyberactivity, primarily distributed denial-of-service (DDoS) attacks. Even off-line structures are vulnerable to online sabotage. The same study established the alarming feasibility of gaining access remotely to electricity generators that are commonly thought to be immune to online threats.

6. Hays says the chip's onshore pedigree reduces the risk of Trojan horses being built into the hard-

ware during the manufacturing process. The 90-nanometer processor is fabricated at IBM's Fishkill, N. Y., foundry—a trusted foundry—which goes through an exhaustive vetting process to be deemed secure enough to manufacture the U.S. military's specialty chips, with security features built directly into the hardware.

7. But despite the built-in security, Hays, who was in Bell Labs' digital signal processing division in the 1980s, says the Acalis chip won't divulge its secrets, even if it's reverse-engineered down to the mask layer. This is to prevent physical scrutiny if a chip falls into the wrong hands. Military experts have speculated that billions of dollars in U.S. military R&D were compromised. CPU Tech anticipates a similar fate for the secure processors it releases into the commercial world. Buying or even stealing a server is much easier than bringing down a spy plane. "We understand the chip itself will find its way to an untrusted source through distribution channels," says Hays, so the chip was designed to be useless if it were to be physically reverse-engineered. Nothing can be gleaned from the hardware, which can be securely configured to work only in concert with CPU Tech's proprietary security software. "We'll be a lot more restrictive about handing out the software that makes it work," says Hays.

8. But reverse-engineering a physical chip is not the only way to break in or create countermeasures. To eavesdrop on communications or impersonate a genuine user, a malefactor needs only decipher the secret encryption key.

9. "Getting the key is the key, so to speak, to being able to generate encrypted data," says David Blaauw, an electrical engineering professor at the University of Michigan, in Ann Arbor.

10. The key is generated using the National Institute of Standards and Technology's Advanced Encryption Standard (AES) algorithm, certified by the National Security Agency. AES algebra is very secure. "But when the key comes out of its cave to do its job once in a while," says Hays, "that's when the key is most vulnerable." Another way of getting the key is a so-called DRAM attack, in which a malefactor freezes the dynamic RAM to ferret out where the key has been temporarily stored. Cooling the DRAM after shutting off a computer can prolong a well-known property of DRAM called remanence—during which the key temporarily remains in memory—for several minutes, giving attackers an ample window to get into the DRAM and extract the key. "Basic disk encryption is very vulnerable," says Hays. "Wherever you put the key, on a chip or in DRAM, the smart bad actor will find a way to get it."

11. The hardware and software of the Acalis chip, Hays says, makes both of these methods impossible for two reasons: For one, the key can be changed at will. The system allows the owner to change the key every day or during every session to guard against side channel attacks. "If you change the key often enough, by the time you figure out the key, it's already irrelevant," says Hays. "There would be no chance to find it in time."

12. Further, instead of depending on secrecy, the system merely ensures that there is no key to be

found. "Through a combination of hardware and software, we never actually store a key," explains Hays. "You obviously have to have something stored or some kind of index or value, but our system completely eliminates key storage."

13. How the chip uses a key without storing it is something CPU Tech executives are not willing to divulge. "Many of the details of our reverse-engineering prevention features are proprietary," says King, "but they include multiple methods of unique chip identification, on-chip memory, and on-chip sensors." Acalis has two CPUs on one chip that operate independently. One processor can run nontrusted code while raising a hardware firewall to isolate it from the second CPU. In this mode, the only communication between the two is through the equivalent of a mailbox built into the chip.

14. Though the company has withheld the details of its process, some security experts are skeptical. "They are addressing the right questions, but the things they are saying are not completely clear to me," says Blaauw.

15. Chris Tarnovsky thinks the idea is smoke and mirrors. The self-taught American engineer was catapulted into notoriety during a major piracy case last year, in which he was accused of reverse-engineering pay-TV security cards and posting the results online, thereby opening the door for hundreds of thousands of nonpaying individuals to get free pay TV. He was (mostly) exonerated and now runs Flylogic Engineering, which performs hardware and software security analysis. He says he has reverse-engineered enough government chips to be unimpressed by Acalis's military pedigree. "I doubt this chip is really that secure and is most likely obscurity mixed with security," he says.

16. Blaauw also has his doubts. "The idea of changing keys is good," he says. But it needs to be changed quickly, before the key is cracked, and that becomes expensive. "It's much more expensive to change a key in terms of resources that to use a key to decrypt or encrypt data, so you may not want to do it every session." Beyond that, it may be possible for a hacker with a good machine to decipher the key even with daily key changes. "We made an encryption engine that was hardware based," Blaauw says. "We cracked it in minutes."

17. As for the key storage trick, neither Blaauw nor Tarnovsky are convinced. "I don't see how," says Blaauw. "At some point in the encryption, you have to apply the bits of the key in the algorithm. If you didn't store it, how do you retrieve it? You could distribute the bits or scramble them, but they need to be stored somewhere in some form— I don't see an easy way around that."

18. But for now, CPU Tech isn't revealing more. "We're still trying to figure out the line between advertising what the chip can do and giving away the company store," Hays says.

19. If everything they have described is accurate, Blaauw says it would be hard to crack the CPU Tech chip. "It doesn't sound like the other approaches people have proposed," he concedes. "They may have something that we don't know about."

(http://www.spectrum.ieee.org/computing/hardware/new-chip-brings-military-security-to-commercial-processors)

Glossary

vendor ['vendɔ:] someone who promotes or exchanges goods or services for money *n*. 厂商,小贩,卖主

grid [grid] a system of high tension cables by which electrical power is distributed throughout a region *n*. 电网

infiltrate [in'filtreit] enter a group or organization in order to spy on the members *v*. 潜入

inspection [in'spekʃən] a formal or official examination *n*. 检查,视察

vulnerability [vʌlnərə'biləti] susceptibility to injury or attack *n*. 漏洞(计算机)

disruptive [dis'rʌptiv] characterized by unrest or disorder or insubordination *adj*. 捣乱的,破坏性的,制造混乱的

malware ['mælwɛə] malicious software *n*. 恶意软件

hysteria [his'tiəriə] state of violent mental agitation *n*. 歇斯底里,不正常的兴奋

grandiose ['grændiəus] impressive because of unnecessary largeness or grandeur; used to show disapproval *adj*. 宏伟的,宏大的,堂皇的

foundry ['faundri] factory where metal castings are produced *n*. 铸造场

thwart [θwɔ:t] hinder or prevent (the efforts, plans, or desires) of *v*. 反对,阻碍

subcontractor [sʌbkən'træktə(r)] someone who enters into a subcontract with the primary contractor *n*. 转包商,次承包商

glean [gli:n] gather, as of natural products *v*. 收集

malicious [mə'liʃəs] intended to harm or upset other people *adj*. 怀有恶意的,恶毒的

sabotage ['sæbətɑ:ʒ] destroy property or hinder normal operations *v*. 从事破坏活动,妨害,破坏

pedigree ['pedigri:] the descendants of one individual *n*. 家谱

fabricate ['fæbrikeit] put together out of components or parts *v*. 制造,建造,装配

divulge [dai'vʌldʒ] make known to the public information that was previously known only to a few people or that was meant to be kept a secret *v*. 泄露,暴露

scrutiny ['skru:tini] the act of examining something closely (as for mistakes) *n*. 研究(推敲)

impersonate [im'pə:səneit] assume or act the character of *v*. 模仿,扮演

algebra ['ældʒibrə] the mathematics of generalized arithmetical operations *n*. 代数学

ferret ['ferit] search and discover through persistent investigation *v*. 搜出

skeptical ['skeptikəl] marked by or given to doubt *adj*. 怀疑的

catapult ['kætəpʌlt] shoot forth or launch, as if from a catapult *v*. 发射

notoriety [nəutə'raiəti] the state of being known for some unfavorable act or quality *n*. 恶名,声名狼籍

exonerate [ig'zɔnəreit] pronounce not guilty of criminal charges *vt*. 使免罪

Exercises

A. Fill in each blank with one of the given words in its correct form.

| grandiose | grid | vulnerability | disruptive | inspection |
| malicious | sabotage | hysteria | infiltrate | divulge |

1. The evolution of America's energy needs has forced scientists and engineers to re-examine the operations, efficiency and security of the national power _____.
2. These tumors _____ normal brain tissue and grow very rapidly.
3. Combing through a child's wet hair may lead to more accurate identification of active head lice infestation than visual _____, according to a new report.
4. The prevalence of frailty and _____ among older cancer patients will pose an increasing challenge for physicians as the population ages.
5. This noise can potentially be _____ to the wiring of connections between brain cells developing at that stage.
6. Herd mentality. Angry mob. Mass _____. As these phrases suggest, we are not always confident that a large group of people will come up with the smartest decisions.
7. Narcissism included _____ views of themselves, inflated feelings of superiority and entitlement, and exploitative interpersonal attitudes, assessed by questions such as, "Without me, our class would be much less fun;" "Kids like me deserve something extra;" and "I often succeed in getting admiration."
8. Computer scientists demonstrated that criminals could hack an electronic voting machine and steal votes using a _____ programming approach that had not been invented when the voting machine was designed.
9. With more than one-third of American workers reporting that their bosses have _____, yelled at or belittled them, the new study challenges previous assumptions that abusive bosses are solely driven by ambition and the need to hold onto their power.
10. Earth, as it turns out, has other secrets to _____.

B. Skim the text and then answer the following questions.

1. What kind of users is CPU Tech targeting?
2. What are the features of the Acalis chip?
3. What are the ways of getting the key?
4. Why does the hardware and software of the Acalis chip make it impossible to get the key?
5. What are the disadvantages of the idea of changing keys?

C. **Read the text and choose the correct answer to each of the following questions.**

1. _____ has been at the center of many U.S. Department of Defense concerns.
   A. Building security into a chip at the start of the chip-design process
   B. Building security into a chip as an afterthought
   C. The prominent line between military and civilian targets
   D. Threat from private hackers

2. _____ is not the feature of Acalis CPU872 that other secure processors don't have.
   A. That each chip is manufactured at a trusted foundry certified by the U.S. Department of Defense
   B. Being integrated on the same board with the processor or functioning as a coprocessor like a graphics-processing unit
   C. That the security key is generated on the chip in a way that thwarts two of the most common attacks on secure systems
   D. Being the first microprocessor born of new methods the Pentagon learned from its hunt for secret kill switches

3. According to the text, which of the following statements is NOT true? _____.
   A. The U.S. military have to use many commercial off-the-shelf chips manufactured outside the US
   B. Even off-line structures are subject to online sabotage
   C. Malicious software and hardware modifications cannot be introduced during the manufacturing process
   D. The line between military and civilian targets has blurred significantly in the Western countries

4. Chris Tarnovsky _____.
   A. received proper education on engineering
   B. was accused of engineering pay-TV security cards and posting the results online
   C. is in charge of a company conducting hardware and software security analysis.
   D. thinks the government chips are secure

5. Which is NOT Blaauw's opinion? _____.
   A. It is not easy to store the key somewhere in a certain form
   B. In the encryption, you will always have to apply the bits of the key in the algorithm
   C. If you do not store the key, you cannot retrieve it
   D. It is good to change keys

D. **Explain the underlined parts.**

1. The government inspections, <u>motivated by</u> a 2007 Idaho National Laboratory demonstration of <u>the vulnerabilities of the U.S. grid</u>, revealed more than the inspectors had bargained for: The invaders had left behind <u>potentially disruptive malware</u>.

2. The 90-nanometer processor is fabricated at IBM's Fishkill, N.Y., foundry—a trusted foundry—which goes through an exhaustive vetting process to be deemed secure enough to manufacture the U.S. military's specialty chips, with security features built directly into the hardware.
3. This is to prevent physical scrutiny if a chip falls into the wrong hands.
4. Getting the key is the key, so to speak, to being able to generate encrypted data.
5. Chris Tarnovsky thinks the idea is smoke and mirrors.

Unit 2　Science Mystery

Text A

The Great Ketchup Mystery

1. Everyone has fallen prey to the ketchup bottle at one time or another.

2. After struggling to dislodge a meager few drops of the red liquid, an avalanche suddenly gushes out and buries your perfectly cooked burger. With suspiciously perfect timing, the ketchup changes from a thick paste to a runny liquid.

3. If you find yourself splattered and wondering "why?", you're in good company. Theoretical physicists are puzzled, too.

4. Ketchup is one of many complex fluids-including whipped cream, blood, film emulsions, nail polish and some plastics-that share a property called "shear thinning". Normally thick like honey, they can become thin and flow like water when stirred or shaken.

5. Paint is another example. How can paint be thin enough at one moment to flow from a stroked brush, and an instant later be thick enough not to drip down the wall? Shear thinning again.

6. The phenomenon is common enough, yet scientists aren't sure why it happens. Researcher Robert Berg of the National Institute of Standards and Technology says, "the details depend on interactions at the molecular level [livil], and that is still poorly understood".

7. Current theories cannot predict the thickness (or "viscosity") of many fluids. It's a problem that vexes physicists and manufacturers alike. Suppose, for instance, that a plastics-maker needs to know how some new polymer "goop" might flow through a pipe. The only way to find out might be to try it-a tedious and sometimes innovation-stifling process. What they really need is a theory that works, a way to anticipate changes in viscosity "before the ketchup explodes from the bottle".

8. Researchers hope that a space-experiment called CVX-2 (short for "Critical Viscosity of Xenon-2") will soon provide new data about the basic physics of such fluids. Berg is the principal investigator for the experiment, which is slated to fly this summer onboard space shuttle Columbia (STS-107).

9. CVX-2 is designed to study shear thinning in xenon, a substance used in lamps and ion rocket engines. Xenon is chemically inert, so its molecules consist of a single atom—it's about as close as you

can get to the flying billiard balls of an idealized gas or liquid. Unlike ketchup, which contains many ingredients ranging from microscopic ions of dissolved salt to visible chunks of pureed tomato, xenon should be relatively easy to understand.

10. Simple liquids like xenon don't normally experience shear thinning. They're either thick or thin, and they stay that way. But this changes near the "critical point"—a special combination of temperature and pressure where fluids can exist as both a liquid and a gas simultaneously. At their critical point, simple fluids should be able to "shear-thin" (a verb) just like ketchup does.

11. Gregory Zimmerli, a scientist at NASA's Glenn Research Centre, explains that "fluids at the critical point resemble a hazy fog-a flurry of little regions constantly fluctuating between liquid-like and gas-like densities. Theory predicts that this fine-grained structure should make the simple fluid shear-thin, like more complex fluids do". (Zimmerli is the project scientist for the CVX-2 experiment.)

12. When CVX-2 reaches orbit, researchers will adjust the pressure and temperature of a xenon sample within the test chamber until it reaches its critical point. A tiny vibrating paddle will then stir the xenon and, if all goes as planned, cause it to thin.

13. Why do the experiment in space? Critical-point fluids are easily compressed. On Earth they collapse under their own weight and become denser at the bottom. In orbital free-fall those density differences vanish—a key requirement for a good experiment.

14. Researchers will probe the physics of shear thinning by varying the temperature of the xenon and amount of stirring it receives. The same paddle that stirs the sample will also measure its viscosity, just as you might estimate the thickness of honey by trying to move a spoon through it.

15. At least that's what scientists are hoping will happen.

16. The ketchup-like behaviour of pure fluids at their critical point is still only theoretical. Even simulations using supercomputers can't prove the theory. "Especially near the critical point, there aren't computers that can simulate the fluid's behaviour," notes Berg. "The chains of interactions between molecules are so long that computers just aren't powerful enough to do it."

17. Consider that the next time you whack the bottom of a ketchup bottle. Even supercomputers can't predict the outcome.

(http://www.firstscience.com/home/articles/mysteries/the-great-ketchup-mystery_1352.html)

Glossary

dislodge [dis'lɔdʒ] remove or force out from a position vt. 逐出，用力移出
meager ['mi:gə(r)] deficient in amount or quality or extent adj. 贫乏的
avalanche ['ævəlɑ:nʃ] a slide of large masses of snow and ice and mud down a mountain n. 雪崩
gush [gʌʃ] come out in a jet; stream or spring forth v. 使涌出，迸出

splatter ['splætə] dash a liquid upon or against v. 使(水等)飞溅

emulsion [i'mʌlʃən] a light-sensitive coating on paper or film; consists of fine grains of silver bromide suspended in a gelati n. 感光乳剂

viscosity [vis'kɔsiti] resistance of a liquid to sheer forces (and hence to flow) n. 粘度,粘性

vex [veks] be a mystery or bewildering to v. 使……困惑

polymer ['pɔlimə] a naturally occurring or synthetic compound consisting of large molecules made up of a linked series of repeated simple monomers n. 聚合体

slate [sleit] designate or schedule v. 计划;安排

xenon ['zenɔn] a colorless odorless inert gaseous element occurring in the earth's atmosphere in trace amounts n. 氙,稀有气体元素,符号 Xe

inert [i'nə:t] having only a limited ability to react chemically; chemically inactive adj. 惰性的,迟钝的

billiard-balls ['biljəd'bɔ:lz] any of several games played on rectangular cloth-covered table (with cushioned edges) in which long tapering cue sticks are used to propel ivory (or composition) balls n. 台球,桌球

puree ['pjuərei] to make fruit or vegetables into a thick smooth sauce by crushing them, usually in a machine v. 制成菜泥/果泥

hazy ['heizi] indistinct in outline adj. 朦胧的,模糊的

flurry ['flʌri] a rapid active commotion n. 疾风,飓风

fluctuate ['flʌktjueit] be unstable v. 变动

orbit ['ɔ:bit] the (usually elliptical) path described by one celestial body in its revolution about another n. 轨道

vibrate [vai'breit] move or swing from side to side regularly v. 摇动

free-fall ['fri:'fɔ:l] the ideal falling motion of something subject only to a gravitational field n. 自由投放

Exercises

A. Fill in each blank with one of the given words in its correct form.

vibrate	flurry	whack	meager	inert	hazy	dislodge	avalanche	splatter	fluctuate

1. Even with its _____ of sunspots, the October sun was mostly blank, with zero sunspots on 20 of the month's 31 days.

2. This startling finding shows the government's _____ investment in pain research is seriously out of proportion with the widespread chronic pain incidence in our society, which is estimated at one in four Americans and accounts for more than 20 percent of all physician office visits.

3. As we pass through the densest part of the plane, gravitational forces from the surrounding giant gas and dust clouds _____ comets from their paths.
4. A tiny patch of graphene could serve as a nanoresonator: clamped on two sides, the graphene would _____ at radio frequencies.
5. The team suggests that distortions in an image due to atmospheric disturbances between camera and distant subjects could be unraveled and a photo taken on a hot, _____ day made acceptable.
6. Judy Wall, a professor of biochemistry at the University of Missouri, is working with bacteria that convert toxic radioactive metal to _____ substances.
7. Why do populations of animals like rabbits and foxes _____ so dramatically?
8. All of these factors have driven the animals to near-endangered species status, and losing the species could badly damage the local ecosystem by throwing the food chain out of _____.
9. The researchers drove semiconducting carbon nanotubes into an _____ process that carries more electrons down more paths, similar to the way a multilane highway carries more traffic than a one-lane road.
10. If you have ever taken a long road trip, the windshield of your car will inevitably be _____ with bugs by the time you arrive at your destination.

B. Skim the text and then answer the following questions.
1. What does "shear thinning" refer to?
2. What are some of the physical properties of critical-point fluids?
3. Why is the experiment carried out in space?
4. Please list some properties of Xenon.
5. Is it possible to predict the behavior of pure fluids at their critical point?

C. Read the text and choose the correct answer to each of the following questions.
1. The phrase "fall prey to" in "Everyone has fallen prey to the ketchup bottle at one time or another (paragraph 1)" means _____.
   A. to suddenly begin to suffer as a result of something or someone bad
   B. to be easy to deceive or be taken advantage of
   C. to think about a problem and worry about it a lot
   D. to hunt for
2. _____ does have a property called shear thinning.
   A. Blood   B. Paint   C. Honey   D. Nail polisher
3. Which statement is true according to the passage? _____.
   A. Scientists are sure why certain liquids have the property of shear thinning
   B. Interactions at the molecular level of liquid are conducive to the understanding of "shear thinning"

C. Phenomena associated with shear thinning are not common
   D. "Shear thinning" concerns thin liquid becoming thick when stirred or shaken
4. At critical points, simple fluids _____.
   A. can exist as a liquid
   B. can exist as a gas
   C. can behave like ketchup
   D. cannot change from one state to another
5. The physics of shear thinning is probed by _____.
   A. varying the pressure of the xenon
   B. varying the temperature of the xenon
   C. varying the way to stir the xenon
   D. varying the frequency of stirring the xenon

D. Explain the underlined parts.
1. Everyone has <u>fallen prey to the ketchup bottle at one time or another.</u>
2. After struggling to <u>dislodge a meager few drops of the red liquid</u>, an avalanche suddenly gushes out and buries your perfectly cooked burger. <u>With suspiciously perfect timing, the ketchup changes from a thick paste to a runny liquid.</u>
3. If you find yourself splattered and wondering "why?", you're in good company.
4. Paint is another example. How can paint be thin enough at one moment to flow from a stroked brush, and an instant later be thick enough not to drip down the wall? <u>Shear thinning again.</u>
5. It's a problem that <u>vexes physicists and manufacturers alike.</u>
6. The only way to find out might be to try it—<u>a tedious and sometimes innovation-stifling process.</u>
7. Xenon is chemically inert, so its molecules consist of a single atom—it's about as close as you can get <u>to the flying billiard balls of an idealized gas or liquid.</u>
8. Fluids at the critical point resemble a hazy fog—<u>a flurry of little regions constantly fluctuating between liquid-like and gas-like densities.</u>
9. The same paddle that stirs the sample will also measure its viscosity, <u>just as you might estimate the thickness of honey by trying to move a spoon through it.</u>

E. Read the passages in this section and decide whether each of the following statements is true or false.

Passage One

   Researchers have released the results of carbon-dating done on human remains found at Stonehenge, one of the world's most famous standing-stone circles.

   Their results, they said, indicate that the sacred site was in fact a burial ground for an elite or royal family thousands of years ago.

"It's now clear that burials were a major component of Stonehenge in all its main stages," said Mike Parker Pearson, a professor of archaeology at the University of Sheffield in England, and the director of the Stonehenge Riverside Archaeological Project.

The radiocarbon-dating of the burnt remains indicates that burials were conducted at the site as long ago as 3000 B.C., and continued for about 500 years.

The remains had been excavated from the Stonehenge site in the 1950s and stored at a nearby museum. The discovery is significant because it is the first time any of the Stonehenge remains had been carbon-dated.

Parker Pearson read a statement to the press which said, "Stonehenge was a place of burial from its beginning to its zenith in the mid third millennium B.C. The cremation burial dating to Stonehenge's sarsen stones phase is likely just one of many from this later period of the monument's use and demonstrates that it was still very much a domain of the dead."

But some Stonehenge experts are careful to point out that while it may have been used as a sacred burial site, that was by no means its sole function.

The ancient site has long been viewed as a place of spirituality, healing, and psychic connection to the mystical world. While the monument was actually built before any formal religions were recorded, modern-day Druids claim that the Druid faith has been connected to Stonehenge for many, many years, even possibly to the time it was built.

While historians have discounted that Druids built Stonehenge, others say that whatever early faith the builders of the site followed, it could have consisted of Druid or pagan-like rituals. Every year groups of Druids still gather at Stonehenge to celebrate midsummer and other pagan holy days. The formation of the stones are said to align precisely with the sunrise on the summer solstice. During the winter solstice, the sun sets between the arches of the largest central stones.

It is partly this phenomenon which has some Stonehenge buffs insisting that the site has astronomical connections. Some say that it was built as an astronomy observatory, particularly in terms of lunar and solar cycles, and posit that it was used primarily as a seasonal calendar to mark the days of the year and signify optimal planting seasons.

Those who insist that the site has more spiritual connections agree with scientists that it may have involved observations of the moon, but say that the ancient people who gathered at the stone circles did so in order to worship the moon, or find a spiritual connection with the heavens and with each other.

Whatever it may have been when it was first built, most will agree that the site itself was very important to the ancient builders. That they managed to drag enormous stones, the lightest of which weighed several tons, over the span of miles before the invention of the wheel, indicates that they really, really wanted them in that particular place.

While its specific origins and ritual intentions may never fully be answered, the fact that thousands of people have visited the ancient stone circles of Stonehenge and had sometimes life-altering, deeply moving spiritual experiences there cannot be discounted. Whatever it once may have been, it remains today a sacred site of spiritual significance.

(http://www.buzzle.com/articles/has-the-mystery-of-stonehenge-been-solved.html)

_____ 1. The radiocarbon-dating of the burnt remains indicates that burials were conducted at the site 3,000 years ago.

_____ 2. Some Stonehenge experts point out that it was used solely as a sacred burial site.

_____ 3. The formation of the stones is said to align precisely with the sunrise on both the summer and the winter solstice.

_____ 4. Some people claim that the ancient people who gathered at the stone circles did so in order to worship the moon.

_____ 5. The origins of Stonehenge are not known yet.

Passage Two

A fortune beyond the imagination of any pirate of the Caribbean has been discovered in the infamously treacherous seas off the Scilly Isles: 17 tonnes of gold and silver coins—500,000 in all—from one of the most lucrative shipwreck sites ever found.

Revealing details of the find, the salvage firm Odyssey Marine Exploration said yesterday it believed the coins were worth an average of $1,000 (£500), giving a total estimated value of $500m.

The site of the 400-year-old wreck, codenamed the Black Swan, has not been disclosed by the company, which flew the coins straight from the salvage site to its headquarters in Florida.

But English experts have heard recent gossip of a spectacular find, and suspect it may be lying just outside UK territorial waters. Many of the coins, most of which are silver with some gold, are believed to be in mint condition. They were described as "unprecedented" by one expert, Nick Bruyer, who has examined a sample. "I don't know of anything equal or comparable to it," he said.

John Morris, co-founder and chief executive of Odyssey, said the company was not yet certain of the identity of the ship. "Our research suggests that there were a number of colonial period shipwrecks that were lost in the area where this site is located, so we are being very cautious about speculating as to the possible identity of the shipwreck."

His partner, Greg Stemm, said: "The remarkable condition of most of the first 6,000 silver coins conserved has been a pleasant surprise, and the gold coins are almost all dazzling mint state specimens. We are excited by the wide range of dates, origins and varieties of the coins, and we believe that the collecting community will be thrilled when they see the quality and diversity of the collection."

In a phrase which will send a shiver up the spine of many maritime archaeologists who fear that unnecessary damage is done during salvage operations, Mr Stemm said: "The outside world now understands that what we do is a real business...not just a lucky one shot deal. I don't know of anybody else who has hit more than one economically significant shipwreck."

Peter Marsden, an internationally recognized expert on maritime archeology and founder of the Shipwreck Centre museum in Hastings, said the find highlighted the need for international agreements on protecting historic wrecks. Even in UK waters only a handful of historic wreck sites have been designated-outside territorial waters it's open season on wrecks-although where ownership can be proved, nation states have frequently laid claim to the contents.

New technology is making the situation acute, Dr Marsden said: many sites that were protected because they were inaccessible for divers, can now be located, searched and salvaged using remote equipment. Odyssey, using such expensive equipment that the company recorded losses in years without a major find, is on the trail of several other wrecks, including HMS Sussex, an English ship which sank in a storm of Gibraltar in 1694, said to be carrying nine tonnes of gold coins.

The new find could exceed the previous biggest haul, a Spanish galleon, Nuestra Senora de Atocha, which sank in a hurricane off Florida in 1622. The wreck was found over 20 years ago by a diver, Mel Fisher, one of the first to turn hobby treasure hunting into a career, and tonnes of coins and other artifacts valued at up to $400m were salvaged.

(http://www.buzzle.com/articles/138354.html)

_____ 6. The site of the Black Swan was disclosed by the company, which flew the coins straight from the salvage site to its headquarters in Florida.

_____ 7. John Morris was quite sure about the identity of the shipwreck.

_____ 8. There are no international agreements on protecting historic wrecks.

_____ 9. The new find mentioned above is unprecedented.

_____ 10. Mel Fisher later became a professional treasure hunter.

F. Cloze. Fill in each blank with one suitable word.

Those of us who study UFOs have more than __1__ information to keep us busy 24/7 if we so desire. There are at least 15~20 reports per day, and usually several photographs and/or videos to __2__. If you ever get behind, there is no catching up.

Of course, the __3__ of these reports are just that: someone sees something that appears to be out of the __4__ in the sky, and reports it to one of the many sources that log sightings.

However, it is very rare that we have a report that claims __5__ contact with an alien being, and it is very interesting to note that although the majority of people __6__ accept the possibility that an unknown object could be __7__, it goes one step beyond for most people to accept the possibility that aliens may already be among us.

Reports of a visual sighting of an extraterrestrial __8__ come under heavy __9__ or disrepute, and are usually written off as a misidentification of a human or animal seen under __10__ conditions.

1. A. ample   B. interesting   C. alarming   D. expected
2. A. collect   B. analyze   C. inspect   D. test
3. A. meaning   B. essence   C. majority   D. theme
4. A. place   B. boundary   C. spectacular   D. ordinary
5. A. actual   B. real   C. genuine   D. true
6. A. unwillingly   B. reluctantly   C. readily   D. willfully
7. A. imaginary   B. imaginative   C. extraterrestrial D. terrestrial
8. A. object   B. being   C. thing   D. matter
9. A. scrutiny   B. exposure   C. inquiry   D. operation
10. A. normal   B. extraordinary   C. illusionary   D. deceptive

G. **Translate the following passages into Chinese/English.**

1. See levels are set to fall over millions of years, making the current rise blamed on climate change a brief interruption of an ancient geological trend, scientists said on Thursday. They said oceans were getting deeper and sea levels had fallen by about 170 meters (560 ft) since the Cretaceous period 80 million years ago when dinosaurs lived, previously, the little-understood fall had been estimated at 40 to 250 meters.

A computer model based on improved understanding of shifts of continent-sized tectonic plates in the earth's crust projects more deepening of the ocean floor and a further sea level decline of 120 meters in 80 million years' time. If sea levels were to fall that much now, Russia would be connected to Alaska by land over what is now the Bering Strait, Britain would be part of mainland Europe and Australia and Papua Island would be the same landmass. The study aids understanding of sea levels by showing that geology has played a big role alongside ice ages, which can suck vast amounts of water from the oceans onto land.

2. 气温的上升会使海平面上升,这是因为当海洋中的水变暖后就会膨胀,而且很多冰川会融化到海洋中。文章指出,如果南极洲和格陵兰岛现在所蕴藏的冰全部融化,就足以使海平面上升50米。在未来的8 000万年中,如果陆地上的冰全部消融,那么,海平面的净下降幅度是70米,而非模型预测的120米。过去人们认为,白垩纪时期的海平面或许比现在仅仅高出40米,该研究对此提出了挑战,指出来自美国新泽西州的测量数据低估了海平面的下降。文章指出,在那个时期,新泽西地区自身就下降了105米至180米,致使读数不准。

Text B

The Mystery of the Bermuda Triangle

1. Miami, Puerto Rico and Bermuda are prime holiday destinations boasting sun, beaches and coral seas. But between these idyllic settings, there is a dark side: countless ships and planes have mysteriously gone missing in the one and a half million square miles of ocean separating them. About 60 years ago, the area was claiming about five planes every day and was nicknamed the Bermuda Triangle by a magazine in 1964. Today, about that many planes disappear in the region each year and there are a number of theories explaining what could be happening.

2. Twins George and David Rothschild are among the first passengers to have experienced bizarre effects in the Bermuda Triangle. In 1952, when they were 19 years old, the two naval men had to make an emergency trip home on a navy light aircraft, north over the Florida Keys, to attend their father's funeral. "We had been flying for probably 20 or 30 minutes when all of a sudden the pilot yelled out that the instruments were dead and he became very frantic," says George Rothschild. He had lost his bearings, and not only did he not know where he was, he also had no idea how much gas was left in the fuel tanks. After what seemed like hours, they landed safely in Norfolk, on the Florida coast.

3. Some speculate that it had nothing to do with the location, but rather the instruments that were available at the time. Pilot Robert Grant says that back in the 1940s, navigating a plane involved a lot of guesswork since they relied completely on a magnetic compass to guide them. Dead reckoning was used, which means that pilots would trust their compass and then estimate how the wind would influence their planned flight path to remain on track. No matter what your mind tells you, you must stay on that course, says Grant. If you don't, and you start turning to wherever you think you should be going, then you're toast.

Wild Weather

4. The landscape of the island of Bermuda is quite unique: it is a remote coral reef precariously perched on a massive extinct volcano. Fisherman Sloan Wakefield, who knows the waters of the Bermuda Triangle very well, thinks that the weather could be responsible for some of the disappearances. Because the island is a dot in the Atlantic Ocean, it gets weather from everywhere and it can change in a heartbeat. One minute, you can be looking at good weather, and the next moment you've got a low front coming through, he says. He has already seen 15 to 20 foot (4.6m to 6m) waves on the sea.

5. Hurricanes are common in the Bermuda Triangle area. In the Atlantic Ocean, they typically originate off the African coast and thrive off the moisture of the warm, tropical waters. Hurricane records from

the past 100 years have shown that they often head west for the United States but swerve into the waters of the Bermuda Triangle at the last minute. Jim Lushine, a meteorologist at the National Hurricane Centre in Miami, Florida studies the weather in the Bermuda Triangle and says that there are more hurricanes in that particular area than in any other in the Atlantic basin.

6. But thunderstorms in the area can be just as dangerous. In 1986, a historic ship called the Pride of Baltimore vanished from radar screens while it was in the Bermuda Triangle, making a trip from the Caribbean to Baltimore. About four and a half days later, the wreckage and eight survivors were found and they revealed that the ship had been hit by a microburst: 80 mile per hour winds emanating from a freak thunderstorm. It happened so quickly that the crew didn't have time to make a distress call. The ship was sunk in the downburst, unfortunately with a great loss of life, says Lushine. Similar downbursts are probably responsible for some of the sunken ships in the Bermuda Triangle.

7. Even more unpredictable than thunderstorms are waterspouts. These can be caused by tornadoes that move out to sea or rotating columns of air that drop from thunderstorms, creating a vortex of spray. When the moisture condenses, it forms a twisting column that connects the sea to the clouds. Jim Edds, an amateur fisherman who chases and films waterspouts for fun, says that if you are out at night and a tornado-like waterspout develops—the really big, strong ones with high velocity—it can flip your vessel over.

Bubbling Methane

8. Seismic activity at the bottom of the ocean can also be an explanation for disappearing ships. Scientists have discovered that huge bubbles of methane gas can violently erupt without warning from the ocean floor and at least one oil rig is thought to have sunk because of this phenomenon. Ralph Richardson, the director of the Bermuda Underwater Exploration Institute, claims that a large pocket of gas could surround a ship, causing it to lose buoyancy and disappear without warning.

9. At the U.S. Navy's research centre in California, Bruce Denardo, an expert in fluid dynamics, has proved that bubbles from methane gas eruptions could be responsible for vanishing ships in the open ocean. Water pressure causes objects to float, and the deeper the water, the greater the pressure exerted to keep the object floating at the surface. If bubbles from methane are introduced, they lower the density of the water. They take up space, but the volume of water stays the same, causing the buoyant force to decrease. In an experiment with a ball in water, Denardo can demonstrate that the ball sinks deeper and deeper down in water as the amount of bubbles increases, until it reaches a critical point where it sinks completely. If a ship were to take on enough water, it would sink to the bottom and stay there, says Denardo.

A Mysterious Time Warp

10. Others have more far out explanations for the Bermuda Triangle disappearances. Property devel-

oper Bruce Gernon claims that on December 4th 1970, when he flew from the island of Andross in the Bahamas to Florida, he experienced a distortion in space time. He had made the same trip on many occasions, but he claims that his journey that day was much faster than usual. "I noticed a huge U-shaped opening in the clouds, but as I approached it, the top of the opening closed and it became a horizontal tunnel that appeared to be 10 to 15 miles long," he says. "When the aircraft entered the tunnel, some lines, which I call time lines, appeared which were rotating counter-clockwise. It was difficult to keep it level and concentrate on the other end of the tunnel which was aiming directly for Miami."

11. Gernon claims that when he came out of the tunnel, it closed fast behind him and he was surrounded by a strange fog. His instruments had stopped working and Air Traffic Control had no radar trace of his plane until they realized that it was actually over Miami beach. Given the time they had been flying, they should still have been about 45 minutes away from Miami. After researching what could have happened, Genon is now writing a book about his experience. "I have come to the conclusion that we experienced a space time warp of a hundred miles in thirty minutes," he says.

12. Is this scientifically feasible? About 80 years ago, Einstein proposed his general theory of relativity which claimed that huge spinning objects could distort space and time in their surroundings. Although NASA researchers have now found signs that black holes and neutron stars appear to warp space time, it is still a far cry from concepts introduced by science fiction like wormholes, or tunnels in space time that provide travellers with an express route between different dimensions and great distances.

13. Explanations for the vanishings in the Bermuda Triangle are all still theories. But especially for people who have witnessed bizarre events in this area, there is a strong desire to find some answers. One author, Gian Quasar, has been investigating every single plane and ship disappearance in the Bermuda Triangle and has listed every case on a massive internet database at http://www.bermuda-triangle.org/. With initiatives like this and further research, perhaps the mystery will come to a conclusion.

(http://www.firstscience.com/home/articles/mysteries/the-mystery-of-the-bermuda-triangle_15176.html)

Glossary

coral ['kɔrəl] a substance like rock, formed in the sea by groups of particular types of small animal, that is often used in jewellery *n*. 珊瑚

idyllic [ai'dilik, i'dilik] excellent and delightful in all respects *adj*. 田园诗的

dead reckoning ['ded'rekəniŋ] navigation without the aid of celestial observations *n*. 推算航行法(计算法定位)

reef [ri:f] a submerged ridge of rock or coral near the surface of the water *n*. 暗礁

precariously [pri'kɛəriəsli] in a way that is likely to fall, be damaged, fail, etc *adv*. 危险地, 不稳固

地

perch [pə:tʃ] to come to rest, settle v. 就位，位于
swerve [swə:v] turn sharply; change direction abruptly v. 突然转向
meteorologist [mi:tjə'rɔlədʒist] a specialist who studies processes in the earth's atmosphere that cause weather conditions n. 气象学家
emanate ['eməneit] proceed or issue forth, as from a source v. 散发，发出
freak [fri:k] very unusual or unexpected adj. 奇异的，不正常的
vortex ['vɔ:teks] the shape of something rotating rapidly n. 漩涡，旋风
seismic ['saizmik] subject to or caused by an earthquake or earth vibration adj. 地震的
oil rig ['ɔilrig] rig used in drilling for oil or gas n. 石油钻塔
buoyancy ['bɔiənsi] the tendency to float in water or other liquid n. 浮力
warp [wɔ:p] a twist or aberration; especially a perverse or abnormal way of judging or acting n. 弯，歪曲

Exercises

A. Fill in each blank with one of the given words in its correct form.

| buoyancy freak perch precariously emanate vortex swerve idyllic warp Seismic |

1. This would be healthier for all of us and might reduce the rural suicide rate to what it was early in the last century, when it was lower than the urban rate, and when rural America, rather than desolate and lonely, was thriving and vibrant, perhaps as _____ as it was in fable.

2. Technology developed by the University of Warwick that can identify partial, distorted, scratched, smudged, or otherwise _____ fingerprints in just a few seconds has just scored top marks in the world's two toughest technical fingerprint tests.

3. We found that if a layer of pure water ice formed near the core, it would have enough _____ to rise upwards, and such a redistribution of mass can generate large tectonic stresses at the surface.

4. The research, led by David Lentink, an assistant professor at Wageningen, and Michael H. Dickinson, the Zarem Professor of Bioengineering at Caltech, revealed that, by swirling, maple seeds generate a tornado-like _____ that sits atop the front leading edge of the seed as they spin slowly to the ground.

5. It's too late to slam on the brakes, and the driver can't _____ either, as there is another car on the neighboring lane. An accident seems inevitable.

6. By storing water, developing thicker skin, or being more tolerant to drying out, the epiphytic ferns could now _____ on a trunk, limb, or twig and live quite happily more than 100 feet off the forest floor, where moisture, temperature and sunlight are very different indeed.

7. The rest of the amoebas pile on, combining to produce spores that sit _____ atop the stalk until wind, insects or other outside forces can carry them to a better place.
8. _____ waves generated by earthquakes pass through the earth. Changes in their direction or velocity indicate variations in the materials through which they pass.
9. The channels appear to _____ directly from material ejected from Hale.
10. To have four fatal stabbings in one day could be a statistical _____.

B. Skim the text and then answer the following questions.
1. What do you know about Bermuda Triangle?
2. What are the possible explanations for the disappearance of aircrafts and ships over Bermuda Triangle?
3. What are the characteristics of Hurricanes in the Atlantic Ocean?
4. Why could bubbles from methane gas eruptions give rise to ship vanishing?
5. Is it possible to warp space time?

C. Read the text and choose the correct answer to each of the following questions.
1. Which of the following statements is true about Bermuda Triangle? _____.
   A. It claims about five planes every day
   B. It lies right between Miami and Puerto Rico
   C. It claims about five planes each year now
   D. It is officially assigned the name
2. In George and David Rothschild's experience over Bermuda Triangle, _____.
   A. George Rothschild became very frantic
   B. the pilot had no idea where they were
   C. they landed safely after hours
   D. things had been out of control for 20 to 30 minutes
3. "If you don't, and you start turning to wherever you think you should be going, then you're toast." What does "you're toast" mean here? _____.
   A. You should propose a toast
   B. You are doomed
   C. You are a celebrity who receives much acclaim and attention
   D. You will be toasted
4. According to Bruce Gernon, _____.
   A. the tunnel warps space time
   B. the tunnel were rotating counter-clockwise
   C. his plane could not be located when he was in the tunnel
   D. the tunnel was closed before he came out

5. It can be induced from the text that _____.
   A. traveling with an express route between great distances is currently impossible
   B. there is proof showing people can travel between different dimensions
   C. the author believes in Bruce Gernon's account on his experience
   D. the author thinks the mystery of Bermuda Triangle couldn't be solved

D. Explain the underlined parts.
1. Some speculate that it <u>had nothing to do with the location, but rather the instruments that were available at the time</u>.
2. Hurricanes are common in the Bermuda Triangle area. In the Atlantic Ocean, they typically <u>originate off the African coast and thrive off the moisture of the warm, tropical waters</u>.
3. About four and a half days later, the wreckage and eight survivors were found and they <u>revealed that the ship had been hit by a microburst: 80 mile per hour winds emanating from a freak thunderstorm</u>.
4. Others have more <u>far out explanations for</u> the Bermuda Triangle disappearances.
5. Although NASA researchers have now found signs that black holes and neutron stars appear to warp space time, it is still <u>a far cry from concepts</u> introduced by science fiction like wormholes, or tunnels in space time that provide travellers with <u>an express route between different dimensions and great distances</u>.

Unit 3   Biometrics

Text A

How will Increasingly Sophisticated Biometric Technologies Affect You?

1. Compared to biometric identification methods, passwords are clunky, insecure dinosaurs. If the burgeoning biometrics industry has anything to say about it, your fingers, face, eyes and even behaviors will be the preferred ways of securely identifying yourself. It's not just for James Bond movies anymore. This is the new reality. Crude fingerprint identification methods may have been around for 100 years, but what is new is the increasingly sophisticated technology applications and ever-improving accuracy of biometrics.

2. Let's take a look at a snapshot of biometrics today. Fingerprint swipers, the most recognized biometric devices, have found their way into laptops, desktops and doors. Entrepreneur Scott Moody uses a fingerprint reader on his laptop. The technology controls access to the computer and keeps data safe. Moody also happens to be the 49-year-old co-founder and CEO of AuthenTec, a leading fingerprint biometrics company that, as you might expect, uses fingerprint sensors to control access to its Melbourne, Florida, offices. In 1998, Moody launched the multimillion-dollar firm with co-founder Dale Setlak, 54.

3. Fingerprints are a doorway into the wide world of biometrics. Forward-looking biometrics companies are involved in everything from hand geometry and iris scans to voice recognition and behavioral biometrics. Grant Evans, CEO of A4Vision, prefers to face up to biometrics. His Sunnyvale, California, company is pioneering 3-D facial imaging technology. "It started out as bleeding-edge technology, and now it's cutting-edge, and it's just entering into the mainstream," says Evans.

4. Biometrics may have started off as technology for governments and law enforcement, but it is working its way into growing businesses and even consumer applications. Turn your gaze to Japan for a moment, and you'll see a proliferation of mobile devices with integrated fingerprint readers. It's a sign of things to come in the U.S. Confirming your identity is even more important now that phones are storing sensitive business and personal data and are even acting as digital wallets.

5. As Vali Ali, distinguished technologist with Hewlett-Packard, says, biometrics isn't just about

security; it's about convenient security. Users don't have to remember lengthy or weak passwords, and you always have your finger or iris with you. "The technologies that are going to win are the types of technologies that people want to use rather than have to use," says Ali. That's one reason fingerprint sensors are so popular. Swiping your fingerprint is a simple, nonintrusive way to identify yourself.

6. The future of biometrics is intriguing and complex. Both AuthenTec and A4Vision are businesses thriving in the field. Evans is pragmatic about A4Vision's prospects. "Someone will probably acquire this company because we're a piece of the puzzle," he says. Consolidation is underway in the biometrics industry, and that trend will likely continue for a while. Entrepreneurs interested in getting in on biometrics need to seriously consider the market realities. As Evans says, "Turning a concept into a viable company in this industry is very tough. It's difficult to compete now unless you have a disruptive technology that is new [and] that no one [else] has."

7. Still, that doesn't mean the pace of innovation will slow down. No technology is fail-safe, which is why multi-modal biometrics is a huge trend for the future. This approach involves combining more than one type of biometric technology. "It's a very common theme to use multiple technologies to tighten the gap for any security leakage or failures in the system," says Evans. Biometric devices are getting smaller, more accurate and more sophisticated. They're also getting more user-friendly. That's a key feature that will help spur adoption of more advanced biometrics. Ali says, "You will see multimodal applications which are very pleasing, human-like and much more natural for interactions."

8. With biometrics, here's what a typical day might look like: You stop at the store on the way to your business and purchase a muffin using your credit card-enabled cell phone after identifying yourself with a fingerprint. To get into your office building, you have your face scanned. You access your laptop by scanning your fingerprint and speaking to the computer so it can recognize your voice. While you're out at lunch, you browse through a database on your smartphone using your fingerprint reader as an intuitive navigation device.

9. The popularity of fingerprint readers in laptops is just a sign of the changing times. The majority of HP business laptops come with fingerprint sensors, as do laptops in Lenovo's ThinkPad line. Most things we use passwords, tokens or keys for today can be replaced with biometrics. Your car, house, office, monetary transactions, computer and mobile devices can be made more secure by embedding these new technologies. "Our product is something that can be virtually ubiquitous in your life," says Moody. "When we're old and in rocking chairs, we can say we were part of making this happen."

(http://www.entrepreneur.com/magazine/entrepreneur/2006/november/168946.html)

Glossary

clunky ['klʌŋki] lacking grace in movement or posture *adj.* 笨拙的

burgeon ['bə:dʒən] grow and flourish v. 迅速发展
snapshot ['snæpʃɔt] an informal photograph n. 快照，印象
bleeding-edge ['bli:diŋ,edʒ] relating to or describing systems, devices or ideas that are so modern that they are still being developed adj. 尖端的
cutting-edge ['kʌtiŋ,edʒ] in accord with the most fashionable ideas or style adj. 最新的，现代的
proliferation [prəulifə'reiʃən] a rapid increase in number n. 增殖
intriguing [in'tri:giŋ] capable of arousing interest or curiosity adj. 吸引人的，有趣的
pragmatic [præg'mætik] solving problems in a realistic way which suits the present conditions rather than obeying fixed theories, ideas or rules adj. 实际的，注重实效的
consolidation [kənsɔli'deiʃən] the act of combining into an integral whole n. 统一
viable ['vaiəbl] capable of being done with means at hand and circumstances as they are adj. 可行的
disruptive [dis'rʌptiv] characterized by unrest or disorder or insubordination adj. 捣乱的，破坏性的，制造混乱的
muffin ['mʌfin] a sweet quick bread baked in a cup-shaped pan n. 松饼
intuitive [in'tju(:)itiv] spontaneously derived from or prompted by a natural tendency adj. 直觉的
embed [im'bed] fix or set securely or deeply vt. 插入，嵌入
ubiquitous [ju:'bikwitəs] being present everywhere at once adj. 到处存在的，遍在的
fail-safe ['feilseif] guaranteed not to fail adj. 自动防止故障危害的，故障安全的

Exercises

A. Fill in each blank with one of the given words in its correct form.

| disruptive | ubiquitous | burgeon | proliferation | intuitive |
| Accuracy | consolidation | intriguing | sophisticated | pragmatic |

1. Baroque classical music in the reading room can help improve radiologists work lives, potentially improving diagnostic efficiency and _____, according to a study performed by researchers at the University of Maryland in Baltimore, MD, Harbor Hospital in Baltimore, MD, and the University of Pennsylvania Health System in Philadelphia, PA.

2. How can we keep our personal location private in a society where GPS-enabled devices and internet-connected computing are _____?

3. The patterns in the third class, _____ coloration, tend to obscure the outline of the animal against certain backgrounds.

4. The LUI provides speech-language pathologists and researchers with a new tool to evaluate a young child's broad _____ use of language.

5. In heart development, prior to birth (embryogenesis) heart cells (cardiomyocytes) _____ and de-

velop into different parts of the heart.
6. In the past, restoration of paintings and other old artwork often involved application of acrylic resins to _____ and protect them.
7. But our findings are the first to show that these specialized neural circuits are there as early as preschool years, and that maturational changes in these areas are associated with preschoolers' abilities to think about their social world in increasingly _____ ways.
8. When solving these problems, humans can use their _____ and visualization skills.
9. Cohousing offers a low-carbon lifestyle, and developers are poised for a market that could soon _____ in the US, according to a new study.
10. Scientists in China are reporting the "_____" discovery that a natural plant hormone, applied to crops, can help plants eliminate residues of certain pesticides.

B. Skim the text and then answer the following questions.
1. How will biometric technologies affect our life?
2. What is the implication of "Fingerprints are a doorway into the wide world of biometrics"?
3. In biometrics, what could be used to identify a person?
4. What is your prediction of a world with advanced biometrics?
5. In what fields could biometrics be used?

C. Read the text and choose the correct answer to each of the following questions.
1. With the development of biometric identification methods, _____ has become a less preferred ways of securely identifying yourself.
   A. your finger   B. your password   C. your behavior   D. your voice
2. The use of biometrics can be found in _____.
   A. governments and law enforcement
   B. businesses and consumer applications
   C. Both A and B
   D. None of the above
3. Even when using a phone, it is important to confirm your identity because _____.
   A. phones can protect your privacy
   B. phones can serve as wallets
   C. phones can store data
   D. phones can store sensitive information
4. The reason why biometrics is about convenient security is that _____.
   A. you can have special ways to remember lengthy passwords
   B. you like to use it instead of having to use it
   C. you can use your own physical traits to identify yourself
   D. you do not need to take with you the thing to identify yourself

5. What is the tone of Moody when talking about the product his company is to provide in the future? _____ .

   A. Optimistic   B. Gloomy   C. Ambivalent   D. Ambiguous

D. Explain the underlined parts.

1. Compared to biometric identification methods, passwords are clunky, insecure dinosaurs.
2. Let's take a look at a snapshot of biometrics today.
3. Fingerprints are a doorway into the wide world of biometrics. Forward-looking biometrics companies are involved in everything from hand geometry and iris scans to voice recognition and behavioral biometrics.
4. It started out as bleeding-edge technology, and now it's cutting-edge, and it's just entering into the mainstream.
5. Biometrics may have started off as technology for governments and law enforcement, but it is working its way into growing businesses and even consumer applications.
6. Evans is pragmatic about A4Vision's prospects. "Someone will probably acquire this company because we're a piece of the puzzle..."
7. No technology is fail-safe, which is why multi-modal biometrics is a huge trend for the future.
8. Turning a concept into a viable company in this industry is very tough. It's difficult to compete now unless you have a disruptive technology that is new [and] that no one [else] has.
9. The popularity of fingerprint readers in laptops is just a sign of the changing times.

E. Read the passages in this section and decide whether each of the following statements is true or false.

Passage One

    Biometrics has become more and more ubiquitous in our daily lives, from ATM machines to check out aisles at your local market, to personal electronics. Continuing innovations and improvements to the various biometric technologies have made them more accessible to consumers and businesses alike.

    Is Biometrics right for your business?

    The answer is probably, yes! ATS offers biometric options to help you maximize the efficiency of your workforce in several ways. For one, Biometrics will eliminate "buddy punching", the practice of one employee clocking in/out for another employee. This practice constitutes time theft and as we know, time is money! Buddy punching also decreases employee morale for the majority of honest workers who become frustrated that they are putting in a full day while a few are not. Biometrics also increases workplace security by ensuring that a user is indeed who they say they are. Through the introduction of biometrics, you know you are receiving an honest day's work and that the employee is receiving an honest day's pay. Furthermore, you can be confident that your strategic business planning is based on accurate and reliable data.

Overcoming Objections to Biometrics in the Workplace

ATS has been helping businesses like yours achieve tremendous ROI by reducing payroll errors, providing visibility to critical trends, eliminating buddy punching, and optimizing the workforce. Biometric systems have been shown to reduce payroll expenses by an average of 3% ~ 5%. Though becoming less of an issue as technology advances, there are still some who may resist the implementation of biometrics. We have seen it all in 10 years!

(http://www.accu-time.com/biometrics.htm)

  _____ 1. Biometrics has become more and more important in our daily lives.

  _____ 2. In a way, biometrics helps to increase employee morale.

  _____ 3. Biometric systems can help to reduce payroll expenses by 3% ~ 5%.

  _____ 4. Biometrics stops advancing.

  _____ 5. All people embrace the implementation of biometrics.

Passage Two

Adware, malware, spyware and computer bots are just a few of the threats that can be named; which prompt the use of a secure computer authentication system. Various methods are used in the authentication processes. The stress has however always been towards a software approach for solving the purpose of authentication.

Passwords

Passwords are the easiest and most common authentication process that are used, not only on desktop computers but also at the network level. However certain rules should be followed when setting a password for your computer or network.

Smart Cards

Smart Cards are among the very few hardware authentication processes in which a simple card with an embedded circuitry is used for accessing the network. Each valid card for a particular network, when inserted into the circuitry it has been made for, gives an output which decides whether you will be allowed to enter into the network or not. The programming logic inserted into each card is different and it is one of the safest methods of authentication.

Fingerprint detection

Almost available in all laptops that are manufactured today; fingerprint detection is another safe method of computer security authentication. Everyone knows that even the iris pattern of two people may even match, but fingerprints can never match.

Face recognition systems

Face recognition system, may amuse you, but of late many people working in the field of security have questioned its user friendly nature and the security it can provide. A simple dimension calculation of the face is done by the computer and the logic used in doing so, has been often found to be prone to errors.

Biometrics

Biometrics is often considered as a far more secure way of authentication than passwords or digital certificates. It is even safer than smart cards, which may be misplaced. The physical and behavioral traits of a person are taken into consideration in this type of authentication.

Captcha Keys

This is the process of authentication that is used to verify whether a human or a computer bot has logged into the system. Captcha keys are randomly generated alphabets and numericals presented in such a form, that only a human can recognise.

(http://www.buzzle.com/articles/computer-security-authentication.html)

_____ 6. Adware, malware and spyware contribute to the use of a secure computer authentication system.

_____ 7. When a password is inserted into the circuitry, an output will decide whether the person using it will be allowed to enter into the network or not.

_____ 8. Fingerprint detection is a safe method of computer security authentication.

_____ 9. Fingerprint detection systems can be found in almost all laptops that are manufactured today.

_____ 10. Digital certificates serve as a far more secure way of authentication than biometrics.

F. Cloze. Fill in each blank with one suitable word.

Since 9/11, the need to secure important facilities __1__ terrorist attack has become a top __2__ around the world. And one of the keys to this is making sure the right people are allowed into __3__ areas and the wrong people are kept out.

A range of technologies and systems have been __4__ in the past few years, but the more successful they are the more __5__ they tend to be, causing disruptions and delays.

For the past three years, a consortium of academic and research __6__ and private-sector companies have been looking at developing new technologies that aim at __7__ both security and safety across a wide __8__ of applications.

At the same time, they have been improving __9__ technologies with the aim of making __10__ techniques much more unobtrusive.

  1. A. off   B. away   C. against   D. from
  2. A. notch   B. significance   C. priority   D. superiority
  3. A. sensitive   B. sensible   C. sentimental   D. sensational

4. A. taken	B. adapted	C. advanced	D. deployed
5. A. disastrous	B. obtrusive	C. sumptuous	D. fallacious
6. A. organizations	B. associations	C. institutions	D. agencies
7. A. enhancing	B. enforcing	C. effectuating	D. enabling
8. A. school	B. host	C. spectrum	D. assembly
9. A. existent	B. existing	C. existed	D. existence
10. A. identifying	B. distinguishment	C. recognition	D. evaluation

G. Translate the following passages into Chinese/English.

1. Biometric technologies are defined as "automated methods of identifying or authenticating the identity of a living person based on a physical or behavioral characteristic".

It is the scientific discipline of observing and measuring relevant attributes of living individuals or populations to identify active properties or unique characteristics.

Unique physical traits, such as fingerprints, iris scans, voiceprints, faces, signatures or the geometry of the hand, can be used. All of those technologies share a methodology involving enrollment and verification. At enrollment, the person offers a "live sample" of the biometric, such as a fingerprint. This is canned electronically, processed and stored as a template.

2. 科学家已经验证了如下三种生物节奏周期:身体生物节奏周期、情感生物节奏周期和智力生物节奏周期。每种周期大约持续28天,并分成时间跨度一样的高能期与低能期两个时期。在身体生物节奏的高能期,我们有较强的抗病能力,身体各部分更协调自如,精力更旺盛;在低能期,我们的抗病能力减弱,身体各部分不太协调一致,而且容易感到疲劳。低能期是为下一个高能期"充电"积蓄能量。

Text B

Financial Institutions Evaluate Biometrics

1. In a bid to boost security in the financial services industry, ISO, the world's largest developer of international standards, recently issued a new biometrics standard for financial firms. Citing the trillions of dollars in daily transactions that "expose the financial community and its customers to severe risks from accidental or deliberate alteration, substitution or destruction of data", ISO pointed to "a strong need for an ironclad authentication method" as a driver behind the new biometrics standard.

2. The new ISO standard presents architectures for implementation, specifies the minimum security requirements for effective management, and provides control objectives and recommendations for biometric solutions. Biometrics includes technologies such as fingerprinting (many new IBM laptops feature finger-

print scanners); voice identification; iris recognition; hand geometry analysis, which measures various points on the hand and examines how the length of one finger relates to your other fingers; and vein recognition, which uses a light source to examine an individual's specific palm vein pattern.

3. Biometrics offers a particularly secure authentication method because—unlike passwords, token and smart cards—biometric patterns cannot be shared, lost, stolen or forgotten, therefore minimizing the risk of identity theft. Biometric techniques, however, have been perceived as somewhat intrusive. As a result, new biometric methods that require less-intrusive examination, such as measuring a user's keystroke rhythm, have become increasingly popular recently.

4. With all types of biometric solutions, individuals' unique patterns are stored in a database. To authenticate a user, his or her biometric characteristic—a fingerprint, for example—is compared to the unique pattern on file.

5. While more and more financial services firms are turning to biometrics to improve security, many companies are reluctant to discuss how they are using biometrics, and the Wall Street firms approached for this article declined to be interviewed on the record. Further, widespread adoption in the U.S. reportedly has been slower than in Europe or Japan.

6. According to Celent senior analyst Ariana-Michele Moore, one reason for the slow adoption has been the high cost of biometrics solutions. "Biometrics are still costly, although the cost is coming down," she relates.

Biometrics behind the Scenes

7. Privacy concerns are another hurdle to widespread adoption, Moore adds, noting that financial institutions aren't yet ready for consumer-facing deployments of biometrics technology. "But behind the scenes, biometrics are being used to go into vaults to access employee-only zones," she says.

8. Phil Alexander, the senior information security officer at a major West Coast financial institution (Alexander asked WS&T not to disclose the firm), says the most obvious use for biometrics is to regulate access to server rooms or other areas that must be kept highly secure. In these cases, he notes, palm and fingerprint recognition are common biometric methods.

9. "I have seen access to admin buildings [authorized] with just one finger," relates Alexander. "It's very clever, for example, after hours—if someone is trying to force you into a building, you can just use a different finger [whose print had not previously been authenticated for secure access], which sets off an alarm."

10. Still, Alexander, who also is the author of a new book on data security, "Information Security: A Manager's Guide to Thwarting Data Thieves and Hackers" (Praeger Security International), points out that biometric authentication on its own is not completely foolproof. "Biometrics is considered a very strong authentication method because it is very difficult to fake somebody's fingerprints or retina pat-

tem," he wrote in his book. "However, as with any form of security control, nothing is foolproof."

Database Vulnerability

11. The fact that biometric patterns are stored in a database creates a point of vulnerability, just as with other forms of authentication, Alexander explains. "This makes the protection of the database that stores the fingerprint data very important," he wrote.

12. Further, while no two people have the exact same fingerprints, for example, it still is possible to foil fingerprint biometrics, Alexander asserts. "When we touch a surface with our hands, we leave a residue called a latent fingerprint," he wrote. "Most of us have heard law enforcement use terms such as 'dusting for prints'. They are using powder to highlight the latent fingerprints and tape to lift them off and preserve them as evidence."

13. Hackers can use similar techniques to steal an individual's fingerprints and try to fool a biometric system, Alexander suggests. In addition, while users can change their passwords if they are lost or stolen, individuals can't change their fingerprints, so that form of biometric identification would be permanently invalidated if users' fingerprints were compromised.

14. On the other hand, Alexander points out, unlike fingerprints, voice patterns based on an established text message can be changed by the user. "Many companies are using text-based voice verification as a form of biometric authentication," he wrote.

15. "The nice thing about this is that the text can be changed," Alexander tells WS&T. "It is then possible to protect a user if a voice pattern that was tied to a specific text is compromised. You simply have them submit another voice sample using a different text, akin to having a user change their password."

16. Still, Michael Barda, manager at SMART Business Advisory and Consulting, contends that voice recognition is not the preferred method due to a very high error rate compared to other biometrics techniques. "If someone changes their pattern of speech on a particular day, it can cause an error," Barda says, noting that a user with a common cold can throw off a voice-verification system.

17. Nevertheless, Ziv Barzilay, founder and CTO of Tel Aviv-based voice biometrics company CellMax Systems, suggests that voice recognition has been gaining momentum due to advances in the technology. He says voice biometrics is the only biometric technology that enables immediate authentication anywhere at any time-simply by using a landline phone, cell phone or microphone. Barzilay also asserts that it is cost effective since it doesn't require additional hardware beyond a common microphone.

18. Solutions such as CellMax's examine the 15-plus parameters that make up a voiceprint, including a user's teeth, nasal cavity, nostrils, lips, tongue, jaw, lungs and diaphragm, Barzilay explains.

Twice the Protection

19. Ultimately, data security expert Alexander says, the best way to boost the effectiveness of a bio-

metric solution is to use it as part of a two-factor authentication approach. "The buzz," he says, "really is two-factor authentication."

20. In his book, Alexander notes that institutions often adopt biometrics as part of a two-factor authentication solution to protect access to sensitive areas. These same buildings generally also have guards posted who check IDs as well, he points out.

21. "So not only would you have to copy my fingerprints, you would have to have a valid ID [to gain unlawful access to the building], and if I am personally known to the security guard, you would also have to look like me to get past them," Alexander writes. "It is also not uncommon for secure buildings to require users to enter a code on a keypad in addition to the fingerprint match."

22. Alexander relates to WS&T an example of one large bank in particular that uses voice recognition to authenticate password resets. He says this actually helps the institution save money. "Some financial institutions have hundreds of thousands of employees, who forget their passwords," he explains, noting that password management can be time-consuming for IT staff. "If you use [biometrics] to have less technology staff on hand, it's actually [cheaper]."

23. Financial services firms, Alexander continues, are beginning to recognize the value of biometrics. "There is wider acceptance," he says. "But ... I'm a big fan of it being matched with something else. It's an added layer of security."

Glossary

ironclad [aiən'klæd] inflexibly entrenched and unchangeable *adj*. 坚固的
vein [vein] a blood vessel that carries blood from the capillaries toward the heart *n*. 静脉
keystroke ['ki:strəuk] the act of pressing an input key *n*. [计算机]按键;键的敲击
relate [ri'leit] give an account of *v*. 叙述
hurdle ['hə:dl] an obstacle that you are expected to overcome *n*. 栏杆,障碍
vault [vɔ:lt] the act of jumping over an obstacle *n*. 撑竿跳
retina ['retinə] the light-sensitive membrane covering the back wall of the eyeball; it is continuous with the optic nerve *n*. 视网膜
foil [fɔil] hinder or prevent (the efforts, plans, or desires) of *v*. 挫败
residue ['rezidju:] matter that remains after something has been removed *n*. 残余
latent ['leitənt] potentially existing but not presently evident or realized *adj*. 潜在的,隐约的
invalidate [in'vælideit] make invalid for use *v*. 使无效
akin [ə'kin] similar or related in quality or character *adj*. 同种的,相似的
advisory [əd'vaizəri] giving advice *adj*. 顾问的,咨询的
momentum [məu'mentəm] an impelling force or strength *n*. 动力,势头

parameter [pər'æmitə] a quantity (such as the mean or variance) that characterizes a statistical population and that can be estimated by calculations from sample data *n*. 参数, 参量

nasal ['neizəl] of or in or relating to the nose *adj*. 鼻的

diaphragm ['daiəfræm] (anatomy) a muscular partition separating the abdominal and thoracic cavities; functions in respiration *n*. 横隔膜

Exercises

A. Fill in each blank with one of the given words in its correct form.

ironclad	parameter	latent	akin	advisory
relate	hurdle	invalidate	residue	momentum

1. It would seem to defy an _____ principle of physics dating to 1873.
2. How do the qualities that manifest themselves in experience _____ to the very different properties that are referred to in scientific descriptions of the physical world?
3. Researchers at North Carolina State University have developed a software tool that will make it faster and easier to translate video games and other software into different languages for use in various international markets addressing a _____ to internationalization that has traditionally been time-consuming and subject to error.
4. Conservation tillage leaves enough crop _____ to cover at least one-third of the soil, while conventional tillage leaves the soil nearly bare.
5. As any TV crime series fan knows, _____ prints are left behind any time someone touches something.
6. So far, no direct and model-independent observation has allowed scientists to validate or _____ any of these existing theories, particularly for the central regions of the quasar.
7. Healthcare providers must carefully consider the unique risk factors related to severe obesity in patients undergoing all types of surgery, according to an American Heart Association scientific _____ published in Circulation: Journal of the American Heart Association.
8. Thus, names appear to carry with them a "_____" that tends to push changes in popularity in the same direction year after year.
9. Without theoretical tools like the new model, drug designers looking to create pills to induce lethal mutagenesis couldn't say for certain under what _____ ranges the drugs really worked.
10. Yet if these women shop when feeling down they risk getting trapped in a vicious cycle of highs and lows _____ to that found in other addictions.

B. Skim the text and then answer the following questions.
1. Why did ISO issue a new biometrics standard for financial firms?

2. Why is biometric authentication not completely foolproof?
3. Through what means can hackers steal an individual's fingerprints?
4. On one hand, voice recognition is not a preferred method; on the other hand, it is gaining momentum. What are the reasons for this?
5. What is the best way to boost the effectiveness of a biometric solution?

C. Read the text and choose the correct answer to each of the following questions.

1. ISO pointed to "a strong need for an ironclad authentication method" to protect the financial community and its customers from severe risks from the following expect _____.
   A. accidental or deliberate alteration of data
   B. accidental or deliberate substitution of data
   C. accidental or deliberate destruction of data
   D. accidental or deliberate misplacement of data

2. According to the text, which of the following is not included in biometric technologies? _____.
   A. Iris recognition   B. Voice identification
   C. Finger geometry   D. Vein recognition

3. _____ is not the preferred method due to a very high error rate compared to other biometrics techniques mentioned in the text.
   A. Fingerprint recognition   B. Text recognition
   C. Voice recognition   D. Key-stroke recognition

4. The word "compromised" in "In addition, while users can change their passwords if they are lost or stolen, individuals can't change their fingerprints, so that form of biometric identification would be permanently invalidated if users' fingerprints were compromised (paragraph 15)" means _____.
   A. destroyed   B. lost   C. shared   D. stolen

5. Which of the following is not an advantage of voice recognition? _____.
   A. It is not time-consuming
   B. Certification of identity can be conducted anywhere
   C. The cost is low
   D. It is free of error

D. Explain the underlined parts.

1. To <u>authenticate a user</u>, his or her biometric characteristic—a fingerprint, for example—is <u>compared to the unique pattern on file</u>.
2. <u>Privacy concerns</u> are <u>another hurdle to widespread adoption</u>, Moore adds, <u>noting that</u> financial institutions aren't yet ready for consumer-facing deployments of biometrics technology.
3. In addition, while users can change their passwords if they are lost or stolen, individuals can't change

their fingerprints, so that form of biometric identification would be permanently invalidated if users' fingerprints were compromised.
4. Ultimately, data security expert Alexander says, the best way to boost the effectiveness of a biometric solution is to use it as part of a two-factor authentication approach.
5. "There is wider acceptance," he says. "But ... I'm a big fan of it being matched with something else. It's an added layer of security."

Unit 4 Psychology

Text A

Gene Plus Stress Equals Depression Debate

1. The last thing depression investigators need is another dead-end research downer. Efforts to find genes that directly contribute to depression have come up empty. And a research team now concludes, after a closer inspection of accumulated research, that a gene variant initially tagged as a depression promoter when accompanied by stressful experiences actually has no such effect.

2. By showing that follow-up studies collectively don't support the study that launched this line of research, two new analyses debunk the proposed pathway to depression. The chances of becoming depressed rise as stressful events mount, regardless of genetic makeup, report statistical geneticist Neil Risch of the University of California, San Francisco, and his colleagues.

3. The new studies, published together in the June 17 Journal of the American Medical Association, also demonstrate the difficulty of replicating reports of any gene variants that appear to work with environmental triggers to foster psychiatric disorders. Individual studies typically lack the statistical power to detect gene-by-environment interactions correctly because most candidate genes and stressful events exert modest effects on mental ailments at best, the scientists say.

4. "I'm supportive of looking for gene-by-environment risk factors, but we'll need much larger samples to find interactions that can be independently replicated," says Risch. In his view, statistically rigorous studies will need tens of thousands of participants.

5. In 2003, scientists led by Avshalom Caspi and Terrie Moffitt, both psychologists at Duke University in Durham, N.C., studied 847 New Zealand volunteers who had been followed since age 3. Between ages 21 and 26, those who encountered several stressful events — such as health crises, money woes and relationship breakups — and who had inherited either one or two copies of a short version of the serotonin transporter gene exhibited high depression rates.

6. The serotonin transporter gene makes a protein that reduces transmission of serotonin, a mood-related chemical messenger in the brain. Many depression medications block the serotonin transporter gene's protein.

7. Caspi and Moffitt's report elicited much excitement among researchers who had been unable to link any genes directly to depression or other psychiatric conditions.

8. But two new meta-analyses directed by Risch challenge the Caspi-Moffitt findings. In the first, Risch's team combined and reanalyzed data on 14,250 participants in 14 studies published through March 2009. A second meta-analysis included unpublished information on 10,943 of the volunteers from 10 of the 14 studies. With that unpublished data, the researchers could identify any interactions between the key gene and stressful events for men and women separately.

9. Both meta-analyses transformed data on participants' depression levels and exposure to stressful events into a format that could be compared with the 2003 study.

10. Meta-analyses have their own problems, though. Chief among them is the difficulty of mixing studies with different sample sizes, participant characteristics and measurements of varying quality into a mathematically meaningful concoction.

11. Although the new meta-analysis could not totally avoid such problems, it raises a valid concern that Caspi and Moffitt's original results have yet to be replicated, says psychiatrist Kenneth Kendler of Virginia Commonwealth University School of Medicine in Richmond.

12. Alleged replications have measured stressful events in a variety of ways and have usually included only male or only female volunteers, he says. Some reports have defined genetic risk as the presence of two copies of the critical gene variant, whereas others have required only one copy.

13. Kendler directed a 2005 study that uncovered an enhanced depression risk for carriers of the short serotonin transporter gene who had been exposed to mild stress levels. Since Caspi and Moffitt reported that high, not mild, stress levels raised the depression risk for people with the gene variant, "we don't really have a replication," Kendler says.

14. In a joint comment, Caspi and Moffitt say the new meta-analyses underscore the need not for larger samples but for "more research of better quality" into gene-by-environment interactions.

15. The team's meta-analyses, like meta-analyses in general, give more mathematical weight to studies with larger samples, Caspi and Moffitt note. But in this case, larger studies — which contained as many as 2,179 participants — assessed stressful life events and depression symptoms via phone or questionnaires, rather than in comprehensive interviews. "Not surprisingly, these big studies with weak measures did not find positive results, and this tilted the meta-analysis toward a null finding," the scientists say.

16. In the past six years, they add, several studies have found that people who possess the short serotonin transporter gene display especially pronounced brain, hormone and mental responses to stressful laboratory situations. None of these studies was included in the new meta-analyses.

17. Epidemiologist Myrna Weissman, a depression researcher at Columbia University, notes that

Caspi and Moffitt's study set the methodological bar high by interviewing a large group of young people over an extended period. Thus, the researchers could determine that stressful life events occurred before rather than after first episodes of depression. Studies that have failed to replicate those findings fall short of that methodological rigor, Weissman asserts.

(http://www.sciencenews.org/view/generic/id/44733/title/Gene_plus_stress_equals_depression_debate)

Glossary

downer ['daunə] a drug that reduces excitability and calms a person n. 镇定剂
variant ['vɛəriənt] something a little different from others of the same type n. 变体
tag [tæg] provide with a name or nickname v. 称为
accompany [ə'kʌmpəni] be a companion to v. 陪伴
debunk [di:'bʌŋk] expose while ridiculing, especially of pretentious or false claims and ideas v. 揭穿真相，暴露
replicate ['replikit] make or do or perform again v. 重复，重做
psychiatric [saiki'ætrik] relating to or used in or engaged in the practice of psychiatry adj. 精神病的
woe [wəu] misery resulting from affliction n. 不幸，困难
serotonin [siərə'təunin] a neurotransmitter involved in e.g. sleep and depression and memory n. 含于血液中的复合胺
elicit [i'lisit] call forth v. 引出
meta-analysis ['metərə'næləsis] any systematic procedure for statistically combining the results of many different studies n. 荟萃分析
concoction [kən'kɔkʃən] an occurrence of an unusual mixture n. 混合物
alleged [ə'ledʒd] declared but not proved adj. 被断言的，假定的
underscore [ʌndə'skɔ:] give extra weight to v. 强调
questionnaire [kwestʃə'nɛə] a form containing a set of questions; submitted to people to gain statistical information n. 调查表
tilt [tilt] to incline or bend from a vertical position v. 倾斜
null [nʌl] lacking any legal or binding force adj. 无效力的，无效的
epidemiologist [ˌepidi:mi'ɔlədʒist] a medical scientist who studies the transmission and control of epidemic diseases n. 流行病学家
methodological [meθədə'lɔdʒikəl] relating to the methodology of some discipline adj. 方法的

Exercises

A. Fill in each blank with one of the given words in its correct form.

downer	woe	accompany	tilt	concoct
underscore	allege	replicate	debunk	null

1. Soil hardening and a loss of soil quality often _____ this approach.
2. Researchers at the University of Pittsburgh School of Medicine have successfully induced human insulin-producing cells, known as beta cells, to _____ robustly in a living animal, as well as in the lab.
3. Our findings _____ the importance of neighborhood safety to healthy aging.
4. "It's a stereotype that men are direct while women are tentative. I _____ that stereotype," said Nicholas Palomares, assistant professor of communication at UC Davis.
5. The children have told us that boredom is the biggest _____, along with adults who expect too much of them and having to work too hard.
6. "In other words," the authors write, "politicians who _____ corruption by their opponents may themselves be perceived as dishonest, critics who praise artists may themselves be perceived as talented, and gossips who describe others' infidelities may themselves be viewed as immoral."
7. "The culture surrounding topics of desertification has always been embedded in this negativity and pessimism that '_____ is us', " added Reynolds, a professor of environmental science and biology at Duke's Nicholas School of the Environment and Earth Sciences.
8. "_____ trials or those with unexpected outcomes should not, however, be viewed as failures; they have and will continue to shed light on the causes of cancer and help us discover the means for its prevention," the editorialist concludes.
9. Seated in swivel chairs that were either upright or at a 30-degree _____, the volunteers performed two listening-related tasks while motionless or spinning in darkness or in light.
10. The silvery white substance is prized as a potent, long-lasting catalyst and is used to _____ antifreeze, detergents and other industrial chemicals as well to make automotive catalytic converters, which cut down on air pollution.

B. Skim the text and then answer the following questions.

1. What is the relationship between genes and depression?
2. What is a major problem with meta-analyses?
3. What is the function of serotonin transporter gene?
4. According to the text, why did big studies fail in finding positive results?
5. Why did the author say that Caspi and Moffitt's study set a high standard for methodology?

C. Read the text and choose the correct answer to each of the following questions.

1. When more stressful events take place, _____.
   A. people will become depressed
   B. genes determine whether the chances of becoming depressed rise or not
   C. people are more likely to be depressed
   D. people will not become depressed easily

2. According to the study made in 2003, _____ exhibited high depression rate.
   A. people undergoing health crises
   B. people suffering from relationship breakups
   C. people with certain characteristics
   D. people inflicted with money woes

3. Serotonin transporter gene _____.
   A. is in the brain
   B. produces a certain kind of protein that can be blocked by depression medications
   C. makes a protein that reduces serotonin
   D. is a mood-related chemical messenger

4. Which statement is true about the two meta-analyses mentioned in the text? _____.
   A. They transformed data so as to make it easy to compare with the 2005 study
   B. They included information of 14 studies
   C. They didn't successfully mix studies with different sample sizes
   D. They confirmed the Caspi-Moffitt findings

5. People who possess the short serotonin transporter gene show _____ brain, hormone and mental responses to stressful laboratory situations.
   A. obvious   B. vague   C. no   D. a few

D. Explain the underlined parts.

1. <u>The last thing</u> depression investigators need is another <u>dead-end research downer</u>.
2. And a research team now concludes, after <u>a closer inspection of accumulated research</u>, that <u>a gene variant initially tagged as a depression promoter when accompanied by stressful experiences</u> actually has no such effect.
3. The chances of becoming depressed rise <u>as stressful events mount</u>, <u>regardless of genetic makeup</u>, report statistical geneticist Neil Risch of the University of California, San Francisco, and his colleagues.
4. In his view, <u>statistically rigorous studies</u> will need tens of thousands of participants.
5. Caspi and Moffitt's report <u>elicited much excitement among researchers who had been unable to link any genes directly to depression or other psychiatric conditions</u>.

6. Meta-analyses have their own problems, though. Chief among them is the difficulty of mixing studies with different sample sizes, participant characteristics and measurements of varying quality into a mathematically meaningful concoction.
7. In a joint comment, Caspi and Moffitt say the new meta-analyses underscore the need not for larger samples but for "more research of better quality" into gene-by-environment interactions.
8. The team's meta-analyses, like meta-analyses in general, give more mathematical weight to studies with larger samples, Caspi and Moffitt note.
9. Not surprisingly, these big studies with weak measures did not find positive results, and this tilted the meta-analysis toward a null finding....

E. Read the passages in this section and decide whether each of the following statements is true or false.

Passage One

Technically, psychology is defined as "the science of mental life". So, how do you apply this science to art and what do you understand upon doing so? Well, from all that I have seen, heard and learnt during the course of my life, I have come to understand that art is nothing but a form of expression. For some, it is an expression of their soul and their inner state of mind. For some, it is a way of venting out their feelings and emotions. For some, it is a way of separating oneself from all worldly attachments and becoming one with the spirit of the universe. Art is something that is unique, simply because of the innumerable ways of both its creation, as well as perception.

Many experts believe (and I personally vouch for this) that there is often a trigger or a certain stimulus that is associated with the creation of any great work of art. That particular trigger could be absolutely anything-an inner emotion, the happening of an external incident, sudden internal awakening, emotional turmoil or even deep anger. Many a time, by observing a work of art, one can get an idea of what could have triggered, stimulated, or inspired the creator to come up with what he or she did. It is simply amazing, how often a true work of art acts as a mirror that reflects the creator's state of mind or being, at the time of creation. To know what I'm talking about, try the following exercise.

The next time you visit an art gallery, try to analyze the paintings and the artifacts from an altogether different perspective. Don't just stand in front of a painting, admire it for ten seconds and then move on to the next one in line. Stand there. Get into the painting. Yes, INTO the painting. Think about what that painting symbolizes, what subject it deals with, what message it gives out. Get an insight into the mind of the artist, try and imagine the creative thinking process that the artist must have gone through while painting it. It is his imagination that helped him in painting this piece of art. Try to get into his mind, think of what must have inspired or stimulated him to paint what he did, to use the patterns and symbols that he did and to use the color combinations that he did. There is a plethora of knowledge and trivia, that is hidden behind that piece of canvas. It is like a treasure to be discovered and you will be amazed, when you actually discover it. In much the same way, you can get into the psychology of art by listening to a piece of music. Select any song or piece of music of your choice. Now listen to it in a totally different way. Put yourself in the shoes of the composer. Think about why a particular musical note has been used in the place that it has been used. What if some other note was used in its place? How would it impact the song or that piece of music? There is always a reason, why the composer has used a particular set of musical notes or chord progressions. Trying to understand that, is like trying to unravel a secret. Getting into the soul of the song will help you to unravel the secret.

(http://www.buzzle.com/articles/the-psychology-of-art.html)

_____ 1. Art is a form of expression.

_____ 2. The author doesn't believe there is an incentive for an artist to create any work of art.

_____ 3. A piece of art itself can offer clue to what inspired the artist into making it.

_____ 4. One can use his heart and soul to get into the psychology of art.

_____ 5. To get into the psychology of art by observing a painting is different from by listening to a piece of music.

Passage Two

Here are some of the major players in human behavior psychology:

Drives and motives: It began with the theory of instincts. Instincts are defined as the innate biological forces like fear, aggression, curiosity and reproduction that decide human behavior. According to Mcdoughall a British psychologist, behavior is result of instincts that are fixed from birth but can be changed as per learning and experience. However, the theory of instincts was replaced by the theory of drives in the 1920s for better explanation of human behavior psychology. This put forth the explanation that it is natural need from which arises a driving force that is accountable for human behavior. However, it was soon realized that other than inner driving forces, there were external factors that played an equally important role in setting the direction of human behavior. One example is the hunger that one feels when on seeing a pastry even after he has had his dinner. This drive does not originate from an internal need, but from an external impetus.

Social influences: Society conditions our behavior by the process of socialization in which an individual picks up attitudes and norms of the society by being exposed to them. As one grows each individual knows the role that he has to play and he accepts the stereotypes of the society. Societal influence explains the differences in the human behavior across various cultures.

Genetics: Behavioral genetics is the branch of science that tries to find the role of genetics behind human behavior psychology. The pioneer in this field was Sir Francis Galton of England who carried out a study on the heredity of genius in families. According to him genius runs in the family. A lot of research has gone into understanding genetic basis of human behavior psychology after sir Galton. These studies indicate that complex behaviors related to personality, cognitive abilities and psychopathology are influenced by human genetics to some extent. However, now it is most widely accepted that genetics alone cannot explain human behavior. Most psychologists today believe that behavior is the result of complex interplay between genetics and behavior.

Hormones: These are chemicals released by the body that control various metabolic processes in the body. They are known to affect the development of cognitive capabilities and also the nervous system. Our cognitive abilities and development of nervous system, both play an important role in how an individual perceives a particular situation and reacts to it. Hormones being secreted in excess or deficient amounts are known to cause behavioral and personality disorders. Also hyperactivity of thyroid gland is known to cause anxiety in individuals that makes them react to the same situation in a different way than that a normal person would.

Human behavior psychology is a vast domain. The factors discussed so far are a few of those that have a major role to play in the psychology of human behavior. Other factors that influence human behavior are cognitive abilities, emotions, personality and behavioral disorders that makes each individual different form another. More research is required to be made in understanding human behavior psychology that is just as perplexing as it seems limitless.

(http://www.buzzle.com/articles/the-psychology-of-behavior.html)

_____ 6. Instincts are forces that decide human behavior.

_____ 7. Learning and experience influence how we behave.

_____ 8. Social influence explains why people from different countries behave differently.

_____ 9. Genetics can be used to explain human behavior.

_____ 10. Behavioral and personality disorders are caused by hormones secretion.

F. Cloze. Fill in each blank with one suitable word.

Studying how people __1__ a work of art is also an important aspect to consider when studying the psychology of art. Different people perceive art in different __2__. The way a man perceives or interprets a work of art __3__ volumes about his mood, his state of mind, his emotional and mental balance, and about him as a person. To understand what I am saying, try this out. The next time you visit a museum or an art exhibition, try and __4__ what people think of a particular painting or artifact. Pay careful attention to each and every person's __5__ of that work of art. Some may find it positive, others may find it negative. Some may be very __6__ of a certain artistic detail, whereas some may find the piece of art to be offensive. It all depends on the person's mind and state of being. A __7__ has two sides, but the number of "sides" (read possibilities) that are __8__ in the human mind are limitless. __9__, you will often see that ten different people, when shown one single painting, will always have ten completely different interpretations, views and understandings of that one single painting. This is a __10__ example of the psychology of art.

1. A. receive   B. conceive   C. perceive   D. deceive
2. A. means   B. methods   C. approaches   D. ways
3. A. speaks   B. expresses   C. indicates   D. announces
4. A. listen   B. imagine   C. observe   D. understand
5. A. account   B. comprehension   C. analysis   D. interpretation
6. A. appreciative   B. understanding   C. considerate   D. amazed
7. A. corn   B. coin   C. sword   D. matter
8. A. presented   B. presenting   C. present   D. presentive
9. A. However   B. Meanwhile   C. Moreover   D. Therefore
10. A. down-to-earth   B. larger-than-life   C. real-life   D. starry-eyed

G. Translate the following passages into Chinese/English.

1. What is it about human behavior psychology that has intrigued human beings since such ancient times? Probably it is the complex and diverse nature of human behavior. Take the case of identical twins. Although they form from the same set of genetic components, as far as behavior is concerned, even they show different reactions to the same situation. So many individuals and each is unique surely on account of physical features, but definitely much more on the basis of behavior. The behavioral differences between identical twins highlights the fact that it is not (at least not just) genetics that governs human behavior. People with similar environmental conditions display relatively similar behavior. However, even such individuals do not behave the same way all the time. Then, what are the factors that govern human behavior psychology?

2. 现在我们都把"心理学"解释为以科学的方法对人类行为进行的研究。这里所用的"行为"一词,不仅仅是指行动、活动范围或举止。它包含着整个生物体的全部正常的和反常的活动,甚至还包括智力迟钝者和精神病患者的那些活动。这种研究的宗旨是要探索行为在自我发现中的作用,以及个人能够发展的各种不同的慈善行为的模式。英语心理学的目的是阐述、预测和控制人类的活动,以便我们可以理解和理智地知道我们的生活并影响他人的生活。

Text B

Work: Kindness and Corporation

1. Does kindness have a proper place at the office? Or is it found mostly on a stool in the corner with a small but definite dunce cap?

2. Kindness, it turns out, is controversial.

3. "Kindness is not a word I would use in my trainings," one executive development coach insists. "The leaders at the level on which I work don't relate to it, because it describes a social value. The closest we come is an emphasis on creating a respectful workplace, avoiding sexual harassment, racial intolerance, or gender bias."

4. Good, of course, but not exactly the tender offer of kindness. Perhaps it's that very sense of tenderness that gives kindness its image problem. One female litigator described her own wariness regarding warm civility: "If a male is pleasant and easy to work with, he's regarded as a nice guy. But if I extend opposing counsel a common courtesy, say, on a scheduling matter where he has a legitimate conflict, I am often seen as a pushover, and that works against my client's interests. I can't afford to be seen as a pleaser."

5. One CEO vigorously defended his own check on compassion: "I'd love to be able to step in and hand a valued employee some cash because I've heard his wife got laid off and I know he needs the money. But people aren't discreet about that kind of thing; they tell. And then every other employee wonders why I didn't do the same for him or her."

6. You could argue that the milk of human kindness is pretty much curdled at the office when it stirs images of weakness, naivete, self-promotion, or self-defense. All the downsides notwithstanding, there is a strong current of kindness stubbornly running through some workplaces. And where it flows, people smile more. They work harder, too.

7. In their book, *Leading with Kindness*, William Baker and Michael O'Malley contend that corporate kindness positively impacts profits. They identify six qualities of kind managers—compassion, integrity, gratitude, authenticity, humility, and humor—and believe a kind management style improves employee performance and retention.

8. Depending on how you define it, kindness can be seen as an individual character trait, present or not as a function of who works where. "Some guys are just total pricks," says a manufacturing rep. "They wouldn't say hello to an entry level associate or look at the cleaning lady. But they would do a favor for a client."

9. The provost of a local college spoke admiringly of the school's president. "He's just a terrific guy who is genuinely interested in the well-being of people. He knows the life story of everyone in the building. He makes everyone feel valued."

10. But kindness can just as readily be a corporate cultural value, one to be supported or snuffed out depending upon the attitude of the people on top. One veteran of five top financial firms said, "These companies were not identical in their basic human spirit. If you had one of those whispering guys at the top, the signal was clear: Do whatever it takes. Losers will be bounced out. Winners will be rewarded.

Kindness was just something that got in the way.

11. "When a decent guy ran the ship, it filtered through, made us more willing to collaborate with each other. It was better for business, not to mention morale. But better or worse, the CEO sets the emotional tone."

12. Overall climate control has its impact, but so does specific strategy. Kindness has found its place as a training tool and as a team-building approach. One physician referred to the importance of correcting staff error in a kind, sensitive fashion. "We try to prevent mistakes. But when they happen, they have to be addressed immediately. I'm a hyper guy, but when I review a staff error I deliberately calm down and give that nurse or that resident a chance to explain her error. If I'm too mad, I take time to get it together. Then we go over the correct course. I'm conscious of mentioning something they've done right recently, so we can end the conversation on a positive note."

13. This same physician sees kindness as a simple staff development strategy. "It's my job to make the people who work for me happy; if they're happy, they'll work harder. So I do stuff like bring them doughnuts, send out for lunch. I make sure to tell them how often my patients say they love you guys, how much the sick people appreciate their efforts."

14. A lot of people would be happier if they worked for him.

15. Each definition of workplace kindness has its own truth, but all have a common thread. Kindness is a step beyond respect or fair play, a step out in front of the corporate policy manual. It is personal, thoughtful, and—for want of a better word—caring. And it exists at the office.

16. I offer anecdotal proof, reported by a senior marketing division manager: "I worked for 10 years at a Fortune 100 firm. When my husband was dying, the CEO called me in and said, 'Go take care of your family. Your job will be here. You've taken care of us all these years. Let us take care of you.'" Chainsaw Al Dunlap took that company over five years later.

Calling for Kindness

17. Yes, work is about making money—that's why it's called work. But money and humanity do not have to be mutually exclusive. Call on your kinder side:

18. In times of emotional distress. You may not know what's wrong, but tuning into the folks around you will probably reveal when something is amiss. An appreciative remark, a supportive comment helps.

19. When giving negative feedback. "I'm just being honest" or "I'm just as hard on myself" are clues to add kindness to your management style.

20. When giving a sensitive personal review. A worker's hygiene problem or slovenly work area needs to be addressed, but keep your awkwardness from becoming harshness.

21. In times of personal emergency. People generally need three times the recovery time we grant

them. Patience and understanding count.

(http://www.psychologytoday.com/articles/200903/work-kindness-and-corporation)

Glossary

dunce cap ['dʌns'kæp] a cone-shaped paper hat formerly placed on the head of slow or lazy pupils *n*. 以前的学生被罚时所戴的纸帽
harassment ['hærəsmənt] the act of tormenting by continued persistent attacks and criticism *n*. 骚扰
litigator ['litiɡeitə] a person employed to litigate, a lawyer skilled in arguing in court *n*. 诉讼律师
wariness ['weərinis] the trait of being cautious and watchful *n*. 注意, 小心
pushover ['puʃəuvə(r)] someone who is easily taken advantage of *n*. (俚)易于征服或控制的人
discreet [dis'kri:t] marked by prudence or modesty and wise self-restraint *adj*. 谨慎的
curdle ['kə:dl] turn from a liquid to a solid mass *v*. 凝结
naivete [nai'i:vətei] lack of sophistication or worldliness *n*. 天真, 质朴
downside ['daunsaid] a negative aspect of something that is generally positive *n*. 消极面, 负面
notwithstanding [nɔtwiθ'stændiŋ] despite anything to the contrary *adv*. 虽然, 尽管
authenticity [ɔ:θen'tisiti] undisputed credibility *n*. 确实性, 真实性
retention [ri'tenʃən] the act of retaining something *n*. 保持(力)
prick [prik] insulting terms of address for people who are stupid or irritating or ridiculous *n*. 刺头
provost ['prɔvəst] a high-ranking university administrator *n*. 负责校政人员
veteran ['vetərən] someone who has given long service *n*. 老手
hyper ['haipə] too excited and energetic *adj*. 精力过旺的
anecdotal [ænek'dəutl] having the character of an anecdote *adj*. 轶事一样的
amiss [ə'mis] not functioning properly *adj*. 有毛病的, 出差错的
hygiene ['haidʒi:n] a condition promoting sanitary practices *n*. 卫生
slovenly ['slʌvənli] negligent of, neatness especially in dress and person; habitually dirty and unkempt *adj*. 马虎的(潦草的)

Exercises

A. Fill in each blank with one of the given words in its correct form.

| retention | downside | prick | veteran | hygiene |
| harassment | notwithstanding | authenticity | anecdotal | discreet |

1. Bullying can also include verbal _____, which can be just as damaging and detrimental to student learning.
2. The increasing number of _____ with posttraumatic stress disorder (PTSD) raises the risk of do-

mestic violence and its consequences on families and children in communities across the United States.
3. Monitoring sensor patterns is an effective and _____ way to ensure the health and privacy of older adults.
4. There is ample _____ evidence that local governments use traffic tickets as a means of generating revenue.
5. Each wireless connection point requires, _____ the name, a cable with a connection to the Internet.
6. The authors say they were intrigued by how consumers were able to judge seemingly mundane objects or mass-market brands as _____.
7. A report published in the October 2008 issue of HortTechnology measures the socioeconomic impact of automation and mechanization on sales, employment, workers' earnings, safety and worker _____ in nurseries and greenhouses.
8. Our research suggests that there may be a _____ to this increase of options affecting people's ability to decide in a particular situation.
9. Testing people for heart disease might be just a finger _____ away thanks to a new credit card-sized device created by a team of researchers from Harvard and Northeastern universities in Boston.
10. Increased hand _____ in primary schools is only a short-term measure in preventing infections such as H1N1 from spreading.

B. Skim the text and then answer the following questions.
1. What is the above-mentioned executive development coach Kindness's view of kindness?
2. According to William Baker and Michael O'Malle, what are the six qualities of kind managers?
3. What is the shared property of different types of workplace kindness?
4. What are the recommended ways to offer kindness?
5. What is your opinion of "kindness on campus"?

C. Read the text and choose the correct answer to each of the following questions.
1. The example given by the female litigator is used to indicate that _____.
    A. people have the same attitude toward male and female tenderness
    B. it is not proper for females to show their kindness
    C. it is human nature that causes people to have different opinions on kindness presented
    D. it is not proper for males to show their kindness
2. According to the CEO mentioned in the fifth paragraph, _____.
    A. personally he wouldn't like to offer help to the employees
    B. it was better not to show kindness to the employees
    C. it was the employees' fault that caused him to hold his compassion

D. the employees are greedy
3. Which of the following is the correct meaning of the phrase "the milk of human kindness"? _____.
   A. Care and compassion for others
   B. Self-promotion, or self-defense
   C. Tenderness
   D. Weakness
4. Which is not the benefit of kindness presented in William Baker and Michael O'Malley's book? _____.
   A. Profits will increase
   B. Employees will work harder
   C. Employee performance will improve
   D. Employee retention will improve
5. Who determines kindness as a corporate cultural value? _____.
   A. The employees   B. The veterans   C. The employers   D. All of the above

D. Explain the underlined parts.
1. But if I <u>extend opposing counsel a common courtesy</u>, say, on a scheduling matter where he <u>has a legitimate conflict</u>, I am often seen <u>as a pushover</u>, and that works against my client's interests.
2. One CEO <u>vigorously defended his own check on compassion</u>... But people aren't <u>discreet about that kind of thing</u>...
3. But kindness can just <u>as readily be a corporate cultural value</u>, one <u>to be supported or snuffed out depending upon the attitude of the people on top</u>.
4. <u>Overall climate control has its impact, but so does specific strategy</u>. Kindness has <u>found its place as a training tool and as a team-building approach</u>.
5. Each definition of workplace kindness has its own truth, but all <u>have a common thread</u>. Kindness is <u>a step beyond respect or fair play, a step out in front of the corporate policy manual</u>.

Unit 5 Energy

Text A

Nuclear Fusion: Energy for the Future?

1. The energy crisis has rocketed from a textbook concept into the most pressing political issue of our time. Future energy supplies are increasingly vulnerable and global consumption is expected to escalate dramatically, increasing by 71% in 2030 and continuing to rise. Energy shortages would have a dramatic impact on every area of modern life: business, transport, food, health and communications. This looming crisis has drawn scientific minds and encouraged radical research into arcane technologies, such as the once neglected area of nuclear fusion.

Why Nuclear Fusion?

2. Our sun, and all the other stars in the universe, are powered by nuclear fusion. Similar to traditional nuclear power, or fission, it can produce huge amounts of carbon-neutral energy. But there is one vital difference: no dangerous, long-lasting radioactive waste. Waste from nuclear fusion is only radioactive for 50~70 years, compared to the thousands of years of radioactivity that result from fission. "This is a long-term supply of energy," says Professor Mike Dunne of the Rutherford Appleton Laboratory in Oxford shire. "You can get a lot of energy from a small amount of fuel and the by-products are benign."

3. Raw materials for nuclear fusion water and silicon are plentiful and widespread on Earth. This should prevent the situations where energy supplies can be threatened by political instability; as demonstrated in January 2007 when Russia shut down a main oil pipeline to Europe after a political spat with Belarus.

4. Nuclear fusion could also help meet international climate change targets, such as those agreed by politicians in Washington last month. Current zero-carbon technologies are unlikely to meet our energy demands this century. Nuclear power is deeply unpopular while renewable energy sources wind, solar and tidal yield relatively little energy for their high cost. But nuclear fusion could render carbon dioxide-producing fossil fuels obsolete by 2100.

The Challenge

5. If we have the potential for unlimited, clean energy, then why wait? Unfortunately, all previous

attempts to produce large amounts of energy from nuclear fusion have failed. Secret tests during the atomic bomb programme in the 1950s discovered fusion was possible, but the continuous nuclear fusion reactions required to generate substantial amounts of energy have remained elusive.

6. Huge amounts of energy are required for nuclear fusion. Atomic nuclei are forced to fuse together, in contrast to fission where nuclei are split apart. In the sun, temperatures of 15 million degrees Celsius and immense pressures force hydrogen nuclei to fuse and produce helium, thus releasing energy. Hydrogen exists as plasma and nuclear fusion reactions occur continually. "The trick is to get a self-sustaining reaction," says Dunne. "It's like setting off an explosive, you have a little bit of energy a detonator and this sets off a chain reaction."

7. Energy production from nuclear fusion has proven an insurmountable challenge so far. Yet scientists are now saying that plans for larger and more sophisticated reactors around the world could finally make this possible in 50 years time. Is this more than just wishful thinking?

Projects Underway

8. Last June, 7 billion ($ 13.5 billion) in funding from the European Union and seven partner countries was agreed, and work has begun on a green hill in Cadarache, France, to construct possibly the world's first viable nuclear fusion reactor. The Europe International Thermonuclear Experimental Reactor (ITER) contains a giant "doughnut", which will spin super-heated hydrogen isotopes in a magnetic field, to produce continuous nuclear fusion. "ITER will produce more energy than you put in," explains Chris Warrick from the UK Atomic Energy Authority. "You need 50 megawatts of power to heat it and you should get around 5,000 megawatts out."

9. Plans for other projects are underway in Britain. The High Power Energy Research (HiPER) project, based in Didcot, is looking at using huge lasers to produce energy from nuclear fusion. "We need to build a laser the size of a football stadium and focus it on a pellet of fuel about 1mm in diameter," says Dunne. "This will collapse the hydrogen isotope fuel until we achieve the same compression you get in the sun."

10. Legitimate concerns remain about investing in such speculative technology and radioactive waste production. "Governments should not waste money on a dangerous toy which will never deliver any useful energy," says Jan van de Putte from Greenpeace. "They should invest in renewable energy, which is abundantly available today." However, scientists argue that all possible solutions to the energy crisis should be explored and any radioactive waste from nuclear fusion is short-lived.

11. Although using nuclear fusion is controversial, it could also be the most significant scientific breakthrough of the century. If it is a success, the energy crisis would be a distant memory, climate change could be halted and we may all be driving around guilt-free in electric cars. It still sounds like science fiction, but we may only have decades to wait before it becomes a reality.

Glossary

escalate ['eskəleit] increase in extent or intensity v. 扩大,升高,增强;(战争)逐步升级

loom [lu:m] come into view indistinctly, often threateningly v. 朦胧地出现,隐约可见,恐怖地出现

arcane [ɑ:'kein] requiring secret or mysterious knowledge adj. 神秘的,秘密的

nuclear fusion: a nuclear reaction in which nuclei combine to form more massive nuclei with the simultaneous release of energy [核]核子融合

fission ['fiʃən] a nuclear reaction in which a massive nucleus splits into smaller nuclei with the simultaneous release of energy n. 裂开,分裂,分体

carbon-neutral: refers to neutral (meaning zero) total carbon release, brought about by balancing the amount of carbon released with the amount sequestered. Various special interests attempt to promote a use of the term that merely refers to carbon reduction, which is clearly not neutral 碳中性,无碳污染的

radioactive ['reidiəu'æktiv] exhibiting or caused by radioactivity adj. 放射性的

radioactivity ['reidiəuæk'tiviti] the spontaneous emission of a stream of particles or electromagnetic rays in nuclear decay n. 放射性

benign [bi'nain] pleasant and beneficial in nature or influence adj. 良性的

silicon ['silikən] a tetravalent nonmetallic element; next to oxygen it is the most abundant element in the earth's crust; occurs in clay and feldspar and granite and quartz and sand; used as a semiconductor in transistors n. 硅

Belarus ['belə,rʌs;'belə,rus] n. 白俄罗斯

renewable energy resource: energy that can be replaced by natural proesses or good management, so that it is never used up 可再生能源

fossil fuel: fuel consisting of the remains of organisms preserved in rocks in the earth's crust with high carbon and hydrogen content 矿物燃料

elusive [i'lju:siv] be difficult to detect or grasp by the mind adj. 难懂的,易忘的,难捉摸的

nuclei ['nju:kliai] the positively charged dense center of an atom n. (nucleus ['nju:kliəs] 的复数形) 核,核心,原子核

celsius ['selsjəs] of or relating to a temperature scale that registers the freezing point of water as 0℃ and the boiling point as 100℃ under normal atmospheric pressure adj. 摄氏的

hydrogen ['haidrəudʒən] a nonmetallic univalent element that is normally a colorless and odorless highly flammable diatomic gas; the simplest and lightest and most abundant element in the universe n. 氢

helium ['hi:ljəm,-liəm] a very light colorless element that is one of the six inert gasses; the most difficult gas to liquefy; occurs in economically extractable amounts in certain natural gases n. 氦

plasma ['plæzmə] (physical chemistry) a fourth state of matter distinct from solid or liquid or gas and present in stars and fusion reactors; a gas becomes a plasma when it is heated until the atoms lose all their electrons, leaving a highly electrified collection of nuclei and free electrons *n.* 等离子体

detonator ['detəuneitə] a mechanical or electrical explosive device or a small amount of explosive; can be used to initiate the reaction of a disrupting explosive *n.* 发爆剂(引燃剂、雷管、炸药、爆鸣器)

insurmountable [insə'mauntəbl] not capable of being surmounted or overcome *adj.* 不能克服的,难以对付的

viable ['vaiəbl] capable of being done with means at hand and circumstances as they are *adj.* 可行的

reactor [ri(:)'æktə] (physics) any of several kinds of apparatus that maintain and control a nuclear reaction for the production of energy or artificial elements *n.* 反应堆

the International Thermonuclear Experimental Reactor (ITER) 国际热核聚变实验堆

isotope ['aisəutəup] one of two or more atoms with the same atomic number but with different numbers of neutrons *n.* 同位素

magnetic field: the lines of force surrounding a permanent magnet or a moving charged particle *n.* 磁场

megawatt ['megəwɔt] a unit of power equal to one million watts *n.* 百万瓦特

pellet ['pelit] a little ball or similarly-shaped object *n.* 小球,球状物,(反应堆燃料)芯块

greenpeace ['gri:npi:s] an international organization that works for environmental conservation and the preservation of endangered species *n.* (保护动物不遭捕猎等的)"绿色和平"组织

science fiction: literary fantasy involving the imagined impact of science on society *n.* 科幻小说

Exercises

A. Fill in each blank with one of the given words in its correct form.

viable	collapse	insurmountable	fiction	benign
fusion	breakthrough	abundantly	rocket	loom
vulnerable	elusive	instability	radioactive	escalate

1. I think that our study is one step toward decreasing the number of invasive procedures in patients with _____ thyroid nodules (甲状腺结节)—while maintaining the same vigilance in detecting thyroid cancer in its early stages.

2. For instance, a bird could decide not to _____ a conflict over territory if it decides the other bird is in better physical condition.

3. Requiring much less effort and materials, the new pipeline will speed up structural studies of protein complexes and will allow to decipher as yet _____ molecular mechanisms of health and disease.

4. When people think of computer science the image that immediately pops into many of their minds is of the computer geek surrounded by such things as computer games, science _____ memorabilia and

junk food.

5. However, quarrying of limestone _____ as a potential threat to wildlife in this area, along with habitat conversion for agriculture.
6. The findings from this study suggest that a genetic and/or an additional environmental factor associated with psychosis (精神病) likely is necessary for the fetal brain to be _____ to the effects of influenza, given that decreases in cognitive performance were only observed in influenza-exposed children who developed a psychotic disorder in adulthood.
7. Carbon-dioxide exists in the atmosphere so _____ that its full possible influence seems probably to be exerted.
8. So what happens if the market rationalizes, if the payment becomes a _____ way to reach the majority of consumers who consume a particular publication?
9. It is possible to achieve nuclear _____ between deuterium nuclei (氘原子核) using high-power lasers, releasing vast amounts of energy.
10. The _____ waste should be buried deeply under the ground in sealed box.
11. Both species' energy demands were relatively low during the months of September and October, but _____ by at least 16% in November and remained high for the rest of the winter.
12. In a _____ for applied physics, North Carolina State University researchers have developed a magnetic semiconductor memory device, using GaMnN thin films, which utilizes both the charge and spin of electrons at room temperature.
13. If certain obstacles, which many believe to be _____, such as scalability and image representation, can be overcome, it is possible that one day machine recognizability can reach that of humans.
14. In their dying days, stars smaller than 2.1 times our sun's mass die and _____ into neutron stars—objects dense enough that the neutrons and protons push against each other.
15. Our model shows how _____ in the grounding line, caused by gradual climatic changes, has the potential to reach a 'tipping point' where disintegration of the ice sheet could occur.

B. Answer the following questions concerning the text.
1. What is energy crisis? And have you ever been confronted with such a problem?
2. What kind of energy does sun produce? What else can do the same thing?
3. What kind of powers can be regarded as renewable powers?
4. What advantage does nuclear fusion have?
5. What do the European Union and seven partner countries want to do by collecting funds?

C. Read the following questions and choose the best answer.
1. According to the text, which aspect of our life is not mentioned in relation to the lack of energy? _____.

A. Commuting by underground   B. Doing operations in the hospital
   C. Migrating to an ecological habitat   D. Plowing with a tractor
2. Compared with nuclear fusion, what disadvantage does nuclear fission have? _____.
   A. Perilous by-products   B. A long-term supply of energy
   C. Free of political intervention   D. Environment-friendly
3. In Paragraph 5, in order to help explain the difficult process of nuclear fusion, what devices are adopted by the author to make such a vivid description as in "the sun" and "with a detonator"? _____.
   A. Contrast and exemplification   B. Exemplification and analogy
   C. Analogy and comparison   D. Comparison and parallel
4. Which of the following is TRUE according to the text? _____.
   A. The government and some scientists are strongly opposed to the program of nuclear fusion
   B. The energy input is similar to the one output in the process of nuclear fusion
   C. Nuclear fission is one of the big breakthroughs in the history of science
   D. Vehicles of transportation may not be a problem-maker of pollution thanks to nuclear fusion
5. What is the author's attitude towards nuclear fusion? _____.
   A. Objective   B. Subjective   C. Optimistic   D. Pessimistic

D. Explain the underlined parts.

1. The energy crisis <u>has rocketed from a textbook concept into the most pressing political issue of our time</u>.
2. This looming crisis <u>has drawn scientific minds and encouraged radical research into arcane technologies</u>, such as the once neglected area of nuclear fusion.
3. <u>Secret tests during the atomic bomb programme in the 1950s discovered fusion was possible</u>, but the continuous nuclear fusion reactions required to generate substantial amounts of energy have remained elusive.
4. The Europe International Thermonuclear Experimental Reactor (ITER) <u>contains a giant "doughnut", which will spin super-heated hydrogen isotopes in a magnetic field, to produce continuous nuclear fusion</u>.
5. <u>Legitimate concerns remain about investing in such speculative technology and radioactive waste production</u>.
6. <u>If it is a success, the energy crisis would be a distant memory, climate change could be halted and we may all be driving around guilt-free in electric cars</u>.

E. Read the passages in this section and decide whether each of the following statements is true or false.

Passage One

Nuclear energy is a way of creating heat through the fission process of atoms. All power plants convert heat into electricity using steam. At nuclear power plants, the heat to make the steam is created when atoms split apart—called fission. (Other types of power plants burn coal or oil for heat to make steam.)

The fission process takes place when the nucleus of a heavy atom, like uranium or plutonium, is split in two when struck by a neutron. The "fissioning" of the nucleus releases two or three new neutrons.

It also releases energy in the form of heat. The released neutrons can then repeat the process. This releases even more neutrons and more nuclear energy. The repeating of the process is called a chain reaction. In a nuclear power plant, uranium is the material used in the fission process.

The heat from fission boils water and creates steam to turn a turbine. As the turbine spins, the generator turns and its magnetic field produces electricity. The electricity can then be carried to your home, so you can work on the computer, watch television, play video games, or make toast!

The U.S. Nuclear Regulatory Commission, also called the "NRC", regulates nuclear power plants. We make sure they are safe for people who work there and live nearby, and for the environment.

The NRC also regulates nuclear material that is used in science, medicine and industry. We issue licenses to those who operate power plants or use nuclear material, and we inspect them to make sure they're following our rules.

DID YOU KNOW?

Nuclear material is used for many things besides nuclear power:

—To detect and treat certain illnesses

—To perform research at universities

—To help in industries for such things as locating cracks in steel, getting rid of dust from film and even measuring the amount of air whipped into ice cream!

(http://www.nrc.gov/reading-rm/basic-ref/students.html)

_____ 1. In contrast, nuclear power seldom involves the production of steam.

_____ 2. Nuclear fission results in multiplication of neutrons.

_____ 3. The flowing water helps the generator to produce electricity.

_____ 4. NRC is an organization to protect the environment and exploit nuclear material.

_____ 5. Uranium has a wide application in people's life.

Passage Two

Fasten your seatbelt. We've got some ground to cover. But it won't be too difficult to grasp the fundamentals. In either fission or fusion, we are taking about nuclear processes, i.e., the physics of nuclear structure and construction/destruction of that nucleus. The big difference is fusion is the "building" of atomic nuclei, and fission is the "breaking" or "splitting" of atomic nuclei.

Fusion is the bonding of atomic nuclei or nuclear particles (nucleons-protons and neutrons) to make "bigger" or "heavier" atomic nuclei. Fission, on the other hand is the splitting of the atom. As the atoms fuse or split they release energy. Lots of it. And most of it is heat energy. In nuclear weapons, the energy is released "all at once" to create a blast. If the energy is released in a "controlled" way, we can release heat at a "useable" rate and apply it to boiling water to make steam.

In fusion, protons or neutrons or the nuclei of atoms are forced together and are fused to make a new atomic nucleus. The release of lots and lots of energy accompanies this reaction. That's what powers stars. Currently we can't really do any fusion reactions to make useful power. There are a few agencies working on fusion devices, but the high temperatures required to attain fusion require very special materials and controls. The current "state of the art" fusion facility is the International Thermonuclear Experimental Reactor (and a link is provided). Fusion is unlikely to become a useful source of power for many years. But what about fission?

Nuclear fission involves the splitting of large atoms, usually uranium (or sometimes plutonium). When large atoms fission, they produce two smaller atoms or fission fragments (and a couple of neutrons and lots of energy). The total mass of the products is less than the mass of the original atom. This mass difference is turned into energy in accordance with the Einstein equation $E = mc^2$. Most of the energy appears in the recoil of the fission fragments, and the heat that is generated is considerable. It is that heat that we capture to turn water into steam to generate electricity.

(http://wiki.answers.com/Q/How_is_nuclear_fission_different_from_nuclear_fusion)

_____ 6. Fusion is the destruction process of the atomic nucleus.

_____ 7. Both in fission and fusion, energy is generated.

_____ 8. Now there are some agencies that can make fusion reactions controllable.

_____ 9. What is lost in the process of fission, in fact, exists in another form.

_____ 10. We use fission reactions more than fusion ones in application.

F. Cloze. Fill in each blank with one suitable word.

With the approval of the Chinese Government, the Chinese Domestic Agency (CN DA) for ITER was __1__ established in June 2008. Registered as the "China International Nuclear Fusion Energy Program Execution Center" (CINFEPEC), the CN DA is an independent legal __2__ under the supervision of the Ministry of Science and Technology. It is composed of 30 permanent staff, together with a dozen __3__ experts and some secondées.

The CN DA consists of five divisions: Project Management, Engineering Technologies, International

Cooperation, Fusion R&D, and Administration. Under the leadership of the Minister from the Ministry of Science and Technology, the CN DA is __4__ the implementation of the ITER project together with other ministries, institutes and entities, and also for the management of __5__ R&D in magnetic confinement fusion.

The CN DA has been busy __6__ the preparation of Procurement Arrangements (PAs) together with the ITER Organization. The CN DA signed two Procurement Arrangements for the TF and PF Conductor Coils in 2008, __7__ for Correction Coils and their conductors will be signed soon.

For its signed PAs, the CN DA has already completed market surveys __8__ the contracts, and is finishing call-for-tender __9__ according to the ITER "Guidelines to the Management of Procurements In Kind".

The CNDA will strictly follow its commitments and __10__ close cooperation and communication with the ITER Organization and other DAs in order to contribute to the success of ITER project. (http://www.iter.org/newsline/Pages/102/1400.aspx)

1. A. basically   B. continually   C. officially   D. appropriately
2. A. department   B. entity   C. existence   D. court
3. A. lawful   B. technical   C. professional   D. governmental
4. A. in accordance with B. in terms of   C. in charge of   D. in respect of
5. A. domestic   B. global   C. regional   D. local
6. A. researching for B. performing for   C. making up   D. working on
7. A. the other two   B. two others   C. two another   D. the another two
8. A. for preparation of B. in preparation for C. in preparation of D. for preparation in
9. A. procedures   B. deteriorations   C. restarts   D. supervisions
10. A. maintain   B. halt   C. activate   D. prohibit

G. Translate the following paragraphs into Chinese/English.

1. Now the "pros" are on a new mission to dispel a generation of scares and suspicion, saying nuclear power is less dangerous to humans and the Earth than burning oil or coal. The "antis" say nuclear energy can never offer 100 percent protection from its radioactive ingredients. The splitting of uranium atoms in a nuclear reactor creates the exceptional heat that drives turbines to provide electricity. The process also creates radioactive isotopes such as cesium-137 and strontium-90 that take about 30 years to lose half their radioactivity. Higher-level leftovers include plutonium-239, with a half-life of 24,000 years.

2. 直接暴露在这些高放射性物质的辐照下，哪怕极短时间，都可能是致命的。通过渗透到地下水的间接辐照可导致生活在附近的居民罹患威胁生命的疾病和生态环境的破坏。目前，摆脱极其致命的放射性废料的最科学的方法是地下深埋。然而还没有任何国家建起了地质型核废料深埋场。每当政府提出要在某处建造一座时，对政府的抗议就随之而来。另一个选择是回收利用。像法国、俄罗斯、日本那样的一些国家把大量核废料重新加工成新的燃料。不过,回收利用会产生可以用于核武器中的钚——所以美国禁止核废料回收利用,害怕引起核扩散。

Text B

Energy Independence and Climate Change: Linked but Separate

1. Politicians love "win-win" solutions. A search of congressional Web sites reveals that the phrase shows up more than 2,500 times. Just as scientists seek to explain multiple facts, policymakers seek to balance the needs of multiple interests. Scientists and policymakers may have little in common, but both value parsimony.

2. Earlier this year, House Speaker Nancy Pelosi (D-Calif.) created a new Select Committee on Energy Independence and Global Warming. In the context of "win-win", the name of the committee is notable, with the conjunction implying both issues may be resolved through the same legislative mechanisms. Although energy independence and global warming are certainly linked, it is also true that, in the words of one Senate committee staff director: "A lot of climate policy is the flip side of energy policy... and vice versa."

3. Increasing energy independence means lowering reliance on foreign energy sources. To achieve this, politicians call for increased domestic energy production or actions to reduce demand. Dealing with climate change can include a wide variety of options, but frequently includes a focus on reducing greenhouse gas emissions.

4. Some of the debate around the recent House and Senate energy packages exemplifies the tension between climate change and energy independence. An analysis by the American Council for an Energy Efficient Economy (ACEEE), for example, found that by 2030, the Senate bill, which calls for everything from an increase in biofuels usage to increasing fuel economy standards, would reduce emissions to 13 percent below projected levels. This is still 15 percent above today's levels, however, and compares poorly with the targets of 60 to 80 percent below 1990 levels by 2050 set by the more aggressive climate change bills currently under consideration.

5. Specific provisions also exemplify this tension, such as coal-to-liquids technologies, which transform coal into liquid fuels. The Senate rejected an amendment to include a coal-to-liquids fuel standard in its bill. In general, technologies that increase reliance on coal at the expense of petroleum are favorable from an energy independence perspective, due to the size of U.S. coal reserves; it is a mantra on Capitol Hill that domestic coal reserves can meet our energy needs for the next 250 years. However, a June as-

sessment from the National Academies found that those reserves may be sufficient for as few as 100 years, but increased use of coal is still considered helpful to achieving energy independence.

6. Coal-to-liquids is not a good choice for reducing emissions, however. A recent MIT study found that deriving fuels from coal produces 2.5 to 3.5 times the amount of carbon produced by burning conventional fuels. Even if technologies are put in place to capture and store some of the carbon, life-cycle emissions from coal-to-liquids are still comparable to those produced by conventional sources.

7. Biofuels have also garnered much recent attention, as they replace fossil fuels with a renewable resource. The Senate energy package calls for production of 36 billion gallons of ethanol per year by 2022 (in 2006, production was less than 5 billion gallons). However, biofuels have weaknesses from both energy independence and emissions standpoints.

8. From the energy independence perspective, the problem is simple. Even if the United States produced 36 billion gallons of ethanol, it would still only be equivalent to about 8 percent of current U.S. oil consumption. And whether this level of production is possible is debatable. A recent Government Accountability Office (GAO) report found that the maximum realistic amount of U.S. corn ethanol production was less than half this value. Meeting the goal requires development and rapid expansion of cellulosic ethanol production.

9. From the emissions perspective, the problem is more complex, but no less real. Devoting more land to ethanol production, be it from corn or cellulose, will mean altering land-use patterns and will require growing, fertilizing, harvesting and transporting fuel stocks — all stages that emit greenhouse gases. Moreover, increasing biofuels production also requires increasing infrastructure to transport, store and sell biofuels, as well as increasing the number of vehicles capable of using them.

10. One of the few options that appears favorable from both energy independence and emissions perspectives is to raise corporate average fuel economy (CAFE) standards, a measure that was passed as part of the Senate energy package. The bill calls for automakers to raise the average mileage of new cars and light trucks to 35 miles per gallon by 2020, compared with about 25 miles per gallon today. The ACEEE analysis found that this alone would reduce emissions by 6 percent below projected 2030 levels, resulting from reduced fuel demand and thus likely contributing to energy independence as well. It remains to be seen whether this provision will make it through the House-Senate conference; the House did not include a fuel economy increase in its energy package. Increased energy efficiency and use of renewable power sources like wind and solar are other options that are favorable from both energy independence and global warming perspectives; they also receive some attention in the new energy packages.

11. Achieving increased energy independence and mitigating climate change impacts are complex but vital issues. Though not the same, they are closely linked, and policy actions that exploit this linkage, such as raising CAFE standards, will aid in helping achieve both goals and creating true "win-win" solutions.

Glossary

congressional [kən'greʃənəl] of or relating to congress *adj*. 会议的，议会的，国会的

parsimony ['pɑ:siməni] extreme care in spending money; reluctance to spend money unnecessarily *n*. 过度节俭，吝啬

conjunction [kən'dʒʌŋkʃən] 1. an uninflected function word that serves to conjoin words or phrases or clauses or sentences; 2. the temporal property of two things happening at the same time; 3. the state of being joined together *n*. 连词，结合，关联，(事件等的)同时发生

flip side: a different aspect of something (especially the opposite aspect) 另一方面，唱片的反面，对等的人物

emission [i'miʃən] the act of emitting or releasing; causing to flow forth *n*. 发射，射出，发行

package ['pækidʒ] 1. a collection of things wrapped or boxed together; a proposition, offer, or thing for sale in which separate items are offered together as a single or inclusive unit *n*. 包裹，整批交易 2. put into a box; to design and produce a package for (retail goods) *vt*. 把……打包，把……进行推销

exemplify [ig'zemplifai] clarify by giving an example of *vt*. 例证，例示

biofuel [baiəu'fju:əl] a gaseous, liquid, or solid substance of biological origin that is used as a fuel *n*. 生物燃料

projected [prə'dʒektid] planned for the future; extending out above or beyond a surface or boundary *adj*. 规划的，设计的；预期的，估计的

aggressive [ə'gresiv] having or showing determination and energetic pursuit of your ends; tending to spread quickly *adj*. 侵犯的，攻击性的，有进取心的，强烈的，迅速生长的

amendment [ə'mendmənt] the act of amending or correcting; a statement that is added to or revises or improves a proposal or document (a bill or constitution etc.) *n*. 改善(正)，修正案，某物质能改善土壤有助生长

mantra ['mʌntrə] a commonly repeated word or phrase; (Sanskrit) literally a "sacred utterance" in Vedism; one of a collection of orally transmitted poetic hymns *n*. 颂歌，咒语(尤指四吠陀经典内作为咒文或祷告唱念的)

garner ['gɑ:nə] acquire or deserve by one's efforts or actions; assemble or get together *v*. 贮藏，积累，得到

ethanol ['eθənɔ:l,-nəul] the intoxicating agent in fermented and distilled liquors; used pure or denatured as a solvent or in medicines and colognes and cleaning solutions and rocket fuel; proposed as a renewable clean-burning additive to gasoline *n*. 乙醇

standpoint ['stændpɔint] a mental position from which things are viewed *n*. 立场，观点

cellulosic ['selju'lousik] a plastic made from cellulose (or a derivative of cellulose) *adj.* 纤维素的

emit [i'mit] expel (gases or odors); give off, send forth, or discharge; as of light, heat, or radiation, vapor, etc.; express audibly; utter sounds (not necessarily words) *vt.* 发出，放射，吐露

infrastructure ['infrə'strʌktʃə] the basic structure or features of a system or organization; the stock of basic facilities and capital equipment needed for the functioning of a country or area *n.* 下部构造，下部组织，基础结构，基础设施

mileage ['mailidʒ] distance measured in miles; the ratio of the number of miles traveled to the number of gallons of gasoline burned *n.* 哩数，里程

mitigate ['mitigeit] lessen or to try to lessen the seriousness or extent of; make less severe or harsh *vt.* 镇静，缓和，减轻

linkage ['liŋkidʒ] an associative relation; a mechanical system of rods or springs or pivots that transmits power or motion; the act of linking things together *n.* 连合，连锁，结合

Capitol Hill: a hill in Washington, D.C., where the Capitol Building sits and Congress meets *n.* 美国国会山，美国国会

House of Representatives: the lower legislative house of the United States Congress or in many state legislatures 众议院

Senate: the upper house of the United States Congress or in many state legislatures 参议员，上议院

Exercises

A. Fill in each blank with one of the given words in its correct form.

| win-win | parsimony | projected | exemplify | garner | amendment |
| conjunction | package | emit | mitigate | aggressive | multiple |

1. Most economists here say that California's economic slump has not bottomed out and that it may grow worse before the earliest _____ recovery in 1995.

2. A few isolated portions of that report, regarding recommended changes for the use of mammography, were widely discussed in the media, and _____ tremendous public attention.

3. The President arrived on Capitol Hill yesterday and immediately set to work reassuring skeptical Republicans about his massive economic stimulus _____ —part of a campaign that earned him praise for seeking their input but questions from those averse to hundreds of billions of dollars in new spending.

4. It was for religious and temperamental reasons — Puritanism and _____ —that Alfred kept his family in such austerity.

5. Dr. Praveen Kolar, assistant professor of biological and agricultural engineering at NC State, has developed an inexpensive treatment process that significantly _____ odors from poultry rendeing op-

erations.

6. Major corporations are addressing common business challenges with "_____" strategies that provide competitive advantage through community investment.
7. But the approach laid out in a draft section of the Senate legislation would pursue the goal so broadly and _____ that even some supporters of the need for data systems fear that it is politically impossible.
8. The proposed system could be used in _____ with a wide range of microsensors and biosensors for monitoring small molecules in the brain.
9. Greenpeace said the top 10 companies, which provided almost 60% of China's total electricity last year, burned 20% of China's coal — 590m tonnes — and _____ the equivalent of 1.44 billion tonnes of carbon dioxide.
10. The recent oil price rises _____ the difficulties which the motor industry is now facing.
11. Among the concerns, the scientists say, is a(an) _____ to the biology standards that attacks one of evolution's key principles: that all living organisms on Earth are dessended from a common ancestor.
12. The study, led by a University of Edinburgh researcher, suggests an underlying difference between the way in which premature births occur in women with single and _____ pregnancies.

B. Answer the following questions concerning the text.

1. What do you think is the relationship between energy consumption and environment protection?
2. What does the author imply by the meaning of "Scientists and policymakers may have little in common, but both value parsimony."?
3. Name some commonly-used renewable fuels, and then talk about their strong points and weak ones.
4. According to the author, what is the proper relationship between energy independence and climate change?
5. From this passage, we can learn some valuable lessons and knowledge from the U.S.A concerning the relationship between energy and environment. And from your point of view, what kind of energy policy should China make compatible with the protection of environment?

C. Read the following questions and choose the best answer.

1. What does "both issues" in Paragraph 2 refer to? _____.
   A. Power production and greenhouse effect
   B. Multiple facts and multiple interests
   C. Resource consumption and global economy
   D. Scientists and policymakers
2. According to the text, what method is proposed to help the U.S.A build up its self-reliance on energy

output and consumption? _____.

A. Lowering energy production abroad

B. Decreasing energy resources dependence overseas

C. Encouraging domestic demand for energy

D. Increasing greenhouse gas emissions

3. Which of the following statements is NOT TRUE according to the text? _____.

A. Coal is considered as a potential fuel to achieve energy independence in the future

B. Energy independence should be in parallel with climate change

C. Global warming leads to climate change

D. Both scientists and policymakers prefer to solve various problems with single method

4. Why can not biofuel replace fossil fuels? _____.

A. Because the application of ethanol cannot be comparable to that of oil

B. Because corn or cellulose is half the value of oil

C. Because biofuel production can worsen the problem of global warming

D. Because the more greenhouse gases it emits, the less independent energy becomes

5. What is mentioned in the 10th paragraph to deal with the issue of energy independence and emissions? _____.

A. Increasing the mileage of the vehicles available in daily life

B. Reducing the consumption of energy

C. Economizing the use of energy in the energy package of the House

D. Renewable power sources are out of the question

D. Explain the underlined parts.

1. Just as scientists seek to explain multiple facts, policymakers seek to <u>balance the needs of multiple interests. Scientists and policymakers may have little in common, but both value parsimony</u>.

2. In general, <u>technologies that increase reliance on coal at the expense of petroleum are favorable from an energy independence perspective</u>, due to the size of U.S. coal reserves; <u>it is a mantra on Capitol Hill that domestic coal reserves can meet our energy needs for the next 250 years</u>.

3. Even if technologies are put in place to capture and store some of the carbon, life-cycle emissions from coal-to-liquids <u>are still comparable to those produced by conventional sources</u>.

4. A recent Government Accountability Office (GAO) report found <u>that the maximum realistic amount of U.S. corn ethanol production was less than half this value</u>.

5. From the emissions perspective, <u>the problem is more complex, but no less real</u>.

6. <u>Though not the same, they are closely linked, and policy actions that exploit this linkage, such as raising CAFE standards, will aid in helping achieve both goals and creating true "win-win" solutions</u>.

Unit 6　Ecology

Text A

Extinction Crisis Looms in Oceania

1. Published in the international journal Conservation Biology, the report is the first comprehensive review of more than 24,000 scientific publications related to conservation in the Oceanic region. Compiled by a team of 14 scientists, it reveals a sorry and worsening picture of habitat destruction and species loss. It also describes the deficiencies of and opportunities for governmental action to lessen this mounting regional and global problem.

2. "Earth is experiencing its sixth great extinction event and the new report reveals that this threat is advancing on six major fronts," says the report's lead author, Professor Richard Kingsford of the University of New South Wales.

3. "Our region has the notorious distinction of having possibly the worst extinction record on earth. This is predicted to continue without serious changes to the way we conserve our environments and dependent organisms. We have an amazing natural environment in our part of the world but so much of it is being destroyed before our eyes. Species are being threatened by habitat loss and degradation, invasive species, climate change, overexploitation, pollution and wildlife disease."

Threats in Oceania

4. Loss and degradation of habitat is the largest single threat to land species, including 80 percent of threatened species.

5. More than 1,200 bird species have become extinct in the Pacific islands and archipelagos.

6. In Australia agriculture has modified or destroyed about 50 percent of woodland and forest ecosystems, and about 70 percent of remaining forests are ecologically degraded from logging.

7. Invasive species, particularly vertebrates and vascular plants, have devastated terrestrial species of the Pacific Islands and caused 75 percent of all terrestrial vertebrate extinctions on oceanic islands.

8. More than 2,500 invasive plants have colonized New Zealand and Australia representing about 11 percent of native plant species.

9. Many invasive weeds, vertebrate pests, and fishes were introduced by government, agricultural-

ists, horticulturalists and hunters.

Species Deceases: Global Snapshot

10. Nearly 17,000 of the world's 45,000 assessed species are threatened with extinction (38 percent). Of these, 3,246 are in the highest category of threat, Critically Endangered, 4,770 are Endangered and 8,912 are Vulnerable to extinction.

11. Nearly 5,500 animal species are known to be threatened with extinction and at least 1,141 of the 5,487 known mammal species are threatened worldwide.

12. In 2008, nearly 450 mammals were listed as Endangered, including the Tasmanian Devil (Sarcophilus harrisii), after the global population declined by more than 60 percent in the last 10 years.

13. Scientists have catalogued relatively little about the rest of the world's fauna: only 5 percent of fish, 6 percent of reptiles, and 7 percent of amphibians have been evaluated. Of those studied, at least 750 fish species, 290 reptiles, and 150 amphibians are at risk.

14. The average extinction rate is now some 1,000 to 10,000 times faster than the rate that prevailed over the past 60 million years.

15. "Many people are just beginning to understand the full extent of these problems in terms of land-clearing, degradation of rivers, pest species and overfishing," says Professor Kingsford. "Climate change is a very important issue but by no means the only threat to biodiversity. The biggest problem seems to be that the policy challenges are just not being taken up by governments. Conservation policies are just seen as a problem for the economy."

16. For each of the major threats to biodiversity and conservation, the scientific team has proposed between three and five specific policy recommendations that should be adopted by governments around the region.

17. Many of these broad policies are being implemented but in a piecemeal way. For example, the scientists recommend setting targets for protected areas such as National Parks of at least 10 percent of terrestrial areas and up to 50 percent of marine areas but these may not be enough.

18. Dr James Watson, President of the Society for Conservation Biology and an author of the report, says: "There is a need for commitment to more protected areas and more effort into rehabilitation of major threatened ecosystems such as wetlands."

19. The report's authors are particularly concerned about the impacts of destructive fisheries and the effects of by-catch from long-line fishing, bottom trawling, cyanide and explosive use in some Pacific nations.

20. "Our recommendations have clearly identified the need for more restrictions on harvesting and better ecosystem management of fisheries," says Professor Kingsford. "There is a real need to have better international mechanisms for protecting against unsustainable fisheries." Of particular importance is the

overwhelming impact of burgeoning human populations in the region on the environment. Populations are set to increase significantly by 2050; for example Australia 35%; New Zealand 25%; Papua New Guinea 76%; New Caledonia 49%.

21. "The burden on the environment is going to get worse unless we are a lot smarter about reducing our footprint on the planet or the human population," says Professor Kingsford. As well, many Pacific Island states have a relatively poor information base for conservation. The study found that 88.5% of all scientific studies were from Australia (53.7%), New Zealand (24.3%) and Hawaii (10.5%). In most other countries in the region, there was relatively poor capacity to inform the community about the state of the environment.

22. There is a real need to invest in building the scientific and government capacity for conservation throughout the region. "Unless we get this equation right, future generations will surely be paying more in terms of quality of life and the environment we live in. And our region will continue its terrible reputation of leading the world in the extinction of plants and animals," says Professor Kingsford.

Glossary

conservation [ˌkɔnsə(ː)'veiʃən] an occurrence of improvement by virtue of preventing loss or injury or other change; the preservation and careful management of the environment and of natural resources *n*. 保存,防止流失,守恒,保护自然资源

oceanic [ˌəuʃi'ænik] relating to or occurring or living in or frequenting the open ocean *adj*. 海洋的, 海洋产出的, 住于海洋的

compile [kəm'pail] get or gather together; put together out of existing material *vt*. 编译, 编纂

habitat ['hæbitæt] the type of environment in which an organism or group normally lives or occurs *n*. (动植物的)产地, 栖息地

deficiency [di'fiʃənsi] the state of needing something that is absent or unavailable or lack of an adequate quantity or number *n*. 缺乏, 不足, 缺点

extinction [iks'tiŋkʃən] no longer in existence or no longer active; extinguished *n*. 消失, 消减, 废止

notorious [nəuː'tɔriəs] having an exceedingly bad reputation *adj*. 臭名昭著的

conserve [kən'səːv] keep in safety and protect from harm, decay, loss, or destruction *vt*. 保存,保持

organism ['ɔːgənizəm] a living thing that has (or can develop) the ability to act or function independently *n*. 生物体, 有机体

degradation [ˌdegrə'deiʃən] changing to a lower state (a less respected state); a low or downcast state *n*. 降格, 堕落, 退化

overexploitation ['əuvərˌeksplɔi'teiʃən] exploitation to the point of diminishing returns *n*. (对资源等的)过度开采, (对工人等的)过度剥削

wildlife ['waildlaif] all living things (except people) that are undomesticated n. 野生动物

Oceania [ˌəuʃi'einiə] a large group of islands in the south Pacific including Melanesia and Micronesia and Polynesia (and sometimes Australasia and the Malay Archipelago) n. 大洋洲

extinct [iks'tiŋkt] no longer in existence; lost or especially having died out leaving no living representatives adj. 灭绝的，熄灭的，耗尽的

archipelago [ˌɑ:ki'peləgəu] a group of many islands in a large body of water n. 群岛，多岛海

ecosystem [ˌi:kə'sistəm] a system formed by the interaction of a community of organisms with their physical environment n. 生态系统

ecologically [ˌi:kə'lɔdʒikəli] with respect to ecology adv. 从生态学的观点看

degrade [di'greid] reduce the level of land, as by erosion or reduce in worth or character, usually verbally v. 降格

logging ['lɔgiŋ] the work of cutting down trees for timber n. 伐木搬运业

invasive [in'veisiv] involving invasion or aggressive attack or gradually intrusive without right or permission adj. 侵入的，侵略性的，攻击性的

vertebrate ['və:tibrit] 1. animals having a bony or cartilaginous skeleton with a segmented spinal column and a large brain enclosed in a skull or cranium n. 脊椎动物; 2. having a backbone or spinal column adj. 有脊椎的

vascular ['væskjulə] of or relating to or having vessels that conduct and circulate fluids adj. 血管的，脉管的

terrestrial [ti'restriəl] of or relating to or inhabiting the land as opposed to the sea or air adj. 陆地的，地上的

agriculturalist [ˌægri'kʌltʃərəlist] someone concerned with the science or art or business of cultivating the soil n. (= agriculturist)农学家

horticulturalist [hɔ:ti'kʌltʃərist] n. 园艺家

snapshot ['snæpʃɔt] an informal photograph, usually made with a small hand-held camera n. 快照，印象

endanger [in'deindʒə] pose a threat to; present a danger to; put in a dangerous, disadvantageous, or difficult position v. 危及

mammal ['mæməl] any warm-blooded vertebrate having the skin more or less covered with hair; young are born alive except for the small subclass of monotremes and nourished with milk n. 哺乳动物

Tasmanian Devil (Sarcophilus harrisii) [tæz'meiniən,-njən] small ferocious carnivorous marsupial having a mostly black coat and long tail n. [动]袋獾

fauna ['fɔ:nə] all the animal life in a particular region or period n. 动物群

reptile ['reptail] any cold-blooded vertebrate of the class Reptilia including tortoises turtles snakes lizards alligators crocodiles and extinct forms *n*. 爬行动物

amphibian [æm'fibiən] cold-blooded vertebrate typically living on land but breeding in water; aquatic larvae undergo metamorphosis into adult form *n*. 两栖动物

biodiversity [ˌbaiəudai'və:siti] the diversity of plant and animal life in a particular habitat (or in the world as a whole) *n*. 生物品种

piecemeal ['pi:smi:l] one thing at a time *adj*. 一片一片的, 逐渐的

marine [mə'ri:n] of or relating to the sea; relating to or involving ships or shipping or navigation or seamen *adj*. 海的, 海事的, 船舶的, 航海的

rehabilitation [ˌri:(h)əˌbili'teiʃən] the conversion of wasteland into land suitable for use of habitation or cultivation *n*. 复原

fishery ['fiʃəri:] a workplace where fish are caught and processed and sold *n*. 渔场(渔业)

by-catch ['baiˌkætʃ,-ketʃ] unwanted fish and other sea animals caught in a fishing net along with the desired kind of fish *n*. 混获, 副渔获物

long-line fishing: 延绳钓

bottom trawling: 水底拖网捕捞法

cyanide ['saiənaid] any of a class of organic compounds containing the cyano radical *n*.

burgeoning ['bə:dʒniŋ] *adj*. 生机勃勃的, 增长迅速的, 发展很快的

Papua New Guinea: *n*. 巴布亚新几内亚

New Caledonia ['nju:ˌkæli'dəunjə] *n*. 新喀里多尼亚(岛)(南太平洋)

Exercises

A. Fill in each blank with one of the given words in its correct form.

| deficiency | extinct | compile | burgeoning | degrade | terrestrial |
| endanger | notorious | habitat | invasive | ecologically | conserve | rehabilitation |

1. With contributions from Japan and other parties, a group called the Borneo Conservation Trust has begun acquiring privately-owned land along the waterway to expand the _____ for the animals.

2. A(An) _____ street gang accused of terrorizing a neighborhood for years, killing a deputy and murdering residents was the target of a coordinated assault by hundreds of law enforcement officials Tuesday.

3. Yet 99 percent of all species that ever lived have gone _____, including every one of our hominid ancestors.

4. Establishing Ecological Demonstration District and Ecological Agriculture County will be promoted in the rural area. Highly efficiency and _____ sound agriculture will be developed to realize sustainable development and build a healthy ecological system.

5. Your noblesse did not deserve punishment; but to _____ is to punish. It was with the same satisfaction I found that the result of my inquiry concerning your clergy was not dissimilar.
6. If we falter in our leadership, we may endanger the peace of the world, and we shall surely _____ the welfare of this nation.
7. My department has been working very long and hard to _____ all the necessary data, but we're having some difficulties getting the required information from the American subsidiary.
8. It is not yet known to what extent new-born babies in Denmark or the Western World suffer from vitamin C _____ but a conservative estimate would be 5 to 10 per cent based on the occurrence among adults.
9. _____ species are organisms that are introduced into a non-native ecosystem and which cause, or are likely to cause, harm to the economy, environment or human health.
10. This is a particular problem for California, where agriculture, industry, a _____ population and environmental needs already clash over limited water supplies.
11. Reducing the loss of natural forest is good for many reasons—it helps to slow global warming by reducing carbon emissions, can _____ threatened species and retain the economically-important ecosystem services upon which forest-dependent people as well as whole economies depend.
12. The studies also indicate that pulmonary _____ results in decreased anxiety and depression for COPD patients because they find they can exercise more, and they enjoy the feeling that they have mastered something important in their lives.
13. Then they compared two ways to stay within that limit: in one, they taxed _____ carbon emissions and industrial and fossil fuel emissions all at the same rate.

B. Answer the following questions concerning the text.
1. What are the "six major fronts" mentioned in the text? And how do you understand them?
2. Do you know what is "invasive species"? And please name some nonindigenous species you are familiar with.
3. How do you understand the sentence "Conservation policies are just seen as a problem for the economy."?
4. How many recommendations concerning the conservation are presented in the text? And what are they?
5. What is the author's attitude toward the problem under discussion?

C. Read the following questions and choose the best answer.
1. What are the ecological conditions the sea areas are involved in as mentioned in the text? _____
   A. Deficient living states   B. Sorry organisms
   C. Global extinctions   D. Notorious conservation
2. Statistics are given in the text to imply that _____.

A. there is a wide variety of flora and fauna in the ecosystem of Oceania
   B. Australian government is responsible for the extinction of bird species
   C. non-native creatures may be the culprit of ecological degradation
   D. habitats can be recovered by colonizing new lands
3. Which of the following is TRUE with regard to global decrease in species? _____.
   A. Animals extinct relatively slower than before thanks to the efforts of scientists
   B. Not all the animals on the earth are judged with their ecological situations
   C. Of the assessed animals, reptiles are considered as the most threatened with extinction or endangered
   D. Many people have a deep impression of the problem of degradation and extinction
4. What is the focus of the policy recommendations proposed by scientists? _____.
   A. Sustainability   B. Conservation
   C. Commitment   D. Rehabilitation
5. What is the writing genre of the text? _____.
   A. Narration   B. Exposition
   C. Argumentation   D. Description

D. Explain the underlined parts.
1. Compiled by a team of 14 scientists, <u>it reveals a sorry and worsening picture of habitat destruction and species loss</u>. It also <u>describes the deficiencies of and opportunities for governmental</u> action to lessen this mounting regional and global problem.
2. Our region <u>has the notorious distinction of having possibly the worst extinction record on earth</u>. This is predicted to <u>continue without serious changes to the way</u> we conserve our environments and dependent organisms. We have <u>an amazing natural environment in our part of the world but so much of it is being destroyed before our eyes</u>.
3. Conservation policies are <u>just seen as a problem for the economy</u>.
4. Many of these broad policies <u>are being implemented but in a piecemeal way</u>.
5. There is <u>a need for commitment to more protected areas and more effort into rehabilitation of major threatened ecosystems such as wetlands</u>.
6. "The burden on the environment is going to get worse unless we are a lot smarter about <u>reducing our footprint on the planet or the human population</u>," says Professor Kingsford.
7. "<u>Unless we get this equation right</u>, future generations <u>will surely be paying more</u> in terms of quality of life and the environment we live in. And our region will <u>continue its terrible reputation of leading the world in the extinction of plants and animals</u>," says Professor Kingsford.

E. Read the passages in this section and decide whether each of the following statements is true or false.

Passage One

Biological invasions of nonindigenous plant pests—plants, pathogens, and arthropods—are serious threats to the rural, urban, and natural ecosystems of the United States. In the agricultural setting, hundreds of millions of dollars are spent each year on pesticides and herbicides to prevent native and nonindigenous pathogens, arthropods, and weeds from ruining crops. There are no treatments for some of them: the glassy winged sharpshooter that is spreading disease in California grapes, Karnal bunt in some wheat-producing states, citrus canker in Florida, and plum pox in Pennsylvania.

Suburban and urban areas have not been spared. The arrival of the Asian long-horned beetle has already led to the destruction of thousands of shade trees on the streets of Chicago and New York. Many suburban areas of the eastern United States have also been subjected to aerial spraying of insecticide to deter the southward spread of the European gypsy moth, which has defoliated thousands of trees in the region.

Equally threatened by nonindigenous plant pests are U.S. forests, wetlands, and other natural areas. Examples of these pests are the chestnut blight fungus, which all but eliminated the American chestnut from northeastern forests early in the 20th century; hemlock woolly adelgid and balsam woolly adelgid, which are killing native hemlock and fir, respectively, in the eastern United States; and the invasive plant Melaleuca quinquenervia, which has changed the hydrological characteristics and plant and animal life of the Everglades. The impact of invasive nonindigenous species on natural areas is likely to be permanent, in part because economic and environmental factors limit eradication or control options that may be appropriate in agricultural settings.

Only a small fraction of introductions of nonindigenous species result in invasions in the United States, but it is not obvious which nonindigenous plants, pathogens, and arthropods are benign and which will become important pests. Moreover, resources are not available to detect the introduction of every nonindigenous pathogen and arthropod or to monitor the fate of every imported plant, so alternative strategies to identify and eliminate pests are needed. The U.S. Department of Agriculture (USDA) asked the National Research Council's Board on Agriculture and Natural Resources (BANR) to examine what is known about nonindigenous plant pests so that it could be determined whether there is sufficient information to list the species that are potential invaders in the United States. To study the issue, BANR created the Committee on the Scientific Basis of Predicting the Invasive Potential of Nonindigenous Plants and Plant Pests in the United States. The committee was charged to

—Consider the historical record of weed, pathogen, and arthropod invaders, including pathways of their introduction.

—Identify and analyze circumstances that could allow nonindigenous species to become invaders, considering the biotic and abiotic characteristics of potentially affected ecosystems, including agricultural systems, and the characteristics of nonindigenous plant pests that contribute to their potential invasiveness.

—Determine the extent to which scientific principles and procedures can characterize the invasive potential of nonindigenous plant pests and determine the degree of uncertainty intrinsic in such characterizations.

—Identify research that should be conducted to enhance the prediction of invasiveness.

(http://www.nap.edu/openbook.php? record id = 10259&page = 1/2)

_____ 1. Non-native species contribute to the transfer of pollen from one flower to another.

_____ 2. It is not unusual to find destructive invasive pests in suburban and urban areas.

_____ 3. Alien species may have a long-lasting effect on American wildlife.

_____ 4. Obviously, most exotic species are not benign, therefore, it is necessary for the government to examine, identify and eliminate the potential pests.

_____ 5. The pathways of ecosystems should be padlocked to keep nonindigenous species out.

Passage Two

The ecological and economic impacts of gene flow between crops and their weedy relatives are significant. Weedy relatives may acquire beneficial genes from cultivated cousins, potentially increasing their invasive ability. Farmers may find that their crop yields decrease or crops may be more difficult to harvest if they hybridize with a weedy relative. These are only a few consequences of the gene flow that occurs all the time between crops and wild relatives.

A recent article in the October issue of the American Journal of Botany by Dr. Adeline Barnaud and colleagues explores the role of gene flow between cultivated sorghum and its weedy relatives in a village in northern Cameroon. Sorghum is a staple food crop that is essential to food security in semi-arid regions of Asia and Africa.

Barnaud and her colleagues used a multidisciplinary approach involving biologists and social scientists in addressing questions of gene flow among the species and how farmers' practices affect this gene flow. The farmers in northern Cameroon distinguish a variety of types of sorghum—ranging from weedy to cultivated with intermediates in between—but whether there is any genetic basis to these types was a question the researchers addressed. "Farmers have quite accurate perceptions about the genetic nature of their sorghum plants, accurately distinguishing not only domesticated landraces from the others, but also among three classes of introgressed individuals, and classing all four along a continuum that corresponds well to genetic patterns," said Barnaud. "Their practices are fairly effective in limiting gene flow."

The researchers found that farmers actively eradicate weedy types from their fields because their presence lowers yields. However, several of the farmers' practices unintentionally favor gene flow. Although farmers actively select against the weedy types, some are maintained to enhance diversity and lower risks of crop failure due to environmental changes, such as with annual rainfall. Also, despite a desire to remove the weedy sorghums, as any farmer or home gardener knows, it is often difficult to identify weeds when the plants are young, and, even if they are properly identified, it may be difficult to fully remove the weeds. As a result, some seeds from the weedy individuals are able to survive in the field and persist year after year. Dr. Barnaud and her colleagues discovered that when harvesting seed for the following year, farmers in this village may not select seed from the middle of the fields where plants are less likely to have been pollinated by weedy types. In addition, the presence of intermediate weedy types may facilitate gene flow between the weediest type and the cultivated type due to their intermediate flowering time and the farmers' mode of management.

(http://www.sciencedaily.com/releases/2009/10/091006155911.html)

_____ 6. Weed can improve its invasion genetically.

_____ 7. In the areas with scanty rainfall, Asians and Africans mainly live on sorghum.

_____ 8. The farmers in northern Cameroon fail to control gene flow.

_____ 9. Whatever the farmers do in their fields leads to the limitation of the gene flow.

_____ 10. It is impossible to eradicate the weed in the field in part because of the farming methods.

F. Cloze. Fill in each blank with one suitable word.

In botany, flora has two meanings. The first meaning, flora of an area or of time period, refers to all plant life occurring in an area or time period, especially the naturally occurring or __1__ plant life. The second meaning refers to a book or other work which describes the plant species occurring in an area or time period, with the __2__ of allowing identification.

The term flora comes from Latin language Flora, the goddess of flowers in Roman mythology. The __3__ term for animal life is fauna. Flora, fauna and other forms of life such as fungi are collectively referred to as biota. Some classic and modern floras are listed below.

Plants are grouped into floras based on region, period, special environment, or climate. Regions can be __4__ distinct habitats like mountain vs. flatland. Floras can mean plant life of an historic era as in fossil flora. Lastly, floras may be __5__ by special environments:

—Native flora. The native and indigenous flora of an area.

—Agricultural and garden flora. The plants that are __6__ grown by humans.

—Weed flora. Traditionally this classification was __7__ to plants regarded as undesirable, and studied in efforts to control or eradicate them. Today the __8__ is less often used as a classification of plant life, __9__ it includes three different types of plants: weedy species, invasive species (that may or may not be weedy), and native and introduced non-weedy species that are agriculturally __10__. Many native plants previously considered weeds have been shown to be beneficial or even necessary to various ecosystems.

Bacterial organisms are sometimes included in a flora, and sometimes the terms bacterial flora and plant flora are used separately.

(http://en.wikipedia.org/wiki/Flora)

1. A. invasive   B. permanent   C. national   D. indigenous
2. A. help   B. aim   C. rest   D. status
3. A. corresponding B. operating   C. promising   D. enterprising
4. A. biologically B. historically   C. geographically D. ecologically
5. A. subdivided   B. multiplied   C. submitted   D. magnified
6. A. carefully   B. deliberately   C. pleasantly   D. silently
7. A. turned   B. appeared   C. classified   D. applied
8. A. designation   B. symbol   C. brand   D. instruction
9. A. when   B. which   C. since   D. however
10. A. available   B. undesirable   C. feasible   D. mandatory

G. Translate the following passages into Chinese/English.

1. In many parts of this affluent coastal region southeast of Rome and northwest of Naples, canals dumping effluent into the Mediterranean from farms and factories coexist with fishermen and beachgoers there is little doubt that this area would need considerable work to return to a more pristine state. For places as far gone as this one, however, a new breed of landscape architect is recommending a radical solution: not so much to restore the environment as to redesign it. Designing nature might seem to be an oxymoron or an act of hubris. But instead of simply recommending that polluting farms and factories be shut, Professor Berger specializes in creating new ecosystems on severely damaged environments: redirecting water flow, moving hills, building islands and planting new species to absorb pollution, to create natural, though "artificial", landscapes that can ultimately sustain themselves.

2. 他希望当地政府在污染最为严重的水路目前所流经的一处关键的山谷购置一片近500英亩(1英亩=4 046.8平方米)的土地。他打算在那里建造一片湿地,作为水流入居民区的大海之前的天然净化站。当然,也需要有更好的规章制度来限制将污染物倾入河道。但是他说,精心混配的一些合适种类的植物、泥土、石头和排水管道也能对缓缓流过的河水过滤净化。这块地面还可以起着一个新公园的作用。

Text B

Bio-Invaders

1. Are we under attack by "non-native" species? Should we care?

2. "That kind of information is dangerous," scolded Jodi Cassell. Cassell, who works with the California Sea Grant Extension program, was speaking at a symposium on "Alien Species in Coastal Waters: What Are the Real Ecological and Social Costs?" at the February American Association for the Advancement of Science meeting in Washington, D.C. She wasn't alone in her alarm. "We have members of the press here," warned a member of the audience. "I am very concerned that they might think that his view is the dominant view."

3. The target of this shushing was Mark Sagoff, a philosopher from the University of Maryland who has worked with Maryland's Sea Grant program to determine how the Chesapeake Bay's unique ecology defines a sense of place. Sagoff's sin? He'd had the temerity to point out the benefits that the much-loathed zebra mussels had brought to the Great Lakes.

4. Introduced via discharged ballast water from European freighters in the mid-1980s, zebra mussel populations have been exploding in the Great Lakes. Tens of thousands of the tiny, striped shellfish can occupy a square meter of any hard surface-like rocks, docks, and boat hulls. Observers initially feared that zebra mussels would clog water-intake pipes for municipalities and power plants and perhaps out-compete native shellfish for food. However, it turns out that the things are voracious "filter feeders." They strain algae and nutrients like fertilizer runoff from the lakes' waters. As a result, zebra mussels have played a significant role in improving water quality by clearing the lakes of polluting organic matter.

5. "There has been a striking difference in water clarity improving dramatically in Lake Erie, sometimes six to four times what it was before the arrival of the zebra mussels," according to the U.S. Geological Survey's Nonindigenous Aquatic Species Database. "With this increase in water clarity, more light is able to penetrate deeper allowing for an increase in macrophytes (aquatic plants). Some of these macrophyte beds have not been seen for many decades due to changing conditions of the lake mostly due to pollution. The macrophyte beds that have returned are providing cover and acting as nurseries for some species of fish." What's more, zebra mussels provide food and habitat for all sorts of native fish and ducks.

6. Having Sagoff point out such positive developments was more than his colleagues on the AAAS panel could bear. To them--and to most professional ecologists--zebra mussels are simply "bad". So too, say ecologists, are all other "non-native" or "invader" species that set up shop in ecosystems different

from the ones in which they originated.

7. Why ecologists feel this way is no small matter. It is one of the hottest questions in contemporary ecology, and one which has tremendous policy implications: Should massive regulatory steps be taken to make sure "non-native species" are kept out of any given ecosystem? This is the same issue that the signatories to the Convention on Biological Diversity are hashing out in Nairobi, Kenya, as this issue goes to print. The convention, an international agreement negotiated during the 1992 Earth Summit, is the first comprehensive global treaty to address all aspects of biological diversity, including genetic resources, species, and ecosystems. The results from Nairobi could well be the start of a global system for controlling non-native species. Delegates from 168 countries, including the U.S. (which has signed but not ratified the convention), are considering the "Guidelines for the Prevention of Biodiversity Loss Caused by Alien Invasive Species" devised by the World Conservation Union earlier this year.

8. Among other things, these guidelines want to apply the very problematic "precautionary principle" to the introduction of alien species. (See "Precautionary Tale", April 1999.) The WCU provisions call for sanctions against people or companies that intentionally introduce species without the prior authorization of national "biosecurity" agencies. They further recommend establishing "appropriate fines, penalties or other sanctions to apply to those responsible for unintentional introductions through negligence and bad practice". The activities of transport companies would "be subjected to appropriate levels of monitoring and control" by the biosecurity bureaucracies. In other words, a decision to regulate non-native species will likely end up regulating international trade, too.

9. The two basic positions regarding the debate over non-native species were laid out in clear relief at the AAAS meeting. So were the essentially aesthetic underpinnings of those who would devote huge resources to keeping "invaders" out of a given ecosystem. Panelist David Pimentel, an ecologist at Cornell, estimated that efforts to clear zebra mussels from municipal and city water-intake pipes, boat hulls, and docks cost about $ 200 million a year. Pimentel noted that he and his colleagues have "conservatively" estimated that the 50,000 non-native species introduced into this continent were costing the American economy $ 137 billion per year. Jodi Cassell and like-minded audience members were clearly worried that if the Sagoffs of the world go around talking about the benefits as well as the costs of non-native species, they might undermine efforts to extirpate invader species from our shores.

10. Sagoff countered by pointing out that even Pimentel admits that the vast majority of introduced species do not have adverse costs. Pimentel's "50,000" is just a big scare number, noted Sagoff. "Besides, more than 60 percent of insect pests are native. So why single out non-natives in toting up the costs?"

11. There's another important point worth making on behalf of the invaders: We have reaped enormous benefits from non-native species. Ninety-nine percent of crop plants in the United States are non-

native, as are all our livestock except the turkey. "There is no basis in either economic or ecological theory for preferring native species over non-native species," said Sagoff. He further challenged his fellow panelists to name any specifically ecological criterion by which scientists can objectively determine whether an ecosystem whose history they don't know has been invaded or not. Are invaded ecosystems less productive? No. Are they less species-rich? No. And so on. Tellingly, the panelists had to agree that there is no objective criterion for distinguishing between "disturbed" ecosystems and allegedly pristine ones.

12. Despite that inability, the Convention on Biological Diversity's Subsidiary Body on Scientific, Technical, and Technological Advice stipulated last year that "it is important to differentiate between natural invasions and human introductions of species".

13. Why? From a strictly ecological point of view, should we care whether a species arrives on a piece of driftwood or on a cargo boat? Why not just regard the introduction of non-native species as fascinating experiments? Science magazine estimated last year that 99 percent of all the biomass—that is, the total of all living matter—in some parts of the San Francisco Bay belongs to non-native species. Yet native species continue to live in the Bay. University of California at Davis evolutionary biologist Geerat Vermeij concluded in a 1991 Science article: "Invasion usually results in the enrichment of biotas [the total flora and fauna] of continents and oceans." In layman's terms, introducing species tends to raise the total number of species living in a given ecosystem, not decrease it.

14. Most recorded extinctions are of species confined to oceanic islands which cannot compete with introduced continental species or humanity's habitat changes. For example, the brown tree snake came to Guam from New Guinea or the Solomon Islands during World War II. (They apparently hitched a ride on either Allied or Japanese ships or planes.) The birds and lizards of Guam were not adapted to snake predators and so were decimated by this alien species. However, continental species are better able to weather invasions. Even the Convention on Biological Diversity's Subsidiary Body concedes, "There are no records of global extinction of a continental species as a result of invasive species."

15. Of course, that isn't to say that non-native species don't sometimes cause economic harm. Take the case of the American chestnut. There was a time when it was said that an enterprising squirrel could travel from Maine to Georgia on the interlocking branches of chestnut trees. Yet an introduced fungus killed off nearly all of them before 1950.

16. The loss of American chestnuts was economically damaging, but the ecological costs are much less clear. The disappearance of such a dominant tree species from the Appalachians might have been expected to have had far more major consequences for the survival of other species in the ecosystem than it apparently has had. If the fungus had arrived before European settlers, it is unlikely that the absence of chestnuts would even have been noted.

17. On the other hand, James Kirkley, a biologist at the Virginia Institute for Marine Sciences, once told me that he would be happy to seed the Chesapeake Bay with Asian oysters. Why? Because overfishing and two fierce diseases have decimated native oysters so that oyster populations are less than 1 percent of their original levels. As a result, Chesapeake Bay waters have become much murkier. Asian oysters are very similar to native ones but resist disease more successfully. "The worst thing that could happen is that the Asian oysters would spread like wildfire," said the biologist, "which is exactly what we would want them to do." In this case a non-native species would be filling an ecological niche that has been opened by disease.

18. Acknowledging the potential benefits of non-native species doesn't necessarily preclude efforts to regulate them--or local species, for that matter. Even Sagoff argues that "good reasons exist for controlling known pests, whether native or exotic. Good reasons exist for taking pride in local flora and fauna". As he told me in an interview, "No good reason, economic or ecological, can be given, however, for waging an expensive battle against exotic species as such."

19. The preference for native over non-native species is essentially "a religious one", says Sagoff. That doesn't mean it isn't valid, but it does mean that ecologists and environmentalists can't simply justify their preference for native species on the basis of economic fiddling that willy-nilly lumps together basically benign alien species along with bad actors. Nor should ecologists attempt to justify their prejudices through recourse to "objective" science. An argument against alien species "must be explicitly an aesthetic one or historical one", he says. "Ecology should not attempt to become a normative science."

20. Arguments over which landscapes are to be preferred are at the heart of a lot of political and environmental debates today: suburban development vs. greenbelts; old-growth forests vs. forests managed for logging; wetlands vs. farmland, etc. They should be recognized for what they are and debated on their proper terms, as value judgments that are rooted not in science, but in aesthetics. The fact is that tastes vary. Some people love to look at fields of amber grain and to hear the gentle lowing of cows in a barn. Others prefer prairie grasses dotted with wildflowers and the rude huffing sounds of bison. Ecology will not and cannot tell us which landscape is "better" or should be favored. The most beautiful landscape or ecosystem, like beauty itself, is in the eye of the beholder.

Glossary

symposium [sim'pəuziəm,-'pɒ-] a meeting or conference for the public discussion of some topic especially one in which the participants form an audience and make presentations *n*. 讨论会(论文集、酒会)

shush [ʃʌʃ] silence (someone) by uttering "shush!" *v*. 嘘,别出声

temerity [ti'meriti] fearless daring *n*. 卤莽,蛮勇

the Great Lakes: 北美洲五大湖

freighter ['freitə] a cargo ship n. 货船(租船人)
shellfish ['ʃelfiʃ] invertebrate having a soft unsegmented body usually enclosed in a shell n. 贝,甲壳类动物
hull [hʌl] dry outer covering of a fruit or seed or nut; the frame or body of ship n. 壳,皮,船体
clog [klɔg] become or cause to become obstructed vt. 阻塞,妨碍,超载
water-intake:进水口,水摄入量
municipality [mju:ˌnisi'pæliti] an urban district having corporate status and powers of self-government n. 自治市,市当局
filter feeder:滤食动物,滤食者
algae ['ældʒi:] primitive chlorophyll-containing mainly aquatic eukaryotic organisms lacking true stems and roots and leaves n. 水藻,海藻
runoff ['rʌnˌɔ:f] the occurrence of surplus liquid (as water) exceeding the limit or capacity n. 径流量(流出,流放口,出轨,决赛)
organic matter:有机物
nonindigenous:非原地的
aquatic [ə'kwætik] 1. a plant that lives in or on water. n. 水生动物,水草; 2. relating to or consisting of or being in water; operating or living or growing in water adj. 水生的,水中的,水上的
macrophyte ['mækrəfait] a macroscopic plant, commonly used to describe aquatic plant, that is large enough to be visible to the naked eye n. [植]大型植物
biosecurity:生物安全性
underpinning ['ʌndəpiniŋ] support from beneath n. 支撑,建筑物下面的基础,支柱
extirpate ['ekstə:peit] destroy completely, as if down to the roots; pull up by or as if by the roots v. 除尽,灭绝
insect pest:虫害
tot up:determine the sum of v. 合计
pristine ['pristain] completely free from dirt or contamination; immaculately clean and unused adj. 远古的,原始状态的,未受损的,新鲜而纯净的
driftwood ['driftwud] wood that is floating or that has been washed ashore n. 流木,浮木
biomass [bai'əutə] the total mass of living matter in a given unit area n. 生物量
biota [bai'əutə] all the plant and animal life of a particular region n. 生物区(系)
flora ['flɔ:rə] all the plant life in a particular region or period n. 植物,群落
layman ['leimən] someone who is not a clergyman or a professional person n. 俗人,门外汉,凡人
Guam [gwɑ:m] the largest and southernmost island in the Marianas which is administered as a territory of the United States; it was ceded by Spain to the United States in 1898 n. 关岛

New Guinea [nju:'gini] a Pacific island north of Australia; the 2nd largest island in the world; governed by Australia and Indonesia *n*. 新几内亚岛(位于太平洋)

Solomon Islands: the northernmost islands are part of Papua New Guinea; the remainder forms an independent state within the British Commonwealth 所罗门群岛

lizard ['lizəd] relatively long-bodied reptile with usually two pairs of legs and a tapering tail *n*. 蜥蜴

predator ['predətə] any animal that lives by preying on other animals; someone who attacks in search of booty *n*. 食肉动物,掠夺者

decimate ['desimeit] kill one in every ten, as of mutineers in Roman armies or kill in large numbers *vt*. 十中抽一(取……的 1/10,毁灭……的大部分)

chestnut ['tʃestnʌt] 1. any of several attractive deciduous trees yellow-brown in autumn; yield a hard wood and edible nuts in a prickly bur; edible nut of any of various chestnut trees of the genus Castanea *n*. 栗子,栗树; 2. (of hair) of a golden brown to reddish brown color *adj*. 栗色的

interlocking [ˌintə(:)'lɔkiŋ] linked or locked closely together as by dovetailing *adj*. 联锁的

fungus ['fʌŋgəs] a parasitic plant lacking chlorophyll and leaves and true stems and roots and reproducing by spores *n*. 真菌,霉菌

Appalachian: in or relating to Appalachia *adj*. 阿帕拉契山脉的

Chesapeake Bay: a large inlet of the North Atlantic between Virginia and Maryland; fed by Susquehanna River 切萨皮克湾

oyster ['ɔistə] marine mollusks having a rough irregular shell; found on the sea bed mostly in coastal waters *n*. 牡蛎

niche [nitʃ] a position particularly well suited to the person who occupies it; (ecology) the status of an organism within its environment and community (affecting its survival as a species) *n*. 壁龛,适当的位置,生态位(一个生物所占据的生境的最小单位)

willy-nilly ['wili'nili] occurring or taking place whether desired or not *adj*. 不容分辨的,犹豫不决的

lump [lʌmp] a large piece of something without definite shape or a compact mass *n*. 团,块状

recourse [ri'kɔ:s] act of turning to for assistance; something or someone turned to for assistance or security *n*. 依赖,救生索,追索权

normative science: 规范科学

amber ['æmbə] of a medium to dark brownish yellow color *adj*. 琥珀色的,琥珀的

huff [hʌf] inhale recreational drugs; blow hard and loudly *vt*. 把……吹胀

bison ['baisn] any of several large humped bovids having shaggy manes and large heads and short horns *n*. 野牛

beholder [bi'həuldə] a person who becomes aware (of things or events) through the senses *n*. 旁观者

Exercises

A. Fill in each blank with one of the given words in its correct form.

| voracious | preclude | explicitly | problematic | enterprising | extirpate |
| fiddle | sin | negligence | exotic | allegedly | niche |

1. The seven deadly _____ — lust, envy, gluttony, sloth, greed, anger and pride — have had an enormous impact on the moral compass of the modern world.
2. But taken collectively, this is a _____ energy grab that could inflate Chinese state companies into the world's biggest corporate monsters, lumbering past even BP and Shell.
3. This combination of good functionality and out-of-the-box ease of use with a price so low that it's almost at the impulse-buy level could prove _____ for Microsoft.
4. Claude was probably a humbug, whose vanity, ambition, and intelligence led him to carve out a _____ as the wickedest man in the world; there is always room for a sadist at the top.
5. Such _____ types of people tend to be competitive and aggressive—and they're often behind the success of thriving businesses.
6. The conference focused on ecological management themes with an emphasis on invasive _____ species issues and the effects of climate change.
7. State authorities yesterday pulled the plug on a Manhattan money-wiring operation that _____ funneled millions of dollars to and from banks in the Dominican Republic, mainly for use by drug dealers.
8. The definition of a global symbol that is not _____ available for reference by modules linked with the module in which the definition occurs.
9. These figures appear to confirm the suspicion that the Government is _____ the exclusion figures by dumping problem pupils in nearby schools.
10. Doctors are human and everyone makes occasional errors, especially when under immense pressure. Of course, gross _____ is indefensible, but illness is never totally as it appears in medical textbooks.
11. In at least one instance, a researcher predicts that global warming will _____ one species from an entire region within 15 years.
12. Though most Iranians are feeling the bite of economic sanctions and expect them to tighten, only a third are willing to negotiate away the right to enrich uranium. However, two-thirds are willing to make a deal that would _____ the development of nuclear weapons.

B. Answer the following questions concerning the text.
1. Based on the information in the text, do you know who questions "Are we under attack by 'non-na-

tive' species? Should we care?"? And what do others think of these questions?
2. What is "Sagoff's sin"? And what does the author think of it?
3. Why do many people insist that massive regulatory steps should be taken to make sure "non-native species" are kept out of any given ecosystem?
4. For the layout of the whole text, how does the author expound the controversial problem of non-native species?
5. From your point of view, what should we do with invasive species?

C. Read the following questions and choose the best answer.
1. What does "this shushing" in the first sentence of Paragraph 3 mean? _____.
   A. Discussing the dominant problem of invasive species at the sea with the media
   B. Warning the government of the dangerous information related to coastal ecological invasion
   C. Withdrawing from considering non-native species as benign
   D. Advancing beneficial policies to protect the Great Lakes from biological attack
2. Instead of destroying ecological environment, zebra mussels in the Great Lakes _____.
   A. block the inlet pipe
   B. provide habitat for its American counterparts
   C. generate nutrients and fertilizers for the fishery
   D. purify the lake to facilitate the photosynthesis
3. Which of the following statements is NOT TRUE according to the text? _____.
   A. Sagoff receives little appreciation from its other ecologists concerning the benefits of zebra mussels
   B. It is suggested that anyone who brings foreign animals or plants to certain country without permission should be put into punishment
   C. At the meeting, several fundamental views concerning exotic species were demonstrated
   D. Nearly all the domestic animals and plants in the US were originated from other places
4. Proponents of non-native species argue that _____.
   A. foreign species cannot get accustomed to the native habitat
   B. a fixed pattern of ecosystem gives birth to the adaptability of invasive species
   C. Biotas are diversified by the introduction of alien species
   D. non-native species usually result in a worldwide extinction
5. What is Sagoff's attitude towards non-native species? _____.
   A. Native species and non-native ones should be treated equally and fairly
   B. Asian oysters are favorable examples of ecological invasion
   C. In a scientific sense, aesthetic taste could be taken into account when dealing with ecosystem
   D. Economic harm is the vital weakness of nonindigenous species

D. Explain the underlined parts.

1. So too, say ecologists, are all other "non-native" or "invader" species that <u>set up shop in ecosystems different from the ones in which they originated</u>.
2. Why ecologists feel this way is <u>no small matter</u>.
3. So were <u>the essentially aesthetic underpinnings of those</u> who would <u>devote huge resources to keeping "invaders" out of a given ecosystem</u>.
4. No good reason, economic or ecological, can be given, however, <u>for waging an expensive battle against exotic species as such</u>.
5. That doesn't mean it isn't valid, but it does mean that ecologists and environmentalists can't simply <u>justify their preference for native species on the basis of economic fiddling that willy-nilly lumps together basically benign alien species along with bad actors</u>.

Unit 7   Agriculture

Text A

Optimistic Future for Agriculture Predicted

1. Despite these recent uncertainties, "up" is precisely the direction an Iowa State researcher believes agriculture is headed for at least the next 10 years.

2. Wally Huffman, professor in agricultural economics and Charles F. Curtiss Distinguished Professor in Agriculture and Life Sciences, predicts supply will go up, demand will go up, and real prices of grain and oilseeds also will go up.

3. "I'm very optimistic about the next 10 years," said Huffman.

4. Huffman presented his research to the Organization for Economic Co-operation and Development in Paris, France, last month. OECD and the Iowa Agricultural Experiment Station supported the research.

5. An important part of Huffman's study was the long-term trend of corn and soybean yields in Iowa, wheat in Kansas and France, rice in Japan and potatoes in the Netherlands. Huffman examined the trends and then made projections about the next decade.

6. The optimism starts with the producers.

7. "Prices right now for corn and soybeans are up about 50 percent relative to two years ago, so those are relatively good prices," he said. "That's good news for grain producers."

8. The impact that the rising demand for biofuels will have on the market for agricultural products is not entirely clear, but grain and oilseed prices will generally be higher than they would be without biofuels.

9. "Overall, biofuels are probably a good thing for farmers," he said. "However, there will be more erratic variation in grain and oilseed prices than there would be without biofuels," he said.

10. The main reasons are the erratic components to both supply and demand of crude oil.

11. While biofuels are pushing demand for grain and oilseeds up, Huffman says the long-term trend in supply of grain and oilseeds is due to new technologies that are being developed by the private sector and marketed to farmers.

12. "Supply is going up, and demand is going up," he said. "I think they will grow at a similar pace. There will be occasional spikes due to bad weather and abrupt restriction in crude oil production, but prices will come down. When they do, they will come down to similar levels to what they are now in real terms, and those are pretty good prices."

13. "For the past 100 years, on average, real agricultural product prices have been falling as technology has been allowing supply to increase faster than demand," he said.

14. But for the past decade, demand has been rising as quickly as supply, he added.

15. Yields for major field crops in major producing areas have been steadily increasing. There is no indication that the rate is slowing and no reason to fear falling crop yields. Huffman predicts that the rate of increase in yields for corn and soybeans in major production areas will rise much faster than it has in the past 50 years.

16. "In the case of corn, since 1955 the average rate of increase in Iowa crop yield has been two bushels, per acre, per year," said Huffman. "That's an amazing accomplishment starting from about 65 bushels, per acre, per year in 1955, up to about 165 bushels, per acre, per year now."

17. Huffman thinks the future will be even better.

18. "From 2010 to 2019, corn yields are going to increase quite substantially, maybe at four to six bushels, per acre, per year," he said.

19. Much of the increase will be due to genetic improvements in hybrid corn varieties associated with new, multiple stacking of genes for insect protection and herbicide tolerance that will permit a major increase in plant populations.

20. These improvements are the result of corn that has been genetically modified (GM) to have certain desirable traits.

21. Also, better equipment, improved farm management, and reduced- and no-till farming will contribute to rising corn yields in the Midwest.

22. Other commodities have also improved yield and will likely see continuing increases, according to Huffman.

23. Soybean yields in Iowa also are increasing, although less dramatically than corn, says Huffman.

24. The trend over the past 50 years is an increase of about .5 bushel, per acre, per year (bu/ac/yr). That rate of improvement in Iowa soybean yields will continue or possibly increase over the next decade. Current soybean yields are about 50 bu/ac/yr.

25. Kansas is the leading producer of wheat in the United States with yields of about 45 bu/ac/yr. Yields have been improving at about .5 bu/ac/yr since about 1950.

26. Farmers in France are producing wheat at about 113 bu/ac/yr. Yields are improving at more than 1.5 bu/ac/yr.

27. France is the leading wheat producer in the European Union, and Huffman attributes much of their production advantage to the French emphasis on wheat advantage. They are also showing faster production improvement. France often puts their best land into wheat production. Huffman predicts wheat yields may increase faster if GM wheat is more successful.

28. Japan is a major rice producer. Yields are improving at a rate of .5 bu/ac/yr, and are now at 113 bu/ac/yr compared to around 90 bu/ac/yr in 1960. GM rice has been tried, but has not measurably increased yields, according to Huffman.

29. Netherlands is the most advanced country in the world when it comes to potato production technology. Yields in the Netherlands have been increasing by about 4.6 bu/ac/yr over the last 50 years and are now at 670 bu/ac/yr.

30. "Potatoes are a major world food crop and they don't get a lot of attention," said Huffman. "They are consumed in large amounts in Europe and other places, including the United States, and yields are phenomenal."

31. Several variables will impact the future of crops.

32. According to Huffman, the biggest are:

—both private companies and government researchers are working on improving production;

—higher yields as a result of new techniques in breeding crops, including methods to condense decades of breeding and testing into a few years;

—change in biofuels from corn-based to biomass-based by 2019;

—GM crops gain more acceptance in Europe.

33. Huffman's report is titled, Technology and Innovation in World Agriculture: Prospects for 2010 ~2019.

Glossary

Iowa ['aiəwə] a state in midwestern United States n. 爱荷华州，美国中西部之一州

oilseed ['ɔilsiːd] any of several seeds that yield oil n. 含油种子(如花生仁、棉籽等)

soybean ['sɔibiːn] a source of oil; used for forage and soil improvement and as food n. 大豆，黄豆

Kansas ['kænzəs] a state in midwestern United States n. 堪萨斯州

Netherlands ['neðələndz] n. 荷兰[国家]

projection [prə'dʒekʃən] a prediction made by extrapolating from past observations; the projection of an image from a film onto a screen; a planned undertaking n. 发射，计划，突出部分

erratic [i'rætik] having no fixed course; liable to sudden unpredictable change; likely to perform unpredictably adj. 无确定路线的，不稳定的，奇怪的，移动的；偏离的，偏执的，固执的，无规律的，漂泊的，反复无常的，漂游的

crude oil: a dark oil consisting mainly of hydrocarbons n. 原油

spike [spaik] 1. a long metal nail; sports equipment consisting of a sharp point on the sole of a shoe worn by athletes; (botany) an indeterminate inflorescence bearing sessile flowers on an unbranched axis n. 长钉, 钉鞋, 穗, 穗状花序; 2. pierce with a sharp stake or point v. 以大钉钉牢, 使……失效

bushel ['buʃl] a United States dry measure equal to 4 pecks or 2152.42 cubic inches; a British imperial capacity measure (liquid or dry) equal to 4 pecks n. 蒲式耳(容量等于八加仑)

acre ['eikə] a unit of area (4,840 square yards) used in English-speaking countries n. 英亩

hybrid ['haibrid] 1. a composite of mixed origin; an organism that is the offspring of genetically dissimilar parents or stock; especially offspring produced by breeding plants or animals of different varieties or breeds or species n. 混血儿, 杂种, 混合物; 2. produced by crossbreeding adj. 混合的, 杂种的

stacking ['stækiŋ] n. 堆垛

herbicide ['hə:bisaid] n. 除草剂

genetically modified (GM): denoting or derived from an organism whose DNA has been altered for the purpose of improvement or correction of defects adj. 转基因的

attribute...to: 归因于

phenomenal [fi'nɔminl] of or relating to a phenomenon; exceedingly or unbelievably great adj. 现象的, 能知觉的, 异常的

condense [kən'dens] undergo condensation; change from a gaseous to a liquid state and fall in drops; make more concise; become more compact or concentrated v. 浓缩, 摘要, 缩短

breed ['bri:d] to bear (offspring); to bring up, raise; to produce and maintain new or improved strains of (domestic animals and plants) v. 生育, 繁殖, (动物的)饲养, (植物的)培植

Exercises

A. Fill in each blank with one of the given words in its correct form.

| genetic | spike | erratic | hybrid | condense | substantially | optimism |
| measurably | breeding | abrupt | phenomenal | projection | | |

1. The debate on global change has largely failed to factor in the inherently chaotic, sensitively balanced, and threshold-laden nature of Earth's climate system and the increased likelihood of _____ climate change.

2. The natural formation in offspring of _____ combinations not present in parents, by the processes of crossing over or independent assortment.

3. The emerging discipline of _____ evolving populations provides insights into the tempo and mode of molecular evolution by combining new statistical techniques with sequences collected through time,

particularly from RNA viruses and ancient DNA.

4. Since then, scientists have tried to understand how such outsized waves arise from the _____ interactions of smaller waves on a choppy sea, with an eye toward creating them on purpose in the form of light traveling in an optical fiber.

5. The dividing cell's chromosomes — the X-shaped coils of DNA — _____ into tight clumps and expel most proteins that cling to DNA to maintain gene expression.

6. Agricultural Research Service (ARS) scientists have developed an efficient and cost-effective method to speed up the _____ of scab-resistant barley cultivars, thus improving crop quality for small-grain breeders in the Northern Plains.

7. The film shows how a high-resolution digital and interactive dome _____ can be combined with three-dimensional sound.

8. Due to its _____ electronic properties, graphene has been considered as a leading material for next generation electronic devices in the multibillion dollar semiconductor industry.

9. As the public climate debate continues, _____ cars with a combination of a combustion engine and an electric motor have increasingly become the focus of research projects.

10. Only rarely do gp120 molecules appear on the surface of the virus in a functional viral _____, which contains a cluster of three gp120 molecules, known as a trimer, in specific alignment.

11. In the largest study to date to prospectively study the health effects of _____ and cynical hostility in post-menopausal women, researchers found that white and black American women's attitudes are associated with health outcomes.

12. In comparison to ordinary Portland cement (OPC), geopolymer concrete (GPC) features greater corrosion resistance, _____ higher fire resistance (up to 2,400°F), high compressive and tensile strengths, a rapid strength gain, and lower shrinkage.

B. Answer the following questions concerning the text.

1. What is the prediction made by an Iowa State researcher concerning future agriculture?
2. What role does biofuel play in pushing up the supply of and demand for agricultural products?
3. According to the text, what may be the "desirable traits" entitled to corn through genetically modified method? And are they safe to both man and environment?
4. List the crops and their corresponding leading producing countries in a table.
5. What is the writing style of the text? And give examples to illustrate it.

C. Read the following questions and choose the best answer.

1. According to Huffman, agricultural prospect is that _____.
   A. uncertainties are overwhelming in the next ten years
   B. economic development is enterprising in the near future

C. farm produce market is promising in the following decade

D. research work is demanding for Organization for Economic Co-operation and Development in recent years

2. Who will benefit first from the optimistic agriculture as mentioned in the text? _____.

   A. Markets   B. Researchers   C. Farmers   D. Private sectors

3. Which of the following statements is TRUE on the basis of the text? _____.

   A. There is no possibility for the price of agricultural products to decrease

   B. In the past century, demand was usually left behind supply in agricultural markets

   C. It is estimated that corn output will grow by at least 20% in the next decade

   D. New chemical technologies contribute to the increase in corn yields

4. In addition to genetic approach, what other method is adopted to help enhance the production of corn? _____.

   A. Soil-less cultivation   B. Aquiculture   C. Herbicide   D. Hybrid

5. Which variable is not included in the suggestions of Huffman in terms of high crop yields? _____.

   A. New technologies ought to be worked out to gain more crop output

   B. GM agricultural products should be protected by Constitution

   C. Experiments on production of crops should be short-term

   D. Official organizations, together with non-official ones ought to endeavor to facilitate crop yields

D. Explain the underlined parts.

1. Despite these recent uncertainties, <u>"up" is precisely the direction</u> an Iowa State researcher believes agriculture is headed for at least the next 10 years.

2. There will be <u>occasional spikes</u> due to bad weather and abrupt restriction in crude oil production, but prices will come down.

3. <u>There is no indication</u> that the rate is slowing and <u>no reason to fear falling crop yields</u>.

E. Read the passages in this section and decide whether each of the following statements is true or false.

Passage One

    "Greens" like cabbages and broccoli are a well-known part of a healthy diet but they don't contain as large an amount of key minerals as they might, according to the lead scientist on the project, Associate Professor of Plant Nutrition, Dr Martin Broadley. He's secured funding to carry out new research into "biofortifying" cabbages and their relatives (Brassica) to boost dietary intakes of calcium and magnesium.

    The project has been funded by Biotechnology and Biological Sciences Research Council and a fertilizer company. It aims to enrich the edible parts of cabbages, broccoli and their more exotic cousins, Chinese cabbage and pak choi, with these minerals using conventional breeding techniques and by devising a recipe for a new type of fertilizer. Dr Broadley says the research could make a real difference to human health worldwide:

"This project is an exciting opportunity which could ultimately deliver real dietary benefits for the UK and globally. Recent studies have shown that leafy Brassica crops are excellent targets for biofortification with calcium and magnesium, even where vegetable consumption is relatively low, such as in the UK. By combining fertiliser-use with the development of more 'blue-skies' conventional breeding tools, we hope that this project will bring benefits in both the short and longer-terms, as well as improve our understanding of plants."

All of us require 22 essential minerals to live. These minerals can be supplied by a balanced and varied diet. Yet billions of people worldwide consume insufficient minerals, including calcium and magnesium. Since most calcium is stored in bones, calcium-deficient diets can reduce bone strength and increase fracture-risks and osteoporosis. In developing countries, calcium deficiency can also cause rickets. Magnesium deficiency is linked to hypertension, cardiovascular disease, and pre-eclampsia in pregnancy.

In the UK, vegetables —excluding potatoes —provide less than one tenth of our calcium and magnesium intakes. It's thought a relatively modest increase in the concentration of these minerals in green leafy vegetables would have a significant beneficial effect on our health. Dr Broadley says this is likely to be achievable by improving fertilizers and breeding programmes:

"Although it seems an obvious solution, we do not yet know how much calcium or magnesium fertiliser to apply to soil to optimise dietary intakes. This is because fertiliser studies tend to focus on crop yield. The 'blue-skies' breeding approaches rely on the fact that each different variety of Brassica represents a unique collection of variants of genes (alleles). However, just like different dog breeds, Brassica varieties are —in theory —interfertile. By crossing different varieties, and finding combinations of alleles which alter the calcium and magnesium content of plant leaves, we can inform conventional breeding programmes. The most exciting part of this project is that it builds directly on recent investment in Brassica research in the UK and elsewhere, which means we will soon have a fully-sequenced genome to work with, alongside other important resources."

(http://www.sciencedaily.com/releases/2009/10/091002124825.htm)

_____ 1. Green vegetables are full of nutrients such as calcium, protein, vitamin which are essential to good health.

_____ 2. Artificial measures are taken to improve mineral content in green vegetables.

_____ 3. People is vulnerable to suffer from fracture due to the lack of the mineral magnesium.

_____ 4. It requires no efforts to apply the method of breeding to enrich the soil with calcium and magnesium.

_____ 5. Brassica crops all possess the genomes peculiar to its own kind.

Passage Two

Bryony Bonning, professor of entomology, and Allen Miller, professor of plant pathology and director of the Center for Plant Responses to Environmental Stresses, are looking at a way to genetically modify soybeans to prevent damage from aphids.

If the research is successful, soybeans will carry in-plant protection from aphids, similar to the way genetically modified corn now keeps the European Corn Borer from destroying corn yields, but using a different molecular tool. Modified corn technology has been in use for about 12 years.

The study is being funded by a Grow Iowa Values Fund Grant. The goal of the grant program is to support development of technologies with commercial potential and to support the growth of companies using those technologies.

The researchers are working with Pioneer Hi-Bred, a DuPont business, as their corporate partner.

Previous research at Iowa State University indicated that if major soybean aphid outbreaks were left untreated, the loss in yield could exceed $250 million in Iowa. The annual cost to prevent the yield loss with insecticides can reach $64 million for Iowa soybean growers.

Soybean aphid outbreaks have become an annual phenomenon in Iowa, according to Miller.

The current research focuses on introducing a gene into soybeans that is harmless to mammals, but creates a toxin that is lethal to aphids that feed on soybean plants.

In order to be effective, the toxin needs to be taken intact into the body cavity of the aphid, not broken down by the digestive system in the bug.

Miller and Bonning identified a plant virus coat protein eaten by soybean aphids that doesn't break down and goes into the aphid body cavity intact.

They know the virus coat protein remains intact because the aphids often spread the virus from plant to plant while they are feeding.

Coat proteins make up the outer shell of a virus particle.

The researchers devised a method to use virus coat proteins to their advantage. The researchers have fused their toxin to the virus' protein coat. Since the protein coat is only part of the virus to be used, there is no risk of an infectious virus. Also, the coat protein is from a virus that normally doesn't infect soybeans.

When the hybrid toxin coat protein is eaten by the aphid, the fatal toxin should get into the aphid body cavity intact.

"What we thought was, if this (virus) protein has this ability to be taken up into the aphid (intact), let's take advantage of that specialization and fuse that to other proteins that are toxic," said Miller.

In addition to possibly curbing the aphid problem and the yield loss it causes, there are other benefits to the farmers and the ecosystems.

"The (potential) economic impact overall is huge," said Bonning. "There will be less insecticide use, and also less fossil fuel used to apply the insecticides."

Also, spraying soybeans with insecticides doesn't just control the aphids, according to Bonning.

"When you spray, you also control beneficial insects," said Bonning. "Lady beetles are affected, for example, and they are a natural enemy of the aphids. So when the aphids come back to a field after spraying, there won't be any lady beetles to naturally control the aphid populations."

Miller adds that if growers spray for aphids and don't eliminate them all, the aphids simply disperse to other fields, making the problem worse.

"There are many reasons not to spray, but you can't tell the growers to stop spraying until you give them an alternative for soybean aphid management," said Bonning.

(http://www.sciencedaily.com/releases/2009/09/090915174457.htm)

_____ 6. Genetically modified soybeans will have an inside protective "immune system" against pests.

_____ 7. The research program concerning insect pests in soybean is of economic significance.

_____ 8. The genetic method used to produce a poisonous chemical in soybean protection is fatal to both aphids and domestic animals.

_____ 9. The coat protein is a safe carrier of poison which is free of infection.

_____ 10. The successful controlling of soybean aphids will trigger a chain of benefits.

F. Cloze. Fill in each blank with one suitable word.

An Agricultural Research Service (ARS) scientist is looking for cover crop perennials that provide the best balance in biofuel production between agronomic success and environmental sustainability. This work is being supported by the Sun Grant Initiative, a national network of land-grant universities and __1__ funded laboratories working together to study, produce, and commercialize renewable, biobased energy technologies.

ARS agronomist Jeremy Singer, __2__ works at the National Soil Tilth Laboratory in Ames, Iowa, is conducting this research as part of a three-component study of optimizing corn __3__ for biofuel production. He's evaluating perennial grass crops to assess their potential for __4__ soil erosion and enhancing soil organic matter even in fields where every bit of corn and stover—stalk, leaves and all—is harvested __5__ for grain or cellulosic ethanol production.

Perennial groundcovers' root systems may contribute enough carbon to the soil to __6__ the loss of carbon when stover is removed. Cover crops also provide __7__ for beneficial insects, facilitate water infiltration, help hold nitrogen in the soil, suppress weeds and reduce the runoff of agricultural chemicals.

Results from Singer's first season in the field indicated that white clover or Kentucky bluegrass were promising cover crop candidates __8__ of additional study. On the other hand, creeping red fescue added notable amounts of carbon to the soil, but was very competitive with corn.

When the optimum groundcover has been identified, using no-till and strip-till cultivation practices in the corn-groundcover system will reduce the amount of fossil fuel needed to prepare and plant the crops. This reduced tillage, __9__, will decrease greenhouse gas emissions and require fewer energy inputs than using conventional tillage—__10__ prospective plus for farmers and fields alike. (http://www.sciencedaily.com/releases/2009/10/091002101613.htm)

1. A. critically   B. federally   C. sufficiently   D. practically
2. A. in which   B. that   C. whom   D. who
3. A. cultivation   B. upbringing   C. training   D. generation
4. A. precipitating   B. worsening   C. mitigating   D. flourishing
5. A. no   B. nor   C. either   D. neither
6. A. banish   B. offset   C. counter   D. retreat
7. A. nest   B. den   C. hollow   D. habitat
8. A. possible   B. worthy   C. available   D. accessible
9. A. in turn   B. in half   C. in effect   D. in that
10. A. other   B. certain   C. another   D. some

G. Translate the following passages into Chinese/English.

1. But even if crops and reserves recover, there are more worrying, long-term influences at work that herald an era of permanently dearer food. Most politically controversial is the diversion of crops to biofuel production. The White House has been the most aggressive in its promotion of biocrops, but others, such as the European Union, have also set ambitious targets for the new technology. US production of ethanol from corn has gone from 1.6 billion gallons in 2000 to 5 billion in 2006. President George Bush has set an interim（中间的，暂时的）target of 35 billion gallons for 2017 on the way to the administration's ultimate goal of 60 billion by 2030. Brazil and Indonesia are accused by their critics of sacrificing food and biodiversity to bio-ethanol and bio-diesel. Should we grow our biofuel crops in verifiable East Anglia（英格兰东部）or more efficient South America?

2. 大多数土壤是细小的岩石颗粒和植物遗体有机物的混合物。它们的形成是由于坚硬岩石的风化产生了砂砾，而这些砂砾又为苔藓类植物所寄生。随时间推移，植物死亡了，死亡的植物又产生了有机的腐殖质。这种物质会像海绵一样保持住水分，帮助将矿物颗粒粘结在一起，并且释放出各种元素和复杂的化学物质，为下一代的植物提供营养。

Text B

Sustainable Agriculture: Perennial Plants Produce More; Landscape Diversity Creates Habitat for Pest Enemies

1. Perennial plants produce more, require less input than annual croplands.

2. The major crops used globally to feed people and livestock wheat, rice, maize and soy are based on an annual system, in which crop plants live one year, are harvested, and are replanted the following year. These systems are notorious, however, for stripping organic nutrients from soils over time.

3. Perennial systems, on the other hand, contain plants that live longer than one year despite being harvested annually. Many agricultural scientists, including Jerry Glover of The Land Institute, say that perennial crops are the key to creating more sustainable agricultural systems.

4. "Across agricultural history, we've fundamentally relied on annual grain crops," says Glover. "But at the same time we rely on them, they're degrading the ecosystems they're in, which reduces their productivity."

5. To compare the long-term sustainability of these two cropping systems, Glover and his colleagues conducted a study on the physical, biological and chemical differences between annual wheat fields and perennial grass fields in Kansas. The fields had each been harvested annually for the past 75 years.

6. In each test, the researchers found perennial fields to be healthier and more sustainable ecosystems. In the perennial fields, the plants' total root mass was more than seven times that of the annuals, and the roots infiltrated about a foot deeper into the ground. The perennial fields also had higher soil microbe biodiversity and higher levels of dissolved carbon and nitrogen in the soil. All these findings, says Glover, suggest that the perennial field soil is healthy enough to maintain high levels of organic nutrients.

7. In addition to being more ecologically sustainable, Glover's team found that the perennial fields were more energy-efficient in providing productive harvests. Although only the annual fields received yearly fertilizer inputs, the perennial fields yielded 23 percent more nitrogen harvested over the 75 years, despite requiring only 8 percent of the energy inputs in the field such as fertilizer and harvesting operations as the annual systems.

8. Glover says that these results clearly show the need to move away from annual crops and increase our use and domestication of perennial crops.

9. "So far, little effort has been made to improve perennial crops," he says. "Some of greatest possibilities for transforming agriculture may well come from overlooked systems such as perennial grasses."

10. Landscape diversity creates habitat for pest enemies.

11. Farmers spend millions of dollars each year on pesticides to kill crop-eating insects. But these insects have natural enemies, too, and new research is investigating what farmers can do to encourage the proliferation of these pest-eaters. One study, presented as a talk at the ESA meeting, shows that increasing the natural habitat in and around farms can boost populations of pests' natural enemies.

12. Rebecca Chaplin-Kramer of the University of California Berkeley surveyed the abundance of flies, ladybugs, wasps and other predators of a common agricultural pest, the cabbage aphid, in croplands ranging from 2 percent to about 80 percent natural vegetation. She found that as the proportion of natural area or complexity increased, so did the numbers of natural enemies in the croplands.

13. Chaplin-Kramer shows that increases in predators didn't always result in fewer aphids in the croplands, but she points out that agents of control are only half of the equation and sources of the pests themselves must also be considered. In the absence of predators, pest levels would likely rise even more dramatically.

14. "By having complexity, you're supplying a community of insects to that farm that will be waiting when" and "if more pests show up," Chaplin-Kramer says.

15. Fostering larger predator communities is time-consuming and can take years to show results, Chaplin-Kramer says, which is why many farmers are skeptical of the idea. But, she says, there's no doubt that a strong predator base is more sustainable than simply using pesticides.

16. "Pesticides are a short-term solution, because pests can build up resistance, and new pesticides are constantly being developed," she says. "Building up predator communities takes time, but the systems are more stable and will provide more ecosystem services in the long term."

17. Reduced tilling improves soil microbe biodiversity.

18. The idea of using biological instead of chemical methods to create healthy croplands doesn't include just above-ground approaches. Soil bacteria can affect the growth and success of crop plants by fixing nitrogen, aiding in the uptake of nutrients and decomposing dead organic matter. Some current farming practices, however, may disrupt the soil ecosystem and decrease the effectiveness of the microbe community.

19. In his poster, Shashi Kumar of Texas Tech University will explore the relationship between conventional tilling and low-tilling practices on farms in semi-arid areas of west Texas. In areas where soil tilling was kept at a minimum, Kumar and his colleagues found a higher diversity of soil bacteria; conventional tilling produced lower bacterial diversity.

20. Kumar says that conventional tillage systems disrupt soil particles and decrease soil pore size, which can lead to decreased water and soil access for microbes. Although he recognizes that tillage is necessary, he thinks that farmers can reduce their tillage, even in semi-arid regions, to promote soil bacterial biodiversity.

21. "We are currently using so many different crop management systems, like pesticides, insecticides and fungicides, which are damaging to our soil system," says Kumar. "Why shouldn't we focus on biological methods, since the bacteria are already there?"

Glossary

perennial [pə'renjəl] lasting three seasons or more; lasting an indefinitely long time; suggesting self-renewal *adj*. 四季不断的，继续多年的

perennial plant: 多年生植物

livestock ['laivstɔk] (not used technically) any animals kept for use or profit *n*. 家畜，牲畜

maize [meiz] tall annual cereal grass bearing kernels on large ears: widely cultivated in America in many varieties; the principal cereal in Mexico and Central and South America since pre-Columbian times *n*. 玉米

infiltrate [in'filtreit] cause (a liquid) to enter by penetrating the interstices; enter a group or organization in order to spy on the members; pass into or through by filtering or permeating *v*. 浸润，渗透，使潜入

microbe ['maikrəub] a minute life form (especially a disease-causing bacterium); the term is not in technical use *n*. 微生物

nitrogen ['naitrədʒən] a common nonmetallic element that is normally a colorless, odorless, tasteless, inert diatomic gas which constitutes 78 percent of the atmosphere by volume; a constituent of all living tissues *n*. 氮

fertilizer ['fə:ti‚laizə] any substance such as manure or a mixture of nitrates used to make soil more fertile *n*. 肥料

domestication [də‚mesti'keiʃən] adaptation to intimate association with human beings *n*. 驯服，教化

proliferation [prəu‚lifə'reiʃən] growth by the rapid multiplication of parts; a rapid increase in number (especially a rapid increase in the number of deadly weapons) *n*. 增殖，分芽繁殖

ladybug ['leidibʌg] small round bright-colored and spotted beetle that usually feeds on aphids and other insect pests *n*. 瓢虫

wasp [wɔsp] social or solitary hymenopterans typically having a slender body with the abdomen attached by a narrow stalk and having a formidable sting *n*. 黄蜂，胡蜂

aphid ['eifid] any of various small plant-sucking insects *n*. 蚜虫

cabbage aphid: 菜蚜(虫)，甘蓝蚜(虫)

bacteria [bæk'tiəriə] (microbiology) single-celled or noncellular spherical or spiral or rod-shaped organisms lacking chlorophyll that reproduce by fission; important as pathogens and for biochemical properties; taxonomy is difficult; often considered plants *n*. (复数)细菌

bacterial [bæk'tiriəl] relating to or caused by bacteria *adj*. 细菌的

uptake ['ʌpteik] the process of taking food into the body through the mouth (as by eating); a process of taking up or using up or consuming *n*. 摄取, 领会

decompose [ˌdi:kəm'pəuz] separate (substances) into constituent elements or parts *v*. 分解, 腐烂

tilling: cultivation of the land in order to raise crops *n*. 耕作, 耕耘

semi-arid: somewhat arid *adj*. 半干旱的

Texas ['teksəs] the second largest state; located in southwestern United States on the Gulf of Mexico *n*. 德克萨斯州, (美国州名)

tillage ['tilidʒ] the cultivation of soil for raising crops *n*. 耕种

insecticide [in'sektisaid] a chemical used to kill insects *n*. 杀虫剂

fungicide ['fʌndʒisaid] any agent that destroys or prevents the growth of fungi *n*. 杀菌剂

Exercises

A. Fill in each blank with one of the given words in its correct form.

| domestication | bacterial | infiltrate | skeptical | strip | proliferation |
| perennial | uptake | abundance | dissolve | fundamentally | decompose |

1. In a partial kill the _____ oxygen level gets low enough to suffocate sensitive species and large fish, but many small fish and hardy species survive.

2. The Environmental Protection Agency may have suppressed an internal report that was _____ of claims about global warming, including whether carbon dioxide must be strictly regulated by the federal government, according to a series of newly disclosed e-mail messages.

3. We found that plastic in the ocean actually _____ as it is exposed to the rain and sun and other environmental conditions, giving rise to yet another source of global contamination that will continue into the future.

4. A _____ or fungal disease of certain plants, such as the cabbage and potato, that causes the stems to turn black at the soil line.

5. It has involved cooperation in developing nuclear energy while ensuring that civil uranium, plutonium and associated plants are used only for peaceful purposes and do not contribute in any way to _____ or nuclear weapons programs.

6. Using original simulations, they have demonstrated that the hole in the ozone layer reduces atmospheric carbon _____ in the Southern Ocean and contributes to the increase in ocean acidity.

7. The spiral galaxy NGC 4522 is located some 60 million light-years away from Earth and it is a spectacular example of a spiral galaxy currently being _____ of its gas content.

8. How you answer those questions will determine how you understand the morphological and physiologi-

cal changes that _____ has brought about—whether as the results of the pressure of natural selection in a new niche, or as deliberately cultivated advantageous traits.

9. Virtualization can and will _____ change infrastructure networks in the same way it changed data centers.

10. A team of scientists in Spain has analyzed 29 esparto fields from Guadalajara to Murcia and has concluded that _____ vegetation cover is an efficient early warning system against desertification in these ecosystems.

11. Although ozone pollution is most often associated with outdoor air, the gas also _____ indoor environments like homes and offices.

12. The promotion of the by the savanna trees increases their own _____ by limiting the establishment and growth of tree species that are better competitors for resources and that might ultimately displace the savanna trees.

B. Answer the following questions concerning the text.

1. Do you know any perennial grasses? And how many of them are served as food in our meals?
2. Judging by the text, what makes one of the researcher think "Some of greatest possibilities for transforming agriculture may well come from overlooked systems such as perennial grasses."?
3. What is the proportional relation between the complexity of natural habitat and the numbers of natural enemies in the fields?
4. According to the text, why are pesticides considered as an expedient solution?
5. What can soil bacteria do to help crops grow successfully?

C. Read the following questions and choose the best answer.

1. Compared with the producers of staple food, perennial grains are more likely to _____.
    A. gain superiority due to short-lived cultivation
    B. achieve sustainability of landscape diversity
    C. diminish fertility of farmland
    D. interfere with agricultural productivity yearly

2. Why is the cropland with perennial plants more fertile than the annual field? _____.
    A. Because it requires less nutrition to obtain a good harvest
    B. Because it has the greatest possibilities for transforming agriculture
    C. Because it is characterized with strong absorption of nutrients
    D. Because it is endowed with tenacious vitality

3. According to the text, which of the following factor is most related to the rapid growth of pest enemies? _____.
    A. Environment   B. Population   C. Predators   D. Cultivation

4. Although proliferating pest-eaters is a long-term task, the favorable side is that _____.
   A. farmers feel doubtful about the sources of predator communities
   B. populations of predators will give up no space for the pest to live on
   C. environment benefits a lot in the long run
   D. chemical methods can totally be replaced by ecological ones
5. Traditional farming practices lead to _____.
   A. a high bacterial content
   B. a great uptake of nutrients
   C. an obvious damage of cropland
   D. a full dissolution of chemicals

D. Explain the underlined parts.
1. These systems are notorious, however, for <u>stripping organic nutrients from soils over time</u>.
2. Some of <u>greatest possibilities for transforming agriculture</u> may well come from overlooked systems such as perennial grasses.
3. Chaplin-Kramer shows that increases in predators didn't always result in fewer aphids in the croplands, but she points out that <u>agents of control are only half of the equation</u> and sources of the pests themselves must also be considered.
4. Soil bacteria can <u>affect the growth and success of crop plants</u> by fixing nitrogen, aiding in the uptake of nutrients and decomposing dead organic matter.
5. Kumar says that conventional tillage systems disrupt soil particles and decrease soil pore size, which can <u>lead to decreased water and soil access for microbes</u>.

Unit 8　Arctic and Antarctic

Text A

The Last Unexplored Place on Earth (Extracted)

　　The landscape could be in upstate New York, western Maine, or any number of other scenic places: a few large lakes, many small ones, wide rivers and slow-flowing streams, water-filled hollows and soggy ground, all set in a stony land. But that's where the resemblance to familiar landscapes ends. Here, no clouds float by, no rain falls, and no stars shine; there is no sunlight or moonshine, and no air at all. Instead, spread over this water-rich landscape, covering it almost completely and sealing it in, is 5 million square miles of glacial ice, roughly two miles thick and a million years old.

　　Antarctica, the coldest place on Earth. If it were possible to lift up the giant ice sheets, that watery, stony terrain is what would remain. But of course it is not possible, so nobody knows what the buried landscape really looks like or how many living things may be down there. As of only a few decades ago, no one knew this world of buried lakes and rivers even existed. Now scientists are paying serious attention to it. Journalists have dubbed it "the last unexplored place on Earth" and "one of Earth's last frontiers". A veteran Russian glaciologist went so far as to call the discovery of one of Antarctica's greatest subglacial lakes, Lake Vostok (now known to be the sixth-largest lake in the world, with a volume of about 1,300 cubic miles), "among the most important geographical discoveries of the second half of the 20th century".

　　One thing that is known for sure about Antarctica's network of subglacial waterways is that they are not some insignificant sideshow to the grand drama of the continent's ice sheets. In fact, learning about the lakes and rivers could shed light (albeit from a very dark place) on weighty matters ranging from ice-sheet stability—how much do the lakes enhance the flow of ice toward the sea? —and the history of glaciation in Antarctica—did some lakes form before the ice? —to the continent's contribution to rising sea levels. According to a recent National Research Council report, the discovery of subglacial lakes "opened an entirely new area of science in a short period of time".

　　Taking advantage of that opening isn't a whole lot easier than mounting an expedition with sled dogs and penguin stew. As the lakes are in remote, extremely cold locations and deeply buried, projects envisioned for studying them directly tend to be logistically challenging, time-consuming, and expensive. "It takes ages to get programs together," says Mahlon Kennicutt II, an oceanographer at Texas A&M University and secretary of the Subglacial Antarctic Lake Environments group (SALE). There's also a long period of environmental review required, largely because subglacial lakes have the potential to harbor life—and the life down there could very well be rare and exotic forms. Bacteria and other microbes that fell on the glacier surface would have spent a million years being carried downward as more snow fell above them before they eventually plopped into the lakes. There, in the near-freezing, totally dark, high-pressure, low-nutrient environment, some might have adapted in novel ways in order to survive. Studying these hardy microbes could provide scientists with clues to how life might exist on Mars or on Jupiter's ice-covered moon Europa.

As yet, no one has touched the waters of a subglacial lake with so much as a drill bit, but a Russian group that has been coring ice over Lake Vostok to get ancient climate records is coming close. The Russians desperately want to be the first to reach a subglacial lake and sample it. "It is important to our country," says Valery Lukin, an oceanographer and director of the Russian Antarctic Expedition. He compares reaching the lake to reaching the moon: "The U.S. made the first flight to the moon. They won. For our country it is very important to be first into a subglacial lake." Russia has put a lot of national resources behind the effort and might be there by 2009. "It's the centerpiece of their polar program," Kennicutt points out.

Some scientists worry that the Russians' drive to be first may put the pristine ecosystem in peril. Drilling equipment and fluid that is dumped down the borehole to keep it open may introduce microbial contaminants into the waters of the lake under the drill station (also called Vostok), making it impossible for scientists to know what was there naturally. John C. Priscu, a professor of land resources and environmental sciences at Montana State University who discovered microorganisms thriving in permanently frozen surface lakes in Antarctica at temperatures as low as 10 degrees Fahrenheit, wants to study microbes in Lake Vostok to learn if they are viable or unique, or both. "What is their lifestyle?" he asks. "Do they form a community? Do they eat each other? Do they make poisons?"

To answer these and other questions, he has to get to the Antarctic lakes before they become polluted.

Only a few decades ago, according to Priscu, most scientists still thought of Antarctica as Robert Falcon Scott did when he realized that he would be second at the South Pole: "Great God! This is an awful place." The prevailing attitude was that Antarctica was a solid block of ice, Priscu says, a continent without life. The idea that there was water underneath either of Antarctica's ice sheets (there is an eastern and a western one) seemed preposterous. "Water under ice sheets? Intuitively, it didn't make sense to me," Kennicutt admits. "It's a very unusual phenomenon." The first person to report evidence of a subglacial lake didn't recognize what he was seeing. In 1958, a Russian airplane navigator named Robinson was making his landing approach at the newly opened Vostok research station when he noticed a large, flat, oval depression "with gentle shores" on the glacier surface. The smooth depression, we now understand, was a result of the bottom of the ice sheet floating free and frictionless as it passed over water instead of bedrock 2 1/2 miles below.

Glossary

upstate ['ʌp'steit] towards, in, from, or relating to the outlying or northern sections of a state, esp. of New York State adj. (美国的一州内)远离大城市的(地);远离海岸线的(地);偏僻的(地)

soggy ['sɔgi] (of soil) soft and watery adj. 湿透的

glacial ice:流动冰

Antarctica [æn'tɑ:ktikə] an extremely cold continent at the south pole almost entirely below the Antarctic Circle; covered by an ice cap up to 13,000 feet deep n. 南极洲

terrain [tə'rein] a piece of ground having specific characteristics or military potential n. 地带,地域,地形

dub [dʌb] give a nickname to; provide (movies) with a soundtrack of a foreign language v. 1.给……起绰号;把……称为;2.配音;复制;3.混声录制,混录(音乐)

glaciologist [ˌglæsi'ɔlədʒist, ˌgleiʃi-] n. 冰河学家

subglacial [sʌb'gleiʃəl] formed or occurring at the bottom of a glacier adj. 冰下的(冰川下的,冰川底部的)

ice sheet:a thick layer of ice covering a large area of land for a long time, esp. those in Antarctica and Greenland n. [地]大冰原,冰盾

albeit [ɔ:l'bi:it] even though conj. 虽然(即使)

glaciation [ˌglæsi'eiʃən] the condition of being covered with glaciers or masses of ice; the result of glacial action; the process of covering the earth with glaciers or masses of ice n. 冻结成冰,冰河作用

envision [in'viʒən] imagine; conceive of; see in one's mind vt. 想像,设想

oceanographer [ˌəuʃiə'nɔgrəfə(r)] a scientist who studies physical and biological aspects of the seas n. 海洋学家

plop [plɔp] drop something with a plopping sound; drop with the sound of something falling into water v. 扑通地坠落

Mars [mɑ:z] a small reddish planet that is the 4th from the sun and is periodically visible to the naked eye; minerals rich in iron cover its surface and are responsible for its characteristic color n. 火星

Jupiter ['dʒu:pitə] the largest planet and the 5th from the sun; has many satellites and is one of the brightest objects in the night sky n. 木星

Europa [juə'rəpə] the 4th largest of Jupiter's satellites; covered with a smooth shell of frozen water *n*. [天]木卫二

fluid ['flu(:)id] a substance that is fluid at room temperature and pressure; a continuous amorphous substance that tends to flow and to conform to the outline of its container: a liquid or a gas *n*. 流体, 液体

borehole ['bɔːhəul] a hole driven into the ground to obtain geological information, release water, etc *n*. 地上凿穿

microbial [mai'krəubiəl] of or involving or caused by or being microbes *adj*. 微生物的, 由细菌引起的

microorganisms [maikrəu'ɔːgəniz(ə)m] any organism of microscopic size *n*. 微生物

fahrenheit ['færənhait,'fɑːr-] 1. of or relating to a temperature scale proposed by the inventor of the mercury thermometer; symbol: F. *adj*. 华氏的; 2. German physicist who invented the mercury thermometer and developed the scale of temperature that bears his name (1686~1736) *n*. 华氏温标, 华氏温度计

preposterous [pri'pɔstərəs] incongruous; inviting ridicule *adj*. 荒谬的, 可笑的

navigator ['nævigeitə] the ship's officer in charge of navigation; the member of an aircrew who is responsible for the aircraft's course *n*. 航海家, 领航员

frictionless: lacking all friction *adj*. 无摩擦的(光滑的)

bedrock ['bed'rɔk] solid unweathered rock lying beneath surface deposits of soil *n*. 岩床, 根底, 基础

Exercises

A. Fill in each blank with one of the given words in its correct form.

| veteran | plop | expedition | fluid | microbial | envision |
| terrain | albeit | pristine | logistically | preposterous | oval | resemblance |

1. This 30-day _____, planned for late December, will involve a 275-mile trek on foot in the dead of winter, crossing the Mojave Desert and into some of most harsh and inhabitable terrain known to man.

2. They think of viruses that infect an organization from the outside. They _____ hackers breaking into their information vaults.

3. That's why I'm passionately for Goldacre, and why I find myself wondering whether we can file a class action against LBC for permitting a presenter to inflict her _____ prejudices on her listeners, to the detriment of someone else's kids.

4. As the first raindrops _____ into Centre Court at 4:34pm, the fourth-round women's singles between Amelie Mauresmo and Dinara Safina was brought to a halt.

5. Mission specialists included _____ spacewalkers John Grunsfeld and Mike Massimino, and first-

time space fliers Andrew Feustel, Michael Good and Megan McArthur, who served as flight engineer.
6. It publishes authoritative articles covering theoretical, computational and experimental investigations of all aspects of the mechanics of _____.
7. The Malaysian property market is showing signs of recovery, _____ at a slow pace, attributed to government spending and developers taking a cautious stance during the economic downturn.
8. Comets move around the sun like planets, but in long _____ course.
9. Although unexpected, our findings are encouraging because determining eligibility for kidney transplantation is a _____ challenging process that requires sequential diagnostic tests and encounters with health care clinicians.
10. Engineers from NASA's Jet Propulsion Laboratory and students at the California Institute of Technology have designed and tested a versatile, low-mass robot that can rappel off cliffs, travel nimbly over steep and rocky _____, and explore deep craters.
11. The report outlines recommendations for large-scale _____ sequencing efforts directed toward cultivated isolates and single cells, as well as a community-scale approach to characterize a set of defined ecosystems of varying complexity.
12. Our results suggest that exposure has a limited role in the ability to process facial _____ in others, which contrasts with the way our brains process facial recognition.
13. While restoration can help reverse losses, this research shows it is critical for human well-being that we conserve _____ habitats and the biodiversity and ecosystem services they provide.

B. Answer the following questions concerning the text.
1. What are the landscapes like in the western Marine?
2. What can we get if we learn the lakes and rivers?
3. What is the desire of the U.S. toward the Antarctica?
4. Are we clear about the ecosystem in Antarctica?
5. How serious does the pollution threatens the atmosphere?

C. Read the following questions and choose the best answer.
1. What does "coldest place" in Paragraph1 refer to? _____.
   A. Power production and greenhouse effect
   B. Heavy rainfalls
   C. Heavy Snowfalls
   D. Large amount of glacial ice
2. Which of the following may not be the role of the buried lakes and rivers in Antarctic area? _____.
   A. Ice-sheet mobility   B. Glacial action

  C. A pioneer activity   D. A mysterious discovery
3. Which of the following statements is NOT TRUE according to the text? _____.
  A. An America oceanographer knows what the buried landscape really looks like
  B. An America oceanographer knows how many living things may be down there
  C. There is an expert, who is from China knows a lot about the Antarctica
  D. Watery, stony terrain remains under the giant ice sheets
4. The study of subglacial lakes is likely to _____.
  A. shed some lights on the research of the life in outer space
  B. have the potential of denying environmental review carried out by oceanographers
  C. prevent bacteria microbes' growth cycle
  D. reveal solar plants' formation process
5. The Russian Antarctic Expedition is not only scientific but also _____.
  A. environment-friendly   B. politics-oriented
  C. highly-efficient   D. Globally-supported

D. Explain the underlined parts.

1. <u>The landscape could be in upstate New York, western Maine, or any number of other scenic places: a few large lakes, many small ones, wide rivers and slow – flowing streams, water – filled hollows and soggy ground, all set in a stony land</u>
2. But of course it is not possible, so nobody knows <u>what the buried landscape really looks like or how many living things may be down there.</u>
3. The Russians <u>desperately want to be the first to reach a subglacial lake and sample it.</u>
4. There's also a long period of environmental review required, <u>largely because subglacial lakes have the potential to harbor life – and the life down there could very well be rare and exotic forms.</u>
5. Studying these hardy microbes could <u>provide scientists with clues to how life might exist on Mars or on Jupiter's ice-covered moon Europa.</u>
6. The prevailing attitude was that Antarctica <u>was a solid block of ice,</u> Priscu says, a continent without life.

E. Read the passages in this section and decide whether each of the following statements is true or false.

Passage One

  These are but a few findings reported in "State of Polar Research", released February 25 by the World Meteorological Organization (WMO) and the International Council for Science (ICSU). In addition to lending insight into climate change, IPY has aided our understanding of pollutant transport, species' evolution, and storm formation, among many other areas.

The wide-ranging IPY findings result from more than 160 endorsed science projects assembled from researchers in more than 60 countries. Launched in March 2007, the IPY covers a two-year period to March 2009 to allow for observations during the alternate seasons in both polar regions. A joint project of WMO and ICSU, IPY spearheaded efforts to better monitor and understand the Arctic and Antarctic regions, with international funding support of about US $ 1.2 billion over the two-year period.

IPY has provided a critical boost to polar research during a time in which the global environment is changing faster than ever in human history. It now appears clear that the Greenland and Antarctic ice sheets are losing mass contributing to sea level rise. Warming in the Antarctic is much more widespread than it was thought prior to the IPY, and it now appears that the rate of ice loss from Greenland is increasing.

Researchers also found that in the Arctic, during the summers of 2007 and 2008, the minimum extent of year-round sea ice decreased to its lowest level since satellite records began 30 years ago. IPY expeditions recorded an unprecedented rate of sea-ice drift in the Arctic as well. Due to global warming, the types and extent of vegetation in the Arctic shifted, affecting grazing animals and hunting.

Other evidence for global warming comes from IPY research vessels that have confirmed above-global-average warming in the Southern Ocean. A freshening of the bottom water near Antarctica is consistent with increased ice melt from Antarctica and could affect ocean circulation. Global warming is thus affecting Antarctica in ways not previously identified.

IPY research has also identified large pools of carbon stored as methane in permafrost. Thawing permafrost threatens to destabilize the stored methane—a greenhouse gas—and send it into the atmosphere. Indeed, IPY researchers along the Siberian coast observed substantial emissions of methane from ocean sediments.

In the area of biodiversity, surveys of the Southern Ocean have uncovered a remarkably rich, colourful and complex range of life. Some species appear to be migrating poleward in response to global warming. Other IPY studies reveal interesting evolutionary trends such as many present-day deep-sea octopuses having originated from common ancestor species that still survive in the Southern Ocean.

IPY has also given atmospheric research new insight. Researchers have discovered that North Atlantic storms are major sources of heat and moisture for the polar regions. Understanding these mechanisms will improve forecasts of the path and intensity of storms. Studies of the ozone hole have benefited from IPY research as well, with new connections identified between the ozone concentrations above Antarctica and wind and storm conditions over the Southern Ocean. This information will improve predictions of climate and ozone depletion.

Many Arctic residents, including indigenous communities, participated in IPY's projects. Over 30 of these projects addressed Arctic social and human science issues, including food security, pollution, and other health issues, and will bring new understanding to addressing these pressing challenges. "IPY has been the catalyst for the development and strengthening of community monitoring networks across the North," said David Carlson, Director of the IPY International Programme Office. "These networks stimulate the information flow among communities and back and forth from science to communities."

The increased threats posed by climate change make polar research a special priority. The "State of Polar Research" document not only describes some of the striking discoveries during IPY, it also recommends priorities for future action to ensure that society is best informed about ongoing polar change and its likely future evolution and global impacts. A major IPY science conference will take place in Oslo in June 2010.

(http://www.sciencedaily.com/releases/2009/02/090225073215.htm)

_____ 1. The narrow IPY findings result in more than 160 endorsed science projects assembled.

_____ 2. It now appears clear that the Greenland and Antarctic ice sheets are losing mass contributing to sea level rise.

_____ 3. Warming in the Antarctic is much more widespread than it was thought superior to the IPY, and it now appears that the rate of ice loss from Greenland is decreasing.

_____ 4. Other IPY studies reveal interesting evolutionary trends such as many present – day deep – sea octopuses having originated from common ancestor species that still survive in the Southern Ocean.

_____ 5. The "State of Polar Research" document not only describes some of the striking discoveries during IPY, it also recommends priorities for future action to ensure that society is best informed about ongoing polar change and its likely future evolution and global impacts.

Passage Two
The Appeal

Antarctica is so vast that only a small portion of it can be explored during a two week period. The Antarctic Peninsula, that part of the continent that points toward the tip of South America, is so long that it spans 12 degrees of latitude, approximately 1,200 km or 800 miles.

Humans never inhabited Antarctica and exploration of the continent is relatively recent. New discoveries continue to be made. In 2007 for example, our vessels sailed uncharted waters while exploring the Antarctic Peninsula!

For many, perhaps, the most appealing aspect of Antarctica is its wildlife. Although there are only a few native species, those that have adapted to the harsh environment thrive in large numbers. Penguin populations are counted in the tens of thousands in some rookeries.

Antarctica is devoid of power lines, billboards, and highways. There are no designer coffee shops or cellular networks. When the engines are turned off, the only sounds you hear are natural-wildlife, water and the occasional boom of icebergs calving. If you listen closely, you can hear your heart beating with excitement!

Getting There

Most visitors to Antarctica arrive by ship, from the closest port, Ushuaia, in the province of Tierra del Fuego, Argentina. Longer expeditions depart (or disembark in) from New Zealand, Australia, and Stanley in the Falkland Islands (Islas Malvinas).

Getting to Antarctica is as much a part of the experience as exploring it. The body of water that separates Antarctica from South America is the Drake Passage. The Drake acts like a funnel, concentrating the energy produced by the winds and currents of the Southern Ocean.

The result can be rough water, some of the roughest in the world. Yet some crossings are relatively quiet, providing extraordinary opportunities for birding and whale watching. The unpredictability of the Drake Passage is intoxicating. A crossing is the perfect introduction to expedition-style travel, where unpredictability is the only thing you can truly count on.

The Cost

Expeditions to Antarctica are diverse in style and cost. Three elements affect the cost of a voyage: the duration of the expedition, the passenger capacity of the vessel, and the activities included

Antarctica does not lend itself to "bare bones" travel. And you cannot upgrade hotels or cut your expedition short if you find you have chosen the wrong itinerary or ship.

So invest wisely—choose an expedition operated by a company with a solid reputation, and ships that are purpose-built for polar waters. Choose one of three styles of ship. For the ultimate experience choose an icebreaker. Nimble adventure ships are for active adventures, and expedition ships offer adventures in comfort.

(http://www.quarkexpeditions.com/antarctic/antarctic-expeditions)

_____ 6. The Antarctic Peninsula points toward the tip of South America, which is so long that it spans 12 degrees of latitude, more than 1,200 km or 800 miles.

_____ 7. Antarctica is powerless, billboards, and highways. There are no designer coffee shops or cellular networks.

_____ 8. The body of water that distinguishes the border of Antarctica from South America is the Drake Passage.

_____ 9. The rough water leads to the winds and currents of the Southern Ocean.

_____ 10. And you can upgrade hotels or cut down your expedition if you find you have chosen the right itinerary or ship.

F. Cloze. Fill in each blank with one suitable word.

Arctic and Antarctic research teams pulled back to warmer climates when the International Polar

Year wrapped last March. But the call has gone out for a __1__ to the poles for a more focused investigation __2__ the effects of global warming. Leading the charge back to the Canadian Arctic is David Hik, a University of Alberta biology professor and a lead researcher with IPY.

"IPY gave us a great __3__ of the state of the planet's polar regions," said Hik. "But in the Arctic we made many observations that need a more __4__ look, especially in the very early spring and the dead of winter."

Hik says university calendars __5__ when most northern research can be done. The only time professors and graduate students have for distant fieldwork is spring and summer.

"We have to be there __6__ the snow begins to melt and we have to be there in the dark of winter to witness and document the effects of reduced snow cover," said Hik.

Hik says having researcher's boots on the ground throughout the year in the Arctic could __7__ intense research into areas touched upon during IPY. Those observations of the effects of a shorter winter and reduced snow cover on Arctic ecosystems include:

—Encroachment by the southern tree line and shrubs on Arctic tundra used by caribou.

—Arctic plants that are growing earlier in the spring and are past their energy yielding __8__ before calving caribou cows and other animals can use them.

—Reduced snow cover and its insulating qualities, which __9__ hibernating species.

To follow through with observations made during IPY, Hik is helping organize a __10__ conference of Arctic and Antarctic research teams for next June in Norway. Hik is co-author of a paper summarizing recent IPY findings and the call for more focused research. It will be published in Science on Sept. 11.

(http://www.sciencedaily.com/releases/2009/09/090910142354.htm)

1. A. return   B. expedition   C. research   D. exploration
2. A. about   B. into   C. for   D. on
3. A. impression   B. imagination   C. snapshot   D. prospect
4. A. attractive   B. thorough   C. authentic   D. thoughtful
5. A. strike   B. manifest   C. dictate   D. symbolize
6. A. as   B. for   C. since   D. while
7. A. impose   B. perform   C. focus   D. terminate
8. A. trough   B. location   C. timing   D. prime
9. A. extirpates   B. impacts   C. endangers   D. starves
10. A. press   B. review   C. follow-up   D. academic

G. Translate the following passages into Chinese/English.

1. Ice at the North Pole melted at an unprecedented rate last week, with leading scientists warning that the Arctic could be ice-free in summer by 2013.

Satellite images show that ice caps started to disintegrate dramatically several days ago as storms over Alaska's Beaufort Sea began sucking streams of warm air into the Arctic.

As a result, scientists say that the disappearance of sea ice at the North Pole could exceed last year's record loss. More than a million square kilometers melted over the summer of 2007 as global warming tightened its grip on the Arctic. But such destruction could now be matched, or even topped, this year.

2. 企鹅中多数品种的总数达到几百万只,有一些品种正以引人注目的速度增长着,这显然是由于南极鲸的数目急剧减少的结果,因为南极鲸同企鹅争夺磷虾——这两种动物都以此为主要食物。多数品种的企鹅都是下两个蛋,不过皇企鹅和王企鹅只下一个蛋。雌企鹅往往出海约两周觅食以恢复下蛋的体耗,一旦回来后,雌、雄企鹅便轮流孵蛋。在这方面皇企鹅已被证明是异于常规的,因为雌皇企鹅通常得步行 50~100 英里到海边,然后再步行相同距离回来,这时蛋已孵化了。

Text B

Arctic Land Grabs could Cause Eco-Disaster

1. After nations carve up the fast-melting region, will there be anything left?

2. Global warming is making the Arctic a hot property. In early August a team of Russian geologists placed a flag in the seabed under the North Pole, claiming it was part of Russia's underwater territory. Earlier this summer Canada's prime minister announced plans to increase patrolling to protect Canadian sovereignty over the Northwest Passage, the fabled shipping route that snakes along Canada's northern border. All this squabbling promises to intensify over the next few years as the Arctic Circle becomes ripe for exploitation.

3. For years, climate scientists have used the Arctic region as an example of how warming temperatures can hurt the environment. The Arctic has been heating up much faster than any other part of the world owing to a variety of climatological factors. In 2006 Arctic ice levels dipped below the record minimum and researchers expect the next few years' levels to be even lower. As the sea ice in the Arctic Ocean continues to melt, more and more ships will be able to pass through waterways like the Northwest Passage. Shipping companies may be drooling over the potential economic benefits, but increased shipping through the Arctic could have devastating environmental consequences, including habitat destruction, introduction of invasive species, and perhaps worst of all, a high chance of oil or chemical spills that could be nearly impossible to clean up.

4. Mariners have been dreaming about using the Northwest Passage above Canada and the Northern Sea route above Siberia for centuries. The two waterways represent a seductive shortcut between Europe

and Asia; the current route from Europe involves looping all the way down to the Panama Canal and back up the U.S. West Coast, a distance of about 12,000 miles. The Northwest Passage route is about 4,000 miles shorter, which could save shipping companies millions of dollars on fuel.

5. To the explorers who, for centuries, tried to navigate the Northwest Passage and failed (hundreds perished in the iceberg-filled waters), the idea of an ice-free Arctic would probably sound ludicrous. Typically, it takes a specially constructed ship with a hardened body to push through the frozen waterway, and even then, only when icebreakers clear its path; the substantial added expense deterred shipping companies from using the passage. But two years ago, the Russian vessel Akademik Fyodorov became the first ship to make it through the Northwest Passage without icebreakers. The window during the late summer when ships could get through used to be a short week or two, but it's been increasing every year. It won't be long before more ships without icebreakers start attempting the journey, Arctic experts say.

6. And ships won't be entering the Arctic just for quick transits through the Northwest Passage. The number one draw to an ice-diminished Arctic is the cache of natural resources like oil and natural gas that are thought to be buried under the ocean floor. The U.S. Geological Survey estimates the Arctic contains up to a quarter of the world's undiscovered oil and natural gas. Once covered by thick sea ice, these treasures could soon become accessible, and Arctic nations like the U.S., Russia, and Denmark want the profits.

7. Environmental groups are not happy about the prospect of increased shipping in the Arctic. Many worry that expanding traffic over the next few years is all too likely to cause an environmentally disastrous accident because the ice won't be completely cleared for decades—it will have cleared just enough that inexperienced mariners will recklessly try to push through. "Freighters of all sorts will be coming through to save some cost on fuel," says Joseph Handley, premier of Canada's Northwest Territories, which border the Arctic Ocean. "They'll come through and there will be accidents."

8. If the worst case does come to pass and there's a large oil or chemical spill in the Arctic, its consequences could be worse than in other areas. The evaporation process is much slower in high latitudes because the water is so cold; breaking down spilled oil would take many decades, says Peter Ewins, director of species conservation for World Wildlife Fund-Canada. In addition, the region is so far removed from population and maritime centers that getting cleanup supplies to a spill site would be much harder, if not impossible. After the Exxon Valdez oil spill in Alaska, the U.S. Coast Guard was near enough that a cleanup effort could start immediately. But if a colossal spill like the Valdez happened much farther north, it could devastate the area. "If you had to clean up a spill in the high Arctic, I don't know how you'd do it," Handley says.

9. The Arctic environment is especially vulnerable to climate change and a large share of the relatively few native species, including polar bears and caribou, are struggling for survival. Increased ship-

ping could send these species over the edge, say ecologists. For example, the Dolphin-Union caribou, which live in the Canadian archipelago in the middle of the Northwest Passage, rely on ice bridges to get into mainland Canada for food in the winter. Ships passing through have already cut up these bridges, Ewins says. This also affects the Inuit community in the northern islands because they rely on the caribou for food. Passing ships have interfered with the Inuit more directly: On more than one occasion, ships barging through the ice have left hunters stranded on newly severed icebergs, according to Handley.

10. Growing numbers of ships in the Arctic could also exacerbate the problem of invasive species, foreign plants and animals that enter and often take over ecosystems. Bacteria and small organisms like crabs and mussels brought in on ships coming from warmer oceans could spread disease and compete with native species for resources. Invasive species are entering the region with or without shipping, says Ted Scambos of the National Snow and Ice Data Center in Colorado; warming of the Arctic Ocean's surface temperatures has already increased mixing with foreign waters and all the microbes they contain. Increased shipping could further accelerate the process, making the situation much worse and harder to repair.

11. Perhaps even more worrisome, there's currently no plan in place to protect the Arctic from the effects of growing maritime traffic. Part of the problem is that no one can agree on which waters belong to whom. Eight countries—Russia, Canada, the United States, Norway, Finland, Iceland, Sweden, and Denmark, through its territory, Greenland—have laid claim to Arctic territory and waters. Each nation is entitled to waters within 200 nautical miles of its continental shelves, according to the U.N.'s Law of the Sea, but over the years confusion has developed as to what constitutes a continental shelf. When a team of Russian geologists claimed part of the North Pole's seabed earlier this month, they argued the seabed is part of a large underwater mountain range that connects to Russia. Should the U.N. accept their claim—an unlikely possibility, given that they've turned down similar claims from the Russian Bear in the past—Russia would be entitled to thousands of miles of the Arctic Ocean and 45 percent of the area's resources, according to some sources. Canadian politicians, meanwhile, say that other countries should be required to get Canadian permission before entering the Northwest Passage because much of the waters weave in and out of Canada's northern islands. The United States and Europe have long ignored Canada's professed sovereignty in this regard, claiming the fast-liquidating Northwest Passage is international and should be unrestricted.

12. With no clear resolution as to who makes the rules in the Arctic, few rules have been adopted. Some international organizations are working on regulation programs in the Arctic, like the U.N.'s Arctic Council, but there is still no plan for how to enforce proposed rules. As countries jockey for land and rights, environmental concerns have been largely ignored.

13. All the Arctic nations are supposedly committed to protecting the Arctic. Back in 1993, they all

signed the Nuuk Declaration, in which they promised to consider the environmental effects of all proposed activities in the region. Still, the economic incentive in this case may be too great for countries to put the environment first, and unlike Antarctica, which the U.N. deemed noncommercial, international territory, the Arctic might never attain protected status—its potential for profit is just too high. "There is a whole series of reasons why people want to venture into the Arctic more and more, so the number of ships will only keep increasing," says Ewins of the WWF.

14. Before long, the concept of an ice-free Arctic won't be a possible future—it'll be present-tense reality, and allied countries like the United States and Canada may find themselves fighting over territory that was quite recently considered a useless wasteland. "This may all be playing out within the next few years, rather than decades from now as had been thought," says Scambos from the National Snow and Ice Data Center. "Things are changing fast."

Glossary

Arctic ['ɑːktik] 1. at or near the north pole; of or relating to the Arctic; extremely cold *adj*. 北极的，极寒的；2. the regions north of the Arctic Circle centered on the North Pole; a waterproof overshoe that protects shoes from water or snow *n*. 北极圈，北极

geologist [dʒi'ɔlədʒist] a specialist in geology *n*. 地质学家

sovereignty ['sɔvrinti] government free from external control; royal authority; the dominion of a monarch; the authority of a state to govern another state *n*. 主权，独立国

squabble ['skwɔbl] 1. argue over petty things. *vt*. 争论(搞乱)；2. a quarrel about petty points *n*. 争论(搞乱)

the Arctic Circle: *n*. 北极圈

climatological: *adj*. 气候的

chemical spill: 化学溢出物，化学滴漏物

mariner ['mærinə] a man who serves as a sailor *n*. 海员

Siberia [sai'biəriə] a vast Asian region of Russia; famous for long cold winters 西伯利亚

Panama Canal: a ship canal 40 miles long across the Isthmus of Panama built by the United States (1904~1914) *n*. 巴拿马运河(穿过巴拿马地峡，接通太平洋和大西洋)

ludicrous ['luːdikrəs] broadly or extravagantly humorous; resembling farce; incongruous; inviting ridicule *adj*. 荒谬的，可笑的

icebreaker ['aisbreikə(r)] a ship with a reinforced bow to break up ice and keep channels open for navigation *n*. 碎冰船

deter [di'təː] try to prevent; show opposition to; turn away from by persuasion *vt*. 阻止，抑制，威吓

cache [kæʃ] a hidden storage space (for money or provisions or weapons) *n*. 隐藏所，贮藏物

evaporation [iˌvæpə'reiʃən] the process of becoming a vapor; the process of extracting moisture *n*. 蒸发，脱水，干燥

latitude ['lætitjuːd] the angular distance between an imaginary line around a heavenly body parallel to its equator and the equator itself *n*. 纬度，界限，自由选择权

caribou ['kæribuː] arctic deer with large antlers in both sexes; called "reindeer" in Eurasia and "caribou" in North America *n*. 北美驯鹿

Inuit ['inuit] a member of a people inhabiting the Arctic (northern Canada or Greenland or Alaska or eastern Siberia); the Algonquians called them Eskimo ("eaters of raw flesh") but they call themselves the Inuit ("the people") *n*. 因努伊特人

barge [baːdʒ] 1. a flatbottom boat for carrying heavy loads (especially on canals) *n*. 驳船；2. push one's way; transport by barge on a body of water *vi*. 猛撞，冲，闯

sever ['sevə] set or keep apart; cut off from a whole *v*. 切断，脱离，分开

exacerbate [igˈzæsə(ː)beit] make worse; exasperate or irritate *vt*. 加重(使……恶化，激怒)

Norway ['nɔːwei] a constitutional monarchy in northern Europe on the western side of the Scandinavian Peninsula; achieved independence from Sweden in 1905 *n*. 挪威

Finland ['finlənd] republic in northern Europe; achieved independence from Russia in 1917 *n*. 芬兰

Iceland ['aislənd] an island republic on the island of Iceland; became independent of Denmark in 1944 *n*. 冰岛

Sweden ['swiːdn] a Scandinavian kingdom in the eastern part of the Scandinavian Peninsula *n*. 瑞典

Denmark ['denmaːk] a constitutional monarchy in northern Europe; consists of the mainland of Jutland and many islands between the North Sea and the Baltic Sea *n*. 丹麦

Greenland ['grinlənd] the largest island in the world; lies between the North Atlantic and the Arctic Ocean; a self-governing province of Denmark *n*. 格陵兰

nautical ['nɔːtikəl] relating to or involving ships or shipping or navigation or seamen *adj*. 海上的，航海的，船员的

continental shelf [ˌkɔntiˈnentl ʃelf] the relatively shallow (up to 200 meters) seabed surrounding a continent 大陆架

liquidate ['likwideit] get rid of (someone who may be a threat) by killing; eliminate by paying off (debts) *v*. 偿付，清算，扫除

jockey ['dʒɔki] defeat someone in an expectation through trickery or deceit *v*. 骗，瞒，骗人使做……

Exercises

A. Fill in each blank with one of the given words in its correct form.

colossal	incentive	sever	evaporation	squabble	drool	deter
seductive	liquidate	exacerbate	recklessly	strand	ludicrous	

1. Experiments were designed to evaluate the ability of the group to find cohesion despite competing _____, while a second series was designed to determine the potential influence of minority power brokers.

2. As global change proceeds, continuing increases in resource availability are likely to _____ such plant invasions.

3. Before the participants judged the photographs for attractiveness, the members of the research team rated the images for how _____, confident, thin, sensitive, stylish, curvaceous (women), muscular (men), traditional, masculine/feminine, classy, well-groomed, or upbeat the people looked.

4. Congress and the White House are _____ over a bill that essentially revises NASA's mission statement.

5. Additionally, it has been shown that the period of mid-adolescence (ages 15 through 19) is the time when teens are more likely to begin high-risk behaviors such as drinking, abusing drugs or driving _____.

6. Some in Iran have been keen to blame foreign media for fuelling the recent protests. This has led to _____ allegations about the BBC which have surfaced in the Iranian media.

7. In this study, we've shown that surgical treatment of migraine headaches is safe, effective, and that this reasonably short operation can have a _____ impact on the patients' quality of life all while eliminating signs of aging for some patients, too.

8. Plants are attacked by a bewildering array of herbivores and in response they have evolved a variety of defences to _____ predators such as thorns and noxious chemicals.

9. Live birds found _____ on beaches around Monterey Bay were starving and severely hypothermic, having lost the insulation normally provided by their waterproof plumage.

10. Individual investors are _____ their holdings at record levels as financial markets sink, often absorbing losses to avoid possibly worse pain later.

11. Temperatures also dropped when higher winds spurred more _____ in this typically humid area, the same process behind household swamp coolers.

12. Many therapies, most still in the conceptual stage, are aimed at restoring the connection between the nerve cell and the _____ nerve fibres that innervate a target tissue, typically muscle.

13. The guidelines also recommend doctors consider offering their patients botulinum (肉毒杆菌) toxin

B to treat sialorrhea (流涎症), also known as _____, if oral medications do not help.

B. Answer the following questions concerning the text.
1. Why did Canada's prime minister announce plans to increase patrolling to protect Canadian sovereignty over the Northwest Passage?
2. What does "drooling" mean in the second passage and why?
3. What is the importance of the icebreakers?
4. What kinds of danger are those inexperienced mariners faced with?
5. What is the reason for breaking the balance of the ecosystems?

C. Read the following questions and choose the best answer.
1. The relationship of Russia and Canada is _____.
   A. very promising   B. bound by promise
   C. more and more intensive D. in dispute
2. Mariners _____ the Northwest Passage above Canada and the Northern Sea route above Siberia hundreds of years ago.
   A. hoped to use   B. hated using
   C. had been using   D. preferred using
3. Ice-diminished Arctic attracts much attention for _____.
   A. its good for traveling
   B. its good place for exploitation
   C. there being lots of gold
   D. its rich in natural resources
4. Consequences in the Arctic could be worse than in other areas for _____.
   A. mariners recklessly try to push through
   B. it is rich in natural resources
   C. its less population
   D. its geographic situation
5. From the last paragraph, we can conclude that _____.
   A. the Arctic will be of no ice
   B. ice will still exist in the Arctic
   C. icebreakers are not needed any more
   D. international conference will be held in the Ice Data Center

D. Explain the underlined parts.
1. They'll <u>come through and there will be accidents</u>.
2. The United States and Europe have long ignored Canada's professed sovereignty in this regard, <u>claiming the fast-liquidating Northwest Passage is international and should be unrestricted</u>.

3. Observations during the alternate seasons in both Polar Regions are carried out in the whole year of 2009.
4. The minimum extent of sea ice decreased to its lowest level since satellite records all the year began 30 years ago.
5. Atlantic storms and ocean sediments are major sources of heat and moisture and methane for the Polar Regions.

Unit 9　Endangered Species

Text A

Wildlife Conservation 2.0

1. Nothing pushes a species to extinction like wiping out its habitat. Consider the Hawaiian Islands: They were originally covered in trees, but by the 1950s three – quarters of the islands' natural forests had been destroyed to make way for animal pastures and crops. Many other habitats were overrun by introduced pigs and rats. The effect on Hawaii's indigenous species was devastating: In the last 200 years, 28 species of birds alone were wiped out, including the large Kauai thrush. Once widespread throughout the Hawaiian Islands, this thrush has not been seen since 1989. It is considered extinct by the World Conservation Union.

2. Conservation biologists face an increasingly difficult job of preserving habitats and, with them, global biodiversity. But Hugh Possingham, an ecologist and mathematician at the University of Queensland in Australia, has developed revolutionary software that will make their work easier and more effective.

3. Traditionally, biologists have drawn up priority lists of places that should be preserved. Sounds straightforward—except that different biologists favor different lists, each list driven by different criteria. One might rank a location according to the overall number of threatened species there, while another ranks locations based on the number of species that are unique to that area. Which list should an organization follow? The most popular list to have emerged, first proposed in the late 1980s by conservation biologist Norman Myers, pinpoints "biodiversity hot spots"—those places with the greatest number of unique species facing the most severe threats, such as the tropical Andes and the Horn of Africa.

4. A new software—based approach may be the key to saving thousands of species.

5. Possingham questions the conventional wisdom that severely threatened places deserve the most attention, and he sees a better path to preservation. "A consequence of our approach is that you do not spend the most money on the most endangered species or the most endangered regions," he says. "You balance cost and biodiversity and threats."

6. For example, last September Possingham, Kerrie Wilson (a biologist at the University of Queens-

land), and a team of researchers assessed the cost and outcomes of various conservation actions in 39 "Mediterranean" ecoregions identified by the World Wildlife Foundation (WWF). These regions—in places like California, South Africa, Chile, and Australia—are among the world's most threatened. Analysis showed that to save the most biodiversity for the buck, scientists might do best to spend money on relatively cheap interventions (such as weed control in a Chilean forest, where weed removal means native trees do not have to compete for nutrients in the soil) and eschew more expensive investments in areas such as Australia's Jarrah – Karri forest, even though it has the highest vertebrate diversity of all the Mediterranean regions analyzed and is home to rare marsupials. The goal is to save more species on the whole, even if they are less newsworthy or photogenic.

7. Possingham began developing this unconventional way of thinking in 1994, when he was on sabbatical at Imperial College London and watched biologists scrambling to try to figure out what to save. He was amazed to see that when they drew up their priority lists, they neglected a crucial factor: cost. Well grounded in math, Possingham began constructing models that performed cost – efficiency analyses of different conservation schemes, ultimately encoding his work into Marxan, a software program written by a Ph.D. student named Ian Ball and first released in 1999. Since then, Possingham has continued to incorporate new factors into his models, including information about the types of threats that species face, the cost of interventions to combat these threats, and the ability to account for how threats and interventions change over time.

8. In practice, Marxan is a tool into which conservationists and policymakers can enter information about their local environment—the distribution of flora and fauna, for example, or the economic value of a patch of land. Based on these data, Marxan designs nature reserves that cost as little as possible to create and maintain, while meeting whatever conservation criteria the user has established; this might mean creating the smallest possible nature reserve that still represents every type of plant life in a given region.

9. Many conservation organizations and governments around the world have enthusiastically adopted Marxan to design and manage protected areas. The Australian government, for example, recently used Possingham's analysis to guide a series of major conservation decisions. Marxan helped identify regions off Australia's northeast coast that collectively maximized biological diversity in the Great Barrier Reef Marine Park, leading to the rezoning of the park boundaries. The government also used Marxan in designating 50 million hectares of new reserves in other parts of the country.

10. Not everyone raves about Possingham's work. Some claim his software – driven approach is at times unnecessary. Conservation ecologist Stuart Pimm of Duke University thinks that Possingham's models make sense in places like Australia, where there is still a lot of intact biodiversity; he has reservations about its use in places where biodiversity is fast declining. For instance, Pimm and a small group of other scientists are now buying up cattle pastures in Brazil to try to connect fragments of highly diverse—and

highly threatened—coastal forests. Pimm calls this action so "obvious" that it requires no methodical cost-benefit analysis. "When you've got a lot of land to play with," Pimm says, "it makes sense to think of these formalized processes [like Possingham's], but in practice, in areas that are particularly badly degraded, you don't have a lot of choices."

11. To many others, though, Marxan's process is part of the appeal. "For years people have sat around with maps and pens and drawn lines on the maps and said, 'We should protect this and protect that,'" says Ray Nias, conservation director for the WWF – Australia, based in Sydney. "What Hugh has done is to make that a mathematical and logical process rather than an intuitive one. It's far more sophisticated and robust than the old way of doing things."

12. Possingham and his colleagues are currently working on making Marxan faster and easier to use and adding additional routines to consider the effects of catastrophes like hurricanes. Not a bad thing, if we are to save as many as possible of the 16,306 species currently listed as threatened by the World Conservation Union.

Glossary

Hawaiian Islands: a group of volcanic and coral islands in the central Pacific n. 夏威夷群岛

kauai ['kauai] an island of Hawaii northwest of Oahu n. 考艾岛(在夏威夷)

thrush [θrʌʃ] songbirds characteristically having brownish upper plumage with a spotted breast; candidiasis of the oral cavity; seen mostly in infants or debilitated adults n. 画眉，鹅口疮，蹄叉腐烂

Queensland ['kwi:nzlənd] a state in northeastern Australia n. 昆士兰州(澳大利亚)

Mediterranean [ˌmeditə'reinjən] 1. the largest inland sea; between Europe and Africa and Asia n. 地中海; 2. of or relating to or characteristic of or located near the Mediterranean Sea adj. 地中海(的)

ecoregion: an area defined by its environmental conditions, esp climate, landforms, and soil characteristics n. 生态区域

chile ['tʃili] a republic in southern South America on the western slopes of the Andes on the south Pacific coast n. 智利

buck [bʌk] mature male of various mammals (especially deer or antelope) n. 雄鹿，雄兔

intervention [ˌintə(:)'venʃən] the act of intervening (as to mediate a dispute); a policy of intervening in the affairs of other countries; (law) a proceeding that permits a person to enter into a lawsuit already in progress; admission of person not an original party to the suit so that person can protect some right or interest that is allegedly affected by the proceedings n. 插入，介入，调停

eschew [is'tʃu:] avoid and stay away from deliberately; stay clear of vt. 避开

marsupial [mɑ:'sju:pjə] 1. mammals of which the females have a pouch (the marsupium) containing the teats where the young are fed and carried n. 有袋类; 2. of or relating to the marsupials adj. 袋

的，袋状的

photogenic [ˌfəutəu'dʒenik] looking attractive in photographs *adj.* 上相的，上镜头的

sabbatical [sə'bætik(ə)l] of or relating to the Sabbath; of or relating to sabbatical leave（公休假）*adj.* 安息日的

conservationist [ˌkɔnsə'veiʃənist] someone who works to protect the environment from destruction or pollution *n.* 自然资源保护论者

Great Barrier Reef Marine Park: 澳洲大堡礁海洋公园

rezone [riː'zəun] *v.* 再分区

hectare ['hektɑː] (abbreviated "ha") a unit of surface area equal to 100 acres (or 10,000 square meters) *n.* 公顷

methodical [mi'θɔdik(ə)l] characterized by method and orderliness *adj.* 有方法的，有系统的

robust [rə'bʌst] physically strong; marked by richness and fullness of flavor; strong enough to withstand or overcome intellectual challenges or adversity; rough and crude *adj.* 强壮的，强健的，粗野的，需要体力的，浓的

catastrophe [kə'tæstrəfi] an event resulting in great loss and misfortune; a state of extreme (usually irremediable) ruin and misfortune; a sudden violent change in the earth's surface *n.* 大灾难，大祸，彻底失败

hurricane ['kʌrikən, 'hʌrikin] a severe tropical cyclone usually with heavy rains and winds moving a 73~136 knots (12 on the Beaufort scale) *n.* 飓风，飓风般猛烈的东西

Exercises

A. Fill in each blank with one of the given words in its correct form.

eschew devastating catastrophe enthusiastically intuitive intervention methodical maximize formalize originally newsworthy robust

1. Alzheimer's might seem hopeless to some, but this research shows that we're closer than ever to unraveling both the protein tangles and mysteries surrounding this _____ disease.

2. The researchers found that health journalists determine what information is _____ by examining the work of their peers and the issues raised by their colleagues and audiences.

3. Educators know children spend 80 percent of their waking time away from school and children are learning deeply and _____ in museums, in community centers, from online games and in all sorts of venues.

4. We propose choosing between different varieties of the same crop species in order to _____ solar reflectivity rather than changing crop type, although the latter could also produce climatic benefits.

5. One way to _____ the value of the gut instinct about chest pain patients would be to introduce ob-

jective tools, like those that already exist for risk stratification of patients with pneumonia and for venous thrombus embolism.

6. Expectant mothers who _____ asthma treatment during pregnancy heighten the risk transmitting the condition to their offspring, according to one of the largest studies of its kind published in the European Respiratory Journal.

7. Brief _____ shows promise for increasing receipt of treatment among alcohol – dependent women, particularly those with higher cognitive functioning or an alcohol – attributable diagnosis.

8. The studies explain, in part, how West Nile Virus spread so rapidly across the United States when experts had been expecting a more plodding, _____ progression of the disease.

9. Americans continue to pull away from organized religion, but the rate of departure previously reported may not have been as abrupt as _____ thought, according to research to be presented at the 104th annual meeting of the American Sociological Association.

10. Material scientists at Washington University in St. Louis have developed a technique for a bimetallic fuel cell catalyst that is efficient, _____ and two to five times more effective than commercial catalysts.

11. The abrupt extinction of marine life we can clearly see in the fossil record firmly links giant volcanic eruptions with global environmental _____, a correlation that has often been controversial

12. Unlike traditional feature based methods, the approach described here utilizes global, whole face, facial characteristics and allows a witness to produce plausible, photo – realistic face images in an _____ way.

B. Answer the following questions concerning the text.

1. What is the duty of conservation biologists? And how do they carry it out?
2. According to Possingham, what is the better path to preservation? Why?
3. How did Possingham develop Marxan? And what is the function of Marxan?
4. Why did people have different opinions towards Marxan?
5. How should we evaluate Possingham and his colleagues' effort?

C. Read the following questions and choose the best answer.

1. The author mentions the Hawaiian Islands in order to _____.
   A. illustrate the disastrous effect of wiping out a species' habitat
   B. show its geographic features
   C. tell people the extinction of a species
   D. compare the indigenous species with the introduced one

2. Which one is not among the world's most threatened? _____.
   A. California   B. South Africa

  C. Chile   D. Austria
3. Which one of the following sentences is TRUE according to the passage? _____.
 A. Possingham created a software program in 1994
 B. He found that people neglected cost when they drew up the priority lists
 C. Marxan was originally a software program written by a student named and first released in 1994
 D. Possingham ceased to incorporate new factors into his models since then
4. Marxan was adopted by many conservation organizations and governments around the world _____.
 A. to design and manage protected areas
 B. to create data of local environment
 C. to establish conservation criteria
 D. to analyze different conservation schemes
5. What is the writing genre of the text? _____.
 A. Narration   B. Exposition   C. Argumentation   D. Description

D. Explain the underlined parts.

1. The most popular list to have emerged, first proposed in the late 1980s by conservation biologist Norman Myers, <u>pinpoints "biodiversity hot spots"—those places with the greatest number of unique species facing the most severe threats</u>, such as the tropical Andes and the Horn of Africa.

2. Possingham questions <u>the conventional wisdom that severely threatened places deserve the most attention</u>, and he sees a better path to preservation. "A consequence of our approach is that <u>you do not spend the most money on the most endangered species or the most endangered regions</u>," he says. "<u>You balance cost and biodiversity and threats.</u>"

3. Analysis showed that <u>to save the most biodiversity for the buck</u>, scientists might do best to spend money on relatively cheap interventions (such as weed control in a Chilean forest, where weed removal means native trees do not have to compete for nutrients in the soil) and <u>eschew more expensive investments</u> in areas such as Australia's Jarrah-Karri forest, even though <u>it has the highest vertebrate diversity of all the Mediterranean regions analyzed and is home to rare marsupials</u>.

4. Since then, Possingham has continued to <u>incorporate new factors into his models,</u> including information about <u>the types of threats that species face, the cost of interventions to combat these threats, and the ability to account for how threats and interventions change over time.</u>

5. In practice, Marxan is a tool into which conservationists and policymakers can enter information about their local environment—<u>the distribution of flora and fauna,</u> for example, or the economic value of a patch of land.

6. Marxan helped <u>identify regions off Australia's northeast coast that collectively maximized biological diversity</u> in the Great Barrier Reef Marine Park, <u>leading to the rezoning of the park boundaries.</u>

7. Possingham and his colleagues are currently working on making Marxan faster and easier to use and adding additional routines to consider the effects of catastrophes like hurricanes.

E. Read the passages in this section and decide whether each of the following statements is true or false.

Passage One

The findings, published October 1 in the journal Bioscience, found that in North America all of the largest terrestrial predators have been in decline during the past 200 years while the ranges of 60 percent of mesopredators have expanded. The problem is global, growing and severe, scientists say, with few solutions in sight.

An example: in parts of Sub – Saharan Africa, lion and leopard populations have been decimated, allowing a surge in the "mesopredator" population next down the line, baboons. In some cases children are now being kept home from school to guard family gardens from brazen packs of crop – raiding baboons.

"This issue is very complex, and a lot of the consequences are not known," said William Ripple, a professor of forest ecosystems and society at Oregon State University. "But there's evidence that the explosion of mesopredator populations is very severe and has both ecological and economic repercussions."

In case after case around the world, the researchers said, primary predators such as wolves, lions or sharks have been dramatically reduced if not eliminated, usually on purpose and sometimes by forces such as habitat disruption, hunting or fishing. Many times this has been viewed positively by humans, fearful of personal attack, loss of livestock or other concerns. But the new picture that's emerging is a range of problems, including ecosystem and economic disruption that may dwarf any problems presented by the original primary predators.

"I've done a lot of work on wildlife in Africa, and people everywhere are asking some of the same questions, what do we do?" said Clinton Epps, an assistant professor at OSU who is studying the interactions between humans and wildlife. "Most important to understand is that these issues are complex, the issue is not as simple as getting rid of wolves or lions and thinking you've solved some problem. We have to be more careful about taking what appears to be the easy solution." The elimination of wolves is often favored by ranchers, for instance, who fear attacks on their livestock. However, that has led to a huge surge in the number of coyotes, a "mesopredator" once kept in check by the wolves. The coyotes attack pronghorn antelope and domestic sheep, and attempts to control them have been hugely expensive, costing hundreds of millions of dollars.

"The economic impacts of mesopredators should be expected to exceed those of apex predators in any scenario in which mesopredators contribute to the same or to new conflict with humans," the researchers wrote in their report. "Mesopredators occur at higher densities than apex predators and exhibit greater resiliency to control efforts."

The problems are not confined to terrestrial ecosystems. Sharks, for instance, are in serious decline due to overfishing. In some places that has led to an explosion in the populations of rays, which in turn caused the collapse of a bay scallop fishery and both ecological an economic losses.

(http://www.sciencedaily.com/releases/2009/10/091001164102.htm)

_____ 1. There are few solutions to the problem that while predators are in decline, mesopredators are expanded in the world.

_____ 2. According to William Ripple, the expansion of mesopredators has both ecological and economic effects.

_____ 3. Primary predators have been dramatically reduced usually on purpose.

_____ 4. It's less important to understand that these issues of predators and mesopredators are complex.

_____ 5. The economic impacts of predators should be expected to exceed those of mesopredators.

Passage Two

Research has previously assumed that animals and plants developed different genetic programs for cell death. Now an international collaboration of research teams, including one at the Swedish University of Agricultural Sciences, has shown that parts of the genetic programs that determine programmed cell death in plants and animals are actually evolutionarily related and moreover function in a similar way.

The findings were published in Nature Cell Biology October 11.

For plants and animals, and for humans as well, it is important that cells both can develop and die under controlled forms. The process where cells die under such forms is called programmed cell death. Disruptions of this process can lead to various diseases such as cancer, when too few cells die, or neurological disorders such as Parkinson's, when too many cell die.

The findings are published jointly by research teams at SLU (Swedish University of Agricultural Sciences) and the Karolinska Institute, the universities of Durham (UK), Tampere (Finland), and Malaga (Spain) under the direction of Peter Bozhkov, who works at SLU in Uppsala, Sweden. The scientists have performed comparative studies of an evolutionarily conserved protein called TUDOR – SN in cell lines from mice and humans and in the plants norway spruce and mouse – ear cress. In both plant and animal cells that undergo programmed cell death, TUDOR – SN is degraded by specific proteins, so-called proteases.

The proteases in animal cells belong to a family of proteins called caspases, which are enzymes. Plants do not have caspases—instead TUDOR – SN is broken down by so – called meta – caspases, which are assumed to be ancestral to the caspases found in animal cells. For the first time, these scientists have been able to demonstrate that a protein, TUDOR – SN, is degraded by similar proteases in both plant and animal cells and that the cleavage of TUDOR – SN abrogate its pro – survival function. The scientists have thereby discovered a further connection between the plant and animal kingdoms. The results now in print will therefore play a major role in future studies of this important protein family.

Cells that lack TUDOR – SN often experience premature programmed cell death. Furthermore, functional studies at the organism level in the model plant mouse – ear cress show that TUDOR – SN is necessary for the development of embryos and pollen. The researchers interpret the results to mean that TUDOR – SN is important in preventing programmed cell death from being activated in cells that are to remain alive.

The research teams maintain that the findings indicate that programmed cell death was established early on in evolution, even before the line that led to the earth's multicellular organisms divided into plants and animals. The work also shows the importance of comparative studies across different species to enhance our understanding of how fundamental mechanisms function at the cellular level in both the plant and animal kingdoms, and by extension in humans.

(http://www.sciencedaily.com/releases/2009/10/091013105335.htm)

_____ 6. Research shows that parts of the genetic programs are actually evolutionarily related and moreover function in a similar way.

_____ 7. It is important that cells both can develop and die under controlled forms for plants and animals, as well as humans.

_____ 8. TUDOR – SN is not important in preventing programmed cell death from being activated in cells that are to remain alive.

_____ 9. TUDOR – SN is necessary for the development of embryos and pollen.

_____ 10. The research made us understand how fundamental mechanisms function at the cellular level.

F. Cloze. Fill in each blank with one suitable word.

The pathogen that causes sudden oak death disease in California has a different genetic fingerprint than fungal strains found in nurseries in Oregon and Washington, according to Agricultural Research Service (ARS) scientists. This __1__, published in the journal PLoS Pathogens, will allow scientists to __2__ infections in other states as likely having originated from either California or the Pacific Northwest.

Sudden oak death is __3__ for the rapid death of live oak and tanoak trees in coastal California forests and in urban and suburban landscapes in the San Francisco Bay area. __4__ that it could spread to other vulnerable forests in the Eastern United States.

The pathogen Phytophthora ramorum affects not only oak and tanoak trees, but also popular __5__ such as rhododendrons, viburnums and camellias. Movement of infected plants from one location to __6__ can contribute to the spread of the disease. Plant pathologist Nik Grunwald, at the ARS Horticultural Crops Research Unit in Corvallis, Ore., has been working on this project for the past four years. He and his research team examined __7__ of the pathogen collected from nurseries on the West Coast of the United States and across the country.

The researchers were able to show that the pathogen from California is different from isolates found in the Northwest. Grunwald and colleagues compared his results to records __8__ by the U.S. Department of Agriculture (USDA) Animal and Plant Health Inspection Service on known shipments of infected plants, and these two sources of data were __9__ each other. The results could help scientists and the nursery industry in __10__ the movement of this pathogen around the country and the world.

(http://www.sciencedaily.com/releases/2009/10/091002105359.htm)

1. A. difference   B. experiment   C. discovery   D. research
2. A. distinguish   B. cultivate   C. eradicate   D. resist
3. A. regretful   B. sophisticated   C. responsible   D. extensive
4. A. It is said   B. It is known   C. It is reported   D. It is feared
5. A. ornamental plants B. perennial plants   C. exotic plants   D. toxic plants
6. A. any   B. other   C. another   D. some
7. A. findings   B. samples   C. infections   D. results
8. A. compiled   B. broken   C. written   D. released
9. A. contrary to   B. disagreeable to   C. comparable with   D. consistent with
10. A. precluding   B. tracking   C. accelerating   D. imitating

G. Translate the following passages into Chinese/English.

1. Polar bears may not be the only Arctic wildlife threatened by global warming. Scientists have discovered that Arctic foxes also struggle as the ice disappears because they rely on the frozen seas to survive the bleak winters.

Researchers tracked the movements of 14 young foxes as they faced their first Arctic winter in northern Alaska, where the temperature plunges to −30℃ and it is dark for 24 hours a day. Only three animals survived the winter, by wandering hundreds of miles across the frozen sea ice looking for seal carcasses left by polar bears. The 11 foxes that remained on the mainland perished.

The scientists said taking to the ice could help foxes survive because there were fewer predators and food was easier to find than on land. But they said the discovery raised new concerns over the foxes' survival in the face of diminishing Arctic ice cover.

2. 不过,动物未能进化出轮子是受阻于无法解决接头问题的说法有一个缺陷。这种理论无法解释为何动物没有进化出由死组织构成而无需动脉和神经的轮子。包括人在内的无数动物都有一些没有血液供应和神经的体外构造,例如:我们的毛发和指甲,其他动物身上的鳞、爪和角。为什么老是不能进化出骨质的、类似滑轮溜冰鞋那样的轮子呢? 在某些情况下,爪子可能比轮子更有用,猫的爪子是可以伸缩的:为什么不是可以伸缩的轮子呢? 这样,我们便得出了一个严肃的在生物学方面被轻率地成为三 R 窘境的怪论:大自然未能产生有可伸缩的滑轮溜冰鞋的老鼠。

Text B

10 Studies that Revealed the Great Global Amphibian Die-Off-and Some Possible Solutions

In our planet's sixth great mass extinction event, amphibians are among the hardest hit.

Amphibian species have been facing a steep decline for decades, in large part because of a fungus, climate change, and environment disruption. As many as one-third of the world's 6,300 amphibian species are threatened with extinction, and researchers fear their loss could wreak havoc on our ecosystem and food webs. Here are landmark studies that have defined the problems and—we hope—will help humans to figure out how to save their froggy friends.

1. The long-term perspective

In August 2008 two researchers at University of California at Berkeley published a meta-analysis titled "Are we in the midst of the sixth mass extinction?" The global assessment highlighted the threat of chytridiomycosis, an infectious, rapidly spreading disease caused by a waterborne fungus.

2. The seminal study

The study "Status and Trends of Amphibian Declines and Extinctions Worldwide" showed one-third of the world's 6,300 amphibian species are threatened with extinction (compared with just 12 percent of all bird species and 23 percent of mammal species). The authors concluded that scientists must begin captive breeding.

3. Problems with captive breeding

A September 2008 study published in Current Biology said captive breeding program accidentally introduced the chytrid fungus that causes chytridiomycosis into Mallorca in 1991; an endangered frog species was housed in the same room as a group of toads, and the frogs spread the chytrid fungus to the toads. The fungus was not known at this time, so health screening of the toads did not reveal the problem.

4. Extinction rates

According to a 2007 study in the Journal of Herpetology, amphibian species are becoming extinct 211 times faster than the "normal extinction rate", the standard rate of extinction in history before humans became a primary contributing factor. And if you count those species "in imminent danger of extinction", that rate climbs to a whopping 45,474 times faster than normal.

5. The global – warming theory

It is unclear how the chytrid fungus spreads. A 2006 study in Nature blamed global warming, for creating ideal conditions shifts temperatures to those more agreeable to the fungus' growth and reproduction—between 63°F and 77°F. But there were many outspoken skeptics of this claim.

6. Skeptics of the global – warming theory

A March 2008 PLoS Biology paper said there is "no evidence to support" the global – warming hypothesis. Instead, researchers said, the pattern of the fungus' spread was typical of an emerging infectious disease; they call their theory the "spreading pathogen hypothesis". The authors suggested governments and environmental agencies can help prevent the fungus' spread by regulating potential infection routes, such as the ornamental plant and aquarium wildlife trade.

7. Problems with insecticides

October 2008's Ecological Applications study suggests malathion, the most common insecticide in the U.S., can devastate tadpole populations even at doses too small to kill individual tadpoles. Researchers created simulated ponds in 300 – gallon outdoor tanks, placed tadpoles inside, and exposed the ponds to no malathion, a single moderately concentrated dose, or low concentrations in weekly doses similar to the exposure tadpoles experience in (human – altered) nature. Even the small amounts of malathion set off a chain of events that caused a decline of tadpoles' primary food source: bottom – dwelling algae. Consequently, half the tadpoles in the experiment did not reach maturity and would have died in nature.

8. A fungus – free country

Oddly, none of the many known amphibian species in Madagascar have been driven to extinction; the island also shows no signs of the chytrid fungus, according to a May 2008 PLoS Biology paper. Because the amphibians in Madagascar are doing so well, the authors argue the region is one of the best places to focus future research efforts. They hope to find out what helps amphibians in Madagascar thrive, as they suffer steep declines elsewhere.

9. Beating the fungus

Introducing probiotic bacteria into the ecosystem could help lessen the effects of chytridiomycosis, according to research presented in June 2008 at the 108th General Meeting of the American Society for Microbiology. The tests indicated that adding pedobacter, a bacterial species that occurs naturally on the skin of red – backed salamanders, to the skin of mountain yellow – legged frogs decreased chytrid's deadly effects.

10. Evolving more slowly than the environment

A May 2007 study in BioScience attributed amphibians' decline to their inability to adapt to the current rapid rate of global change. The authors noted the aforementioned pesticide pollution and chytrid infections, as well as habitat loss and UV – B light exposure that causes mutations in amphibian eggs. Amphibians are particularly vulnerable because they have permeable skin, ability to live on both land and water, and eggs without shells. Perhaps most detrimental is their complex life cycle, which makes evolution an even slower process.

Glossary

die – off: becoming extinct n. 衰减,死尽,绝种
wreak [riːk] cause to happen or to occur as a consequence v. 造成巨大破坏;引起严重问题
havoc ['hævək] violent and needless disturbance n. 大破坏,蹂躏
froggy ['frɔgi] of, like, or relating to frogs; full of frogs adj. 蛙的
meta – analysis [ˌmetə'nælisis] n. 元分析,荟萃分析
chytridiomycosis: 壶菌病
seminal ['siːminl] pertaining to or containing or consisting of semen; containing seeds of later development adj. 精液的,种子的,生殖的
captive breeding: 圈养繁殖;人工繁殖
chytrid: 壶菌
Mallorca [mɑːˈjɔːkə, mɑːlˈjɔːrkɑː] 马略卡岛[西班牙东部](巴利阿里群岛中的最大岛)
toad [təud] any of various tailless stout – bodied amphibians with long hind limbs for leaping; semiaquatic and terrestrial species n. 蟾蜍,癞蛤蟆
screening ['skriːniŋ] the display of a motion picture; fabric of metal or plastic mesh; the act of concealing the existence of something by obstructing the view of it; testing objects or persons in order to identify those with particular characteristics n. 遮蔽(屏蔽,筛,防波,筛屑)
imminent ['iminənt] close in time; about to occur adj. 逼近的,即将发生的
whopping ['(h)wɔpiŋ] (used informally) very large adj. 巨大的,天大的
outspoken [autˈspəukən] given to expressing yourself freely or insistently; characterized by directness in manner or speech; without subtlety or evasion adj. 直言无讳的,坦率的,坦白无隐的
skeptic ['skeptik] someone who habitually doubts accepted beliefs n. 怀疑者,怀疑论者,无神论者
hypothesis [haiˈpɔθisis] a proposal intended to explain certain facts or observations; a tentative theory about the natural world; a concept that is not yet verified but that if true would explain certain facts or phenomena; a message expressing an opinion based on incomplete evidence n. 假设,猜测,前提
pathogen ['pæθədʒ(ə)n] any disease – producing agent (especially a virus or bacterium or other microorganism) n. 病原体
aquarium [əˈkwɛəriəm] a tank or pool or bowl filled with water for keeping live fish and underwater ani-

mals n. 水族馆，养鱼池

ornamental plant：观赏植物

malathion ['mælə'θaiɔn] a yellow insecticide used as a dust or spray to control garden pests and house flies and mites n. 杀虫剂的一种，其商标名

tadpole ['tædpəul] a larval frog or toad n. 蝌蚪

simulated ['simjuleitid] not genuine or real; being an imitation of the genuine article; reproduced or made to resemble; imitative in character adj. 伪装的，模仿的

concentration [ˌkɔnsen'treiʃən] (chemistry) the strength of a solution; number of molecules of a substance in a given volume (expressed as moles/cubic meter) n. 集中，专心，浓度

probiotic [prəˌbai'ɔtik] of or relating to probiotics adj. [生]前生命期的

pedobacter n. 土地杆菌属

salamander ['sæləmændə] any of various typically terrestrial amphibians that resemble lizards and that return to water only to breed; reptilian creature supposed to live in fire n. 蝾螈

aforementioned [ə'fɔ:menʃənd] being the one previously mentioned or spoken of adj. 上述的，前述的

mutation [mju(:)'teiʃən] (biology) an organism that has characteristics resulting from chromosomal alteration; (genetics) any event that changes genetic structure; any alteration in the inherited nucleic acid sequence of the genotype of an organism; a change or alteration in form or qualities n. 变化，转变，母音变化

Exercises

A. Fill in each blank with one of the given words in its correct form.

| wreak | steep | moderately | highlight | imminent | reproduction | accidentally | dose |
| midst | maturity | simulated | oddly | outspoken | hypothesis | infectious | |

1. With the U.S. Congress beginning to consider regulations on greenhouse gases, a troubling _____ about how the sun may impact global warming is finally laid to rest.

2. "Evolution Canyon" has _____ slopes and runs approximately east–west, which means that the south-facing slope receives up to eight times as much solar radiation as the north-facing slope.

3. The _____ crew module, faithful to the vehicle that will ferry astronauts to the International Space Station by 2015, to the moon in the 2020 timeframe and ultimately to points beyond, will measure approximately five meters (16.4 ft) in diameter.

4. With different countries using varied approaches to produce tens of thousands of food alerts each year, there is an urgent need to filter this enormous body of information to _____ where to place concentrated efforts.

5. The scans showed that when the children saw animations of someone hurt _____, the same portion

of the brain that registered pain when they are hurt also was highlighted upon seeing someone else hurt.

6. Computed tomography (CT) scans are responsible for more than two thirds of the total radiation _____ associated with medical imaging exams.
7. The cost – benefit of particle film must be decided by growers and wine makers and its potential benefit of more uniform fruit _____, increased yield, and berry size.
8. By attaching light – emitting genes to _____ bacteria in an experimental system, researchers at University College, Cork, Ireland, have been able to track where in the body the bacteria go—giving an insight into the path of the infection process leading to the development of more targeted treatments.
9. Monkeys interpret rising and falling tones differently than humans. _____, their only response to several samples of human music was a calming response to the heavy – metal band Metallica.
10. Northern Europe has so far been free from invasive pest ants, but it seems just a matter of time until Lasius neglectus, a new ant that was discovered in 1990, will reach these latitudes and _____ havoc in parks and gardens of Northern Germany, Scandinavia and the British Isles.
11. In the "subtle guide" theory, a small number of scout bees, which had been involved in selecting the new nest site, guide the swarm by flying unobtrusively in its _____; near neighbors adjust their flight path to avoid colliding with the guides while more distant insects align themselves to the guides' general direction.
12. An approaching object on a collision course projects an expanding image on the retina, providing information that the object is approaching and how _____ the danger is.
13. When given the choice between surgery, watchful waiting or external beam radiotherapy, patients younger than 50 with _____ and poorly differentiated prostate cancers have better long – term overall and cancer – specific survival when they opt for surgery.
14. Though the options for communicating are limited to a few simple words it is the first time such people have had any such options at all and their loved ones are able to be more _____ in their gratitude.
15. The basic premise is that individuals use environmental cues to predict population declines, causing them to delay _____ until the decline has occurred, when each offspring will make a bigger contribution to the gene pool.

B. Answer the following questions concerning the text.
1. How seriously are amphibian species threatened with extinction?
2. What is chytridiomycosis in the first paragraph?
3. What makes amphibian species become extinct?

4. Why do we introduce probiotic bacteria?
5. Why don't the amphibian species in Madagascar go extinct?

C. Read the following questions and choose the best answer.

1. How many amphibian species are threatened with extinction? _____.
   A. About a quarter   B. Less than a half   C. Thrice   D. More than a half
2. According to the research presented in June 2008 at the 108th General Meeting of the American Society for Microbiology, _____.
   A. all the countries start to introduce the bacteria
   B. Asian countries start to introduce the bacteria
   C. people found probiotic bacteria into the ecosystem could help lessen the effects of chytridiomycosis
   D. African countries start to introduce the bacteria
3. Half the tadpoles in the experiment did not reach maturity resulted in _____.
   A. small amounts of malathion   B. the exposure tadpoles experience
   C. amphibian eggs   D. bottom-dwelling algae
4. Why did the authors argue the region is one of the best places to focus future research efforts? _____.
   A. The amphibians in Madagascar are doing so well
   B. The island also shows no signs of the chytrid fungus
   C. They suffer steep declines elsewhere
   D. For the exceptional landscape around the world
5. Amphibians have permeable skin, ability to live on both land and water, and eggs without shells, which lead to _____.
   A. a lower possibility for them to be ill   B. a higher potential for them to be ill
   C. a strong and fragile body   D. greener skin than before

D. Explain the underlined parts.

1. In our planet's sixth great mass extinction event, amphibians are <u>among the hardest hit.</u>
2. As many as one-third of the world's 6,300 amphibian species are <u>threatened with extinction,</u> and researchers fear their loss could <u>wreak havoc on our ecosystem and food webs.</u>
3. The authors concluded that scientists must <u>begin captive breeding.</u>
4. But there were <u>many outspoken skeptics of this claim.</u>
5. Because the amphibians in Madagascar <u>are doing so well,</u> the authors argue the region is one of the best places <u>to focus future research efforts.</u>
6. A May 2007 study in BioScience <u>attributed amphibians' decline to their inability to adapt to the current rapid rate of global change.</u>

Unit 10　Genetic Engineering

Text A

Evolution by Intelligent Design

1. "There are no shortcuts in evolution," famed Supreme Court justice Louis Brandeis once said. He might have reconsidered those words if he could have foreseen the coming revolution in biotechnology, including the ability to alter genes and manipulate stem cells. These breakthroughs could bring on an age of directed reproduction and evolution in which humans will bypass the incremental process of natural selection and set off on a high-speed genetic course of their own. Here are some of the latest and greatest advances.

Embryos from the Palm of Your Hand

2. In as little as five years, scientists may be able to create sperm and egg cells from any cell in the body, enabling infertile couples, gay couples, or sterile people to reproduce. The technique could also enable one person to provide both sperm and egg for an offspring—an act of "ultimate incest", according to a report from the Hinxton Group, an international consortium of scientists and bioethicists whose members include such heavyweights as Ruth Faden, director of the Johns Hopkins Berman Institute of Bioethics, and Peter J. Donovan, a professor of biochemistry at the University of California at Irvine.

3. The Hinxton Group's prediction comes in the wake of recent news that scientists at the University of Wisconsin and Kyoto University in Japan have transformed adult human skin cells into pluripotent stem cells, the powerhouse cells that can self-replicate (perhaps indefinitely) and develop into almost any kind of cell in the body. In evolutionary terms, the ability to change one type of cell into others—including a sperm or egg cell, or even an embryo—means that humans can now wrest control of reproduction away from nature, notes Robert Lanza, a scientist at Advanced Cell Technology in Massachusetts. "With this breakthrough we now have a working technology whereby anyone can pass on their genes to a child by using just a few skin cells," he says.

Gene Targeting

4. When we create egg and sperm on demand, we may not have to pass along our complement of genes as is. A process known as homologous recombination could allow us to remove undesirable traits

· 145 ·

and replace them with helpful ones, one gene at a time. Homologous recombination occurs naturally during sexual reproduction, when DNA from the two parents mixes to form offspring that are genetically unique. But as Mario Capecchi of the University of Utah, Sir Martin Evans of Cardiff University in Wales, and Oliver Smithies of the University of North Carolina proved in 2007 with their Nobel Prize winning work on mice, homologous recombination can also be achieved in the lab. By selectively adding or deleting stretches of DNA in the (artificially) fertilized cell, scientists could knock out genes for a disease like diabetes or insert genes coding for extra height or intelligence.

Artificial Chromosomes

5. Changing an offspring's DNA gene by gene can be tedious. A speedier route would be to introduce a multiplicity of new traits all at once by inserting an entire new chromosome, a structured strand of DNA containing many genes. Several researchers, including genetics pioneer J. Craig Venter, have already constructed centromere—work together. The centromere contains proteins that control the delicate process of cell division. How it does so is "an extremely difficult problem", says Bill Earnshaw, a cell biologist at the Institute of Cell and Molecular Biology at the University of Edinburgh in Scotland. In part that's because in order to study the centromere's functions, researchers have had to use techniques that kill the cell. Earnshaw, along with colleagues from the National Institutes of Health and the University of Nagoya in Japan, have finally found a way around the problem and are now conducting the foundational research needed to build functional artificial chromosomes.

6. Earnshaw believes the synthetic chromosome could eventually be used to shuttle genes like a kind of Trojan horse. Some of those genes, he speculates, could convert ordinary cells into stem cells that might reseed the immune system, aid in rejuvenation, and more. Once the genes were delivered, the centromere needed for that chromosome to survive could be turned off. In subsequent generations, some cells would contain the extra chromosome, and these would be discarded because of their potential to become cancerous. Other daughter cells would not have the reprogramming genes.

7. "Based on what we know, the artificial chromosome is going to be the best way to modify the genome," says Lee Silver, a professor of molecular biology and public policy at Princeton University. "Nature doesn't care about individual children. Instead of rolling the dice, why don't we take the dice and put them down in the way that parents think is best for their children." He anticipates the development of specialized artificial chromosomes—a "good health" artificial chromosome, for instance—that could routinely be inserted into human embryos. "You could create a generic version that has lots of good genes like the ones known to protect against cancer, strokes, and heart disease," says Silver.

Our Post-Darwinian Future

8. Pluripotent stem cells, gene targeting, and artificial chromosomes could leapfrog over evolution and let us take control of our genome, maybe even turn ourselves into a whole new species. "There is no

scientific basis for thinking that we couldn't," says Silver. "There's nothing really special about the human genome. There's nothing that says this is the end."

9. Bioethicist John Harris of the University of Manchester in England, a member of the Hinxton Group's steering committee, believes that achieving our potential "might require some deliberate changes" to our genes. He predicts that genetic engineering will eventually lead to what he calls "enhancement evolution". Through the nuanced use of biotechnology, enhancement evolution will gradually introduce genes that improve the species, one person at a time. At that point, deliberate selection will replace natural selection as the driving force for species change. "We are not suited to survive designed as we are," says Harris. "We are hugely vulnerable to diseases, and new diseases come along all the time. It's amazing we haven't been entirely wiped out by one."

10. The first changes to the human genome, Harris believes, will happen within small test populations. This will allow us to assess the risks and benefits of the modifications and then decide how to proceed. "It will be an experiment," says Harris. "You do it for a time, and if it looks good and doesn't have any disastrous consequences, you continue it. We'll have plenty of time to manage it in that way."

11. Enhancement evolution has plenty of critics. Lanza, for one, is uneasy about giving parents the power to design their children's genomes. What if a couple wants a world-class athlete in the family and provides those genes, but the child grows up wanting to play chess, he asks. And what if some of the modifications go seriously wrong? Who should have the final say on when and how the human genome should be changed?

12. On the other hand, if technology can enable us to eliminate disease and disabilities from our children or insert genes that might make them smarter or better looking, why wouldn't we use it? As DNA guru James Watson once said, "Evolution can be just damn cruel." At least it is today. Tomorrow the responsibility for evolution may rest on our own shoulders—for better or for worse.

(http://discovermagazine.com/2009/mar/02-evolution-by-intelligent-design)

Glossary

famed [feimd] widely known and esteemed *adj.* 著名的
incremental [inkri'mentəl] increasing gradually by regular degrees or additions *adj.* 增量的, 增加的
embryo ['embriəu] an animal organism in the early stages of growth and differentiation that in higher
  forms merge into fetal stages but in lower forms terminate in commencement of larval life *n.* 胚胎
sperm [spə:m] the male reproductive cell; the male gamete *n.* 精液, 精子
infertile [in'fə:tail] incapable of reproducing *adj.* 不能生育的
sterile ['sterail] incapable of reproducing *adj.* 无生育能力的
incest ['insest] sexual intercourse between persons too closely related to marry *n.* 乱伦

consortium [kən'sɔːtjəm] an association of companies for some definite purpose *n*. 联合，合伙
pluripotent [pluə'ripətənt] able to develop into or effect any (or most) cell type, i.e. not restricted to a specific system *adj*. [生]多能(性)的
wrest [rest] obtain by seizing forcibly or violently, also metaphorically *v*. 夺取，猛扭，歪曲
homologous [hɔ'mɔləgəs] having the same evolutionary origin but serving different functions *n*. [生]同种异体的；同源的
diabetes [ˌdaiə'biːtiːz] any of several metabolic disorders marked by excessive urination and persistent thirst *n*. 糖尿病
chromosome ['krəuməsəum] a threadlike body in the cell nucleus that carries the genes in a linear order *n*. 染色体
multiplicity [ˌmʌlti'plisiti] a large number *n*. 多数，多样
strand [strænd] a pattern forming a unity within a larger structural whole *n*. 绳索(之一股)
centromere ['sentrəˌmiə] a specialized condensed region of each chromosome that appears during mitosis where the chromatids are held together to form an X shape *n*. [生]着丝点，着丝粒
rejuvenation [riˌdʒuːvi'neiʃən] the act of restoring to a more youthful condition *n*. 复原，再生
genome [dʒi'nerik] the ordering of genes in a haploid set of chromosomes of a particular organism; the full DNA sequence of an organism *n*. [生]基因组，染色体组
generic [dʒiːnəum] applicable to an entire class or group *adj*. [生物]属的，类的
stroke [strəuk] any one of the repeated movements of the limbs and body used for locomotion in swimming or rowing *n*. 中风
leapfrog ['liːpˌfrɔg] progress by large jumps instead of small increments *v*. 跃过，飞越
steer [stiə] be a guiding force, as with directions or advice *v*. 引导
nuanced [njuː'ɑːnst] with a subtle difference *adj*. 有细微差别的
vulnerable ['vʌlnərəb(ə)l] susceptible to attack *adj*. 易受伤害的，有弱点的
modification [ˌmɔdifi'keiʃən] the act of making something different *n*. 修正，修饰
guru ['guruː] a recognized leader in some field or of some movement *n*. 专家

Exercises

A. Fill in each blank with one of the given words in its correct form.

| Strand | steer | wrest | famed | enhance |
| modification | vulnerable | nuance | rejuvenation | multiplicity |

1. Weather forecasts equate to an enormous volume and _____ of information, when you account for the array of forecast providers, communication channels, and the size and diversity of the U.S. population

2. _____ road users (VRUs) like pedestrians, cyclists and motorcyclists are more difficult to protect because they are hard to see, difficult to track and they often emerge suddenly from unexpected quarters.

3. In contrast to previous applications of genomics technologies where the goal is to distinguish existing disease from absence of disease, nutrigenomics aims to discern _____ differences in predisease states such that personalized dietary interventions can be designed to prevent or modify future disease susceptibility.

4. Many of the strategies scientists propose depend on a way to _____ hydrogen, which is an energy carrier, from water.

5. However, the utility of these drugs is often limited by the _____ ability of cancer cells to repair their DNA.

6. The result is a chain reaction of biodiversity where the _____ of one species triggers the sequential _____ of a second, dependent species.

7. The study could form the basis of "an effective facial _____ program", and lead to a new understanding of the effect reactive oxygen species on cellular aging, they note.

8. The approach is promising because it allows multiple segments of a DNA _____ to be threaded simultaneously through numerous tiny pores and for each fragment to move slowly enough through the opening so that the base pairs can be accurately read.

9. Policymakers and economists often promote managed-care plans based on the assumption that they prevent the overuse of unnecessary surgical procedures or help _____ patients to high-quality providers, compared to traditional fee-for-service insurance plans.

10. Scientists report use of a new X-ray imaging technique to reveal for the first time in a century unprecedented details of a painting hidden beneath another painting by _____ American illustrator N.C. (Newell Convers) Wyeth.

B. Skim the text and then answer the following questions.

1. In your opinion, how can mankind benefit from genetic engineering?
2. According to the text, why is it not correct to say "there are no shortcuts in evolution"?
3. What is the function of homologous recombination?
4. What can help mankind to skip part of the course of evolution?
5. What does the author mean by saying "Tomorrow the responsibility for evolution may rest on our own shoulders—for better or for worse."?

C. Read the text and choose the correct answer to each of the following questions.

1. Who can benefit the most from the creation of sperm and egg cells from any cell in the body? _____.

A. Old couples   B. Gay couples   C. Fertile couples   D. All couples

2. Which of the following statements is not true? _____.

   A. Scientists can transform adult human skin cells into pluripotent stem cells

   B. Pluripotent stem cells can develop into any kind of cell in the body

   C. Human skin cells can be transformed into cells with the ability to self-replicate

   D. Technique to transform skin cells into stem cells enables humans to control reproduction to a certain degree

3. Centromere is _____.

   A. a structured strand of DNA containing many genes

   B. a kind of protein that controls the delicate process of cell division

   C. posing an extremely difficult problem to scientists

   D. an entire new chromosome

4. According to John Harris, enhancement evolution _____.

   A. brings about improved species

   B. is a part of natural selection

   C. requires deliberate changes to our genes

   D. leaves us vulnerable to diseases

5. People's attitudes toward enhancement evolution are _____.

   A. positive   B. negative   C. ambivalent   D. indifferent

D. Explain the underlined parts.

1. He <u>might have reconsidered those words</u> if he could have foreseen the coming revolution in biotechnology, <u>including the ability to alter genes and manipulate stem cells.</u>

2. ... according to a report from the Hinxton Group, an international consortium of scientists and bioethicists <u>whose members include such heavyweights as</u> Ruth Faden, director of the Johns Hopkins Berman Institute of Bioethics...

3. The Hinxton Group's prediction <u>comes in the wake of</u> recent news that scientists at the University of Wisconsin and Kyoto University in Japan...

4. <u>By selectively adding or deleting stretches of DNA</u> in the (artificially) fertilized cell, scientists could <u>knock out genes for a disease like diabetes or insert genes coding for extra height or intelligence.</u>

5. <u>A speedier route would be to introduce a multiplicity of new traits all at once</u> by inserting an entire new chromosome, a structured strand of DNA containing many genes.

6. Earnshaw believes the synthetic chromosome <u>could eventually be used to shuttle genes like a kind of Trojan horse.</u> Some of those genes, <u>he speculates, could convert ordinary cells into stem cells that might reseed the immune system,</u> aid in rejuvenation, and more.

7. Nature doesn't care about individual children. Instead of rolling the dice, why don't we take the dice and put them down in the way that parents think is best for their children.
8. Pluripotent stem cells, gene targeting, and artificial chromosomes could leapfrog over evolution and let us take control of our genome, maybe even turn ourselves into a whole new species.
9. Tomorrow the responsibility for evolution may rest on our own shoulders—for better or for worse.

E. Read the passages in this section and decide whether each of the following statements is true or false.

Passage One

Throughout the article I have been mentioning genetic engineering in humans. You must have got it by now, that it is an advance science that helps modify genes. But you may be plagued with the question, "What are the uses and benefits of genetic engineering in humans?". There are a few major advantages of genetic engineering in humans, like:

Genetic engineering in humans could help prevent life threatening and incurable diseases like cancer, Alzheimer's disease, even HIV/AIDS. There are cases like cardiomyopathy or susceptibility to viruses, that can be overcome with the help of genetic engineering.

Better drugs could be produced that are disease or gene specific and attack the specific genetic mutation in an individual, to help over come a disease or disorder.

Many people want to live a longer, healthier life or are just afraid of death. Such people with a love of life, can place their bets on genetic engineering to help them live longer. It is possible to increase the average life span of an individual to 100 ~ 150 years. And not just a longer life, but a healthy, long life, free from diseases and disorders.

Women have a craze to look young and maintain their beauty for all eternity. The benefits of genetic engineering in humans may make it possible to slow down or reverse certain cellular metabolism, that may be able fulfill this desire to remain "forever young" for many dreamers in the near future.

You may have heard of designer clothes, designer bags, designer shoes and even a designer nose. But have you heard of designer babies? Yes, designer babies are possible to be produced with the help of genetic engineering in humans. Parents can choose the characteristics of their babies, like blond with blue eyes, high IQ, fair skin, etc. It may even be possible to choose the talent in your favorite idol to be manufactured (pun intended!) in your baby, like for example, a singer like Elvis Presley or maybe a great dancer like Micheal Jackson. No, I am not joking, this is all possible with a little bit of genetic engineering, within the blueprint of life-DNA.

Do you remember "Dolly Sheep"? This was a genetically modified, cloned sheep that is now dead for over 6 years. This world famous sheep was cloned using the cell from the mammary gland of another sheep. Cloning, another aspect of genetic engineering in humans can also be possible. There are many ethical issues of cloning and it is considered illegal by many governments around the world. It is a crime to clone humans now, but may be in our quest to produce the perfect beings, cloning will soon become a part of life.

(www.buzzle.com/articles/genetic-engineering-in-humans.html)

_____ 1. Life span can be increased by 100 ~ 150 years.

_____ 2. Genetic engineering in humans can slow down or reverse certain cellular metabolism.

_____ 3. Characteristics of a person can be modified with the help of genetic engineering.

_____ 4. Parents can choose the characteristics of their babies now.

_____ 5. Cloning poses many ethical issues to mankind.

Passage Two

Under the pretext of producing a cure for diseases and hereditary disorders, many researchers carry out experiments on genetically modifying humans. This genetic engineering can prove to be a bane if:

In the pursuit of producing babies without any genetic defects or hereditary disorders, we may end up producing super humans. Just as the example I mentioned in the beginning of my article, we may have a line of humans that may spell doom to those who are not genetically modified.

Smarter humans means, larger brains, that may lead to babies with larger heads that have trouble passing through the birth canal of their mothers. This may cause trouble during birth and a rise in cesareans.

Long life could lead to population problems. There may be stress on the natural resources and less living space. Although, you may live free of diseases, you may have a fight for survival for securing the basic necessities.

Just like in the movie Gataca, there may be a division between genetically engineered humans and those that are normal (just imagine, begin normal may prove to be a curse in the future!). People will no longer be discriminated on the basis of race, religion or creed, but actually on their genes!

Human cloning may create problems of copies of men moving about freely around the world. If your clone turns out to be the one with a criminal streak, you may end up in jail for a crime committed by your clone. It is possible, if you can't prove your innocence. Imagine someone else taking over your life, family, work, etc!

The problem faced by many developing countries today, is female infanticide. Genetic engineering may help stop this cruel and barbaric custom of killing the innocent girl child. You may think this is an advantage, I say otherwise. Genetic engineering may help such narrow minded, biased parents to actually choose the gender of the child. Therefore, more parents opting for a male child over a girl child. Thus, directly bringing an end to girl child killing as there will be no birth of the girl child!

I can go on and on regarding the benefits of genetic engineering in humans, like end of hunger, no disease, cure for all ailments, long life, ageless beauty, super intelligent humans, etc. But, one should always give a second thought to all the disadvantages listed. It is often said, man should not attempt to "play God". That's correct, but if God has bestowed us the power to make some beneficial changes to his creations, then we should surely do so wisely. Genetic engineers have turned into modern day alchemists, who are searching for the ultimate elixir of life, to produce the genetically modified, perfect human. This precious knowledge is being exploited by greedy men, who are using it just to earn more money. Nothing is bad if exploited within limits. When we harness our present, we should keep in mind all the possible effects it will have on our future. We may not be alive to view the beauty and the ugliness of the future, but our beloved children may be facing the consequences. With caution in mind, man should tap the benefits of genetic engineering in humans, with full understanding of the genetic engineering ethics.

(http://www.buzzle.com/articles/genetic-engineering-in-humans.html)

_____ 6. In the future, people who are not genetically modified will be threatened in a certain way.

_____ 7. Human cloning helps to relieve the stress on the natural resources.

_____ 8. Human cloning may lead to serious problems in society.

_____ 9. Human cloning can impact female distribution.

_____ 10. Genetic engineering should be exploited wisely.

F. Cloze. Fill in each blank with one suitable word.

In humans, the most __1__ benefit of genetic engineering is gene therapy which is the medical treatment of a disease __2__ the defective genes are repaired and replaced or therapeutic genes are __3__ to fight the disease. __4__ the past decade, many autoimmune and heart diseases have been treated using gene therapy. Certain diseases __5__ the Huntington's disease, ALS and cystic fibrosis is caused by __6__ genes. There is hope that a(n) __7__ for such diseases can be found by either inserting the corrected gene or modifying the defective gene. __8__, the hope is to __9__ eliminate genetic diseases and also treat non-genetic diseases with __10__ gene therapy.

1. A. promising   B. expected   C. needed   D. imperative
2. A. whereupon   B. whereabouts   C. wherein   D. whereof
3. A. inserted   B. introduced   C. modified   D. removed
4. A. For   B. Over   C. By   D. From
5. A. concerning   B. namely   C. like   D. as
6. A. deteriorated   B. deficient   C. default   D. defective
7. A. cure   B. method   C. means   D. remedy
8. A. Ultimately   B. Consequently   C. Contrarily   D. Eventually

9. A. completely   B. wholly   C. totally   D. entirely
10. A. fruitful   B. appropriate   C. desirable   D. relative

G. Translate the following passages into Chinese/English.

1. British and American scientists are breeding genetically modified pigs in the hope of providing organs for transplant to humans, the project leader wrote in a newspaper. Scientists in London and California have begun conducting the genetic experiments to find a solution to record - long waiting lists for organ transplants, fertility specialist Robert Winston said in a commentary written for Britain's The Sunday Times. In Britain alone, about 8,000 patients are waiting for a transplant.

2.《星期日泰晤士报》报道说,试验在英国遭遇资金及法律规章困境后将转移到美国。报道说,这些转基因猪将在密苏里州进行饲养与繁殖。温斯顿写道:"我们的美国朋友会因我们的技术而获益,但又一项英国创新将会受到损害,而我们本可以为英国带来的收益也会流失。"在此之前,一些科学家曾批评把动物器官用于人类移植的观点,他们说,这项技术有把动物病毒传染给人类的风险。温斯顿则表示,他的研究项目旨在培育无病菌的猪。

Text B

Building Better Humans

1. The sci-fi possibilities of genetic tampering may soon become real. And there's no law against them.

2. A young couple having difficulty conceiving a child undergoes tests to pinpoint the problem. As they sit in the doctor's office, awaiting the results, each wonders whose reproductive system has failed.

3. "There's nothing wrong with either of you," the doctor tells them, at last.

4. "So what's the problem?" they ask.

5. "You're two different species. You can't interbreed."

6. Science fiction? Perhaps for now. But according to the eminent physicist Freeman Dyson, this is where the human genome project will inevitably lead us. He and his Princeton colleague, molecular biologist Lee Silver, say that rapidly emerging genetic technology will ultimately split humanity into many species.

7. They draw their conclusion from cold, complex science, but their point is simple, and frightening: Once we figure out how to safely manipulate our genes, people will start adding and deleting them to their perceived advantage. Different sorts of humans will emerge. And it's safe to assume that each will decide that it is superior.

8. While anyone who watched even a minute of "Britney in Hawaii" might believe that this has al-

ready occurred, rest assured it has not.

9. But the development and use of genetic engineering are the subject of ferocious debate among the scientific elite. Some influential scientists, notably James D. Watson, the father of DNA research, are pushing for experiments that were once unthinkable: tampering with the human germline—sperm and egg cells. In other words, genetically altering not only an individual, but future generations.

10. "Some people are going to have to have some guts and try germline therapy without completely knowing that it's going to work," Watson said at a UCLA conference in 1998. "And the other thing, because no one has the guts to say it, if we could make better human beings by knowing how to add genes (from plants or animals), why shouldn't we do it? What's wrong with it?"

11. Human germline engineering is prohibited in federally funded research. But there is no ban on such experiments in the private sector. Last weekend, a coalition of activists and organizations met in San Francisco to form the Exploratory Initiative on New Genetic Technologies. On Wednesday, the group will announce efforts to develop a broad movement to push for limitations on genetic technologies, including statutory bans on germline genetic engineering and human cloning.

12. "A ban," says Watson, "would be a disaster."

13. To get a glimpse of what might very well be our future, it helps to understand some boring science. All current human genetic therapy trials are called somatic: they involve genes in various parts of the body, but not the sex cells, which produce eggs and sperm. Tampering with sex cells—producing genetic alterations that will be passed to your offspring, and their descendents—takes genetic engineering into an entirely new technological and ethical realm.

14. While many experts believe that germline engineering is at least a decade away, Hamilton Smith, a Nobel laureate biochemist, sees the technology developing much more rapidly. "It might come pretty quickly," he says.

15. Smith knows something about the speed of technological advance. He is the director of DNA Resources for Celera Genomics Corp., which, in just nine months, produced a rough map of the human genome—a feat that most scientists said would take years.

16. The pressure for germline engineering is also likely to come from another direction—you and me. We want children better than ourselves. We certainly don't want them to suffer unnecessarily. David Baltimore, a Nobel laureate who heads the California Institute of Technology, believes that consumer demand will encourage the rapid development and utilization of germline engineering.

17. Genetic screening is already standard in prenatal care. It is not farfetched to imagine that prospective parents will one day turn to clinics to produce embryos that can not only be tested for genetic defects, but also "corrected". And is there any reason to think people will stop at fixing disease-causing defects? Is it such a stretch to imagine people demanding genetic enhancements—mental, physical, be-

havioral?

18. Prominent scientists not only believe the possibility is real; they are also preparing for it. At a retreat of the premier geneticists and policy analysts last summer at the Jackson Laboratory in Bar Harbor, Maine, LeRoy Walters, director of the Kennedy Center of Ethics, gave a speech on methods for guaranteeing equal access to the enhancement of intelligence.

19. How close are we to being able to alter the human gene book? Germline genetic manipulation of other mammals is already occurring. Genes are routinely deleted from and added to mice for experiments. Five years ago a University of Pennsylvania researcher discovered how to alter the genes in the sperm of mice, and applied for a patent on it. In the wake of that advance, ethicists called for national and international meetings on germline engineering. Mice and humans are estimated to share 90 percent of their genomes.

20. The implications of germline engineering are so profound, and scary, that some leading scientists dismiss the possibility that anyone would seriously contemplate doing it. Asked Monday whether any reputable scientists are advocating germline engineering in humans, Celera founder and president J. Craig Venter said that he knew of nobody.

21. But in a new book, Watson, perhaps the most influential figure in biological research in the last half-century, is quoted as calling for germline engineering during a 1998 conference at UCLA. Watson co-discovered the double helix structure of DNA, the basis for all the genetics research, including the mapping of the genome. He was the first director of the publicly funded Human Genome Project, and is now president of the Cold Spring Harbor Laboratory on Long Island. On July 4, he is scheduled to receive the $100,000 Liberty Medal in Philadelphia for his life's work.

22. However shocking Watson's opinion might sound, he provides sound reasons for germline engineering, according to the transcript published in "Engineering the Human Germline: An Exploration of the Science and Ethics of Altering the Genes We Pass to our Children", edited by Gregory Stock and John Campbell. For one, germline engineering is more efficient than treating patients one by one. "You delete a bad gene from the gene pool, and no future generation need worry about it or undergo genetic therapy for it. Also, if a deadly infection broke out across the globe, humanity would be saved by implanting disease resistance into the germline."

23. Watson offers scientists a strategy for confronting the social challenges that will face germline engineering.

24. "I'm afraid of asking people what they think. Don't ask Congress to approve it. Just ask them for money to help their constituents. That's what they want ... Frankly they would care much more about having their relatives not sick than they do about ethics or principles."

25. Although other nations, including Britain, Japan and China, cooperated in and contributed to

the sequencing of the human genome, Watson believes that attempts to coordinate globally on the genome manipulation would retard the effort. "I think it would be a complete disaster to try and get an international agreement," he says. "I just can't imagine anything more stifling. You end up with the lowest common denominator."

26. As for regulating genetic engineering, he says: "I think our hope is to stay away from regulations and laws whenever possible."

27. Watson ridicules the notion that human genome has sanctity, or that civil rights should somehow enter the debate. "I think it's complete nonsense. I mean, what or who sanctifies? ... Evolution can just be damn cruel, and to say that we've got a perfect genome and there's some sanctity? ... Terms like sanctity remind me of animal rights. Who gave a dog a right? The word 'rights' gets very dangerous. We have women's rights, children's rights; it goes on forever."

28. "I'd like to give up saying rights or sanctity. Instead, say that humans have needs, and we should try as a social species to respond to those needs ... To try to give it more meaning than it deserves in some quasi-mystical way is for Steven Spielberg or somebody like that. It's just plain aura, up in the sky—I mean, it's crap."

29. Watson is not alone in his support for germline engineering. But in science circles there is also strong emerging opposition to such experiments, and growing support for regulation.

30. Last month, Eric Lander, a friend of Watson and director of the largest publicly funded genome sequencing center, at the Massachusetts Institute of Technology, called for a ban on human germline gene therapy because of our limited knowledge. The human genome, Lander says, "has been 3.5 billion years in the making. We've been able to read it for the last year or so. And we suddenly think we could write the story better?"

31. Lander acknowledges that there are potential benefits to germline engineering. "There is the prospect that by changing things we might put off aging, prevent cancer, improve memory." The dazzling possibilities, he says, makes it tough to recommend reining in scientists. "I find it a very difficult question," he said. "For my own part, I would have a ban in place, an absolute ban in place on human germline gene therapy. Not because I think for sure we should never cross that threshold, but because I think that is such a fateful threshold to cross that I'd like society to have to rebut that presumption some day, to have to repeal a ban when it thought it was time to ever try something like that."

32. Though Celera's Hamilton Smith and Lander were competitors in the race to complete the mapping of the human genome, they agree on this point. "The only thing I'm certain of is that we don't possess the knowledge to monkey with our germline," says Smith. "We don't fully understand the consequences of changes that even look like they would be good." As an example, Smith cites the single genetic mutation responsible for sickle cell disease, which has now been found to simultaneously provide re-

sistance against malaria.

33. Francis Collins, the director of the National Institutes of Health Human Genome Project, also has repeatedly urged caution on germline, which he views as humans fully taking charge of their evolution. But asked Monday whether he would support a ban, he demurred, afraid that opening that door for legislation could lead to other prohibitive measures that would impede important biomedical progress.

34. Princeton's Dyson has his own ideas on what is to be done. In his view, the speciation of humans into different groups is inevitable—and it would be a disaster to allow such diversification without restraint. "We must travel the high road into space, to find new worlds to match our new (genetic) capabilities," Dyson writes in "The Sun, The Genome and The Internet," published last year. "To give us room to explore the varieties of mind and body which our genome can evolve, one planet is not enough."

35. More sci-fi fantasy? The ravings of an aging academic? I asked Celera's Smith what he thought. He paused, and then said, "Dyson's a very smart guy. I think there's a lot to what he says for the future. It's hard to tell where mankind is going here."

(http://www.salon.com/health/feature/2000/06/27/germline/)

Glossary

tamper ['tæmpə] interfere unwontedly v. 干预
pinpoint ['pin,point] locate exactly v. 精确地找到
interbreed [,intə'bri:d] breed animals or plants using parents of different races and varieties v. 使异种繁殖
ferocious [fə'rəuʃəs] marked by extreme and violent energy adj. 十分强烈的，极度的
germline ['dʒə:mlain] a set of cells destined to be organized into eggs or sperm n.【医】性细胞系
coalition [,kəuə'liʃən] the union of diverse things into one body or form or group; the growing together of parts n. 结合
statutory ['stætjut(ə)ri] relating to or created by statutes adj. 法令的，法定的
somatic [səu'mætik] affecting or characteristic of the body as opposed to the mind or spirit adj. 身体的
descendent [di'send(ə)nt] a person considered as descended from some ancestor or race n. 子孙，后代
laureate ['lɔ:riit] someone honored for great achievements n. 授予荣誉者
prenatal ['pri:'neitl] occurring or existing before birth adj. 产前的，出生前的
farfetched ['fɑ:'fetʃt] highly imaginative but unlikely adj. 牵强的，不自然的
contemplate ['kɔntempleit] consider as a possibility v. 沉思，打算
reputable [repjutəbl] having a good reputation adj. 受好评的，有声望的，卓越的
retard [ri'tɑ:d] slow the growth or development of v. 妨碍，迟延
denominator [di'nɔmineitə] the divisor of a fraction n. 分母，平均水平

sanctity ['sæŋktiti] the quality of being holy *n.* 神圣,尊严,圣洁
quasi ['kwɑ:zi(:),'kweisai] having some resemblance *adj.* 类似的,外表的
aura ['ɔ:rə] an indication of radiant light drawn around the head of a saint *n.* 光环,光圈
crap [kræp] something which is not worth anything, not useful, nonsense or of bad quality *n.* 废话,胡说,胡扯
rein [rein] control and direct with or as if by reins *v.* 统制
rebut [rein] prove to be false or incorrect *v.* 反驳
repeal [ri'pi:l] annul by recalling or rescinding *v.* 废止,撤消
mutation [mju(:)'teiʃən] any event that changes genetic structure; any alteration in the inherited nucleic acid sequence of the genotype of an organism *n.* (生物物种的)突变
sickle ['sikl] an edge tool for cutting grass or crops; has a curved blade and a short handle *n.* 镰刀
malaria [mə'lɛəriə] an infective disease caused by sporozoan parasites that are transmitted through the bite of an infected Anopheles mosquito; marked by paroxysms of chills and fever *n.* 疟疾
demur [di'mə:] to express disagreement or refuse to do something *v.* 提出异议,反对,抗辩
speciation [ˌspi:ʃi'eiʃən] the evolution of a biological species *n.* 种形成
raving ['reiviŋ] speaking in an uncontrolled way, usually because you are upset or angry, or because you are ill *n.* 胡说,怒吼

Exercises

A. Fill in each blank with one of the given words in its correct form.

| repeal | coalition | statutory | rebut | ferocious |
| retard | denominator | tamper | pinpoint | rein |

1. Until we have that information in hand, we should not _____ with these vulnerable ecosystems, particularly at a time when climate change is already threatening them.
2. A researcher has developed probes that can help _____ the location of tumors and might one day be able to directly attack cancer cells.
3. The _____ tiger mosquito invaded Illinois in the 1990s.
4. A shocking decline in the Russian Federation's wild tiger population highlights the importance of eliminating trade in and demand for tiger parts, the International Tiger _____ (ITC) said today.
5. In 2005, about 14 million children and adolescents were prescribed drugs under the _____ health insurance funds.
6. Polysaccharides, a type of carbohydrate that includes starch and cellulose, may benefit people with diabetes because they help _____ absorption of glucose.
7. Whether you are bleeding to death from an injury, having a heart attack, or having a stroke, the com-

mon _____ is time.

8. It is not always advisable to give free _____ to one's emotions.
9. The _____ of the federal speed control law in 1995 has resulted in an increase in road fatalities and injuries, according to researchers at the University of Illinois at Chicago School of Public Health.
10. A key argument used to _____ such findings relates to satellite records of temperature change in the troposphere the lowest layer of Earth's atmosphere.

B. Skim the text and then answer the following questions.
1. How would genetic engineering be taken advantage of?
2. For what reasons should germline engineering be banned?
3. What are the benefits of germline engineering?
4. What are the possible consumer needs for germline engineering?
5. What is your prediction of a world with germline engineering?

C. Read the text and choose the correct answer to each of the following questions.
1. What can be inferred from the story about the young couple? _____.
   A. They are not humans
   B. They cannot have a baby
   C. Different species cannot interbreed
   D. Maybe one of them is a genetically modified or a clone
2. Which of the following statements is not true concerning germline engineering? _____.
   A. Prohibition on it would be a disaster
   B. Consumer demand will encourage the rapid development of it
   C. Human gerline engineering is not allowed everywhere
   D. It is already a reality for a decade
3. Which of the following is not the reason why Watson advocate germline engineering? _____.
   A. Germline engineering saves us treating patients
   B. Deleting a bad gene can prevent future generations from trouble that would be caused by it
   C. Implanting disease resistance into the germline can save humanity from a deadly infection
   D. Germline engineering can helps us combat diseases
4. The word "retard" in "Watson believes that attempts to coordinate globally on the genome manipulation would retard the effort (paragraph 25)" means _____.
   A. accelerate　　　　B. slow down　　　　C. prevent　　　　D. terminate
5. According to the text, which of the following statements is true? _____.
   A. Congressmen are definitely opposed to germline engineering
   B. According to Lander, the benefits germline engineering would bring about outweighed its threats

C. Legislation is, to a certain extent, a hindrance to scientific development

D. Dyson believed that it was better for regulations not to be involved in the development of genetic engineering

D. Explain the underlined parts.

1. Once we figure out how to safely <u>manipulate our genes,</u> people will start adding and deleting them to <u>their perceived advantage</u>.
2. It is <u>not farfetched</u> to imagine that prospective parents will one day turn to clinics to produce embryos that can not only be tested for genetic defects, <u>but also "corrected"</u>.
3. The implications of germline engineering are <u>so profound</u>, and scary, that some <u>leading scientists dismiss the possibility</u> that anyone would seriously contemplate doing it.
4. I just can't imagine <u>anything more stifling. You end up with the lowest common denominator.</u>
5. Not because I think for sure we should never cross that threshold, but because I think that is <u>such a fateful threshold to cross</u> that I'd like society to have to <u>rebut that presumption</u> some day, to have to <u>repeal a ban</u> when it thought it was time to ever try something like that.

Unit 11   Disease and Treatment

Text A

Mosquito and Cucumber Salad Anyone?

1. Could a genetic hybrid of a mosquito and a sea cucumber spell the end of malaria—one of the World's most deadly diseases? Do you live in a developed country and feel unconcerned about malaria? Perhaps you should think again. With the explosion of easy international travel, imported cases of malaria are reported more frequently. And the emergence of drug-resistant strains means the disease is appearing again in areas where it was previously under control.

2. There has never been a greater need for innovative preventative measures and new anti-malarial drugs. But have we found an unlikely ally in a gelatinous blob from the bottom of the Ocean.

Malaria's Deadly Toll

3. Malaria is an infectious disease caused by the plasmodium parasite that's transmitted by mosquitoes. Although malaria is largely a preventable and treatable disease, one person dies of malaria every 30 seconds. It rivals HIV and tuberculosis as the world's most deadly infection and the majority of its victims are under five years old.

4. Malaria causes severe illness in 500 million people worldwide each year, and kills more than one million. It is estimated that 40% of the world's population are at risk. Malaria transmission occurs primarily in large areas of Central and South America, sub-Saharan Africa, the Indian subcontinent, Southeast Asia and the Middle East.

5. In addition to an impact on individual health, malaria also has a significant socioeconomic impact. The disease causes an average loss of 1.3% annual economic growth in countries with a high incidence of infection. Furthermore, malaria has lifelong effects through increased poverty, impaired learning and decreased attendance in schools and the workplace.

How it All Begins—the Malaria Parasite Life Cycle

6. The transmission of the parasite plasmodium begins with the female mosquito, which needs blood to make eggs. When the mosquito bites an infected human it ingests parasite sperm and eggs. These then unite in the stomach of the mosquito to form what's known as ookinetes-cells that become embedded in the

stomach wall.

7. These ookinetes migrate through the mosquito's stomach wall and produce thousands of infectious daughter cells known as sporozoites. After 10~20 days they move to the mosquito salivary glands and are ready to infect another human.

8. Once inside the human body, the sporozoites are carried by the blood to the victim's liver where they hide from the immune system. In the liver they invade the cells and multiply into thousands of cells. After 9~16 days they return to the blood and infiltrate red blood cells where again they stay invisible to immune surveillance. Within the red blood cells they multiply once more forming parasite sperm and egg cells. This process destroys the victim's red blood cells which releases the parasitic cells into the bloodstream to be ingested by a mosquito-thus renewing the transmission cycle.

9. Patients with malaria exhibit extreme feverish attacks, flu-like symptoms, tiredness, diarrhea, nausea, vomiting and shivering while the malarial parasite damages the liver and blood cells. The severity of the symptoms depends on several factors, such as the species (type) of infecting parasite and the patient's acquired immunity and genetic background.

Cucumbers that Eat themselves Alive—and Malaria

10. The malaria parasite plasmodium has been studied for decades, but because of its ability to evade the immune system a vaccine has been hard to develop.

11. Most drugs that are available are active against the parasites while they are in the human blood. However, there is an emergence of parasite strains that are resistant to many of the existing anti-malarial drugs thus making the discovery of new therapies essential.

12. Recently, an International team of researchers, led by Professor Bob Sinden from the Imperial College in London, has found that the sea cucumber makes a chemical that is toxic to the fatal malarial parasite.

13. The sea cucumber is a worm-like scavenger that feeds on plankton and debris in the ocean and is made of a tough gelatinous tissue. A slimy mass of muscular tissue, the cucumber has the unusual ability to violently expel its internal body organs during times of stress. These can later be regenerated. Another fascinating feature is their ability to slowly digest themselves to cope with periods of starvation.

Cucumbers that Cure

14. Some varieties of sea cucumbers are said to have excellent healing properties so it may be no surprise that this creature has found medicinal use, both formally and in alternative therapies. Extracts have found their way into oils, creams and cosmetics. Sea cucumber extract has also been shown to heal wounds more quickly and reduce scarring. Other extracts from sea cucumbers inhibit blood vessel formation thus making it an excellent potential therapy for cancer.

15. Researchers have now found that this slug like creature also produces a protein which impairs

development of the malaria parasite. Called lectin (CEL-III), this protein has been shown to damage human and rat red blood cells. Lectin is poisonous to the parasites when they are still in the early ookinete stage of development before they migrate out of the mosquito's stomach to produce the millions of sporozoites which end up in the insect's saliva.

16. Inhibiting this ookinete development is a potential way to eliminate the transmission of sporozoites to the human host thus breaking the transmission cycle.

Part Cucumber and Part Fly

17. In order to inhibit ookinete development within the stomach, the research team has developed genetically modified mosquitoes. They are just like regular mosquitoes accept for one gene. This newly introduced gene is part lectin-making gene from the sea cucumber and part gene from the mosquito that makes a substance that is released into the stomach during feeding. In this way the toxin can be introduced into the stomach where it can kill the ookinete cells.

Still No Solution (of should we say "dressing")

18. The concept of genetically modifying mosquitoes to disrupt parasite development prior to human infection is a novel approach to control the disease that is gaining recognition due to limited success elsewhere.

19. Currently, the only treatments against the parasite once they are in human blood are chloroquine, quinine, doxycycline, mefloquine and a few others. Unfortunately, since the most afflicted countries tend to be the poorest there has been little commercial incentive to develop new drugs. But with the disease now on our doorsteps perhaps activity here will step up.

20. The rapid spread of antimalarial drug resistance over the past few decades has required more intensive monitoring to make sure there is proper management of clinical cases and early detection of changing patterns of resistance. Countries are being assisted in strengthening their drug resistance surveillance systems.

21. Mosquitoes have also built up resistance to insecticides which have been used in abundance.

22. But the deployment of super mossies that can fight off infection, like the cucumber salad, faces considerable challenges. In order to carry out this endeavor, thousands of mosquito embryos must be injected with a gene encoding for the anti-malarial protein and then the genetically modified adult mosquitoes released into the wild. And, unfortunately the toxic protein does not totally remove all parasites from all mosquitoes and as such, at this stage of development, would not be effective enough to prevent transmission of malaria to humans.

23. Furthermore, the genetically modified version of the mosquito would have to become the predominant species which is very difficult to achieve.

24. More research needs to be done but this finding is a first step toward developing a new method

of preventing transmission of malaria thanks to the lowly sea cucumber.

(http://www.firstscience.com/home/articles/humans/mosquito-and-cucumber-salad-anyone-page-1-1_45364.html)

Glossary

malaria [mə'lɛəriə] an infective disease caused by sporozoan parasites that are transmitted through the bite of an infected Anopheles mosquito; marked by paroxysms of chills and fever *n*. 疟疾

melatinous [mi'lætinəs] thick like gelatin *adj*. 胶粘的

blob [blɔb] an indistinct shapeless form *n*. 一滴

infectious [in'fekʃəs] caused by infection or capable of causing infection *adj*. 传染的

plasmodium [plæz'məudiəm] parasitic protozoan of the genus Plasmodium that causes malaria in humans *n*. 疟原虫

parasite ['pærəsait] an animal or plant that lives in or on a host (another animal or plant); it obtains nourishment from the host without benefiting or killing the host *n*. 寄生虫

impair [im'pɛə] make worse or less effective *v*. 损害，削弱

ingest [in'dʒest] serve oneself to, or consume regularly *v*. 摄取

salivary ['sælivəri] of or relating to saliva *adj*. 唾液的

infiltrate [in'filtreit] enter by penetrating the interstices *v*. 渗透，潜入

surveillance [sə:'veiləns] close observation of a person or group (usually by the police) *n*. 监视，监督

diarrhea [ˌdaiə'riə] frequent and watery bowel movements; can be a symptom of infection or food poisoning or colitis or a gastrointestinal tumor *n*. 痢疾，腹泻

toxic ['tɔksik] of or relating to or caused by a toxin or poison *adj*. 有毒的

scavenger ['skævindʒə] any animal that feeds on refuse and other decaying organic matter *n*. 清道夫

plankton ['plæŋkt(ə)n] the aggregate of small plant and animal organisms that float or drift in great numbers in fresh or salt water *n*. 浮游生物

gelatinous [dʒi'lætinəs] thick like gelatin *adj*. 胶粘的

slug [slʌg] any of various terrestrial gastropods having an elongated slimy body and no external shell *n*. [动]鼻涕虫

saliva [sə'laivə] a clear liquid secreted into the mouth by the salivary glands and mucous glands of the mouth; moistens the mouth and starts the digestion of starches *n*. 唾液

chloroquine [ˌklɔ(:)rə'kwi:n] an antimalarial drug used to treat malaria and amebic dysentery and systemic lupus erythematosus *n*. 疟疾的特效药之一种

quinine [kwi'ni:n; (US) 'kwainain] a bitter alkaloid extracted from chinchona bark; used in malaria therapy *n*. 奎宁

doxycycline [dɔksi'saiklin] an antibiotic derived from tetracycline that is effective against many infections *n*. [微]强力霉素

mefloquine ['mefləkwi:n;(US)'mefləkwain] an antimalarial drug (trade name Larium and Mephaquine) that is effective in cases that do not respond to chloroquine; said to produce harmful neuropsychiatric effects on some people *n*. 甲氟奎

Exercises

A. Fill in each blank with one of the given words in its correct form.

infectious	parasite	impair	lowly	surveillance
infiltrate	incentive	vaccine	afflicted	toxic

1. Researchers at Monash University in Victoria, Australia have found an increase in _____ compounds, a decrease in protein content and a decreased yield in plants grown under high CO_2 and drought conditions.
2. She says that patients with malignant glioma often die within a year of being diagnosed, since the tumor cells rapidly _____ normal brain tissue and are difficult to treat.
3. If progression of the cancer occurs during active _____, patients may undergo radical therapy.
4. This is a significant first step in developing a universal _____ to help protect against pandemic influenza.
5. "The most important variable for reducing diarrheal illness in the worst _____ countries is rural sanitation, a message that can be obscured with a 'one size fits all' linear regression model" like those used in the past, the researchers said.
6. A preliminary study suggests that economic _____ appear to be effective for achieving short-term weight loss, according to a new report.
7. In many animal species, however, stable hierarchies are routinely formed in which some individuals seem to slip naturally into their dominant role whereas others resign themselves to play the part of _____ subordinates.
8. A recent survey of infectious diseases specialists regarding the diagnosis and treatment of syphilis appears in the November 15, 2009 issue of Clinical _____ Diseases, now available online.
9. Virginia Commonwealth University Life Sciences researchers have discovered a new mechanism the malaria _____ uses to enter human red blood cells, which could lead to the development of a vaccine cocktail to fight the mosquito-borne disease.
10. Scientists have created a mouse to help understand human neuronal diseases that _____ a patient's ability to feel and to move their arms and legs.

B. Skim the text and then answer the following questions.
1. What do you know about malaria?
2. In what places can sporozoites or ookinetes be shielded from the immune system?
3. Where could sea cucumber extracts be found?
4. Why can't toxic proteins prevent transmission of malaria to humans satisfactorily?
5. Please list some of the characteristics of the sea cucumber.

C. Read the text and choose the correct answer to each of the following questions.
1. Which statement is true about malaria? _____.
   A. It is not fatal to catch malaria
   B. It only appears in underdeveloped countries
   C. It cannot be eliminated in a region
   D. Cases of malaria are reported more frequently
2. Which of the following diseases claims the most of lives? _____.
   A. HIV　　　　　　　B. Tuberculosis　　　C. Malaria　　　D. Cancer
3. Among the Four, _____ is most likely to be influenced by malaria.
   A. China　　　　　　B. Alaska　　　　　　C. Algeria　　　D. Russia
4. The severity of the symptoms of malaria depends on several factors except _____.
   A. the type of infecting parasite
   B. the patient's intrinsic immunity
   C. the patient's genetic background
   D. the patient's acquired immunity
5. It is true that _____.
   A. there has been little to gain in developing new drugs in the most afflicted countries
   B. the only treatments against malaria parasites are conducted in human blood
   C. there is no possibility that people in poor countries would try to produce new drugs
   D. antimalarial drugs spread rapidly over the past few decades

D. Explain the underlined parts.
1. <u>Could a genetic hybrid of a mosquito and a sea cucumber spell the end of malaria</u>—one of the World's most deadly diseases?
2. <u>It rivals HIV and tuberculosis as the world's most deadly infection</u> and the majority of its victims are under five years old.
3. <u>In addition to an impact on individual health</u>, malaria also <u>has a significant socioeconomic impact</u>.
4. These ookinetes <u>migrate through the mosquito's stomach wall</u> and produce thousands of <u>infectious daughter cells known as sporozoites</u>.

5. In the liver they invade the cells and multiply into thousands of cells.
6. However, there is an emergence of parasite strains that are resistant to many of the existing anti-malarial drugs thus making the discovery of new therapies essential.
7. Inhibiting this ookinete development is a potential way to eliminate the transmission of sporozoites to the human host thus breaking the transmission cycle.
8. Unfortunately, since the most afflicted countries tend to be the poorest there has been little commercial incentive to develop new drugs. But with the disease now on our doorsteps perhaps activity here will step up.
9. Furthermore, the genetically modified version of the mosquito would have to become the predominant species which is very difficult to achieve.

E. Read the passages in this section and decide whether each of the following statements is true or false.

Passage One

If mainstream media has made one thing clear, it's that we the people crave the bizarre. And sometimes, the bizarre is beyond what anyone could have imagined. Such is the case with certain rare and crazy diseases—disorders that seem to defy reality. Unfortunately for the many sufferers out there, some diseases, however crazy they may be, are very real—and equally as frightening. Here are just a few crazy diseases to whet your appetite for the bizarre.

Polyglandular Addison's Disease

Type of Disease: Hormonal disorder

Crazy Because: Can cause instantaneous death from sudden emotional distress

Cure: None, but manageable by medication

In February 2008, media reports swirled around the story of Jennifer Lloyd, a 10-year-old from Prestwich, who is one of only six known sufferers in the U.K. of polyglandular Addison's disease. Addison's disease is a hormonal disorder named after Dr. Thomas Addison who first described the disease in 1855. The polyglandular form is much rarer than the ordinary disorder, leaving affected patients literally unable to produce adrenaline in response to stress. Adrenaline, or epinephrine, is the "fight or flight" hormone that prepares the body for action. Without adrenaline, the body's organs cannot respond to stress and instead go into shock and shut down, leaving those affected critically ill. Patients such as Jennifer require constant attention and steroidal medication just to live out their daily lives: "Something as simple as walking the dog can be a worry," Jennifer's mother told the BBC. In Jennifer's case, even watching a movie, playing sports or dancing requires strict supervision in case she becomes overly excited. Despite the mundane outlook for Jennifer and other patients with this crazy disease, most can lead normal lives with the help of medication.

Reflex Sympathetic Dystrophy
Type of Disease: Nerve disorder
Crazy Because: Causes searing pain as if on fire
Cure: Complex; disease may spontaneously resolve, but treatment usually only lessens symptoms

Imagine being tormented every waking moment of every day by searing pain in your limbs. Your arms feel like they are on fire, they are swollen, hot to the touch, and you sweat excessively. These are just a few of the symptoms of reflex sympathetic dystrophy (RSD), a poorly understood disorder defined by pain in the limbs that is way out of proportion from what is expected following a particular injury or harmful event, such as surgery or stroke. The disease is believed to be caused by an abnormal chain reaction of the sympathetic nervous system, the body system that regulates blood flow and other aspects of the skin. Experts liken the pain response to that of an engine revving out of control.

While the disease may spontaneously disappear on its own, many patients undergo intensive treatments for years just to lessen the pain. And for some patients, the pain can become so profound that they must undergo the most extreme and expensive of therapies—being placed under a Ketamine coma—to essentially reset the pain connections of the body. In 2003, under the guidance of German colleagues of renowned RSD specialist Dr. Robert Schwartzman, 14-year-old Lindsay Wurtenberg of the U.S. underwent Ketamine coma-therapy and successfully recovered from a particularly debilitating case of RSD that developed following a harmless spider bite. "I don't think there is a worse pain problem," said Dr. Schwartzman of Lindsay's condition. He was probably right.

(http://www.askmen.com/sports/health _ 150/189 _ mens _ health.html)

_____ 1. It is said that people yearn for something unusual.
_____ 2. It is dangerous for people with Polyglandular Addison's diseases to be overexcited.
_____ 3. Medication can help people get rid of Polyglandular Addison's disease.
_____ 4. Hormonal disorder gives rise to reflex sympathetic dystrophy.
_____ 5. Reflex sympathetic dystrophy can only be cured by medication.

Passage Two

But first, diabetes. Beaulieu chose diabetes as a context in which to spark discussion on organizational and financial systems for several reasons, she said. It is a very prevalent disease: as Beaulieu and co-authors David Cutler and Katherine Ho noted in their study, it is the seventh leading cause of death in the U.S. Its economic burden is also high, since it is linked to other afflictions such as heart and renal disease and blindness.

And, she added, one of the most important aspects of this disease is that the medical profession already knows how to treat it. "We have the medical knowledge to do it. And it's not being done. Just under one-half of identified diabetics in this country don't have their blood sugar under control," she said.

Diabetes manifests as Type I or Type II and, as one participant pointed out, the most appropriate care involves some tailoring. But in general, it is well recognized that diabetes can lead to long-term complications and short- and long-term costs. As Beaulieu and her co-authors learned, diabetics may make up between 3 and 10 percent of a typical health plan's membership. It typically costs about $1,000 a year to treat a newly diagnosed diabetic patient; obviously, the numbers go up if a diabetic suffers serious complications.

Healthcare providers have attempted a number of disease management strategies over the last ten years or so. The diabetes programs have varied, but all are linked by the idea that patients can and should become educated about their disease and be proactive in taking care of their health. According to Beaulieu and her co-authors, disease management is focused on prevention and control, not acute care. "The aim is to improve the coordination of care and to reduce the number of hospitalizations and severe complications among diabetic patients," they wrote.

Disease management, then, can take several approaches. The simplest is probably for the healthcare provider to offer a monitoring system for patients who have already been diagnosed as diabetics, sending out e-mail or making phone calls to remind patients of test and checkup dates. Another route is to offer a combined monitoring, tracking, and alert system. This method automatically lets the healthcare provider know if patients skip their tests or if a more intensive treatment seemed warranted by the latest test results. A third approach—less common—is to create a coordinated "virtual team" around the patient, by sharing lab data, insurance claims data, and pharmacy data in an attempt to enhance overall care.

Another part of diabetes disease management programs aims not at current diabetics but at identifying members of the health plan who seem at particularly high risk of developing the disease within the next couple of years. This kind of program is harder for health plans to implement, according to Beaulieu and her co-authors, because it requires data collection and analysis tools, since potential diabetics are identified on the basis of pharmacy and lab data as well as questionnaires and surveys. Not many organizations have ventured into this element of disease management.

In their case-study discussion, participants at the conference mulled over the strategies of HealthPartners, an independent nonprofit that is one of three health maintenance organizations (HMOs) in the Minneapolis market. HealthPartners has an enrollment of about 675,000 people, and its network consists of approximately 3,700 primary care physicians and 4,500 specialists, according to Beaulieu and her co-authors. In the 1990s, it began a program with two elements similar to those outlined above: one to focus on plan members who already had diabetes, and another to focus on members at risk of developing diabetes.

Analyzing HealthPartners, Beaulieu and her co-authors found that such programs could lose money in the first one to three years and so would not break even in a three-year time period. Allowing an eight-to twelve-year period, however, would be more realistic for a break even, they suggested.

(http://hbswk.hbs.edu/item/3792.html)

_____ 6. Diabetes leaves people suffering from even more diseases.

_____ 7. It costs about $1,000 a year to treat a diabetic patient.

_____ 8. It is not necessary for people diagnosed with diabetes to take active part in treatment.

_____ 9. It is harder for health plans aiming at current diabetics to carry out.

_____ 10. HealthPartners is the name of a hospital engaged in the study of diabetes.

F. Cloze. Fill in each blank with one suitable word.

What used to be __1__ is now commonplace: traveling abroad to receive medical __2__, and to a developing country at that.

So-called medical tourism is on the rise for everything from cardiac care to plastic surgery __3__ hip and knee replacements. As a recent Harvard Business School __4__ study describes, the globalization of health care also __5__ a fascinating angle on globalization generally and is of great interest to __6__ strategists.

"Apollo Hospitals—First-World Health Care at Emerging-Market Prices" explores how Dr. Prathap C. Reddy, a cardiologist, opened India's first for-profit hospital in the southern city of Chennai in 1983. Today the Apollo Hospitals Group __7__ more than 30 hospitals and __8__ patients from many different countries, according to the case. Tarun Khanna, a Harvard Business School professor __9__ in global strategy, coauthored the case with professor Felix Oberholzer-Gee and Carin-Isabel Knoop, __10__ director of the HBS Global Research Group.

1. A. weird   B. extraordinary   C. rare   D. scarce
2. A. treatment   B. abroad   C. tourism   D. study
3. A. to   B. on   C. in   D. at
4. A. medical   B. tourism   C. case   D. strategy
5. A. provides   B. sets   C. focuses   D. visualizes
6. A. medical   B. academic   C. tourism   D. corporate
7. A. controls   B. manages   C. merges   D. establishes
8. A. cures   B. heals   C. treats   D. remedies
9. A. specializing   B. dealing   C. authoritative D. expertising
10. A. exclusive   B. executive   C. excessive   D. exemplary

G. Translate the following passages into Chinese/English.

1. ECT (electroconvulsive therapy): Most people do not like the idea of electroconvulsive therapy (ECT). It is a treatment that is reserved only for patients who have severe depression, for which it is highly effective and can work faster than medication. It involves having a brief anaesthetic that sends the

person to sleep for 5~10 minutes. While asleep, a muscle-relaxing drug is given and a small electric current is passed through the brain for a fraction of a second. Once the person has woken, it takes half an hour or so to get over the effects of the anaesthetic. ECT is only given under the close supervision of an anaesthetist, a psychiatrist and nursing staff. Most commonly, ECT is administered twice a week and around 6~10 treatments are necessary to treat the depression, though an effect may be seen after the first one or two treatments. There is no evidence that properly administered ECT damages the brain in any way.

2. 对抑郁症的病因我们还不完全清楚。基因或早年的生活经历可能会使一些人容易患上此病。应激性生活事件,如失业或失恋,都可能引发一段时间的抑郁症。某些躯体疾病、药物治疗以及在娱乐场所吸食毒品,也可能引发抑郁症。在很多人中,确定他们患抑郁症的某一个"病因"是很困难的。而这使他们感到痛苦,因为他们想知道为什么会得这种病。然而抑郁症,就像任何疾病一样,可能没有明显致病原因。

Text B

Is Hypnosis Moving Closer to Mainstream Medicine?

1. Throughout the developed world, people are increasingly turning to hypnosis for a variety of reasons, from stopping smoking to alleviating the pain of cancer treatment. It's surprising, therefore, that there is little consensus among medical professionals about what hypnosis is, let alone whether it's effective for these purposes.

2. The word hypnosis is derived from Hypnos, the Ancient Greek god of sleep, and was coined by James Braid (1795~1860), the first person to conduct formal medical research on the subject. In fact, however, hypnosis bears little relation to true sleep, and is more accurately described as a state of highly focused attention. James Braid himself later realised this, and attempted to change the name to monoideaism, but the catchier hypnosis had stuck. Subjects under hypnosis remain conscious throughout the process. Andrew Barrett, a London based practitioner, told me: "People [who come to me] are vaguely aware [of what hypnosis is] but apprehension is based on what they see on TV such as Derren Brown or Paul McKenna. The initial fear is 'will I be in control?' I give them a taste and then they feel more comfortable and we can get down to real work." Approximately 95% of subjects can be hypnotised to some degree, although many cannot attain the deep, trance-like states often associated with hypnosis.

3. Jenny Fenfham, who used hypnosis for help managing anxiety, remembers, "[The hypnotist] told me to think of a door. He told me to open the door and to go inside, to imagine a room on the other side. He asked me to see what was in this room and to throw away what I didn't want."

4. Perhaps the fundamental dividing line in the hypnosis debate is between those who argue that it is an "altered state of consciousness" and those who insist that supposedly "hypnotised" patients are in fact subconsciously acting out a role. It has long been universally accepted that, contrary to popular perception, it is not possible to hypnotise someone against his (or her) will. While this does not invalidate the notion of an altered state, it does leave open the possibility that the subject simply wants to be hypnotised and therefore behaves in the way he believes a hypnotised person should behave.

5. This latter explanation is often given for the bizarre behaviour exhibited by subjects in stage hypnosis: that, since people believe that they are not responsible for their actions, their inhibitions are removed. The Hypnotherapy Association comments, "Entertainment hypnosis relies on compliance, expectation from the audience and perception of what the audience expects. In fact, if you should choose to go to an entertainment hypnotist, you are going with the express intention of having fun and being asked to do silly things."

6. One might hope that modern brain imaging techniques such as EEG (Electroencephalography), PET (Positron Emission Tomography) and fMRI (functional Magnetic Resonance Imaging), which allow activity in different parts of the brain to be measured, might provide a definitive resolution to this so-called "state/non-state" argument. Instead they have made the question itself seem ill-defined since, while patients under hypnosis do show changes in cerebral activity, so do patients asked to complete or imagine various activities. The American website Skepdic comments dryly: "One might as well call daydreaming, concentrating, imagining the colour red, or sneezing altered states, since the experience of each will show electrical changes in the brain and changes in brain waves from ordinary waking consciousness."

7. Nevertheless, brain imaging has provided us with some tantalizing hints. A 1998 study in patients pre-screened for their ability to suffer auditory hallucinations under hypnosis scanned their brains using PET under four conditions: when a tape was playing, when it was not playing, when they were asked to imagine hearing the tape, and when they were under hypnosis and told that they were hearing the tape. One region of the brain, activated when they were hearing the tape but inactivated (initially) when they were not hearing the tape, was found to be activated by hypnotic suggestion that the tape was playing despite remaining inactive when they simply imagined hearing it. In other words, their brains were fooled into genuinely believing they were hearing it.

8. Whether hypnosis is a genuine transcendence of normal consciousness or a kind of elaborate subconscious role-play is fundamentally irrelevant to whether or not it is effective as a medical tool. The term hypnotherapy refers to the use of hypnosis as a therapeutic tool, but the distinction between a hypnotist and a hypnotherapist is somewhat ill-defined, as some (including Andrew Barrett, who calls himself a hypnotist) reserve the term hypnotherapist for psychotherapists who use hypnosis as one part of in-depth

psychological counselling. Perhaps the most common reason people visit a hypnotherapist is for help with smoking cessation. Many hypnotherapists claim that hypnosis has been clinically proven to assist in the battle against the evil weed. However, a review conducted by the Cochrane Library in 1998 concluded that "The effects of hypnotherapy on smoking cessation claimed by uncontrolled studies were not confirmed by analysis of randomized controlled trials." More recently, a 2004 review by two scientists at the Centre for Tobacco Control concluded "the evidence of any effect is anecdotal". Evidence supporting the use of hypnotherapy to treat drug addiction is similarly lacking.

9. Hypnotherapy is also widely used in pain management, and here there is good evidence that it works, both epidemiological and from laboratory studies. A 2006 meta-analysis (an analysis of other analyses, considered the gold standard of evidence in medicine) by the Cochrane Library of five studies on a total of 729 patients concluded that women taught self-hypnosis techniques were only half as likely to require painkillers during childbirth as those who were not. Formal research on hypnotherapy to treat emotional problems is still unavailable, but anecdotal evidence suggests many have found it helpful. Jenny Fenfham, who used hypnotherapy to treat anxiety attacks, told me, "At the end of the session I felt really tired but good, like after a heavy workout, but I didn't feel any positive change. But over the next couple of days I felt less stressed and more confident."

10. A 1999 laboratory study by the Arnold and Mabel Beckman centre in Canada performed PET scans of the brains of hypnotised volunteers as they dipped their hands into painfully hot water. Half were told that the water would be painfully hot, while half were told that it would be pleasantly warm. While the parts of the brain that process physical stimuli were unaffected by hypnotic conditioning, the somatosensory (literally "sensing the body") cortex, which is involved in the conscious suffering aspect of pain, was significantly less active in the brains of those who had not been told to expect pain. This may explain the effectiveness of hypnotherapy in pain relief.

11. Another use of hypnosis has been to help witnesses to crimes to "recover" memories to which their conscious minds may not have access. This, however, has fallen out of favour owing to recent research suggesting that hypnosis does not enhance the accuracy of the memory in any special way and that the subject may subconsciously "fill in" gaps in memories with the imagination. The technical term for this is confabulation. Many states in the US have blanket bans on testimony recovered under hypnosis and, in Britain, the Crown Prosecution Service advises against hypnotising potential witnesses, saying, "A witness who has been hypnotised will often tell a story full of detail which may appear utterly convincing. No expert will be able to tell if it is the truth or confabulation. The story told under hypnosis will become so firmly fixed in the subject's mind that he or she will become unshakeable in cross examination." Nevertheless, the police sometimes use hypnosis when searching for a lead from someone who is unlikely to be asked to testify in any resulting court case.

12. The debate surrounding the true nature of hypnosis will perhaps never be resolved, but what seems certain is that people will continue to seek help from it for a variety of purposes, and that modern medical science suggests that at least for some ailments hypnosis is a perfectly rational treatment.

(http://www.firstscience.com/home/articles/humans/is-hypnosis-moving-closer-to-mainstream-medicine_32925.html)

Glossary

hypnosis [hip'nəusis] a state that resembles sleep but that is induced by suggestion *n*. 催眠状态

alleviate [ə'li:vieit] provide physical relief, as from pain *v*. 减轻, 使……缓和

consensus [kən'sensəs] agreement in the judgment or opinion reached by a group as a whole *n*. 共识, 一致, 合意

practitioner [præk'tiʃənə] someone who practices a learned profession *n*. 从业者

trance [trɑ:ns] a state of mind in which consciousness is fragile and voluntary action is poor or missing; a state resembling deep sleep *n*. 梦幻之境, 恍惚

inhibition [ˌinhi'biʃən] (psychology) the conscious exclusion of unacceptable thoughts or desires *n*. 压抑

compliance [kəm'plaiəns] a disposition or tendency to yield to the will of others *n*. 顺从, 遵从

cerebral ['seribrəl] of or relating to the cerebrum or brain *adj*. 脑的

tantalizing ['tæntəlaiziŋ] very pleasantly inviting *adj*. 诱人的

pre-screen ['pri:skri:n] to screen in advance for potential problems *v*. 预检

hallucination [həlu:si'neiʃən] illusory perception; a common symptom of severe mental disorder *n*. 幻觉

transcendence [træn'sendəns] the state of excelling or surpassing or going beyond usual limits *n*. 超越

cessation [sə'seiʃən] a stopping *n*. 停止

epidemiological [ˌepiˌdi:mi'ɔlədʒikəl] of or relating to epidemiology *adj*. 流行病学的

cortex ['kɔ:teks] the layer of unmyelinated neurons (the grey matter) forming the cortex of the cerebrum *n*. 脑皮层

confabulation [kənˌfæbju'leiʃən] (psychiatry) a plausible but imagined memory that fills in gaps in what is remembered *n*. 虚构(症)

Exercises

A. Fill in each blank with one of the given words in its correct form.

| compliance | cessation | tantalizing | confabulation | consensus |
| inhibition | hallucinations | transcendence | hypnosis | alleviate |

1. Although there is no doubt that _____ can impact the mind and behavior, the underlying brain mechanisms are not well understood.
2. A new study shows that a blanket can also help _____ shivering in patients who have been cooled to prevent brain damage.
3. Researchers have demonstrated that standardized neurobehavioral assessment is more sensitive than diagnoses determined by clinical _____.
4. Studies have suggested that _____ of return (in which our attention is less likely to return to objects we've already viewed) helps make visual search more efficient—when searching a scene to find an object, we have a bias toward inspecting new regions of a scene, and we avoid looking for the object in already searched areas.
5. They found that _____ with guidelines was significantly increased and that there was an improvement in outcome in intensive care unit patients.
6. The findings, published online April 26 in Nature Medicine, demonstrate the _____ potential of immunotherapy in cancer treatment, says principal investigator Dr. Pamela Ohashi, co-director, CFIBCR.
7. New findings suggests that all individuals, regardless of cultural background or religion, experience the same neuropsychological functions during spiritual experiences, such as _____.
8. _____ is a devastating memory disorder consisting in the uncontrolled production of "false memories".
9. Changes in food and drink consumption, including caffeine intake, could place people in a better position to cope with _____ or possibly impact on how frequently they occur, say the scientists.
10. Varenicline is a recently introduced smoking _____ product of proven effectiveness, but there have been concerns that it may increase the risk of suicidal behaviour and suicide.

B. Skim the text and then answer the following questions.

1. For what reasons do you think a person would like to be hypnotised?
2. In what areas can hypnosis be used?
3. What are the features of the brain of people hypnotised?
4. Is testimony recovered under hypnosis reliable or not? Why?
5. Do you know of some case studies in hypnosis? If you do, please share with the class.

C. Read the text and choose the correct answer to each of the following questions.

1. Hypnosis is a state in which a person _____.
   A. is in deep sleep
   B. is with highly focused attention
   C. is controlled by a psychologist
   D. is total relaxed physically and mentally
2. The word "subject" in "approximately 95% of subjects can be hypnotised to some degree (paragraph

2)" means _____.
   - A. a topic under discussion
   - B. a person who owes allegiance to that nation
   - C. a person who is subjected to experimental procedures
   - D. a person or object selected by an artist or photographer for graphic representation
3. Which of the following statements is true about a hypnotised person? _____.
   - A. He is not against being hypnotised
   - B. He doesn't want to be hypnotised
   - C. He behaves at will
   - D. He behaves in the way he believes a hypnotised person should behave
4. _____ cannot result in electrical changes in the brain and changes in brain waves from ordinary waking consciousness.
   - A. Daydreaming
   - B. Imagining various activates
   - C. Imagining various colors
   - D. Imagining the color red
5. It can be inferred from the text that _____.
   - A. hypnosis is a perfect treatment for ailments
   - B. people will stop turning to hypnosis because of its unknown nature
   - C. Hypnosis will be here to stay
   - D. Hypnosis is unreliable

D. Explain the underlined parts.

1. In fact, however, hypnosis <u>bears little relation to true sleep</u>, and is more accurately described as a state of highly focused attention.
2. While this does not <u>invalidate the notion of an altered state</u>, it does leave open the possibility that <u>the subject simply wants to be hypnotised</u> and therefore behaves in the way he believes a hypnotised person should behave.
3. Whether hypnosis is <u>a genuine transcendence of normal consciousness or a kind of elaborate subconscious role-play</u> is fundamentally irrelevant to whether or not it is effective as a medical tool.
4. Another use of hypnosis has been to help witnesses to crimes to <u>"recover" memories to which their conscious minds may not have access</u>.
5. This, however, has <u>fallen out of favour</u> owing to recent research suggesting that hypnosis does not enhance the accuracy of the memory in any special way and that the subject may <u>subconsciously "fill in" gaps in memories with the imagination</u>.

Unit 12 Nuclear Power

Text A

Oil Is Out; Is Nuclear In?

1. Put yourself in an imaginary time machine and set the dial to around the year 2040. The exorbitant price of oil, now at $500 a barrel, has pushed a good chunk of the globe toward nuclear power.

2. If the world is on the cusp of such an era, will it result in weapons proliferation or accidents such as meltdowns? Or will a new way to harness energy emerge to compete with nuclear power?

3. Currently, more than 400 reactors in 30 countries supply about 16 percent of the world's electricity, according to the World Nuclear Association. Nuclear power is increasing steadily, with about 30 reactors under construction in 12 countries. Most reactors being ordered or planned are in Asia. And more than 40 developing countries have recently approached U.N. officials to express interest in starting nuclear power programs.

4. Nuclear energy advocates see the technology as a clean way to wean the world from expensive and environmentally damaging fossil fuels.

5. But for critics, the thought of a nuclearized world stirs controversy.

6. "The G8 countries can't even maintain adequate safety and security," said Paul Walker at Global Green USA, an environmental and arms control organization and affiliate of a group founded by former Soviet President Mikhail Gorbachev. "So the developing world presents a dangerous potential for terrorist attack or diversion of radioactive materials or major accident."

7. Experts are also concerned that the spread of nuclear power could spur weapons proliferation. Arab states could learn the wrong lessons from Iran, a nation that thumbs its nose at the West while it allegedly builds a nuclear weapons program, said Charles Ferguson, senior fellow at the Council on Foreign Relations.

8. Neighbors of the Persian giant could follow its lead in sidestepping full disclosure of its nuclear program, or repeat its argument that unfriendly relations with the few Western countries that supply nuclear fuel have forced it to build it's own enrichment program, Ferguson said. Most countries that rely on nuclear power have only small programs without the ability to produce highly enriched uranium, which

can be used in bomb making, he added.

9. "Iran thinks of itself as a top dog in the region, and that can appear threatening to Saudi Arabia and other Arab states," Ferguson said.

10. Surrounding nations could establish nuclear programs with the intent of supplying electricity but could later flirt with the idea of nuclear weapons, Ferguson said. Fear of a dominant Iran could prompt regional governments to keep their nuclear weapons options open, he added. Some could decide it's more cost effective to start enriching their own uranium.

11. "It's kind of a slow train wreck," Ferguson said.

12. Commercial reactors use low enriched uranium, which is non-weapons grade, although some research reactors use highly enriched uranium, Ferguson said. An enrichment facility can make low enriched uranium for commercial reactor fuel or highly enriched uranium for nuclear bombs, he said. "That's why there is such a big concern about the spread of enrichment technology," he said.

13. A turning point for the Middle East could come when its oil begins to dry up and the region starts clamoring for nuclear power.

14. "At that point Saudi Arabia will feel some economic pain," said Ferguson. "So they can legitimately say 'let's invest in nuclear.'"

15. To curtail moves from peaceful technology to weapons material production, experts recognize the need for strong regulatory bodies. But some authoritarian governments may not warm to the idea of answering to an independent government body, Ferguson said.

16. Ernie Moniz, director of Massachusetts Institute of Technology's energy initiative, said one way to curtail nuclear weapons proliferation is to push "fuel leasing", in which a country would receive a secure, fresh supply of low enriched uranium fuel and return the spent fuel to the supplier. The user would agree not to pursue further enrichment or reprocessing. Spent fuel can also be used to make weapons.

17. The United Arab Emirates is moving toward such an arrangement, although no country has formally adopted it, Moniz said.

18. The spread of nuclear power could also increase terrorists' access to nuclear materials, experts said. Even now, some of the world's research reactors, which contain fuel suitable for bomb making, are lightly guarded and vulnerable to security breaches, Ferguson said.

19. Safety is another concern. There have been two major accidents — Chernobyl and Three Mile Island. Chernobyl was a result of major design deficiencies, violation of operating procedures and the absence of a safety culture, according to the World Nuclear Association.

20. "Chernobyl used an old design that could never have been licensed in the West," said Moniz. "I would expect that any future plant built anywhere will use modern safety features."

21. Regardless, it takes just one Chernobyl or Three Mile Island to spur panic, the fallout of which

could halt nuclear power expansion worldwide, Ferguson said. The 1979 Three Mile Island accident raised many public questions about the safety and reliability of nuclear power and dealt a death blow to new plant construction in the United States, Walker said.

22. George Friedman, chief executive officer of Stratfor.com, a private intelligence firm, said nuclear weapons proliferation is unlikely. "The most remarkable thing is the lack of nuclear proliferation," he said. "In fact we've seen very little."

23. Nearly 200 states are party to the Nuclear Non Proliferation treaty, five of which have nuclear weapons. Other known nuclear powers are India and Pakistan. Iran and Syria are alleged to have nuclear weapons and Israel's nuclear weapons status remains unknown. Pakistani scientist A.Q. Khan is alleged to have shared nuclear secrets with North Korea, Libya and Iran, although he recently recanted his confession.

24. "Simply creating a nuclear explosion is easy," said Friedman. "But creating a nuclear weapon is fiendishly difficult," he said, explaining why weapons proliferation fears are unfounded.

25. "Iran, for example, does not have the advanced electronics or other engineering capabilities to deliver such an explosion," he said. "Eighty percent of a weapons program has nothing to do with nuclear weapons."

26. But he does expect increased civilian use of nuclear power in a future with a dwindling supply of affordable fossil fuels.

27. One problem is that the electricity that nuclear plants produce cannot be stored well. An airplane, for example, cannot be flown on batteries, said Friedman. "And you can't drive a truck using electricity," he added. Building a reactor can also take years.

28. "So the real issue is going to be storage," said Friedman.

29. Friedman expects Japan, which imports 100 percent of its oil, to move increasingly toward nuclear power. Other countries would likely include industrial nations with limited domestic resources like South Korea and Taiwan, he said. European countries would also fall into the mix, at least until a better technology comes along.

30. But nuclear power's limitations could spur a drive toward other technologies.

31. "If I were to bet, I would bet on space-based solar power," Friedman said.

32. Direct conversion of solar energy on earth is inefficient, mostly because of the amount of land it uses, Friedman said. But beaming microwave energy to earth would be more viable later in the century. This would especially be the case if the military's use of space soars, which would eventually cause launch costs to decline, he said.

33. In line with such predictions is a 2007 report by the Pentagon's National Security Space Office entitled Space-Based Solar Power as an Opportunity for Strategic Security, which encourages the govern-

ment to start developing space power.

34. As for which energy source will reign later in the century, Friedman expects a range of competing ideas but says that one dominant one will emerge, just as hydrocarbons did in the 19th century.

35. "I expect ferment, crisis and then a single solution (will) emerge," he said.

(http://www.nationaldefensemagazine.org/ARCHIVE/2008/AUGUST/Pages/OilIsOut; IsNuclearIn.aspx)

Glossary

exorbitant [ig'zɔ:bitənt] greatly exceeding bounds of reason or moderation *adj*. 过高的
cusp [kʌsp] point formed by two intersecting arcs *n*. 尖头，尖端
proliferation [prəuˌlifə'reiʃən] a rapid increase in number (especially a rapid increase in the number of deadly weapons) *n*. 增殖
meltdown ['meltdaun] severe overheating of the core of a nuclear reactor resulting in the core melting and radiation escaping *n*. 熔化
wean [wi:n] detach the affections of *v*. 戒掉
affiliate [ə'filieit] a subsidiary or subordinate organization that is affiliated with another organization *n*. 联号(联播台，同伙)，附属机构
flirt [flə:t] behave carelessly or indifferently *v*. 轻率对待
clamor ['klæmə] make loud demands *v*. 大声地要求
curtail [kə:'teil] place restrictions on *v*. 限制
emirate [e'miərit] the domain controlled by an emir *n*. 酋长国
breach [bri:tʃ] a failure to perform some promised act or obligation *n*. 违背
recant [ri'kænt] formally reject or disavow a formerly held belief, usually under pressure *v*. 放弃主张
fiendishly ['fi:ndiʃli] as a devil; in an evil manner *adv*. 恶魔似地，极坏地
viable ['vaiəbl] capable of being done with means at hand and circumstances as they are *adj*. 可行的
ferment ['fə:mənt] a state of agitation or turbulent change or development *n*. 动乱

Exercises

A. Fill in each blank with one of the given words in its correct form.

| viable | exorbitant | wean | breach | ferment |
| clamor | proliferation | reign | curtail | affiliate |

1. It's easier to rebuild trust after a _____ if you already have a strong relationship.
2. Producers already make grain ethanol by using yeast to _____ six-carbon plant sugars like glucose.

3. Different coins were minted during this emperor's _____.
4. This behavior is so unconscious that there is little that can be done to _____ it.
5. A major reason explaining why women are underrepresented not only in math-intensive fields but also in senior leadership positions in most fields is that many women choose to have children, and the timing of childrearing coincides with the most demanding periods of their career, such as trying to get tenure or working _____ hours to get promoted.
6. The more that are implemented, the more we will _____ people away from sole reliance on their cars when they could be walking and/or riding, and improving their health as a result.
7. Other authors of the paper include Peijun Li of GUMC and Uwe Rudolph of McLean Hospital, a Harvard Medical School _____.
8. However, given current environmental and economic pressures the recuperation of such heat energy could become _____.
9. A new University of Colorado at Boulder study shows the strongest evidence yet that noise pollution negatively influences bird populations, findings with implications for the fate of ecological communities situated amid growing urban _____.
10. They found that SOCS-1 blocks _____ of prostate cancer cells and that inhibition of SOCS-1 expression stimulated tumor cell growth.

B. Skim the text and then answer the following questions.
1. What is your opinion of the use of nuclear power?
2. According to the text, what are the possible negative effects of the use of nuclear power?
3. What does "Persian giant (line 1, paragraph 8)" refer to?
4. What is the problem with the electricity produced by nuclear plants?
5. According to Friedman, what will be the best energy source in the future?

C. Read the text and choose the correct answer to each of the following questions.
1. Which of the following statements is true? _____.
    A. In 30 countries, about 16 percent of the electricity is supplied by reactors
    B. 40 countries have started nuclear power programs
    C. There are about 30 reactors under construction in 12 countries
    D. 40 countries have reactors
2. Which is not the viewpoint of people mentioned in the text? _____.
    A. Nuclear energy can help to reduce the use of fossil fuels
    B. Nuclear energy is safe to use
    C. The use of nuclear energy can result in controversy
    D. The use of nuclear energy have certain negative results

3. It is correct that _____.
   A. Iran sets a good model for Arab states
   B. Iran has nuclear weapons program
   C. Iran tries to involve the Western world in its nuclear weapons program
   D. Iran is very advanced in the use of nuclear energy
4. The reason why some people are beset with the spread of enrichment technology is that _____.
   A. it can make highly enriched uranium for commercial reactor fuel
   B. it can make low enriched uranium for nuclear bombs
   C. it can make highly enriched uranium for nuclear bombs
   D. it can make uranium non-weapon grade
5. The example of Chernobyl and Three Mile Island is used to indicate that _____.
   A. the spread of nuclear power could increase terrorists' access to nuclear materials
   B. improper management in certain aspects could give rise to accidents
   C. nuclear power causes panic
   D. design deficiency courts disaster

D. Explain the underlined parts.

1. <u>The exorbitant price of oil</u>, now at $500 a barrel, has <u>pushed a good chunk of the globe toward nuclear power</u>.
2. If the world is <u>on the cusp of such an era</u>, will it result in <u>weapons proliferation or accidents such as meltdowns?</u> Or will <u>a new way to harness energy emerge to compete with nuclear power?</u>
3. Nuclear energy advocates see the technology <u>as a clean way to wean the world from expensive and environmentally damaging fossil fuels.</u> But for critics, the thought of <u>a nuclearized world stirs controversy.</u>
4. Arab states could <u>learn the wrong lessons from Iran,</u> a nation that <u>thumbs its nose at the West</u> while it allegedly builds a nuclear weapons program, said Charles Ferguson, senior fellow at the Council on Foreign Relations.
5. <u>A turning point</u> for the Middle East could come when its <u>oil begins to dry up and the region starts clamoring for nuclear power.</u>
6. <u>To curtail moves from peaceful technology to weapons material production,</u> experts recognize <u>the need for strong regulatory bodies.</u> But some authoritarian governments may not <u>warm to the idea of answering to an independent government body,</u> Ferguson said.
7. But he does <u>expect increased civilian use of nuclear power</u> in a future with <u>a dwindling supply of affordable fossil fuels.</u>
8. European countries would also <u>fall into the mix</u>, at least until a better technology comes along.

9. "I expect ferment, crisis and then a single solution (will) emerge," he said.

E. Read the passages in this section and decide whether each of the following statements is true or false.

Passage One

  I am addicted to electricity. So are you. And so is your business. We live in an "always on" world—air conditioners, streetlights, TVs, PCs, cell phones, and more. And with forecasts that we'll need 40% more electricity by 2030, determining how we can realistically feed our energy addiction without ruining our environment is the critical challenge of the new century. Of course, we could buy energy-saving appliances or drive fuel-efficient cars. We can recycle cans, bottles, and newspapers. We can even plant carbon-absorbing trees. But, no matter how much we may wish they would, these acts by themselves won't satisfy our energy demands. To do that, we need a diverse energy mix that takes a practical, rather than emotional, approach.

  Enter nuclear energy. Nuclear alone won't get us to where we need to be, but we won't get there without it. Despite its controversial reputation, nuclear is efficient and reliable. It's also clean, emitting no greenhouse gases or regulated air pollutants while generating electricity. And with nuclear power, we get the chance to preserve the Earth's climate while at the same time meeting our future energy needs.

  The cost of failing to meet these needs will be steep. The global economy relies on world-class power grids to trade stocks, to communicate instantly, and to buy and sell around the clock. If anything points to the frustrating effect that a failed power grid can have on profits, it's the San Francisco power outage that took down Silicon Valley enterprises like Craigslist and Netflix (NFLX) in July. Although it only cost them two hours of online business, that minor power blip illustrates how a lack of electricity can render even a tech-savvy company impotent.

  Nuclear power also provides a valuable tool for businesses: cost stability. Unlike other power suppliers, nuclear plants buy their uranium at set prices three years in advance. And uranium prices comprise just 26% of production costs at nuclear plants; by comparison, coal accounts for 78% of costs at coal-fired plants. So despite big increases in uranium prices over the past three years, industry production costs have remained low, at less than 2 cents per kilowatt-hour (a quarter of those at gas-fired plants).

  Moreover, many of the management woes that gave the early nuclear business a black eye have finally been overcome. The Tennessee Valley Authority recently demonstrated the industry's ability to manage large capital projects by successfully refurbishing the Browns Ferry 1 reactor in Alabama and returning it to commercial operation. The five-year project was completed on time and very close to budget. Also, U.S.-designed reactors have been built in about four years in Asia, and new nuclear plants (Business-Week, 6/26/07) on the drawing board for installation here in America will be licensed by the Nuclear Regulatory Commission under a speedier process that should be far more efficient than the one in place when the 104 nuclear facilities operating today were licensed.

But this streamlined process will not compromise nuclear safety and security. The NRC holds nuclear reactors to the highest safety and security standards of any American industry. (The Bureau of Labor Statistics finds that accident rates at nuclear plants are lower than in the manufacturing, real estate, or finance industries.) A two-day national security simulation in Washington, D.C., in 2002—conducted by the Center for Strategic & International Studies—concluded nuclear plants "are probably our best defended targets". And because of their advanced design and sophisticated containment structures, U.S. nuclear plants emit a negligible amount of radiation. Even if you lived next door to a nuclear power plant, you would still be exposed to less radiation each year than you would receive in just one round-trip flight from New York to Los Angeles.

Here's the reality: The U.S. needs more energy, and we need to get it without further harming our environment. Everything is a trade-off. Nothing is free, and nuclear plants are not cheap to build (although costs should drop as we build more of them). But we have a choice to make: We can either continue the 30-year debate about whether we should embrace nuclear energy, or we can accept its practical advantages. Love it or not, expanding nuclear energy makes both environmental and business sense.

(http://www.businessweek.com/magazine/content/07_38/b4050098.htm)

_____ 1. Nuclear energy can cause air pollution.

_____ 2. A company may suffer greatly from power outrage.

_____ 3. Uranium takes up a great proportion of production costs at nuclear plants than coal does at coal-fired plants.

_____ 4. U.S. nuclear plants emit a tiny amount of radiation.

_____ 5. Take environment and business into account, the use of nuclear energy shouldn't be expanded.

Passage Two

The UK government has formally announced its long-awaited decision to support a new generation of nuclear power stations.

Keeping the country's electricity supply secure and meeting carbon dioxide emission targets were behind the government's approval for nuclear. The costs of constructing, operating, and decommissioning the plants would be borne by the private sector, explained John Hutton, head of the Department for business, enterprise and regulatory reform. "The evidence in support of new nuclear power stations is compelling," he told members of parliament on 10 January.

Nuclear plants could, in theory, be constructed in the UK whatever the government's view. But private investors would not risk their money without political support. The government's public approval now reassures investors that power plants will not be delayed by such obstacles as planning permission, explained Adrian Bull, UK stakeholder relations manager for Westinghouse, the US-based nuclear construction company.

Looming Threat

The UK's 19 nuclear power stations supply a fifth of the country's electricity, but all except one are due to close by 2023. Replacing them with new nuclear build would fill the electricity shortfall and limit greenhouse gas emissions-and the government has committed to a 60 per cent cut in carbon dioxide emissions by 2050. "If the UK is to meet its carbon reduction targets, a nuclear replacement programme is essential," said David White, energy spokesperson at the Institution of Chemical Engineers.

Despite Hutton's announcement, new nuclear plants are still a decade away in the UK. Power companies such as E.ON and Electricite de France have already expressed interest in building the plants, and British Energy will decide in the next few months which partners it prefers to help it replace reactors at existing atomic sites. Four designs, from Toshiba-Westinghouse, Areva, Atomic Energy of Canada Ltd (AECL), and General Electric, are being examined by the Health and Safety Executive, together with the Environment Agency. But it will take another four years before a design and site is selected, and a further five before a plant can operate.

Environmental groups said that nuclear plants would be built too late to have an effect on carbon emissions in the next decade, and that the government had ignored the views of the public. Last year, a public consultation on nuclear was condemned by a High Court judge as "inadequate" and "misleading", forcing a second round of consultation which finished in October 2007.

International Boost

The UK's approval could bolster the resolve of private investors in nuclear power in other countries. France and Finland are already building new nuclear power stations, and many nuclear designs have been submitted to the US Nuclear Regulatory Commission for safety approval. Investors' confidence in the economics of nuclear electricity generation has been boosted by the high price of oil, now over \$100 a barrel, and the hope that a global price might be set on carbon emissions.

Scientists, while welcoming the government's decision, also warned that plenty of detailed decisions remained, around such issues as radioactive waste disposal and skills shortages. "The UK must maintain a high level of science teaching and research," said RSC chief executive Richard Pike. "If we fail to provide sufficient numbers of qualified scientists, the country will risk losing its way in providing energy for the future."

(http://www.rsc.org/chemistryworld/News/2008/January/10010801.asp)

_____ 6. The UK government approved of nuclear station on condition that it should make the country's electricity secure and emit only a reasonable amount of carbon dioxide.

_____ 7. It was probably disapproval of the government that prevented the development of nuclear station in UK.

_____ 8. It will take eight years from the selection of a design and site to the operation of a plant.

_____ 9. The high price of oil is one reason why some investors prefer nuclear power.

_____ 10. UK has already had a perfect mastery of operational technique in the use of nuclear energy.

G. Translate the following passages into Chinese/English.

1. Currently 435 nuclear reactors operate around the world, with an electrical generating capacity of approximately 370 gigawatts (GW), providing about 17 percent of the world's electricity. Various analysts have optimistically foreseen a steep rise in those numbers. For instance, a 2003 interdisciplinary study by the Massachusetts Institute of Technology outlined a scenario of "low" nuclear growth that would still allow a tripling of nuclear generation by 2050. The contribution of the developing nations would soar to a third of the whole, from 10 to 307 GW. To reach that level, however, would demand about 8 percent annual growth sustained over 45 years.

2. 有关能量的一些事情很难理解。能量不断地从一种形式转变为另一种形式,就像一位化装艺术家一样。当你自认为了解它的时候,它突然变成了另一种完全不同的形式。但是有一点是肯定的:能量永远不会消失,同样,它也不会无端地产生。过去,人们认为能量和物质是两种完全不同的东西。现在我们知道,能量和物质是可以相互转换的。微量的物质可以转换为令人难以执行的巨大核能。太阳利用氢气制造核能,随着物质转化为能量,其质量日复一日在减小。

F. Cloze. Fill in each blank with one suitable word.

After 20 years of __1__, nuclear energy again finds favor in the eyes of many __2__ planners. In __3__ with electricity generated from coal or natural gas, nuclear power contributes __4__ to greenhouse gas emissions and could __5__ help in the effort to reduce global warming. The establishment of a tax on carbon __6__, which has been widely proposed as an __7__ to move away from fossil-fuel use, would make nuclear energy even more __8__. Such arguments may ultimately prove __9__ to industrial nations—but to __10__ that the developing nations will follow suit is to ignore some important realities.

1. A. stagnation   B. development   C. application   D. suspension
2. A. policy   B. environment   C. energy   D. electricity
3. A. contrast   B. comparison   C. line   D. harmony
4. A. a lot   B. a little   C. little   D. much
5. A. however   B. therefore   C. furthermore   D. nevertheless
6. A. uses   B. deposits   C. emissions   D. reduce
7. A. incentive   B. prevention   C. prohibition   D. promotion

8. A. environment-friendly   B. attractive   C. cost-effective   D. intriguing
9. A. propelling   B. compelling   C. repelling   D. dispelling
10. A. assume   B. resume   C. consume   D. desume

Text B

The Necessity of Nuclear Power

1. Nuclear energy has been a controversial topic ever since the first reactor powered four 200-watt light bulbs in the Idaho desert in 1951. Today, the United States is gearing up for the next generation of reactor designs, breathing new life into the decades-old debate. Here, Patrick Moore and Anna Aurilio present compelling arguments both for and against pursuing nuclear power as an answer to the country's energy problems.

Nuclear Energy Provides Practical Baseload Power
by PATRICK MOORE

2. When I helped found Greenpeace in the 1970s, my colleagues and I were firmly opposed to nuclear energy. But times have changed. I now realize nuclear energy is the only non-greenhouse gas-emitting power source that can effectively replace fossil fuels and satisfy growing demand for energy.

3. Nuclear power plants are a practical option for producing clean, cost-effective, reliable and safe baseload power.

4. Nuclear energy is affordable. The average cost of producing nuclear energy in the United States is less than two cents per kilowatt-hour, comparable with coal and hydroelectric.

5. Nuclear energy is safe. In 1979, a partial reactor core meltdown at Three Mile Island frightened the country. At the time, no one noticed Three Mile Island was a success story; the concrete containment structure prevented radiation from escaping into the environment. There was no injury or death among the public or nuclear workers. This was the only serious accident in the history of nuclear energy generation in the United States. Today, 103 nuclear reactors quietly deliver 20 percent of America's electricity.

6. Spent nuclear fuel is not waste. Recycling spent fuel, which still contains 95 percent of its original energy, will greatly reduce the need for treatment and disposal.

7. Nuclear power plants are not vulnerable to terrorist attack. The five-feet-thick reinforced concrete containment vessel protects contents from the outside as well as the inside. Even if a jumbo jet did crash into a reactor and breach the containment, the reactor would not explode.

8. Nuclear weapons are no longer inextricably linked to nuclear power plants. Centrifuge technology now allows nations to produce weapons-grade plutonium without first constructing a nuclear reactor. Iran's

nuclear weapons threat, for instance, is completely distinct from peaceful nuclear energy generation, as they do not yet possess a nuclear reactor.

9. New technologies, such as the reprocessing system recently introduced in Japan (in which the plutonium is never separated from the uranium) can make it much more difficult to manufacture weapons using civilian materials.

10. Finally, excess heat from nuclear reactors offers a practical path to the "hydrogen economy", and can address the increasing shortage of fresh water through desalinization.

11. A combination of nuclear energy, wind, geothermal and hydro is the most environmentally-friendly way to meet the world's increasing energy needs. Nuclear power plants can play a key role in producing safe, clean, reliable baseload electricity.

12. An advisor to government and industry, Dr. Patrick Moore is a co-founder and former leader of Greenpeace, and chair and chief scientist of Greenspirit Strategies Ltd. in Vancouver, Canada. He and former Environmental Protection Agency administrator Christine Todd Whitman are co-chairs of the Clean and Safe Energy Coalition, which supports increased use of nuclear energy.

Nuclear Energy is Simply Not Necessary
by ANNA AURILIO

13. Nuclear energy is too expensive, too dangerous, and too polluting. And despite claims from the nuclear industry, it's simply not necessary either for our future electricity needs or to meet the very real challenge of global warming. Worldwide, renewable alternatives such as wind, solar and geothermal power, along with small decentralized heat and power cogeneration plants, already produced 92 per cent as much electricity as nuclear power did in 2004—and those sources are growing almost six times faster. A recent study prepared by Synapse Energy Economics found that by using clean energy technologies in the next twenty years, the U.S. could cut our reliance on nuclear in half, reduce projected carbon dioxide emissions from electricity by 47% and save consumers $36 billion annually.

14. After 50 years and more than $150 billion dollars in subsidies, the nuclear industry is still unable to build a plant on its own. With the new incentives in the 2005 Energy Policy Act, taxpayers would be covering 60 to 90 per cent of the generation cost of electricity from a new nuclear plant. What do we get for our money?

15. In a post-9/11 world, nuclear facilities will always be a tempting target for terrorists, and government studies have highlighted the weaknesses in our current safeguards.

16. Even without attackers, the danger of an accident is ever-present. The Davis-Besse plant in Ohio narrowly avoided a disaster in 2002 when inspectors found a hole that had corroded almost all the way through a pressure vessel, leaving just 3/16 of an inch of steel preventing the release of radioactive steam. Instead of clamping down, the Nuclear Regulatory Commission seems more intent on loosening

safety rules to help aging plants keep operating for longer.

17. And when plants are operating perfectly, they're still producing high-level radioactive waste. No country in the world has solved the problem of how to dispose of it, and even the most optimistic advanced reactor designs will continue adding to the lethal mountain of waste already produced.

18. The argument that nuclear energy is our best bet to reduce global warming emissions only makes sense if you pretend that coal is the only other option. That's a false choice, and it ignores the rapidly developing range of energy efficiency and clean, renewable energy sources. Whatever challenges still face technologies like solar and wind power, they pale compared to the fundamental security and environmental problems that won't be fixed by any new reactor design. For 30 years, no one has ordered or built a new nuclear plant, for very good economic reasons. Now Congress and the nuclear industry are trying to distort the market with new subsidies. They're pushing a technology with serious health, safety and economic risks, and in doing so diverting research dollars away from better alternatives.

19. Anna Aurilio is the Legislative Director for U.S. PIRG responsible for policy development, research and advocacy on energy issues and anti-environmental subsidies. She has testified numerous times before House and Senate Science, Energy and Appropriations committees. Ms. Aurilio received a bachelor's degree in Physics from the University of Massachusetts at Amherst in 1986 and a Master's degree in Environmental Engineering from the Massachusetts Institute of Technology in 1992. Prior to receiving her Master's degree, Ms. Aurilio was a Staff Scientist with the National Environmental Law Center, and the PIRGs' National Litigation Project for three years.

(http://www.popularmechanics.com/science/earth/3900086.html)

Glossary

compel [kəm'pel] force somebody to do something *v*. 强迫

baseload ['beisləud] the minimum amount of power that a utility or distribution company must make available to its customers, or the amount of power required to meet minimum demands based on reasonable expectations of customer requirements *n*. 基底负载,基极负载

jumbo ['dʒʌmbəu] of great mass; huge and bulky *adj*. 巨大的,大型的

breach [bri:tʃ] make an opening or gap in *v*. 在……上打开缺口

centrifuge ['sentrifju:dʒ] separating substances by whirling them *n*. 离心分离

plutonium [plu:'təuniəm] a solid silvery grey radioactive transuranic element whose atoms can be split when bombarded with neutrons; found in minute quantities in uranium ores but is usually synthesized in nuclear reactors; 13 isotopes are known with the most important being plutonium 239 *n*. 钚(放射性元素)

desalinization [di:ˌsælini'zeiʃən] the removal of salt (especially from sea water) *n*. 脱盐作用

geothermal [ˌdʒi(:)əu'θəməl] of or relating to the heat in the interior of the earth *adj.* 地热的

decentralize [di:'sentrəlaiz] make less central *v.* 分散

cogeneration [kəuˌdʒenə'reiʃən] the use of a heat engine or a power station to simultaneously generate both electricity and useful heat *n.* 热电联供

subsidy ['sʌbsidi] a grant paid by a government to an enterprise that benefits the public *n.* 补助金，津贴

corrode [kə'rəud] cause to deteriorate due to the action of water, air, or an acid *v.* 腐蚀

Exercises

A. Fill in each blank with one of the given words in its correct form.

environmentally-friendly	jumbo	decentralize	vessel	
affordable	geothermal	subsidy	corrode	lethal	compel

1. For example, laws in the US already _____ TV adverts to instruct patients experiencing negative side effects to report their symptoms to the FDA.
2. The catalogue of emissions that the researchers have compiled are taken from their own American context but the concept and framework is applicable universally-looking at the full range of vehicles, from hatchbacks and pick-ups to light and heavy railways, small aircrafts and _____ jets.
3. _____ energy is increasingly contributing to the power supply world wide.
4. As a condition of receiving loans from the World Bank and International Monetary Fund, Mexico had to reduce its public expenditure, including spending on healthcare services, and _____ the Ministry of Health in a manner that according to the authors did not devolve decision-making authority adequately.
5. The _____, called the Affordable Medicines Facilitymalaria (AMFm), will be rolled out in 2009 and is designed to address concerns of poor access to artemisinin combination therapies (ACTs) for malaria, and fears about growing resistance to the drugs.
6. Released as gases, these substances can _____ copper pipes, wiring, and air conditioning coils, the article notes.
7. The vaccines provided complete protection against the _____ challenge of the homologous and heterologous H5N1 avian influenza A virus with no evidence of morbidity, mortality, or shedding of the challenge virus.
8. Researchers at the University of Bath and the food & drinks research centre at Campden BRI are leading a project to create a new high speed _____ packaging process that will use recycled materials and reduce the amount of plastic used, cutting the waste that goes into landfill.
9. Researchers at The Medical College of Wisconsin in Milwaukee have linked higher levels of the hor-

mone aldosterone to high blood pressure and blood _____ disease in African Americans.

10. A new generation of simple, _____ medical diagnostic tests is heading toward the developing world where they may protect impoverished people from AIDS, tuberculosis, malaria and other infectious diseases.

B. Skim the text and then answer the following questions.

1. What is the major difference between the views of Patrick Moore and Anna Aurilio?
2. How do you understand "nuclear energy provides practical baseload power"?
3. What is the most environmentally-friendly way to meet the world's increasing energy needs?
4. What are the potential dangers of the use of nuclear energy?
5. According to Anna Aurilio, is nuclear energy our best bet to reduce global warming emissions? Why or why not?

C. Read the text and choose the correct answer to each of the following questions.

1. According to Patrick, nuclear energy _____.
   A. will work together with fossil fuels to provide mankind with energy
   B. can produce gases that cause global warming
   C. is able to provide the world with enough energy, though its need is ever-increasing
   D. is safe to use

2. The accident taking place at Three Mile Island _____.
   A. resulted in radiation pollution
   B. was the only serious accident in the history of nuclear energy generation
   C. proves that concrete containment structure can prevent radiation from escaping into the environment
   D. resulted from the meltdown of a major reactor core

3. Which of the following is not the negative aspect of nuclear power mentioned by Anna Aurilio? _____.
   A. It causes nuclear weapon threats
   B. Radioactive materials may be released by accident
   C. It may court terrorist attack
   D. It brings about air pollution

4. According to Anna, which of the following statements is not true? _____.
   A. A large amount of money to cover the generation cost of electricity of a nuclear plant would come from the tax
   B. The current ability of safeguards in the country cannot prevent nuclear facilities from outside danger
   C. Nuclear Regulatory Commission helps aging plants with their maintenance to make their work longer

D. When plants are operating perfectly, they're still producing high-level radioactive waste
5. The phrase "clamp down" in "Instead of clamping down, the Nuclear Regulatory Commission seems more intent on loosening safety rules to help aging plants keep operating for longer(paragraph 18)" shares similar meaning with the expression _____.
   A. crack down   B. crush down   C. clip down   D. crumble down

D. Explain the underlined parts.

1. Today, the United States is <u>gearing up for the next generation of reactor designs, breathing new life into the decades-old debate</u>.
2. Nuclear power plants are <u>not vulnerable to terrorist attack</u>.
3. Finally, excess heat from nuclear reactors <u>offers a practical path to the</u> "hydrogen economy", and can <u>address the increasing shortage of fresh water through desalinization</u>.
4. With <u>the new incentives</u> in the 2005 Energy Policy Act, taxpayers <u>would be covering 60 to 90 per cent of the generation cost</u> of electricity from a new nuclear plant.
5. Whatever challenges still face technologies like solar and wind power, <u>they pale compared to the fundamental security and environmental problems</u> that won't <u>be fixed</u> by any new reactor design.

Unit 13 Material Science

Text A

The Kilogram Isn't What It Used to Be — It's Lighter

1. What I love best about the kilogram is its tangibility, its solid, sculpted form of shiny platinum and iridium. I'm referring to not just any kilogram but the quintessential one that resides here—the actual International Prototype Kilogram, or IPK, created in 1879 as the official standard of mass. It's a smooth cylinder of alloy, only an inch and a half high and an inch and a half in diameter. Though petite, the IPK is necessarily dense; it weighs 2.204 6 pounds. If you went to pick it up, you might think someone had cemented it to the tabletop for a prank. Even if you knew what to expect, its compact heft would still boggle your senses.

2. Of course, they won't let you pick it up. They won't even let you anywhere near it. If you touched it—if you so much as breathed on it—you would change its mass, and then where would we be? That's why the IPK leads such a sheltered life. It is kept under a triple bell jar inside a temperature- and humidity-controlled vault in a secure room within the Parc de Saint-Cloud enclave of the International Bureau of Weights and Measures, or BIPM (Bureau International des Poids et Mesures). Thus protected, it reigns over a world's worth of measurement. Every hill of beans, every lump of coal, every milligram of medication—in short, every quantity of any substance that can be weighed—must be gauged against this object.

3. The IPK is, in and of itself, the International System of Units' definition of mass. Through a complex dissemination protocol, the essence of the kilogram is transferred from the IPK to its counterparts at standards laboratories around the world, and from there to centers of industry and scientific research, ending up in grocery stores, post offices, and bathrooms everywhere.

4. Although I have come to pay my respects to the IPK, I am denied even a glimpse of the thing. Nor can I see one of its six official copies, for these reside alongside the prototype in guarded seclusion. I must content myself with replicas —with the working standards that fill the ultraclean laboratory of Richard Davis, an American physicist in Paris who for the past 15 years has headed the Mass Section at the BIPM.

5. Gloved for work, Davis wears a lab coat over his street clothes, blue paper bootees over his shoes, and a net over his hair. Around him kilogram weights of various shapes and materials sit on colored plates under glass bell jars, like an assortment of fine cheeses. They have been delivered here from other countries to be reckoned in comparison with the IPK.

6. "That one belongs to Ireland," Davis says, indicating a stainless-steel kilogram on a red dish. Member states—signatories to the Meter Convention—pay dues to the BIPM that cover the cost of periodic checks on their national reference standards.

7. It takes a minimum of four days to calibrate a single kilogram according to the BIPM's cautious regimen of repeated comparison weighings. Visiting kilograms could theoretically go home after a week, but they typically stay in the lab for months, allowing the time it takes them to become thermally stable in their new surroundings, undergo cleaning by the BIPM method, and prove themselves, through repeated trials, to be worthy ambassadors of mass. Given the uncertainty, however minuscule, in every measurement, such repetitions are essential before these national standards can leave with a calibration certificate stating how they compare with the IPK, along with a precise correction factor.

8. En route to or from Paris, the visiting kilograms disdain ordinary transport. Zeina Jabbour, group leader of Mass & Force at the National Institute of Standards and Technology in Gaithersburg, Maryland, recently brought two of the four U.S. kilograms here for calibration. She carried one herself in a specially designed case inside a padded camera bag that was all but handcuffed to her wrist, and she entrusted the other to a colleague who flew on a different plane. ("That way, if something happened to one of us.") Soon after her flight touched down at Charles de Gaulle, she grabbed a taxi straight to the BIPM on the other side of the city for a handover directly to Davis.

9. Before picking up a kilogram with a pair of widemouthed forceps called lifters, Davis flicks off suspected specks of dust with a fine-tipped brush. ("My wife paints.") He has modified the artist's brush for his purposes by degreasing its fibers and covering its metal ferrule with plastic, "so if you accidentally hit the kilogram, you won't scratch it." On a balance precise to 10 decimal places, a scratch counts.

10. Davis tests the Irish kilogram in a sealed chamber against three BIPM working standards that are also made of stainless steel. He doesn't weigh it against the platinum-iridium standard, since stainless weights are only one-third as dense, and therefore three times as large, displacing a much greater quantity of air. "You'd have to make an air buoyancy correction that would amount to almost a tenth of a gram," he explains. "That is huge."

11. Although Davis serves as the IPK's official guardian, even he rarely sees the original prototype, which is too precious and vulnerable to damage to remain in constant use. Over the course of its century-plus lifetime, the IPK has emerged only three times to serve "campaigns" of active duty, most recently in

1988 ~ 1992, when it participated in a formal verification of all kilogram prototypes belonging to the 51 Meter Convention member states. On that occasion, however, the IPK itself was found wanting. Despite all the protective protocols and delicate procedures, it had mysteriously changed. No one can say whether the IPK has lost weight (perhaps by the gradual escape of gases trapped inside it from the start) or if most of the prototypes have gained (possibly by accumulating atmospheric contaminants). The difference is approximately 30 micrograms —30 billionths of a kilogram—in a hundred years. (Imagine 30 cents out of a $10 million stack of pennies.)

12. This alarming show of instability is driving global efforts to redefine the kilogram, so that mass need not depend on the safety or stability of some manufactured item stored in a safe. In fact, more than mass hangs in the balance, for the kilogram is tied to three other base units of the International System of Units (SI), namely the ampere, the mole, and the candela. Several more quantities—including density, force, and pressure—are in turn derived from the kilogram.

13. Other 19th-century artifacts of measurement have long since been retired in favor of fundamental constants of nature. In 1983, for example, the platinum-iridium bar that described the length of the meter yielded to a new benchmark: A meter is now defined as the distance light travels in a vacuum in 1/299,792,458 second (a second being the time it takes an atom of cesium-133 to vacillate 9,192,631,770 times between the two hyperfine levels of its ground state). These figures fail to give the average person any real feel for the quantities in question, but to a metrologist —one who specializes in the science of measurement—such equivalences rooted in physics have the advantage of permanence and reproducibility.

14. One invariant vying to replace the IPK is Planck's constant, which could be determined via an experimental device called a watt balance. Alternatively, researchers may successfully express mass in terms of Avogadro's number (which is tied to the unchanging mass of individual atoms), provided they can count the atoms in a crystal of silicon-28.

15. But neither of these complex, costly endeavors is likely to yield a new standard in time for the next meeting of the General Conference of Weights and Measures, scheduled for 2011. For now, the International Prototype Kilogram stands firm on metrology's last frontier.

(http://discovermagazine.com/2009/mar/08-kilogram-isn.t-what-it-used-to-be-its-lighter)

Glossary

tangibility [ˌtændʒiˈbiliti] the quality of being perceivable by touch *n*. 确实性，确切性，真实性

platinum [ˈplætinəm] a heavy precious metallic element; grey-white and resistant to corroding; occurs in some nickel and copper ores and is also found native in some deposits *n*. 白金，铂

iridium [iˈridiəm] a heavy brittle metallic element of the platinum group; used in alloys; occurs in natural alloys with platinum or osmium *n*. 铱

quintessential [ˌkwintisenˈtʃəl] representing the perfect example of a class or quality *adj*. 精粹的，精髓的，典型的

prototype [ˈprəutətaip] a standard or typical example *n*. 原型

cylinder [ˈsilində] a solid bounded by a cylindrical surface and two parallel planes (the bases) *n*. 圆柱体

petite [pəˈtit] very small *adj*. 小的

prank [præŋk] a ludicrous or grotesque act done for fun and amusement *n*. 开玩笑，恶作剧

heft [heft] the property of being large in mass *n*. 重量，分量

boggle [ˈbɔgl] overcome with amazement *v*. 使因吃惊而不知所措

dissemination [diˌsemiˈneiʃən] the opening of a subject to widespread discussion and debate *n*. 传播，宣传

protocol [ˈprɔtəkɔl] forms of ceremony and etiquette observed by diplomats and heads of state *n*. 外交礼仪

seclusion [siˈkluːʒən] the quality of being secluded from the presence or view of others *n*. 隔离

replica [ˈreplikə, riˈpliːkə] copy that is not the original; something that has been copied *n*. 复制品

bootee [ˈbuːti] a slipper that is soft and wool *n*. 毛线鞋

assortment [əˈsɔːtmənt] a collection containing a variety of sorts of things *n*. 分类，各色俱备之物

signatory [ˈsignətəri] someone who signs and is bound by a document *n*. 签署者，签约国

calibrate [ˈkælibreit] mark (the scale of a measuring instrument) so that it can be read in the desired units *v*. 查看刻度，校正刻度

regimen [ˈredʒimen] any set of rules about food and exercise that someone follows, especially in order to improve their health *n*. 养生法，生活规则

minuscule [miˈnʌskjuːl] very small *adj*. 极小的

en route [ɔnˈruːt] on a route to some place *adv*. 在途中

disdain [disˈdein] reject with contempt *v*. 蔑视

handcuff [ˈhændkʌf] confine or restrain with or as if with manacles or handcuffs *v*. 上手拷

forceps [ˈfɔːseps] a metal instrument with two handles used in medical operations for picking up, pulling and holding things *n*. 钳状骨针

speck [spek] a very small spot *n*. 斑点，灰尘，污点

degrease [diːˈgriːz] remove grease or oil from *v*. 脱脂，清除油渍

ferrule [ˈferuːl] a metal cap or band placed on a wooden pole to prevent splitting *n*. (棍棒顶端等的)金属箍，金属环，套圈

stack [stæk] an orderly pile *n*. 堆

ampere ['æmpeə] a former unit of electric current n. 安培

mole [məul] the molecular weight of a substance expressed in grams n. 摩尔,克分子量

candela [kæn'di:lə] the basic unit of luminous intensity adopted under the Systeme International d'-Unites; equal to 1/60 of the luminous intensity per square centimeter of a black body radiating at the temperature of 2,046 degrees Kelvin n. 烛光(发光强度单位)

benchmark ['bentʃmɑ:k] a standard by which something can be measured or judged n. 基准点,参照点

cesium ['si:zjəm] a soft silver-white ductile metallic element (liquid at normal temperatures); the most electropositive and alkaline metal n. [化]铯

vacillate ['væsileit] move or sway in a rising and falling or wavelike pattern v. 游移不定,摇摆

hyperfine ['haipə:fain] extremely fine or thin, as in a spectral line split into two or more components adj. 超精细的

vie [vai] compete for something; engage in a contest; measure oneself against others v. 竞争

Exercises

A. Fill in each blank with one of the given words in its correct form.

| benchmark | en route | quintessential | tangible | speck |
| boggle | disdain | signatory | dissemination | vie |

1. New research by the Carbon Disclosure Project (CDP) with responses from 80 of CDP's _____ investors across the globe revealed that three-quarters factor climate change information into their investment decisions and asset allocations.

2. Mental patients are either violently dangerous or docile and incompetent. We fear the first and _____ the latter.

3. She found that the subjects who received a lot of traffic information _____ opted more often for a route that was unreliable but fast.

4. In the case of the Crab Nebula pulsar, located in the constellation Taurus, some 6,300 light years from Earth, the numbers _____ the mind: Plasma clouds in the pulsar's atmosphere send out the radio emission blasts in times as short as four-tenths of a nanosecond.

5. Then, through the course of his editorial, Weissmann explains how and why the dietary supplement industry is at odds with the FDA's origins and mission, and that these supplements represent little more than unregulated drugs that have _____ personal and professional consequences that go well beyond anything described on their labels.

6. Yet the essential freedoms users have on shared networks such as the Internet-described famously by political scientist Dana Ward as the "_____ example of a large-scale anarchist organisation"

makes them difficult to manage efficiently.
7. As a result there is now, for the first time, an objective _____ for measuring a surgeon's basic skills in the field of minimally invasive surgery.
8. Dr. Amanda Harvey and colleagues at Brunel University have demonstrated that the protein Brk plays a role in breast cancer progression and _____.
9. Conversely, players who are near or slightly below the top 30 on the money list must work extremely hard at the end of the season as they _____ for a spot in the Tour Championship.
10. This device, the size of a _____ of dust, might enable measurements of the untwisting of DNA and have applications in spintronics, fundamental physics, chemistry and biology.

B. Skim the text and then answer the following questions.
1. Please list some properties of the IPK.
2. Why does a single kilogram typically stay in the lab for months before going home?
3. What is the reason why other objects used for measurement in the 19th century have been out of use?
4. What is likely to compete with IPK to become a new standard?
5. According to the text, how is a meter and a second determined?

C. Read the text and choose the correct answer to each of the following questions.
1. The IPK _____.
   A. is kept in a museum
   B. can be affected by changed in humidity
   C. is used to measure the weight of things
   D. is on display
2. In his visit, the author was _____ the IPK.
   A. not allowed to have a look at
   B. allowed to see the official copies of
   C. allowed to see
   D. allowed to see either the official copies or
3. Davis modified the artist's brush and covered its metal ferrule with plastic _____.
   A. because his wife liked painting
   B. to flick off suspected specks of dust more efficiently
   C. in case possible scratches should make the result of calibration different
   D. as a decoration
4. Which of the following statements is incorrect on Davis' test of the Irish kilogram? _____
   A. He weighed it against three BIPM standards and the platinum-iridium standard
   B. The stainless standard has a density which is higher than that of the platinum-iridium one

C. Even air buoyancy would change the result of the test

D. The test was conducted in a sealed chamber

5. The IPK has _____.

   A. been in existence for almost 100 years

   B. been put into practical use for three times

   C. gained a tiny amount of weight by accumulating atmospheric contaminants

   D. changed for about 300 micrograms in a hundred years

D. Explain the underlined parts.

1. What I love best about the kilogram is <u>its tangibility, its solid, sculpted form</u> of shiny platinum and iridium.

2. If you touched it—if you so much as breathed on it—you would change its mass, and then <u>where would we be</u>? That's why the IPK <u>leads such a sheltered life</u>.

3. Although I have come to <u>pay my respects to the IPK, I am denied even a glimpse of the thing</u>. Nor can I see one of its six official copies, <u>for these reside alongside the prototype in guarded seclusion</u>.

4. Member states—<u>signatories to the Meter Convention—pay dues to the BIPM that cover the cost of periodic checks on their national reference standards</u>.

5. <u>Visiting kilograms</u> could theoretically go home after a week, but they typically stay in the lab for months, <u>allowing the time it takes them to become thermally stable in their new surroundings</u>, undergo cleaning by the BIPM method, and prove themselves, through repeated trials, to <u>be worthy ambassadors of mass</u>.

6. She carried one herself in a specially designed case inside a padded camera bag that was <u>all but handcuffed to her wrist, and she entrusted the other to a colleague</u> who flew on a different plane. ("That way, if something happened to one of us.")

7. Although Davis serves as the IPK's official guardian, even he <u>rarely sees the original prototype</u>, which is <u>too precious and vulnerable to damage to remain in constant use</u>.

8. Other 19th-century artifacts of measurement <u>have long since been retired in favor of fundamental constants of nature</u>.

9. These figures fail to give the average person <u>any real feel for the quantities in question</u>, but to a metrologist —one who specializes in the science of measurement—<u>such equivalences rooted in physics have the advantage of permanence and reproducibility</u>.

E. Read the passages in this section and decide whether each of the following statements is true or false.

Passage One

Engineers one day may not have to guess when a bridge is about to break. New materials that flush red in response to damage may provide a visible warning sign of trouble to come, scientists report in the May 7 Nature.

"I think it could be a milestone," says Christoph Weder, a polymer chemist at Case Western Reserve University in Cleveland and at the University of Fribourg in Switzerland, who wrote a commentary in the same issue of Nature.

The materials' chameleon-like abilities are thanks to a small four-ringed molecule called a mechanophore. When the weakest bond in the mechanophore breaks, the molecule creates a dog-bone shape, and the reaction causes the molecule to redden.

"It's a really simple detection method," says study coauthor Nancy Sottos, a materials scientist at the Beckman Institute for Advanced Science and Technology at the University of Illinois at Urbana-Champaign. "We're opening up this one bond, and it changes color."

But the small color-changing molecule isn't so useful on its own, she says. "It's hard to apply force to something so small, so we hooked it into the backbone of a long polymer. That's the trick."

Sottos and her colleagues spiked two kinds of polymers — a stretchy, soft one and a hard, glassy one — with the molecule. The team tested the first material, which stretched about as much as a Stretch Armstrong doll, by pulling on it until it broke. The bright red color appeared a few seconds before the material snapped, suggesting the molecules acted as an early warning sign that the material had incurred damage. In another test, the researchers mimicked repetitive stress by repeatedly stretching and relaxing the soft polymer. "After a few cycles of that, we got this brilliant color change in the material, without it breaking," says Sottos.

Hard, glasslike beads of a second polymer also changed color when the beads were squeezed, indicating that the color change was indeed due to mechanical forces.

Other researchers have done neat tricks with color-changing molecules but never before in a solid, Weder says. "The question is can you do this in a nice solid material? And this is what they have done."

Sottos says the material could eventually be used to make solid objects including rollerblade wheels, thin films such as coats of paint, or even thin fibers that could turn red when tiny deformations develop.

The team is also working on another property of mechanophores: self-healing. Shining bright light on the molecule triggers the broken bond to re-form, at which point the red warning disappears.

But this ability to heal introduces a new problem: If light can trigger the molecule to lose its red color, then color won't be a reliable indicator of damage to the material as a whole, Weder says.

"This is really a proof-of-concept paper," he says. "Before the material can be used as a mechanical force sensor, there are practical issues that need to be addressed," including how light may interfere with the desired signal and how the color-change might be made permanent.

(http://www.sciencenews.org/view/generic/id/43524/title/Molecule_turns_red_at_breaking

_ point _)

_____ 1. When the material is made into a dog-bone shape, the molecule will redden.

_____ 2. The color-changing molecule isn't so useful on its own because it is too small to allow force being applied to it

_____ 3. Shining bright light on the molecule helps it to turn red.

_____ 4. The material mentioned above is used as a mechanical force sensor.

_____ 5. There are still some problems unsolved concerning the material.

Passage Two

Finding a way to reduce the temperature requirements for solid oxide fuel cells, which now require temperatures of 800 to 1,000 degrees Celsius to use fuel other than pure hydrogen, is a key step toward widespread adoption of fuel cells.

Solid oxide is one of five basic types of fuel cells, and is a promising type for municipal, home and mobile electricity generators.

Researchers from the California Institute of Technology have devised a cathode that allows solid oxide fuel cells to operate at 500 to 700 degrees Celsius. This temperature range is high enough to support a variety of fuels, but low enough that the fuel cell components need not be made from costly high-temperature materials, said Sossina Haile, an associate professor of materials science and chemical engineering at the California Institute of Technology.

The method promises to lower the cost of fuel cells, which could spur broader adoption of the technology.

Fuel cells extract chemical energy from fuel rather than burning it like combustion engines. Like batteries, fuel cells contain a pair of electrodes, and supply a flow of electricity by pushing electrons from the anode to the cathode. This happens when oxygen reacts with electrons at the cathode to form oxygen ions, which then migrate through the electrolyte to the anode where they react with fuel to produce water and release electrons. Some fuels also produce carbon dioxide at this step.

The researchers' fuel cell looks much like existing cells, said Haile. "It's like developing a recipe for a cake that bakes at 150 degrees Fahrenheit rather than 325 degrees Fahrenheit," she said. "The oven still looks pretty much the same, but it's a lot cheaper because it doesn't have to withstand such high temperatures."

Until the researchers' new cathode, all known cathode materials have been effective only at temperatures near 1,000 degrees Celsius at catalyzing, or speeding up the reaction of the oxygen gas molecule with electrons to form negatively-charged oxygen ions, said Haile.

Haile's research colleague Zongping Shao developed the material, made from barium, strontium, cobalt, iron and oxygen, and dubbed BSCF, for a different application—oxygen purification membranes.

It was natural that the researchers test the material as a fuel cell cathode because some of the properties that make the material useful as an oxygen purification membrane also tend to make it good as a fuel cell cathode, said Haile.

But the chemical formula was different enough from typical fuel cell cathodes that the rest of the fuel cell community was not looking in this direction, said Haile. Fuel cell cathodes traditionally use an alkaline-earth-based oxide. The researchers' material instead contains an oxide based on rare-earth metals. Alkaline-earth and rare-earth elements are types of metals than readily react with oxygen. "It was a classic situation of taking results from one field and applying them to another that lead to the breakthrough," she said.

In addition to catalyzing the oxygen ion reaction at lower temperatures, the cathode is also particularly efficient at conducting oxygen ions, said Haile. Conventional solid oxide fuel cell cathodes are made from two different types of materials—one that catalyzes the oxygen reduction reaction, and a second that conducts oxygen ions well to provide an efficient pathway for oxygen ions to travel to the electrolyte.

The new material does both, said Haile. "It turns out that BSCF not only has excellent catalytic activity, it also has excellent oxygen ion conductivity, better than any material we could add as a second component."

"It's hard to believe that a significantly better cathode has been overlooked because there are so many studies on [similar materials], but if this is true this cathode material could represent quite a breakthrough for the low temperature solid-oxide fuel cells," said James Ralph, and assistant materials scientist at Argonne National Laboratory.

(http://www.trnmag.com/Stories/2004/102004/Cooler_material_boosts_fuel_cells_102004.html)

_____ 6. A cathode is devised to allow solid oxide fuel cells to operate at 800 to 1,000 degrees Celsius.

_____ 7. Fuel cells extract chemical energy by burning it like combustion engines.

_____ 8. The new cathode mentioned above has been effective only at temperatures near 1,000 degrees Celsius at catalyzing, or speeding up the reaction of the oxygen gas molecule with electrons to form negatively-charged oxygen ions.

_____ 9. The new cathode can conduct oxygen ions efficiently and has excellent catalytic activity.

_____ 10. So many studies on similar materials have been overlooked.

F. Cloze. Fill in each blank with one suitable word.

Diamond is the __1__ material known to man. But with most __2__ (including drilling) diamonds must be __3__ after each use, which is expensive. Scientists at UCLA have created a lower-cost material that __4__ diamond's strength. This ultra-hard material, called rhenim diboride, is made from a __5__ of the relatively soft metal osmium with rhenium, a fairly dense, soft metal that is next to osmium on the __6__ table. Richard B. Kaner, a UCLA professor of inorganic chemistry and materials science and engineering, says his team made the material "ultra-__7__" (resistant to shape deformation—a necessary condition for hardness) by finding metals that are already incompressible and working to __8__ them. The scientists have tested the material's properties by heating it in a furnace to achieve a powder and bonding it through arc melting. The material could be __9__ for oil drills, scratch-resistant coatings for precision __10__ or computer cases, and watch faces.

1. A. most expensive   B. rarest   C. hardest   D. strongest
2. A. applications   B. functions   C. features   D. machining
3. A. cleaned   B. tested   C. replaced   D. removed
4. A. rivals   B. beats   C. offset   D. challenge
5. A. cooperation   B. association   C. collaboration   D. combination
6. A. periodic   B. periodical   C. cyclic   D. cyclical
7. A. dense   B. incompressible   C. soft   D. moldable
8. A. melt   B. compress   C. harden   D. heat
9. A. applied   B. equipped   C. installed   D. used
10. A. devices   B. gauges   C. apparatuses   D. instruments

G. Translate the following passages into Chinese/English.

1. The research for alternative transportation fuels has become a major national challenge. One substitute fuel that could help reduce the nation's dependence on petroleum is anhydrous ammonia, which is widely used as a fertilizer. Due to its hydrogen content, anhydrous ammonia can be used in internal combustion engines with minor modifications, can be used in direct ammonia fuel cells, and also provides hydrogen feed stock for standard hydrogen fuel cells. The use of ammonia as transportation fuel became cost effective once gasoline broke the $3-barrier. The United States consumes approximately 25 million barrels of petroleum daily.

2. 严格地说，虽然氨没有毒性，但最令人担心的是它的安全性和吸入物的危险性。和空气混和时，与汽油(gasoline)和乙醇(ethanol)相比，氨的着火能量高、燃点高，而爆炸范围窄。拿一个破损的氨油箱来说，它就不像破损的汽油或乙醇油箱那样容易爆炸和着火。氨的最佳特点都是与氢共有的。它既可以用于内燃机中也可以用于燃料电池里，燃烧时不产生温室气体，还可以从多种矿物和可再生资源中生产出来。

Text B

How to Build an Invisibility Cloak

1. Rare is the moment when Harry Potter fans, Star Trek aficionados, H. G. Wells enthusiasts, and theoretical physicists unite in a moment of ecstasy. But that instant came last May with a flurry of dramatic headlines. "Scientists may be able to make magic like Harry Potter," wrote the Associated Press. "Here's how to make an invisibility cloak," shouted MSNBC. "Cast no shadows," said The Economist. For Duke University physicist David Smith, though, the oddest moment was seeing his work flashed on the CNN crawl the same day it appeared in Science Express, the online edition of the journal Science. "It was surreal," he says. "The story was generating a huge splash before the scientific community had a chance to take a critical look."

2. Smith hardly fits the profile of a media celebrity: soft-spoken, patient, and bespectacled, he has the pale-skinned hue of a man who has perhaps spent too much time in a windowless lab fiddling with wires. All at once, however, he and his postdoc Dave Schurig became the targets of intense public interest. Reporters called from around the world, crackpots sent long letters hand-scrawled with dubious hypotheses, and a Korean television crew flew in to the leafy Duke campus, posing Schurig, graduate student Jonah Gollub, and technician Bryan Justice in lab coats in front of their intricate machinery. "They wouldn't film until we put the white coats on. We didn't even have any—we had to borrow them," recalls Schurig.

3. All this fuss over a theory not only unproved but so dense with equations it is all but incomprehensible to the average person. What sparked such fascination was the mind-bending notion itself: Smith, Schurig, and their coauthor John Pendry of Imperial College London proposed that by using a novel class of composite materials, they could manipulate light so as to render an object invisible to the eye. Suddenly, Harry Potter's invisibility cloak, Star Trek's Romulan ship-concealing devices, and H. G. Wells's bandaged Invisible Man seemed the stuff of testable science. In a more practical vein, the finding could have profound implications for military technology, wireless communication, and even interplanetary exploration.

4. In September, the journal Science accepted a paper from Smith and Schurig that proved that their method was more than just a thrilling hypothesis. They had succeeded in cloaking a small cylindrical object—shielding it not from visible light but from microwaves, a form of electromagnetic radiation with a substantially longer wavelength, which makes the cloaking effect considerably easier to achieve. The way they did it most closely recalls not Harry Potter but another fictional character: the Invisible Woman, a

Marvel Comics superhero who can bend light waves at her command, rendering her body and clothing imperceptible. By tightly controlling the bending, or refraction, of microwaves as they pass through a custom-built material, the Duke researchers could force them to detour around an object so that the microwaves are neither absorbed nor reflected. If they performed the same feat with visible light, a viewer looking directly at the object would see only what lies behind it, as if the object were not even there.

5. To explain their technique, Smith and Schurig invoke the example of a mirage on a hot summer road. When light rays from the sky hit the hot, thin air just above the surface of the asphalt, they bend. Although light moves through a vacuum at a constant speed, it slows down when traveling through any transparent medium, like water or glass. Light travels faster in the hot, thin air close to the road than it does in the cold, dense air above, and that difference in speed is what causes it to shift direction as it crosses the boundary between the two. Rays once headed from the sky to the ground are redirected to your eye, making the road shimmer like water. In effect, the mirage is cloaking the (now invisible) road behind an image of the blue sky.

6. To similarly cloak something from electromagnetic radiation, Smith and Schurig must bend the incoming beam around the object in a tightly controlled manner. They managed to do so using a class of recently created "metamaterials" that possess an ability, not found in nature, to bend light at extreme angles (a property known as negative index of refraction). The team's metamaterials consist of thin, rigid sheets of fiberglass insulator stamped with neat rows of conducting metal shapes like loops, coils, or tiny rectangles. The metal circuitry is designed to direct incoming electromagnetic radiation—in this case, microwaves—so it moves in a specific way.

7. All electromagnetic radiation has two intertwined components: a magnetic field and an electric field. As Schurig explains, these can be redirected when they interact with a material. "Materials are made of atoms, and these atoms respond to electromagnetic waves by acting like a little tiny magnet," he says. Electrons begin moving in circles in response to the magnetic field, as well as back and forth in reaction to the electric field—and the moving charges produce fields of their own. The challenge for the Duke team was to find the right shapes and dimensions for the metal circuitry on the metamaterials so they could precisely dictate how the electrons move around, which in turn controls how the incoming radiation is bent.

8. To demonstrate their system in action, Smith and Schurig walk into their lab, a room lit with fluorescent bulbs and littered with wires, pliers, plugs, pulleys, flashlights, foam cladding, microscopes, computer terminals, and a lone bicycle. The object to be cloaked is just a small copper cylinder filled with black foam: 5 centimeters (2 inches) in diameter and 1 centimeter (0.4 inch) tall. For the experiment it is sandwiched between two horizontal aluminum plates, the bottom one 3 feet square and the top one 4 feet square. Leading in from the front of the apparatus is a wire that feeds microwaves toward the

cylinder as it sits in the center of the bottom plate. Around it, Smith and Schurig have arranged concentric rings of metamaterials, with the empty spaces between the rings forming narrow channels. Having carefully varied the properties of the circuits on those surrounding rings, they can now bend microwaves to flow around the cylinder like water flowing around a pebble in a stream. This makes the object undetectable to an instrument downstream that measures microwaves.

9. According to the Duke team, this experiment shows it should be possible to make an object invisible to the human eye as well, but there are major technical hurdles. For cloaking to work, the metal shapes stamped on the metamaterial must be smaller than the wavelength of the electromagnetic radiation that is aimed at them. The wavelength of the microwaves is a little over 3 centimeters (just over an inch), and the shapes on the surface of the metamaterials are closer to 3 millimeters long. Green light, by contrast, has a wavelength of 500 nanometers—60,000 times smaller—so the shapes that could cloak it would have to be around 50 nanometers long. Theoretically, you could pattern metamaterials at that tiny scale using specialized methods like focused beams of charged atoms, but such materials would be difficult to mass-produce.

10. At this point, then, cloaking objects from visible light is still pie in the sky. In the meantime, the far more accessible applications of microwave cloaking have already garnered intense interest—mainly from the military. Smith is up-front as he rattles off their funding sources: DARPA (the Defense Advanced Research Projects Agency); the Air Force, the Army, the Navy, the intelligence community. One of the technique's most practical and immediate uses would be to hide obstructions that block wireless communication. But since Smith and Schurig's technique bends electromagnetic radiation in a controlled manner, it could someday also be co-opted to focus or concentrate energy in highly efficient ways. For example, it could be used to create supersensitive solar cells or even to power a Mars rover that would gather energy from a microwave beam sent by a satellite orbiting the Red Planet.

11. The Duke researchers are not the only ones scrambling to create cloaking devices. When their theory first appeared in the May 26 edition of Science Express, it was published alongside an independent article that outlined a similar proposal. The author of that paper, theoretical physicist Ulf Leonhardt of the University of St. Andrews in Scotland, proposed using slightly different types of engineered materials to accomplish the trick. A few weeks before that, a pair of math-loving physicists, Graeme Milton of the University of Utah and Nicolae Nicorovici of the University of Sydney in Australia, came up with yet another, drastically different scheme for making objects the size of dust specks invisible.

12. The Milton-Nicorovici hypothesis, which is based on rigorously proved mathematical calculations, relies on the use of a superlens, a thin transparent film that can resolve light finer than its wavelength (long considered a theoretical impossibility), producing extremely sharp images. A superlens made from a thin film of silver could have a negative index of refraction, bending light outside of its normal

path. "What we found was that if you put a speck of dust near the superlens and shine light on the dust, then part of the scattered light gets trapped at the front surface of the superlens," Milton explains. "That trapped light builds up in intensity until it almost exactly cancels the incoming light," in the same way that two colliding sound waves can zero each other out. It is as if there is no light there at all, and the dust particle becomes invisible.

13. So how far off is a real invisibility device? Could such a contraption ever be used to cloak an airplane, a tank, or a ship? Smith doesn't want to be snared by such hypothetical questions. "Reporters, they call up and they just want you to say a number," he says. "Number of months, number of years. They push and push and push and then you finally say, well, maybe 15 years. Then you've got your headline, right? 'Fifteen years till Harry Potter's cloak!' So I have to resist giving you a number."

14. One major problem with masking objects from visible light, says Schurig, is that light is composed of a range of colors, each with its own wavelength. "We don't know how much of that spectrum we could cloak all at once," he explains. "If you could get past these fabrication issues, you could cloak one color of light, and maybe you could cloak some range of visible light. We might be able to make the cloak work for a brief time, for a microsecond at red, a microsecond at green, a microsecond at blue, and you could make it look translucent. But we don't know that you could make something 100 percent invisible to the whole spectrum simultaneously."

15. Milton sounds a further note of caution. Of the Duke research, he says: "I think it's a brilliant idea. But there's a certain amount of skepticism in the scientific community in so far as the time line. I remember reading claims that you could cloak some factory that would be an eyesore. I think that's a bit far-fetched. You can make some small things invisible, but making larger things invisible will be a longer time in coming."

16. There are other factors that neither Harry Potter fans nor the series' fabulously wealthy author, J. K. Rowling, seem to have considered. Ulf Leonhardt—the only one of the researchers who admits to enjoying the books—explains that Harry can see through his cloak, which is made of a thin material in which he can walk and climb. "The present scheme assumes you have something very rigid" surrounding the object, Leonhardt says. "It's not a cloak, it's like a suit of armor. If you want to have something flexible, then the material also has to change its properties, like a chameleon. That is also possible in principle, but with present technology we're a long way away from that."

17. The other, bigger problem is that to see, the eyes must absorb light—which, of course, makes them visible. "If Harry Potter wants to see through his cloak, then his eyes would be visible, because they have to see. And if they have to see, they have to be seen," says Leonhardt. "For example, a fish that camouflages itself by being transparent has eyes that are not transparent, because they have to see. Yet Harry Potter can see through the invisibility cloak. That, I think, is not possible. He would be blind

behind it."

(http://discovermagazine.com/2006/nov/building-invisibility-cloak)

Glossary

flurry ['flʌri] a rapid active commotion *n.* 忙乱

surreal [sə'ri:l] characterized by fantastic imagery and incongruous juxtapositions *adj.* 不现实的，梦幻的，怪异的

bespectacled [bi'spektəkld] wearing, or having the face adorned with, eyeglasses or an eyeglass *adj.* 带眼镜的

fiddle ['fidl] manipulate manually *v.* 瞎搞，乱弄

postdoc [pəust'dɔk] a scholar or researcher who is involved in academic study beyond the level of a doctoral degree *n.* 博士后

crackpot ['krækpɔt] a whimsically eccentric person *n.* 疯子，怪人，狂想家

refraction [ri'frækʃən] the change in direction of a propagating wave (light or sound) when passing from one medium to another *n.* 折光，折射

mirage ['mirɑ:ʒ] an optical illusion in which atmospheric refraction by a layer of hot air distorts or inverts reflections of distant objects *n.* 海市蜃楼

intertwine [ˌintə(:)'twain] spin or twist together so as to form a cord *v.* 纠缠，缠绕

fluorescent [fluə'resənt] emitting light during exposure to radiation from an external source *adj.* 萤光的

pliers ['plaiə(r)z] a gripping hand tool with two hinged arms and (usually) serrated jaws *n.* 钳子

pulley ['puli] a simple machine consisting of a wheel with a groove in which a rope can run to change the direction or point of application of a force applied to the rope *n.* 滑车，滑轮

cladding ['klædiŋ] a protective covering that protects the outside of a thing *n.* 覆层

concentric [kɔn'sentrik] having a common center *adj.* 同中心的

garner ['gɑ:nə] acquire or deserve by one's efforts or actions *v.* 得到

up-front ['ʌp'frʌnt] frank and honest *adj.* 坦率的

rigorously ['rigərəsli] in a way demanding strict attention to rules and procedures *adv.* 严格的，严厉的

contraption [kən'træpʃən] a device or control that is very useful for a particular job *n.* 奇妙的装置

snare [snɛə] catch in or as if in a trap *v.* 诱惑

scramble ['skræmbl] struggle or compete with others to get or reach something *v.* 竞争

fabrication [ˌfæbri'keiʃən] the process of making or producing something *n.* 制造

translucent [trænz'lju:snt] almost transparent; allowing light to pass through diffusely *adj.* 半透明的

camouflage ['kæmuflɑ:ʒ] disguise by camouflaging; exploit the natural surroundings to disguise something *v.* 伪装

Exercises

A. Fill in each blank with one of the given words in its correct form.

| crackpot | camouflage | flurry | surreal | translucent |
| resolve | contraption | rigorously | mirage | concentric |

1. In nature, animals like cuttlefish and chameleons use the awe-inspiring tricks of _____ to hide from theirs.
2. Much of the pale spiral structure in the outer parts of the galaxy is unusually smooth and gives the whole galaxy the ghostly look of a vast _____ jellyfish.
3. Now researchers at The Rockefeller University and colleagues in Japan have devised a _____ sensitive enough to probe and ply these microscopic spindles and have used it to measure for the first time the structure's stiffness and deformability.
4. While it is disappointing that NPL-2008 was not found to be effective for reducing repetitive behaviors, this study does highlight the importance of high quality, _____ controlled clinical trials.
5. The underlying cloaking phenomenon is similar to the _____ seen ahead at a distance on a road on a hot day.
6. Noller proposed in the early 1970s that the RNA component was responsible for carrying out the ribosome's key functions. At the time it was considered a "_____ idea", but subsequent findings by Noller and others proved he was right.
7. The team, which includes graduate students Shakiba Jalal and Ryan Arsenault, has already received a _____ of emails from scientists interested in the technique.
8. Even in the _____ environment, users, who were unaware that they were part of a psychological study, succumbed to very down-to-earth effects of social influence.
9. The results of the study are promising. If it proves successful here, we could gain an effective technique to _____ crocodile-human conflicts.
10. In computer simulations, the researchers have demonstrated an approximate cloaking effect created by _____ rings of silicon photonic crystals.

B. Skim the text and then answer the following questions.

1. How is a mirage formed on a hot summer road?
2. What is a most practical and immediate use of the technique mentioned in the text? And what could the future applications be?
3. According to Smith, when will they finally present an invisible cloak before the world?
4. What is the difference in the material of the current technology to make things invisible and that of Harry's cloak?

5. Why are the eyes of "transparent" fish nontransparent?

C. Read the text and choose the correct answer to each of the following questions.

1. According to the text, _____ would not be crazy about the method to build an invisibility cloak.
   A. Harry Potter fans
   B. Star Trek aficionados
   C. H. G. Wells enthusiasts
   D. physicians

2. Light could be manipulated so as to render an object invisible to the eye, which has profound implications for practical applications like the following except _____.
   A. military technology
   B. wireless communication
   C. interplanetary exploration
   D. Romulan ship-concealing devices

3. The word "co-opted" in "But since Smith and Schurig's technique bends electromagnetic radiation in a controlled manner, it could someday also be co-opted to focus or concentrate energy in highly efficient ways (paragraph 10)" means _____.
   A. taken for its own use
   B. chosen as an alternative
   C. cooperated
   D. used

4. Which of the following statements is not incorrect? _____.
   A. Smith succeeded in cloaking a small cylindrical object
   B. Ulf Leonhardt proposed using certain types of engineered materials to create cloaking devices
   C. Some researchers worked out method to make objects the size of dust specks invisible
   D. The above-mentioned researchers have their findings published in different journals

5. According to Schurig, what is the major problem with masking objects from visible light? _____.
   A. We cannot cloak certain range of visible light
   B. Light is composed of a range of colors with different wavelengths
   C. We cannot make a cloak look translucent
   D. We do not know how much of spectrum we could make invisible simultaneously

D. Explain the underlined parts.

1. Smith hardly <u>fits the profile of a media celebrity: soft-spoken, patient, and bespectacled</u>, he has the pale-skinned hue of a man who has perhaps spent too much time in a windowless lab fiddling with wires.

2. Invisible Woman, a Marvel Comics superhero who can bend light waves <u>at her command, rendering her body and clothing imperceptible.</u>

3. At this point, then, cloaking objects from visible light is <u>still pie in the sky</u>. In the meantime, <u>the far more accessible applications of microwave cloaking have already garnered intense interest</u>—mainly from the military.

4. The Duke researchers are not <u>the only ones scrambling to create cloaking devices</u>.

5. Milton <u>sounds a further note of caution</u>.

Unit 14 Mars

Text A

Terraforming Mars

1. In August, NASA's unmanned Phoenix Mars Mission blasted off from the Kennedy Space Center as the first mission of NASA's Mars Scout Program. Phoenix will reach the Red planet in May 2008, and is part of NASA's strategy to "follow the water" on Mars. This will pave the way for manned Martian missions, which President George W. Bush made a NASA priority in 2004. No date has been set for the crewed mission to Mars, but NASA is drawing up plans. The ultimate goal: making Mars a human outpost.

2. The renewed focus on Mars has rejuvenated the idea of terraforming Mars, which once belonged to the realm of science fiction, but is becoming increasingly possible today. Terraforming—or earthforming—is a Herculean feat of planetwide engineering that will change the Martian atmosphere and allow humans to make uninhabitable Mars into a planet fit for natural life. Space suits will still be necessary for human habitation, but food will be available from plants that grow on a more temperate Mars.

3. "Now we have fairly accurate maps of the Red Planet, and can imagine how it might be modified—terraformed—to make it nearer to our heart's desire," said space visionary Arthur C. Clarke recently. A little more than a decade ago, Clarke wrote a book, The Snows of Olympus: A Garden on Mars (W.W. Norton & Co., 1994) that dealt with how to create a biosphere on Mars. He envisioned a huge garden on the slopes of Olympus Mons, the giant Martian volcano.

4. Mars, the only likely candidate for terraforming in the solar system, has numerous features in common with Earth. Like Earth, it has a rocky composition and marked seasons. Clearly, an environment different from the cold, dry world we see today once existed on Mars, as has been clear from recent NASA missions. Liquid water flowed on the Martian surface in the past: there are vast dry gorges and canyons etched by water and ice. The reddish color of the soil indicates hydration of the surface rocks, and is evidence of the role of water in the evolution of the planet.

5. Earlier this year the NASA rover Spirit confirmed that Mars was once a wet place. Spirit was exploring an area called Gusev Crater, when it found a piece of nearly pure silica. Silica is a component of

window glass, and it is often a main ingredient in sand. The sort of silica found on Mars is usually formed in the presence of a significant amount of water. And if water flowed once on this frigid planet, will it not be possible to make it flow again?

6. Given that most astronomers and space scientists believe that humans have been responsible for global warming on Earth, some scientists think so.

7. "Humans are effectively warming the Earth", says NASA's Christopher McKay, who says we "can, and should, do the same on Mars". McKay has written extensively about terraforming Mars, which he terms "planetary ecosynthesis". McKay is one of a handful of NASA scientists who have begun to think about creating a permanent outpost on Mars even though many years may pass before a human sets foot there.

8. The first step to terraforming Mars would be to warm up the planet. It has a lot of frozen carbon dioxide (dry ice) at its poles. Increasing the temperature from its current 60℃ to just above 0℃ would turn the dry ice into gas. The ensuing thick atmosphere of carbon dioxide would create a greenhouse effect and would allow water to flow on Mars; in principle, plants could then grow slowly.

9. The first Martian plants would probably be lichens. In a few decades, there would be a seasonally ice-free lake on the summit of Olympus, Mars's largest volcano. Soon thereafter, a terraformed Mars would witness a veritable green revolution characterized by pines and oaks, allowing it to become our second home.

10. Of course, questions remain as to what is the best way to warm up Mars. One possibility, espoused by James Oberg in his book New Earths in 1981, is to use giant mirrors in orbit around the planet to increase the temperature by reflecting sunlight onto the poles. NASA researchers are currently investigating large solar sails in an effort to provide spacecraft with solar power. Such solar sails could be adapted for this purpose.

11. Another warming idea, as proffered by McKay, is to generate gases known as halocarbons that would create a greenhouse atmosphere. They would exclude gases like bromine and fluorine, which can damage an ozone layer. It would involve building a factory on Mars to make halocarbons through chemical reactions. The raw materials would be the Martian soil and the Martian atmosphere. Mars has a thin atmosphere, and many light gases such as hydrogen aren't trapped by Martian gravity. However, the heavier halocarbon molecules would be trapped, and they would contribute to a greenhouse effect. McKay says that real chemical studies have yet to be done, but he favors this method because we already have "produced halocarbons on Earth that have contributed to global warming".

12. In addition, there are more speculative ideas, such as using nuclear-powered rockets to divert asteroids to crash on Mars. This would create a catastrophe that would release a lot of heat into the atmosphere, which would increase the planet's temperature dramatically.

13. Most ideas put forward by scientists such as McKay budget about five to 10 decades for the temperature increase. Most space scientists agree that we now have the technological capability to attempt some of these schemes; of course, the execution of any particular one on a planetary scale will be quite challenging, according to McKay.

14. Scientists also say that carbon dioxide and water alone will not be enough to sustain life. "A biosphere requires large amounts of carbon dioxide and water but also nitrogen," says McKay. "Nitrogen gas is essential for a breathable atmosphere and nitrogen is needed by life as an essential macronutrient."

15. As far as scientists know, there is very little nitrogen in the Martian atmosphere and there is no data on the amount of nitrates in the Martian soil that could be converted to nitrogen. Theoretical arguments suggest lightning and meteorites should have produced nitrates on Mars that could be adequate, says McKay.

16. "The question of the nitrogen supply is probably the key question in terms of the feasibility of ecosynthesis on Mars," he stresses.

17. Ethical questions also abound. As Clarke pointed out recently, "Whether we should embark on such a venture should be decided very carefully, and future Martian inhabitants must be allowed to have their say."

18. Many who have thought about the topic view it from an anthropocentric view. Anthropocentrism puts human interests foremost.

19. In a 2002 article in Environmental Law Reporter on the ethics of terraforming, Robert D. Pinson wrote, "The most applicable environmental ethic to terraforming Mars is anthropocentrism. It puts our interests at the forefront while still ensuring the existence of all life. It seems obvious that we should give ourselves the highest level of intrinsic worth since we are the ones placing the value. Life, of course, has the ultimate intrinsic worth, but we are a part of that life. It is in our best interest to preserve and expand life. What better way than by changing a planet that is currently unable to sustain life into one that can."

20. And of course there is the business of getting to Mars and back safely, while sustaining the crew through the long multiyear trip. Unmanned missions like Phoenix are technologically possible today because we do not need to worry about transporting a big payload. There are ideas for manned missions that involve getting to Mars with the aid of nuclear rockets, but a lot of work remains to be done before we can send humans there.

21. "We cannot, of course, begin terraforming today, but we can research and plan the future," Pinson had said in 2002. That sentiment, if anything, has gotten stronger.

22. "Given the situation here on Earth, I think it prudent that we try to colonize Mars," Pinson told IEEE Spectrum recently. "Since the evidence for water on Mars is becoming stronger and stronger, I really believe we should make an effort to get over there and investigate further."

(http://www.spectrum.ieee.org/aerospace/space-flight/terraforming-mars)

Glossary

scout [skaut] someone who can find paths through unexplored territory *n*. 侦察员
outpost ['autpəust] a settlement on the frontier of civilization *n*. 前哨
rejuvenate [ri'dʒu:vineit] return to life; get or give new life or energy *v*. 复原, 更新
herculean [ˌhə:kju:'ljən] extremely difficult *adj*. 极困难的
gorge [gɔ:dʒ] a deep ravine (usually with a river running through it) *n*. 山峡, 峡谷
canyon ['kænjən] a ravine formed by a river in an area with little rainfall *n*. 峡谷, 溪谷
etch [etʃ] make an etching of *v*. 蚀刻, 铭刻
hydration [hai'dreiʃən] the process of combining with water; usually reversible *n*. 水和
rover ['rəuvə] someone who leads a wandering unsettled life *n*. 漫游者
lichen ['laikən] any thallophytic plant of the division Lichenes; occur as crusty patches or bushy growths on tree trunks or rocks or bare ground etc. *n*. 地衣, 青苔
veritable ['veritəbl] not counterfeit or copied *adj*. 真实的, 真确的, 真的
espouse [is'pauz] choose and follow; as of theories, ideas, policies, strategies or plans *v*. 支持, 赞成
proffer ['prɔfə] present for acceptance or rejection *v*. 提供
halocarbon [ˌhæləu'kɑ:bən] one of various compounds of carbon and any of the halogens *n*. 卤代烃(卤化碳)
bromine ['brəumi:n] a nonmetallic largely pentavalent heavy volatile corrosive dark brown liquid element belonging to the halogens; found in sea water *n*. [化]溴
fluorine ['flu(:)əri:n] a nonmetallic univalent element belonging to the halogens; usually a yellow irritating toxic flammable gas; a powerful oxidizing agent; recovered from fluorite or cryolite or fluorapatite *n*. 氟
speculative ['spekjulətiv] not based on fact or investigation *adj*. 推理的
asteroid ['æstərɔid] any of numerous small celestial bodies composed of rock and metal that move around the sun (mainly between the orbits of Mars and Jupiter) *n*. [天文]小游星, 小行星
catastrophe [kə'tæstrəfi] an event resulting in great loss and misfortune; a sudden violent change in the earth's surface *n*. 大灾难
macronutrient [ˌmækrəu'nju:triənt] the elements required in large amounts by all living things *n*. [生]大量养料, 大量营养素, 常量营养元素
meteorite ['mi:tiərɑit] stony or metallic object that is the remains of a meteoroid that has reached the earth's surface *n*. 陨石, 陨星
abound [ə'baund] be abundant or plentiful; exist in large quantities *v*. 富于, 充满

embark [im'bɑːk] set out on *v*. 着手，从事

anthropocentric [ˌænθrəpə'senˌtrik] human-centered *adj*. 以人类为中心的

payload ['peiˌləud] The total weight of passengers, crew, equipment, and cargo carried by an aircraft or spacecraft *n*. 负载

Exercises

A. Fill in each blank with one of the given words in its correct form.

abound	divert	speculative	catastrophe	prudent
embark	rover	release	Herculean	etch

1. Our study shows that neither plant nor animal life escaped the impact of this global _____.
2. It is considered _____ for people who are ill to delay international travel and for people developing symptoms following international travel to seek medical attention, in line with guidance from national authorities.
3. Two teams of one astronaut and one geologist each have been driving the _____ through the Arizona desert, trying it out in two different configurations.
4. He looks, for example, at suggestions that scientists themselves could take a financial risk in _____ research depending on whether they do or do not think it will pay off, as well as proposals-through, say, 10-year fellowships-that allow scientists to pursue really "hard", long-standing problems without the pressure for rapid results.
5. Agents that _____ nitric oxide (NO) within the body can help to treat such angina pectoris attacks because NO dilates arteries thereby improving blood circulation.
6. The team has undertaken the _____ task of reconstituting the history of about one hundred remote galaxies that have been observed with both Hubble and GIRAFFE on the VLT.
7. This makes sense because where predators _____, one might not get a second chance to reproduce.
8. HIAPER, one of the nation's most advanced research aircraft, is scheduled to _____ on an historic mission spanning the globe from the Arctic to the Antarctic.
9. We are able to "tune" the cloak to the differing frequencies of incoming waves which means we can _____ waves of a variety of frequencies.
10. A carbon dioxide laser beam was used to _____ information into the first few outer cells of the fruit peel. The mark can't be peeled off, washed off or changed, offering a way to trace the fruit back to its original source.

B. Skim the text and then answer the following questions.

1. What is the significance of terraforming Mars?

· 216 ·

2. Please list some methods to warm up Mars.
3. Why is nitrogen supply probably the key question in terms of the feasibility of ecosynthesis on Mars?
4. How do you understand the anthropocentric views concerning the issue mentioned in the text?
5. What are the problems that need to be solved before we can send humans to Mars?

C. Read the text and choose the correct answer to each of the following questions.

1. _____ is not the feature of Mars.
   A. That liquid water existed in the past
   B. The surface rocks being red
   C. Having distinct seasons
   D. Sharing some similarities with the Earth

2. Which of the following would not happen after humans warm up Mars? _____.
   A. Carbon dioxide on Mars will change into frozen form
   B. A greenhouse effect will be found there
   C. Plants will appear on Mars
   D. Dry ice will turn into gas

3. A biosphere requires large amounts of the following except _____.
   A. carbon   B. water   C. nitrogen   D. carbon dioxide

4. Which of the following statements is incorrect concerning missions to Mars? _____.
   A. We can sustain the crew through the long multiyear trip now
   B. Unmanned mission are possible today
   C. We cannot sending men to Mars with the aid of nuclear rockets now
   D. There is still a lot to be done before we can send men to Mars

5. The word "prudent" in "Given the situation here on Earth, I think it prudent that we try to colonize Mars" means _____.
   A. sensible   B. unconsidered   C. feasible   D. unrealistic

D. Explain the underlined parts.

1. In August, NASA's <u>unmanned Phoenix Mars Mission blasted off</u> from the Kennedy Space Center as the first mission of NASA's Mars Scout Program... This will <u>pave the way for manned Martian missions</u>...

2. <u>The renewed focus on Mars has rejuvenated the idea of terraforming Mars</u>, which once <u>belonged to the realm of science fiction</u>, but is becoming increasingly possible today.

3. Mars, <u>the only likely candidate for terraforming in the solar system</u>, <u>has numerous features in common with Earth</u>.

4. <u>Given that most astronomers and space scientists believe that humans have been responsible for global</u>

warming on Earth, some scientists think so.
5. In addition, there are more speculative ideas, such as using nuclear-powered rockets to divert asteroids to crash on Mars.
6. Most space scientists agree that we now have the technological capability to attempt some of these schemes; of course, the execution of any particular one on a planetary scale will be quite challenging, according to McKay.
7. The most applicable environmental ethic to terraforming Mars is anthropocentrism. It puts our interests at the forefront while still ensuring the existence of all life.
8. And of course there is the business of getting to Mars and back safely, while sustaining the crew through the long multiyear trip. Unmanned missions like Phoenix are technologically possible today because we do not need to worry about transporting a big payload.
9. "Given the situation here on Earth, I think it prudent that we try to colonize Mars," Pinson told IEEE Spectrum recently. "Since the evidence for water on Mars is becoming stronger and stronger, I really believe we should make an effort to get over there and investigate further."

E. Read the passages in this section and decide whether each of the following statements is true or false.

Passage One

With each passing day, new images beamed from Mars by American rovers and European spacecraft build a stronger case for the argument that the red planet was not only awash in water at one time, but also chock-full of the basic building blocks of life. Conclusive proof of life—for example, an old fish bone kicked up by a wheel of one of NASA's Mars rovers—has yet to be found. Nevertheless, there is a growing conviction among scientists that the discovery of evidence of past life on Mars is all but inevitable.

The rover Opportunity, which landed in the Meridiani Planum in 2004, came to rest on a patch of terrain that NASA's planetary scientists believe was once the floor of a giant sea. A closeup look at a small outcrop revealed it to be made of layered sedimentary rock, the sort that builds up as finely dispersed solids from eroded rock settle out of water and become cemented together. On Earth, similar geologic formations are riddled with fossils of early forms of life. Because the laws of nature hold true throughout the universe, there is every reason to believe the same chemical processes that sparked life in the rich chemical soup that filled the primitive oceans on Earth, also took place in Martian seas. "If you have an interest in searching for fossils on Mars, this is the first place you want to go," says Ed Weiler, NASA Associate Administrator.

And it is not only within the Meridiani Planum that the water needed to support life is likely to be found. Data from the European Space Agency's (ESA) Mars Express orbiter shows a substantial amount of ice also exists at the planet's south pole.

As the chemical past of Mars begins to unfold, old ideas about Martian history once dismissed as speculative have gained scientific currency. The most provocative idea surrounds ALH84001, the so-called Mars meteor. It blasted into space when an asteroid struck Mars 16 million years ago. Eventually, it crossed paths with Earth, survived the fiery trip through Earth's atmosphere, and landed in the pristine Antarctica wilderness where it lay undiscovered for more than 13,000 years. After being picked up by a sharp-eyed geologist in 1984, NASA put the 3.5 billion-year-old rock on the shelf until the late 1990s. When scientists finally got around to examining it in detail, they found that it contains magnetic spheres that could have been created only by bacteria.

This totally defied reason. Mars, after all, was believed to have dried up. Its atmospheric pressure is so low, any liquid water would immediately boil away. The recent discovery of evidence of an ancient water source where Opportunity touched down suggests that the watery conditions needed for a rock like ALH84001 to form, existed on the red planet when the Mars meteor began its multimillion-year journey to Earth. Naysayers who argue magnetic spheres could also be produced by chemical processes are now in the minority. "The process of evolution has driven magnetotactic bacteria to make perfect little bar magnets," says Joseph Kirschvink, a NASA geobiologist who studied ALH84001. "An entire industry devoted to making small magnetic particles for magnetic tapes and computer discs has tried and failed for the past 50 years to make similar particles." Today, the mainstream scientific community recognizes that the spherical, magnet-containing structures found inside meteorite ALH84001 could only have been produced by a living organism.

With the question of whether Mars was once alive settled to the satisfaction of most, a more important question arises: If the red planet were once alive, how did it die?

(http://www.popularmechanics.com/science/space/1283126.html)

_____ 1. NASA's Mars rovers have kicked up an old fish bone.

_____ 2. There is evidence showing that certain chemical processes that could spark life took place on Mars.

_____ 3. ALH84001, the so-called Mars meteor, has been on earth for about 3.5 billion ears.

_____ 4. A great portion of scientists believe that the spherical, magnet-containing structures found inside meteorite ALH84001 could have been produced by chemical processes.

_____ 5. People know why Mars was once alive, but not why it died.

Passage Two

Many of the ideas about life and death on Mars begin with assumptions that arise from our understanding of the geology and biology on Earth. Regardless of whether they align themselves with the live Mars or dead Mars side of the equation, there are several points upon which most scientists concur. Chief among these is the age of the Earth, agreed to be between 3.9 billion and 4.5 billion years old. There is also a growing consensus on when life first appeared. Hubert Staudigel and his colleagues at the Scripps Institution of Oceanography, in San Diego, have found evidence of life more than 3.5 billion years old in the form of a primitive microfossil in lava in South Africa. Finally, there is agreement on the overall structure of the two planets' environments. During their formative years, both Earth and Mars were surrounded by a thick cloud of carbon dioxide. The gas created the well-known greenhouse effect: By preventing heat that entered the atmosphere during the day from escaping into the night, the gas creates a sort of incubator for new types of organisms.

Scientists are divided on what happened after the formative years. Many believe that factors such as the small size and low density of Mars caused it to rapidly cool. This school of thought holds that from its youngest years, Mars was a cold and desolate landscape, an inhospitable environment where any life that took shape was prevented from evolving into a more sophisticated form. The recent discovery of what appears to be sedimentary rock in the Meridiani Planum casts doubt on that pessimistic theory, and lends credence to the idea that Mars was once, perhaps recently, a warm and wet planet.

Cold and dry or warm and wet, the one fact about early life on Mars on which there is complete agreement relates to its planetary neighborhood. Earth and Mars started out in a rough part of town. For about 500 million years, during the period when the first primitive forms of life on both planets were establishing themselves, both planets were hammered by meteors large enough to rip holes in the atmosphere and evaporate entire oceans. Mars is roughly half the diameter of Earth, which means that all other things being equal, Mars sustained fewer hits. And that, of course, would have been good news for any primitive life that might have taken root. Then just about the time things began calming down, they also chilled out, which brings us to the moon. Earth has one, which is large. Mars has two, which are small. Size matters a lot.

Bruce M. Jakosky, a professor of geological sciences at the University of Colorado in Boulder, explains. Earth and Mars are tilted on their axes 23.5° and 25.2°, respectively. These angles, however, are not fixed. Over time, the tug of the other planets' gravitational fields increases the angle—picture a wobbling, spinning top and the way it leans. On Earth, the tug of the planets—chiefly giant Jupiter—has been dampened by the gravitational tug of the moon. And so the Earth wobbles less than 1.5°. Being less massive, the moons of Mars exert a smaller dampening effect. Mars is believed to have at times wobbled as far as 40° away from its normal 25.2° dip.

On Earth, and presumably on Mars, shifts from the normal tilt are important. On Earth, they created the Milankovitch cycle, which is believed to have driven the emergence of ice ages.

On Mars, the effects of the increase in the planet's tilt were more dramatic. They produced what is referred to as the "runaway refrigerator", or reverse greenhouse effect (illustrated above). Extreme cold will cause carbon dioxide, the gas that creates the greenhouse effect, to solidify. On Earth we call this material dry ice. Turning atmospheric carbon dioxide into dry ice increases the amount of heat that escapes from a planet at night. Each year becomes colder. The net result is a planet that resembles Antarctica, but with a most alien atmosphere.

Extreme cold on Mars would have killed off any life that had begun by asphyxiation or starvation. Just as it does during a hard frost here on Earth, extreme cold would have snuffed out any oxygen-producing plants. Their demise would have been followed by the death of any other forms of life dependent upon oxygen. Oxygen, of course, is not a prerequisite for life. For example, the common septic tank relies upon the fact that there are anaerobic bacteria that thrive in an oxygen-free environment. The extreme cold created by the runaway refrigerator would have killed any anaerobic organisms by depriving them of nutrients. Liquid water not only leaches essential minerals out of rock and soil but also it delivers them. Immobilize the water by freezing it, and any primitive life-forms simply starve.

On Earth, organisms are found in temperatures ranging from polar cold to desert hot, from pressure extremes of crushing deep-sea depths to the almost-airless upper reaches of the atmosphere. And for when conditions become too severe, nature has provided some creatures with the ability to shut down. Not long ago, scientists found a type of Siberian moss that had lain dormant for 40,000 years, then began to grow when it was warmed. Mars may have been inhabited by distant cousins of this hearty plant, but nature still dealt them a losing hand when it failed to provide the red planet with a protective magnetic field.

From time to time, residents in far northern latitudes are treated to a rare celestial show: the northern lights. These undulating bands of color are produced when the high-energy particles that form the solar wind collide with the Earth's magnetic field. Without what amounts to this electromagnetic force field, the solar wind would penetrate the atmosphere and cook any organisms in its path, just as if they had been placed in a microwave oven. Organisms that were not killed outright would likely suffer damage to their genetic makeup.

(http://www.popularmechanics.com/science/space/1283126.html)

_____ 6. The Earth was once shrouded by a thick layer of carbon dioxide.

_____ 7. There is evidence showing Mars was warm and wet.

_____ 8. Theoretically, Mars has received more meteors than the Earth does.

_____ 9. The gravitational tug of the moons of Mars can serve as an account for the extreme cold on Mars now.

_____ 10. If there were life form like the Siberian moss on Mars, it could survive.

F. Cloze. Fill in each blank with one suitable word.

In the mid-1990s the U.S. __1__ on a new strategy for exploring the Red Planet. In __2__ to the 1993 failure of the Mars Observer mission—a billion-dollar, decade-in-the-making probe that mysteriously lost __3__ with ground controllers just before it was scheduled to go into orbit around the planet—

NASA administrator Daniel Goldin decided to shift to smaller, less __4__ spacecraft and create a sustained exploration campaign by sending one or two probes to Mars at every launch opportunity. (These opportunities come every two years or so, when Earth and Mars are properly aligned.) The new strategy __5__ out the inherent risk of interplanetary travel and __6__ that the engineering experience and scientific data __7__ by one mission could be rapidly used by the next. The approach has proved a brilliant success _____, putting three NASA spacecraft into __8__ around Mars and three rovers on the planet's surface (Pathfinder, Spirit and Opportunity). The Phoenix Mars Lander, which left Earth in August, is __9__ to reach the Red Planet next May, and NASA plans to __10__ the Mars Science Lab in 2009.

1. A. put   B. concentrated   C. moved   D. embarked
2. A. aspect   B. response   C. respect   D. accordance
3. A. contact   B. contract   C. contest   D. content
4. A. time-consuming B. sophisticated   C. expensive   D. spacious
5. A. spread   B. put   C. remove   D. send
6. A. assured   B. ensured   C. reassured   D. sured
7. A. conducted   B. collected   C. acquired   D. presented
8. A. position   B. movement   C. orbit   D. circulation
9. A. planed   B. arranged   C. bound   D. expected
10. A. launch   B. send   C. release   D. emit

G. Translate the following passages into Chinese/English.

1. For astronomers, the main difference between midtown Manhattan and rural Mongolia is the darkness of the night sky. In dense urban areas the sky is 25 to 50 times brighter than in less populated places, blotting out all but the heartiest celestial sights. Stray light is not just an urban problem, however. Even far from Times Square and Broadway, a pervasive glow fills the spaces between the stars. The intensity of this background varies with the season and with solar activity, but the sky itself always outshines all the visible stars combined.

2. 去遥远的山顶可以排除天空的部分光干扰,但是你仍然不能逃脱散射的阳光和稀疏的星光。这种光辐射到处都是——包括外层空间。哈勃太空望远镜——在地面上方370英里环绕地球运行——察觉出一个黑暗度几乎无星光天空两倍的背景。尽管如此,黄道光会照亮那里的天空并遮住那些发光微弱的天体;这是在可见光波长里的主要漫射背景。哈勃望远镜还必须全力对付下面地球那几乎遍及半边天的耀眼光辉。

Text B

The Truth about Water on Mars: 5 New Findings

1. In its few months of roaming the polar area on Mars last year, the Phoenix Lander found water ice beneath the red planet's surface and snow in the atmosphere. But for those hoping that life once existed on Mars—or still might—liquid water would be the crown jewel. While Phoenix died this past November as the winter brought on shorter and colder days, project leader Peter Smith of the University of Arizona, along with a number of colleagues from NASA's Jet Propulsion lab and universities all over the world, have spent the intervening months confirming those early finds and poring over the lander's massive amounts of data. Most of the attention is focused on whether Phoenix's data conclusively shows evidence that liquid water once flowed across Mars. There is a lot of complex analysis, but, in short, signs point to yes. Here are five lessons taken from today's analysis, which was published today in four separate studies in the journal Science.

Lesson 1: Clean White Ice Can Come From Breathing Soil — Find a Solid Layer of Ice, and You Can Bet on Liquid Water

2. The picture Phoenix took on Mars that captured the world's attention showed clean white ice, which had been just below the surface, exposed by the lander's own tracks. But, the latest studies now confirm, the lander also found the same hard ice table, about 2 to 7 inches deep in the ground, every place it looked.

3. The purity surprised Smith. He'd thought that if ice lies beneath Mars' surface, it might come from water vapor that freezes and attaches to soil particles at night and then sublimes directly back into a gas during the day. This cycle happens on Mars; as JPL researcher and study co-author Michael Hecht puts it, "The soil breathes." But, Smith says, a solid layer of ice like the Phoenix team found is the signature of liquid water freezing.

4. The Phoenix Lander followed up its find of ice below the surface with a much more controversial image: what appeared to be liquid water on the rover's legs. Hecht and Smith still disagree whether or not the image shows evidence of "thin films" of water that Smith says could exist on the surface and could have splashed onto the lander. However, Smith acknowledges, even if that water does exist, it's only a small amount. Mars is still an extraordinarily dry place that makes Antarctica look hospitable by comparison.

Lesson 2: Calcium Carbonate is a Sign of Liquid Water—That, or Low-Temperature Volcanoes

5. The mineral calcium carbonate shows up all over the Earth—it's the key ingredient in limestone

and some chalk, and people take it as a calcium supplement. Researchers have confirmed that the Phoenix Lander's examination of Martian soil turned up lots of calcium carbonate. The mineral, which the researchers found by cooking the soil, is a promising sign that liquid water existed at some point, Smith says, because it almost always needs water to form.

6. Carbon dioxide in the atmosphere first reacts with the water in the soil, then the water leaches calcium out of the ground to form calcium carbonate. The only other way the mineral is naturally created is through low-temperature volcanoes, Smith says, but only one of the Earth's many volcanoes is known to do it, so that explanation is unlikely.

7. Calcium carbonate carries another bonus for life-seekers: It prevents the soil from becoming too acidic, keeping it at a pH close to that of seawater on Earth.

Lesson 3: Martian Clouds—and Snowfall—Are Not Evidence of Liquid Water

8. When the Phoenix Lander beamed home images of snow on Mars, the scientists were taken aback. Jim Whiteway of York University in Canada, the lead author of the study dealing with Martian cloud cover, says scientists always assumed the ice crystals in Mars' atmosphere were tiny and suspended in the air. Close review of the data, however, revealed that rather than being 2 to 3 microns in size as the team expected, the snow they saw on Mars was 50 to 100 microns—large enough to fall back to the ground as precipitation.

9. Unlike the other studies, the Martian clouds don't point one way or the other regarding liquid water's existence. Clouds on Mars don't need liquid water to form—water vapor rises into the lower atmosphere when it's warm, freezes into ice crystals when it cools and falls back down, and the cycle starts over when the day warms again.

10. But Martian clouds and precipitation can be a lot like the Earth's, with the ice crystals akin those in our cirrus clouds. "They turned out to be so similar to the clouds you fly through in a jet airliner," Whiteway tells PM. His study doesn't rule out liquid water once existing, he says, and if our neighbor has clouds like ours, perhaps it had liquid water, too.

Lesson 4: The Lack of Perchlorate Streaks Contradicts Evidence of Liquid Water Deposits Underground

11. When scientists found perchorate on Mars last year, there was a heated discussion in the scientific community. Rocket scientists worried about contamination because perchlorate is a constituent of rocket fuel. Others worried that finding the chemical would mean that Martian soil was less hospitable to life because it's a water contaminant here on Earth. The latest study from Hecht shows that both concerns were overblown. The fuel used for landing doesn't contain perchlorate, which makes contamination unlikely, and while perchlorate can have harmful health effects on humans, bacteria have no trouble feasting on the chemical.

12. Perchlorate's relationship with water, Hecht says, bears both good news and bad news. The good news is that perchlorate salts are highly soluble—they easily dissolve in water, and when they do they lower its freezing point by anywhere from 35 to 70 degrees Celsius, depending on their chemical composition. That would widen the temperature range that liquid water could exist on the surface.

13. However, because perchlorates dissolve so easily into water, you'd expect to see grains or streaks of them left over when the water evaporates, Hecht says. These streaks are not evident on Mars. Instead, perchlorates appear to be more randomly distributed through soil. That argues against recent wetness on Mars, Hecht says, but doesn't preclude the possibility that "thin films" of water could still be on the surface.

Lesson 5: Phoenix Reveals Much About Water, But if We're Going to Find Life, We'll Need to Go Back to Mars

14. "What we know isn't everything," says Hecht. "We do leave potential discrepancies, and that's fine." There's a lot left to learn, especially about the big question—the possibility of life. While bacteria enjoy a meal of perchlorate, which packs plenty of energy, they usually eat in diluted form on Earth. The chemical absorbs water so easily that it acts as a desiccant, and that could be deadly for microbes on a dry place like Mars.

15. While there are more papers yet to come, Phoenix may have gone as far as it can on the life question, Smith says. The lander took the first big step by finding ice, and he says upcoming studies could take the second big step by giving further evidence that Mars was once a habitable zone, and could be again. If there are Martian microbes, he speculates, they're probably in an underground crack where there's more heat and moisture. It'll take another lander to go find them.

(http://www.popularmechanics.com/science/air_space/4323651.html)

Glossary

roam [rəum] move about aimlessly or without any destination, often in search of food or employment v.
    漫游，闲逛，徜徉
propulsion [prə'pʌlʃən] a propelling force n. 推进，推进力
sublime [sə'blaim] vaporize and then condense right back again v. 升华，
calcium ['kælsiəm] a white metallic element that burns with a brilliant light; the fifth most abundant element in the earth's crust; an important component of most plants and animals n. 钙
carbonate ['kɑ:bəneit] a salt or ester of carbonic acid n. 碳酸盐
limestone ['laimstəun] a sedimentary rock consisting mainly of calcium that was deposited by the remains of marine animals n. 石灰石
leach [li:tʃ] remove substances from by a percolating liquid v. 过滤，萃取

micron ['maikrɔn] a metric unit of length equal to one millionth of a meter *n*. 微米

precipitation [pri‚sipi'teiʃən] the falling to earth of any form of water (rain or snow or hail or sleet or mist) *n*. 坠落,凝结

cirrus ['sirəs] a wispy white cloud (usually of fine ice crystals) at a high altitude (4 to 8 miles) *n*. [气]卷云

perchlorate [pə'klɔːreit] a salt of perchloric acid *n*. 高氯酸盐

streak [striːk] a marking of a different color or texture from the background *n*. 条理,痕迹

overblow ['əuvəbləun] bigger or more important than it should be *v*. 夸张;过分渲染

preclude ['preljuːd] serve as a prelude or opening to *v*. 作为前奏,作为开端,引出

discrepancy [dis'krepənsi] a difference between conflicting facts or claims or opinions *n*. 相差,差异,差别

dilute [d(a)i'ljuːt] lessen the strength or flavor of a solution or mixture *v*. 冲淡,稀释

desiccant ['desikənt] a substance that promotes drying (e.g., calcium oxide absorbs water and is used to remove moisture) *n*. 干燥剂

microbe ['maikrəub] a minute life form (especially a disease-causing bacterium); the term is not in technical use *n*. 微生物

Exercises

A. Fill in each blank with one of the given words in its correct form.

| leach | preclude | streak | discrepancy | dilute |
| distribute | contradict | feast | roam | precipitation |

1. Although inner city rodents appear to _____ freely, most form distinct neighborhoods where they spend the majority of their lives.

2. The researchers identified two classes of chemical compounds in commonly-used plastic lab ware that could _____ into solutions.

3. For example, in the southwestern coast, where it is hot and dry, _____ played a very strong role and temperature a lesser role in dengue transmission.

4. "It is common to find that people consider luck to be contagious—they are likely to believe that being near a person on a winning _____ somehow enhances their own chances of winning," writes author Arul Mishra (University of Utah, Salt Lake City).

5. The potential of forest biotechnology to help address significant social and environmental issues is being "strangled at birth" by the rigid opposition of some groups and regulations that effectively _____ even the testing of genetically modified trees, scientists argue in a new report.

6. But Myhre's article now points at what might have been a defect in these estimates. By doing this, he

brings scientists a big step closer to the explanation of the _____ between models and estimates from observations.

7. The research team, led by Dr Doug Stewart from the School of Civil Engineering and Dr Ian Burke from the School of Earth and Environment, has discovered that adding _____ acetic acid (vinegar) to the affected site stimulates the growth of naturally-occurring bacteria by providing an attractive food source.

8. It identifies issues and threats associated with using these methods to register voters, _____ blank ballots and return voted ballots.

9. The team has now found the optimal conditions for the Daqing microbe to _____ on hydrocarbon, which could point the way to a more effective approach to bioremediation of spill sites.

10. The findings also _____ the conventional interpretation of experimental results obtained by other researchers studying the fragmentation rate of certain proteins containing sulfur-sulfur bonds when stretched with a microscopic force probe.

B. Skim the text and then answer the following questions.

1. What is the phenomenon Michael Hecht referred to using the expression "the soil breathes"?
2. Why cannot the finding of perchorate serve as strong evidence showing liquid water could exist on the surface of Mars?
3. What is evidence indicating the existence of water on Mars?
4. If there had been life forms on Mars, what do you think are reasons for their extinction?
5. Why does the lack of perchlorate streaks contradict evidence of liquid water deposits underground?

C. Read the text and choose the correct answer to each of the following questions.

1. What does the word "die" mean in "While Phoenix died this past November as the winter brought on shorter and colder days (paragraph 1)"? _____.
   A. Be discarded as worthless
   B. Break down
   C. Stop functioning for a while
   D. Pass away

2. According to Lesson 1 in the text, which of the following is not the opinion held by Smith? _____.
   A. There could be water exist on the surface of Mars
   B. The water on Mars could be only of a tiny amount
   C. Mars is not too dry to be inhospitable
   D. A solid layer of ice is indicative of liquid water freezing

3. Which of the following statements is not true about calcium carbonate? _____.
   A. Water is usually needed in the formation of calcium carbonate
   B. It makes seawater acidic

C. Not all volcanoes give birth to calcium carbonate

   D. It can be found in limestone and some chalk

4. In accordance with what has been mentioned in Lesson 3, it is correct that _____.

   A. liquid water helps to form cloud is Mars' atmosphere

   B. the ice crystals in Mars' atmosphere were too tiny to contribute to snowfall

   C. water vapor forms cloud in Mars' atmosphere

   D. he ice crystals in Mars' atmosphere is different from those in our cirrus clouds

5. Which of the following is true about the current probe of life on Mars? _____.

   A. Bacteria were found on Mars

   B. It has been found that Mars was once a habitable zone

   C. The lander would carry out missions find life on Mars sometime

   D. Microbes have been found in underground cracks

D. Explain the underlined parts.

1. But for those hoping that life once existed on Mars—or still might—liquid water <u>would be the crown jewel</u>.

2. The picture Phoenix took on Mars that <u>captured the world's attention</u> showed clean white ice, which had been just below the surface, <u>exposed by the lander's own tracks</u>.

3. Mars is still <u>an extraordinarily dry place</u> that <u>makes Antarctica look hospitable by comparison</u>.

4. The mineral, which the researchers found by cooking the soil, <u>is a promising sign that liquid water existed at some point,</u> Smith says, because it almost always needs water to form.

5. The fuel used for landing doesn't contain perchlorate, <u>which makes contamination unlikely,</u> and <u>while perchlorate can have harmful health effects on humans, bacteria have no trouble feasting on the chemical</u>.

Unit 15 Space Travel

Text A

Russia's Dark Horse Plan to Get to Mars

1. Mars has been nothing but bad luck for the Russians. They have launched 20 probes to the planet since 1960, and all either failed or suffered from severe technical problems. But soon—as early as this October—Russia will attempt to reverse its fortunes with one of the most ambitious unmanned space missions ever.

2. Instead of aiming straight for Mars, the Russians are going after Phobos, the larger of its two little satellites and one of the oddest objects around. Their probe, called Fobos-Grunt ("Phobos soil" in Russian), will not only land on Phobos but also scoop up some samples of the surface and send them to Earth. Understanding Phobos could tell us a lot about the early history of the solar system. "It may give us clues to the formation of Earth's moon and the moons of the other planets, and the role played by asteroid impacts in shaping the terrestrial [rocky] planets," says Alexander Zakharov of the Moscow-based Space Research Institute and chief scientist for Fobos-Grunt. Even more important, this mission could lay the groundwork for an innovative strategy for exploring—and even colonizing—Mars itself.

3. Phobos is very different from our moon. It is a potato-shaped rock measuring only 12 miles by 17 miles, nearly as dark as coal, and dominated by a six-mile-wide crater called Stickney, evidence of a collision that nearly shattered the puny satellite. Phobos circles just 3,721 miles above the Martian surface (Earth's moon averages a distance of 239,000 miles) and completes an orbit in 7 hours and 39 minutes, making a Phobos "month" on Mars less than one-third of a Martian day. In fact, Phobos circles so close to Mars that tidal forces are slowly causing its orbit to decay. Within the next few tens of millions of years it will crash into the planet; we are catching it at the tail end of its 4.5-billion-year life.

4. The same proximity to Mars that will one day doom Phobos makes it an extremely attractive staging post for human explorers. One side of Phobos always faces Mars, and on that "hemisphere" the planet dominates the sky. This makes Phobos a good place for monitoring most of the Martian surface. Moreover, any manned outpost on Phobos would be well shielded from space radiation—protected on one side by Mars and on the other by the satellite's own bulk. From Phobos humans could explore the planet's sur-

face remotely using robots, eliminating the agonizing 10- to 20-minute delay that the operators of NASA's Mars rovers currently have to endure. Phobos would also be a natural staging area for manned excursions to Mars.

5. Before we start drawing up plans for outposts on Phobos, though, we need a much better grasp of what kind of place it is. Right now scientists do not even know exactly what Phobos is made of. It appears similar to a group of asteroids known as carbonaceous chondrites. These primitive objects contain amino acids, the building blocks of life, and appear to be nearly unchanged fragments of the material from which the solar system formed. Scientists have speculated that a rain of carbonaceous chondrites may have seeded early Earth with the raw material for biology here. Phobos's distinctive composition has led some scientists to suspect that it (along with Deimos, Mars's other miniature satellite) might be a captured asteroid. But that is far from a foregone conclusion.

6. "Phobos is a funny object," says David Beatty, chief scientist of the NASA Mars Exploration Directorate. "It's kind of a mystery why Phobos is there and where it came from." RKA, the Russian space agency, hopes to get some answers by having Fobos-Grunt gather samples of Phobos's battered surface. Back on Earth, detailed analysis will identify their precise composition and age. (A suite of onboard instruments will also do some analysis on Phobos.) From this we should get new insights into the history of Phobos and a broader snapshot of what our solar system was like in its formative days.

7. In this mission, Fobos-Grunt will get a huge assist from the laws of orbital mechanics. Owing to the counterintuitive rules of space navigation, it takes remarkably little energy to get to Phobos from Earth. In fact, the energy required to travel between two spots in the solar system has virtually nothing to do with the distance between them. What really matters is a quantity called delta-v, the amount that a spaceship's velocity must change to shift from one trajectory to another. Delta-v depends on how strong the gravitational fields are at your departure and arrival points; how much energy you need to swing farther out from (or in toward) the sun; and how much assistance you can get from atmospheric braking—that is, skimming through a planet's atmosphere to help slow down.

8. The total delta-v required for a mission to land on Phobos and come back is startlingly low—only about 80 percent that of a round trip to the surface of Earth's moon. (That is in part because of Phobos's feeble gravity; a well-aimed pitch could launch a softball off its surface.) It is actually easier to send a probe or cargo to Phobos than to the moon. The comparison for a manned flight is more complicated, since a crew would need much more food and air for the six-month journey to Phobos than for the three-day trip to our moon. But the huge additional delta-v needed to get down to the Mars surface and back up into orbit again means it would be vastly cheaper and easier to maintain an outpost on Phobos than on the Martian surface.

9. If the mission is successful, Fobos-Grunt will be the first probe to explore the Earth-Phobos-Earth space highway. The one-ton probe will enter orbit around Mars in August or September 2010 (as-

suming Russia's schedule does not slip) and begin studying Phobos remotely. Once the mission scientists have selected a good landing spot, the spacecraft will touch down on the satellite's surface sometime in March or April 2011. Then Fobos-Grunt will extend a robot arm and start collecting samples of regolith—surface soil and rocks—for return to Earth. The main body of the probe will serve as a launchpad for the small return module and remain permanently on Phobos. When the 233-pound return module reaches Earth in June or July 2012, it will drop off a soccer-ball-size capsule containing a thumb-size canister of precious Phobos soil; finally, the canister will make a hard landing in a remote region of Kazakhstan.

10. Planetary scientists hope that analysis of Phobos's regolith will shed light on the nature of the satellite's deep interior because of the turnover between the surface and the interior over the eons. Phobos's density is very low, about two-thirds that of ordinary basalt. This could mean that it is similar to water-rich objects in the outer edge of the asteroid belt, or it could mean that Phobos is a rubble pile, with many empty cavities between rock fragments. "The single most important issue to address on Phobos regarding the future human exploration of Mars is the question of water," says Pascal Lee, chairman of the Mars Institute, a research organization. "Does Phobos contain any water, and if so, in what amount, form, and location? Answers to these questions will help determine how we will travel to Mars."

11. Phobos's exterior poses some riddles of its own. Its most striking visual structures (aside from the giant Stickney crater) are sets of crater chains that line up across the surface. Deimos does not have anything like them, nor do any of the half-dozen regular asteroids imaged by space probes so far. One theory is that the craters are old steam vents, relics of an ancient catastrophe that cracked Phobos's crust and heated its interior, sending steam blasting outward. This would be good news for future human visits to Mars, as vents would mark the location of water-bearing minerals, perhaps even buried deposits of water ice. Another, less enticing possibility is that the holes are crevices opened by tidal forces or by impacts that caused the entire moon to flex.

12. A third theory holds that the crater chains are tied to ancient impacts on Mars. Some meteor strikes in Mars's past were powerful enough to propel pieces of the planet's crust at speeds greater than escape velocity, some 3.1 miles per second. We know this because scientists have found meteorites on Earth that clearly originated on Mars; these pieces evidently drifted around the solar system before landing here. If some fragments of the Martian surface reached Earth, many more of them should have hit Phobos on the way out. The swarms of rocks sent flying by a major impact on Mars might have created the crater chains seen on Phobos. In fact, by some estimates, up to 10 percent of the satellite's surface might consist of material that originated on Mars.

13. Seen in this light, Russia's Fobos-Grunt strategy looks rather clever. Despite its low profile, Phobos may turn out to be one of the most intriguing places in the solar system. And, located in a sweet spot of accessibility, it is a natural outpost for future space exploration, whether with people or with probes. If there is a key stepping-stone from Earth to Mars, this odd, intriguing space rock could be it.

(http://discovermagazine.com/2009/jun/21-russias-dark-horse-plan-to-get-to-mars)

Glossary

phobos ['fəubɔs] the larger of the two satellites of Mars *n*. [天]火卫一
crater ['kreitə] a bowl-shaped depression formed by the impact of a meteorite or bomb *n*. 火山口
puny ['pju:ni] inferior in strength or significance *adj*. 微小的,弱的
proximity [prɔk'simiti] the property of being close together *n*. 接近
agonize ['ægənaiz] cause to agonize *v*. 折磨
carbonaceous [kɑ:bə'neiʃəs] relating to or consisting of or yielding carbon *adj*. 碳的,碳质的,含碳的
chondrite ['kɔndrait] a rock of meteoric origin containing chondrules *n*. [地]球粒状陨石
deimos ['deimɔs] the outer of two small satellites of Mars *n*. 火卫二
foregone [fɔ:'gɔn] be earlier in time; go back further *adj*. 先前的,过去的,已知的
directorate [di'rektərit] a group of persons chosen to govern the affairs of a corporation or other large institution *n*. 董事,董事会
batter ['bætə] strike violently and repeatedly *v*. 猛击
counterintuitive [ˌkauntərin'tju:itiv] contrary to what common sense would suggest *adj*. 违反直觉的
delta-v ['deltə'vi:] a scalar which takes units of speed that measures the amount of "effort" needed to carry out an orbital maneuver, i.e., to change from one trajectory to another *n*. 加速度
trajectory [trə'dʒekətəri] the path followed by an object moving through space *n*. 轨道,弹道,轨线
regolith ['regəliθ] the layer of rocky debris and dust made by metoritic impact that forms the uppermost surface of planets, satellites and asteroids *n*. 风化层;土被;表皮土
eon ['i:ən] an immeasurably long period of time *n*. 千万年,永久
basalt [bə'sɔ:lt] the commonest type of solidified lava; a dense dark grey fine-grained igneous rock that is composed chiefly of plagioclase feldspar and pyroxene *n*. 玄武岩
enticing [in'taisiŋ] provoke someone to do something through (often false or exaggerated) promises or persuasion *adj*. 引诱的,迷人的
crevice ['krevis] a long narrow depression in a surface *n*. 裂缝
flex [fleks] form a curve *v*. 弯曲,褶曲

Exercises

A. Fill in each blank with one of the given words in its correct form.

| Enticing agonize eon puny counterintuitive |
| permanent swarm proximity foregone profile |

1. The words were either positive (e.g. cheerful, flower and peace), negative (e.g. _____, despair and murder) or neutral (e.g. box, ear or kettle).

2. Therefore, cancer vaccines, like vaccines against influenza or other diseases, offer the hope of _____ the immune system to recognize proteins found on the surface of cancerous cells.

3. These are the most significant results of a study on two boreholes drilled in _____ of the mouth of the Amazon River by Petrobras, the national oil company of Brazil.

4. More than a million cancer survivors living in the United States are _____ what they believe is necessary medical care due to the cost, and Hispanics and African-Americans are twice as likely to go without services, according to data presented at the American Association for Cancer Research conference on the Science of Health Care Disparities.

5. Individuals on dialysis have their blood removed, filtered, and then returned several times a week—a process that can be performed through a removable tube or catheter or through a _____ vascular access.

6. Researchers writing in the open access journal BMC Evolutionary Biology now report that it also occurs in a strictly monogamous species of bird, suggesting that the black-legged kittiwake possesses the ability to choose partners with a very different genetic _____.

7. The second largest earthquake _____ ever recorded in Yellowstone National Park occurred during the two weeks from 27 December 2008 and 7 January 2009 and included more than 1000 earthquakes.

8. _____ as it may seem, those healthful phytoestrogen nutrients that consumers usually associate with fruits and vegetables also exist in foods of animal origin.

9. The future internet will link billions of devices, or at least must be capable of doing so. It makes the most powerful network paradigms of today appear _____.

10. Because physical evidence of Earth's early bombardment has been erased by weathering and plate tectonics over the _____, the researchers used data from Apollo moon rocks, impact records from the moon, Mars and Mercury, and previous theoretical studies to build three-dimensional computer models that replicate the bombardment.

B. Skim the text and then answer the following questions.

1. Why is it important for man to probe Phobos?
2. What are some features of Phobos?
3. What is decisive for traveling between two spots in the solar system?
4. What are the differences between Phobos and the moon?
5. In what aspects is Phobos different from Deimos?

C. Read the text and choose the correct answer to each of the following questions.

1. Which of the following statement is incorrect on the features of Phobos? _____.
   A. It is an irregularly shaped mass
   B. It survived tremendous outside impact

C. It moves in an unchanged orbit around Mars

   D. It is different from the moon

2. Phobos is a good place for monitoring most of the Martian surface because _____.

   A. it is shielded from space radiation

   B. it is a natural staging area for manned excursions to mars

   C. one side of it always faces Mars

   D. humans could explore the planet's interior remotely using robots

3. Delta-v depends on _____.

   A. the relationship between the gravitational fields at your departure and arrival points

   B. the energy needed to swing out from or in toward the sun

   C. the help of atmospheric braking to accelerate

   D. the weight of the spacecraft

4. Which of the following statements is incorrect? _____.

   A. The total delta-v required for a mission to land on Phobos is only about 80 percent that of a trip to the surface of Earth's moon

   B. Missions to the Mars costs more than that to Phobos

   C. It's easier to send a probe to Phobos than to the moon

   D. The comparison for a manned flight to Phobos is more complicated than to our moon.

5. According to paragraph 9, it is correct that _____.

   A. Fobos-Grunt is to enter orbit around Mars in August or September 2010 definitely

   B. the main body of the probe will not retain to Earth

   C. a soccer-ball-size canister of Phobos soil will be sent back to Earth

   D. a robot will be send to correct samples

D. Explain the underlined parts.

1. Mars has been nothing but bad luck for the Russians.

2. It may give us clues to the formation of Earth's moon and the moons of the other planets, and the role played by asteroid impacts in shaping the terrestrial rocky planets.

3. It is a potato-shaped rock measuring only 12 miles by 17 miles, nearly as dark as coal, and dominated by a six-mile-wide crater called Stickney, evidence of a collision that nearly shattered the puny satellite.

4. From Phobos humans could explore the planet's surface remotely using robots, eliminating the agonizing 10- to 20-minute delay that the operators of NASA's Mars rovers currently have to endure. Phobos would also be a natural staging area for manned excursions to Mars.

5. Phobos's distinctive composition has led some scientists to suspect that it (along with Deimos, Mars's

other miniature satellite) <u>might be a captured asteroid</u>. But that is far from a foregone conclusion.

6. The one-ton probe will enter orbit around Mars in August or September 2010 (<u>assuming Russia's schedule does not slip</u>) and begin studying Phobos remotely.
7. <u>Once the mission scientists have selected a good landing spot</u>, the spacecraft will <u>touch down on the satellite's surface</u> sometime in March or April 2011.
8. Planetary scientists hope that analysis of Phobos's regolith will <u>shed light on the nature of the satellite's deep interior</u> because of the <u>turnover between the surface and the interior over the eons</u>.
9. <u>Seen in this light,</u> Russia's Fobos-Grunt strategy looks rather clever. <u>Despite its low profile,</u> Phobos may <u>turn out to be one of the most intriguing places in the solar system</u>.

E. Read the passages in this section and decide whether each of the following statements is true or false.

Passage One

Space is cool, that much is clear. Being in space—well, that's even cooler. Getting there, however, can be a problem. In the past you had to undergo years of schooling and become somewhat of a "rocket scientist". And, well, that's a lot of work and can really be a drag. However, what if there were an easier way to get into space, you know, simply by paying your way there? Well, it's been done before and it most certainly will be done again. Here are a few things you probably didn't know, but may want to remember, if you're interested in space tourism.

1. A Californian billionaire was the world's first space tourist

On April 28, 2001, Dennis Tito became the world's first paying space tourist to embark on space tourism when he forked over $20 million for the trip of a lifetime: an eight-day holiday aboard the International Space Station (ISS). A former NASA employee, Tito founded Wilshire Associates, a California-based powerhouse in consulting, technology and investment management that helped the entrepreneur amass billions of dollars in personal assets. However, money can't buy you everything—Tito faced numerous setbacks in his bid to buy his way into space tourism.

First, NASA rejected his proposal on the grounds that he was not sufficiently trained. Tito then turned to Russia, only to have his proposal rejected when the original destination—the Mir Space Station—was decommissioned and fell out of orbit. Finally, through partnership with Space Adventures, Ltd., Tito secured a spot on Soyuz TM-32, a Russian supply ship bound for the ISS. However, the sudden change in plans generated great political tension between Russia and the United States, with NASA agreeing to allow Tito to board the ISS only if he agreed to take full responsibility for his actions and not sue over injury or illness.

Despite the political row, Mr. Tito described his space tourism experience as euphoric; "I spent 60 years on Earth and eight days in space, and from my viewpoint it was two separate lives," the U.S. tycoon told CNN.

2. By 2009 suborbital tours may go for a cool $100,000

Imagine being boosted 62 miles straight up into the sky, seated comfortably in a six-passenger suborbital spacecraft. At the apex of your flight, on the verge of where space begins, you'll sit weightless in dead silence, just below orbiting satellites, where the curvature of the Earth and a dark, star-filled sky meet your eye. This space tourism odyssey could all be yours for a mere $100,000.

Starting in late 2009, companies such as Virgin Galactic and Space Adventures, Ltd. will begin offering weekly suborbital flights of space tourism to the wealthy and adventurous. Despite the rather hefty price tag, ranging between $100,000 and $200,000, surveys show considerable interest among wealthy executives, and the price is expected to drop considerably as suborbital flights become routine and as competition grows. With a handful of private space tourism companies expected to offer suborbital flights in the coming years, the competition will certainly grow. However, some questions arose about whether the supply will meet the insane demand for space tourism: "[it's] an experience that sells itself," says TheSpaceReview.com. After looking at the awesome designs of some of the spacecrafts, we couldn't agree more.

(http://www.askmen.com/entertainment/special_feature_150/195_special_feature.html)

_____ 1. In order to travel in the outer space, one needs to study for years and become somewhat of a "rocket scientist".

_____ 2. Tito had worked in NASA before he became the first world paying space tourist.

_____ 3. Tito's request to travel to ISS was rejected by Russia because he was not sufficiently trained.

_____ 4. That more companies would engage themselves in offering space tours will leads to a great decrease in the price charged.

_____ 5. Not every company can offer qualified spacecraft for space tourists.

Passage Two

US and Russian scientists are planning the ultimate in fuel-economy travel: they hope to launch a space sailing ship driven only by the pressure of sunlight later this year.

Cosmos 1, an unfurled fan of 15 metre sails, each far thinner than a dustbin bag but stiffened and coated with mirror material, could be launched from a Russian nuclear missile submarine.

A rocket designed during the cold war to attack Britain or the US will be fired from beneath the Barents Sea with the furled sail in place of its warhead.

The Russians will use a second piece of cold war rocketry-designed to take spy satellites out of orbit-to push the spacecraft to its ideal orbit of 800km, far above the last wisps of the Earth's atmosphere.

Then it will unfurl its sails. According to theory, as the solar rays hit the mirrored surface of the sails and then bounce away, they will exert pressure. Even in the pure vacuum of space this pressure will be barely perceptible: five millionths of the push exerted, for instance, by an apple in the palm of a hand.

But under this lighter-than-featherweight touch, the spacecraft will begin to move. The 100kg object will accelerate at a barely measurable fraction of a millimetre per second, but will gain speed with every second in the sun. By the end of the first day it will have increased its velocity by 100mph. In 100 days, it could reach 10,000mph.

Cosmos 1 is a venture by the Planetary Society—an independent international group of enthusiasts and space veterans—backed by a film and television company called Cosmos Studios and working with the Russian Academy's space research, Russian contractors and the Russian navy.

Space sailing ships were first proposed in 1924, more than 30 years before the first successful rocket launch.

Rocket fuel is the biggest single cost in a space mission, and the US, European and Japanese space agencies all have solar sailing projects. The first to go up, however, will be an entirely private venture.

A suborbital test in 2001 failed, but only because the third stage of the rocket failed to separate. The Cosmos 1 team had hoped to launch last year, and then again earlier this year. Launch could still slip to early 2005.

"We had a couple of setbacks in difficulties with the radio system development, and the software testing took longer than planned," said Louis Friedman, the director of the Planetary Society, who once worked on a Nasa solar sail project. "Also the Russians, with our agreement, kept adding capabilities to the spacecraft. Progress isn't really slow-developing anything new is a complex process in which hope always exceeds reality."

The spacecraft has now passed all its electronic tests. The sails and control console, made in Russia, will be packed and shipped to the launch area. Progress will be tracked by Russian ground stations, the US air force and US government agencies. The best hope is that once launched, Cosmos 1 will spiral away from Earth for a month: proof that theorists got their sums right.

The sails could be adjusted like helicopter blades to alter flight direction and speed.

Solar sails are, for the moment, the only hope for interstellar missions. Although far slower than a chemically powered rocket, a space clipper would continue to accelerate as long as there was sunlight. Craft like Cosmos 1 could reach Pluto in five years. The fastest orthodox mission planned so far would take nine years.

Ann Druyan, a founder of Cosmos Studios and the wife of the late astronomer and writer Carl Sagan, said: "If Cosmos 1 succeeds it will be visible throughout much of the world to the naked eye, a signal flare of hope for the wise use of science and high technology. Over the past four years I've imagined Cosmos 1's vast silvery sails unfurling in space countless times. If it does come to pass, it will be a thing of beauty and a milestone of progress on the long human journey to the stars."

(http://www.buzzle.com/editorials/8-15-2004-57890.asp)

_____ 6. Cosmos 1 could be launched from a Russian nuclear missile.

_____ 7. As the solar rays hit the mirrored surface of the sails and then bounce away, they will exert pressure which cannot be detected.

_____ 8. The first rocket was launched more than 30 years before space sailing ships were proposed.

_____ 9. Flight direction and speed of the sails could be adjusted.

_____ 10. Although far slower than a chemically powered rocket, a space clipper would continue to accelerate at anytime.

F. Cloze. Fill in each blank with one suitable word.

Data from public opinion __1__ indicate that nearly fifty million people would like to visit space. In __2__ as many as two million people each year would take the journey __3__ the outer limits of Earth's gravity. The public's fascination with space travel means the potential development of a space travel tourism industry with revenues that could __4__ to $10 billion or more every year.

__5__, it really is not hard to understand the interest in commercial space travel by private business. In fact, more than six companies are working to making commercial space travel a __6__. However, the company that is closest to becoming the industry pioneer is Virgin Galactic. The company is a well __7__ joint venture of Richard Branson, Burt Rutan, and Paul Allen.

Eager future space travelers should consider that the development of Virgin Galactic's Space Ship Two is nearly completed and could be __8__ test flights by the end of the year into space. The spacecrafts successful predecessor, Spaceship One, __9__ reached space on October 4, 2004, winning the $10m Ansari X Prize. The larger and more powerful, Space Ship Two, is being built to __10__ two pilots and six passengers. Indeed, there will be enough room on board to experience the freedom of movement in the zero gravity of space. Initially, Virgin Galactic has ordered five spaceships to begin the business of commercial space travel and tourism.

1. A. studies   B. polls   C. researches   D. investigations
2. A. theory   B. fact   C. practice   D. principle
3. A. away   B. from   C. beyond   D. off
4. A. amount   B. account   C. add   D. count
5. A. Therefore   B. But   C. Moreover   D. Firstly
6. A. dream   B. reality   C. matter   D. practice
7. A. found   B. find   C. fund   D. funded

8. A. performed   B. performing   C. experienced   D. experiencing
9. A. last   B. first   C. next   D. ever
10. A. carry   B. take   C. accommodate   D. present

G. Translate the following passages into Chinese/English.

1. From cyborg housemaids and waterpowered cars to dog translators and rocket boots, Japanese boffins have racked up plenty of near - misses in the quest to turn science fiction into reality. Now the finest scientific minds of Japan are devoting themselves to cracking the greatest sci - fi vision of all: the space elevator. Man has so far conquered space by painfully and inefficiently blasting himself out of the atmosphere but the 21st century should bring a more leisurely ride to the final frontier. For chemists, physicists, material scientists, astronauts and dreamers across the globe, the space elevator represents the most tantalising of concepts: cables stronger and lighter than any fibre yet woven, tethered to the ground and disappearing beyond the atmosphere to a satellite docking station in geosynchronous orbit above Earth.

2. 日本对其覆盖范围广泛的学术基础及工业基础能够解决这些工程学难题越来越有信心,甚至开出了1万亿日元(50亿英镑)这个低得惊人的太空电梯建造账单。日本因其在精密工程学和优质材料制造领域国际领先而享有盛誉,没有这二者太空电梯这一创意也许永远无法实现。线缆是最大的障碍。把太空电梯从地球表面送上同步卫星需要总长为其间距离两倍的线缆来实现配重,以确保维持线缆自身的张力。线缆还必须特别轻和出奇的坚韧,同时能承受住大气层内外所有抛射体对它的撞击。据一些设计小组的说法,解决之道在于应用碳质纳米管——能够合成为纤维的微小粒子。日本的一些大型纺织公司如今都在关注碳质纳米管的大规模生产。

Text B

Solar Sailing

1. Long ago, someone stood alone on a sandy shore and gazed longingly out at the seemingly endless expanse of ocean, over a horizon suffused softly with ocean mist, musing "I wonder, what's out there?". Then, they fashioned a boat, rigged it with a large cloth to catch the wind, and set sail.

2. Not quite so long ago, someone stood alone on a sandy shore and gazed longingly up at the seemingly endless expanse of space, suffused softly with sparkling stars, musing "I wonder, what's out there?". Then, they fashioned a spacecraft, rigged it with a large cloth to catch the Sun, and set sail.

3. The first paragraph: Already happened. The second: Any day now.

May the Solar Force be with You

4. To fully appreciate how spacecraft can deploy a solar sail to harness the power of sunlight, let's travel back in time for a brief history of solar sailing. Almost 400 years ago, German astronomer Johannes Kepler observed comet tails being blown by what he thought to be a solar "breeze." This observation inspired him to suggest that "ships and sails proper for heavenly air should be fashioned" to glide through space.

5. Little did Kepler know, the best way to propel a solar sail is not by means of solar wind, but rather by the force of sunlight itself. In 1873, James Clerk Maxwell first demonstrated that sunlight exerts a small amount of pressure as photons bounce off a reflective surface. This kind of pressure is the basis of all modern solar sail designs.

6. In 1960, the large balloon-like satellite Echo-1 felt these solar pressure effects loudly and clearly. "Photon pressure played orbital soccer with the Echo-1 thin-film balloon in orbit... The shards were flung far and wide by sunlight."

NASA Blazes the Trail

7. NASA had a more positive experience with solar sailing in 1974 when the Mariner 10 spacecraft ran low on attitude control gas. Because Mariner 10 was on a mission to Mercury, there was plenty of sunlight around and this gave mission controllers an idea. They angled Mariner's solar arrays into the Sun and used solar radiation pressure for attitude control. It worked. Though Mariner 10 was not a solar sail mission, and though the radiation pressure it used was incredibly small, this ingenious use of Mariner's solar arrays did demonstrate the principle of solar sailing.

8. Also in the 1970s, Dr Louis Friedman, then at NASA's Jet Propulsion Laboratory, led a project to try the first solar sail flight. Halley's Comet was to make its closest approach to Earth in 1986, and NASA conceived the exciting idea of propelling a probe via solar sail to rendezvous with the comet. Eventually, the project was scrapped. Still the year-long work on preliminary design demonstrated that, indeed, solar sailing was a feasible spacecraft-propulsion technique.

Russia Sails the Space Frontier

9. In 1993, the Russian Space Agency launched a 20-meter diameter, spinning mirror called Znamya 2 (pictured), hoping to beam solar power back to the ground.

10. "Some call Znamya 2 a sail because it was made of a large, lightweight reflector and unfurled like a solar sail might be unfurled," says Les Johnson of the NASA Marshall Space Flight Center, co-author of the newly published book Solar Sails: A Novel Approach to Interplanetary Travel. "In fact, if I were asked to demonstrate solar sail technology and was constrained to deploy it from a large spacecraft, I might design a 'sail' like Znamya."

11. The foil reflector unfurled and when illuminated produced a spot of light which crossed Europe

from France to Russia. Unable to control its own flight, however, the mirror burned up in the atmosphere over Canada. Russia's proto-sail program was abandoned in 1999 after a larger, follow-up mission (Znamya 2.5) failed to deploy properly.

12. Solar sails were an accessory on India's INSAT 2A and 3A communications satellites, circa 1992 and 2003. The satellites were powered by a 4-panel solar array on one side. A solar sail was mounted on the north side of each satellite to offset the torque resulting from solar pressure on the array.

13. In 2004, the Japanese deployed solar sail materials sub-orbitally from a sounding rocket. Although it was not a demonstration of a free-flying solar sail that could be used for deep-space exploration, the deployment was nevertheless "a valuable milestone" remarks Friedman, who appreciates the challenges of deploying gossamer sheets from fast-moving spacecraft.

14. To date, no solar sail has been successfully deployed in space as a primary means of propulsion.

The Challenges Ahead

15. The Planetary Society hoped to demonstrate the technology with its Cosmos 1 mission in 2005. "Cosmos 1 was a fully developed solar sail spacecraft intended to fly only under the influence of solar pressure for control of the spacecraft's orbit," says Friedman, now the director of the Planetary Society.

16. "If all had gone as planned, the US-based Planetary Society, working with Russia, would have been the first to fly a fully functional, though performance-limited, solar sail in space," says Johnson. "It would have been the first spin-stabilized, free-flying solar sail to fly in space." Cosmos 1, however, was lost when the launch vehicle failed.

17. Meanwhile, NASA has also continued to dabble in solar sailing. Between 2001 and 2005, the Agency developed two different 20-meter solar sails (fabricated by ATK Space Systems and L'Garde, Inc., respectively) and tested them on the ground in vacuum conditions. "These sail designs are robust enough for deployment in a one atmosphere, one gravity environment and are scalable to much larger solar sails-perhaps as much as 150 meters on one side. A NASA flight test is possible by the year 2010."

18. Edward E. Montgomery's team from the Marshall Space Flight Center has been working in cooperation with Elwood Agasid's Ames team toward deploying the NanoSail-D solar sail, which was launched on a SpaceX Falcon 1 rocket, from Omelek Island in the Pacific Ocean on August 2. Unfortunately, that launch vehicle too failed when the second stage separated from the first. Before the mission, Montgomery stated: "Our primary objective is to demonstrate successful deployment of a lightweight solar sail structure in low Earth orbit." They hoped to measure two types of pressure as NanoSail-D circled Earth: (1) aerodynamic drag from the wispy top of Earth's atmosphere and (2) the pressure of sunlight.

19. And what of Cosmos 2? The mission is a privately funded project, a partnership of The Planetary Society and Cosmos Studios. Work has begun at the Russian Space Research Institute on some Cos-

mos 2 spacecraft hardware. They are also studying possible launch configurations on a reliable launch vehicle.

Interstellar Flight

20. If successful, Cosmos 2 and its successors could profoundly affect the future of science and exploration missions.

21. "Success would be huge for the future of space exploration," says Montgomery.

22. "Solar sailing is the only means known to achieve practical interstellar flight," says Friedman. "It is our hope that the first solar sail flight will spur the development of solar sail technology so that this dream can be made real."

23. Each effort is a stepping stone, in the great visionary Carl Sagan's words, along "the shore of the cosmic ocean," leading us closer to sailing among the stars. Future attempts will surely take us the rest of the way.

24. "'Twas all so pretty a sail it seemed

As if it could not be,

And some folks thought 'twas a dream they'd dreamed

Of sailing that beautiful sea."

—Eugene Field

(http://www.firstscience.com/home/articles/machines/solar-sailing_51134.html)

Glossary

suffuse [sə'fju:z] spread or flush or flood through, over, or across v. 遍布，弥漫，充满

muse [mju:z] reflect deeply on a subject v. 冥思

rig [rig] equip with sails or masts v. 装配帆具

deploy [di'plɔi] to distribute systematically or strategically v. 配置，部署

harness ['hɑ:nis] control and direct with or as if by reins v. 控制

comet ['kɔmit] (astronomy) a relatively small extraterrestrial body consisting of a frozen mass that travels around the sun in a highly elliptical orbit n. 彗星

photon ['fəutɔn] a quantum of electromagnetic radiation; an elementary particle that is its own antiparticle n. 光子

bounce [bauns] spring back v. 弹回

shard [ʃɑ:d] a broken piece of a brittle artifact n. 碎片（薄硬壳）

ingenious [in'dʒi:njəs] marked by independence and creativity in thought or action adj. 有独创性的

propel [prə'pel] cause to move forward with force v. 推进

rendezvous ['rɔndivu:] to meet at a certain planned time and place v. 约会

preliminary [pri'liminəri] designed to orient or acquaint with a situation before proceeding *adj.* 初步的，预备的

unfurl [ʌn'fə:l] unroll, unfold, or spread out or be unrolled, unfolded, or spread out from a furled state *v.* 展开

interplanetary [ˌintə(:)'plænitəri] between or among planets *adj.* 行星间的

constrain [kən'strein] restrict *v.* 限制

illuminate [i'lju:mineit] make lighter or brighter *v.* 照明

accessory [æk'sesəri] a supplementary component that improves capability *n.* 附件

offset ['ɔ:fset] compensate for or counterbalance *v.* 弥补，抵销

torque [tɔ:k] a twisting force *n.* 转力矩

gossamer ['gɔsəmə] characterized by unusual lightness and delicacy *adj.* 薄弱的

dabble ['dæbl] work with in an amateurish manner *v.* 装出什么都知道的样子，充内行

robust [rə'bʌst] physically strong *adj.* 强壮的，强健的

scalable ['skeiləbl] capable of being scaled; possible to scale *adj.* 可以测量的

aerodynamic [ˌɛərəudai'næmik] designed or arranged to offer the least resistant to fluid flow *adj.* 空气动力的

wispy ['wispi] thin and weak *adj.* 稀的

configuration [kənˌfigju'reiʃən] an arrangement of parts or elements *n.* 结构，布局

Exercises

A. Fill in each blank with one of the given words in its correct form.

| configuration | bounce | preliminary | wispy | rendezvous |
| interplanetary | torque | propulsion | robust | deploy |

1. Two teams of one astronaut and one geologist each have been driving the rover through the Arizona desert, trying it out in two different _____.

2. The gas being lit up in these star-forming regions looks very _____ and fragile, but looks can be deceiving.

3. The catalysts have a high surface area, invaluable for a number of applications besides in fuel cells, and are _____ and stable.

4. However, to counter the effects of gravity and remain in place, they would have to be equipped with cutting-edge electric ion _____.

5. Researchers at Boston University working with collaborators in Germany, France and Korea have developed a nanoscale torsion resonator that measures miniscule amounts of twisting or _____ in a metallic nanowire.

6. The _____ design review is one of a series of checkpoints that occurs in the design life cycle of a complex engineering project before hardware manufacturing can begin.
7. Working together they are studying the best ways to _____, maintain, continuously collect environmental and water quality data and evaluate the effects of long-term sensor deployment on water quality monitoring systems and sensor data from a number of sites, and disseminate the findings to the widest possible audience.
8. A group of physicists from the University of Liege, Belgium, is publishing research in the New Journal of Physics today, Tuesday, 18 November, which shows how lab technicians can make droplets dance, float and _____ above a surface, keeping small amounts of fluid free of contamination and ripe for testing.
9. When the lunar module took off from the surface of the moon 40 years ago Neil Armstrong and Buzz Aldrin were relying on 4 cubic tonnes of N2O4 — one of the most important rocket propellants ever developed — to return them to lunar orbit and _____ with the Apollo Command and Service Module.
10. The solar wind, which carries the particles from the sun's magnetic field, known as the _____ magnetic field, takes about three or four days to reach the Earth.

B. Skim the text and then answer the following questions.
1. What is the function of the comparison presented in the first two paragraphs?
2. What is the reason why Znamya can be called a sail in a certain sense?
3. What are the challenges facing scientists in solar sailing?
4. What do you learn about Cosmos 2 from the text?
5. What is your thought on the implication of the poem by Eugene Field?

C. Read the text and choose the correct answer to each of the following questions.
1. Which is the best way to propel a solar sail? _____.
   A. A solar breeze　　　B. Heavenly air　　　C. The force of sunlight　　　D. Photons
2. Which of the following statements is not true? _____.
   A. Mariner 10 was on a mission to Mercury
   B. Solar pressure was used for attitude control of Mariner 10
   C. A considerable amount of solar force was employed on Mariner 10
   D. Solar arrays of Mariner 10 could be adjusted
3. The word "scrapped" in "Eventually, the project was scrapped (paragraph 9)" means _____.
   A. abandoned　　　B. failed completely　　C. separated in parts　D. refused
4. According to the text, solar sails _____.
   A. are made of a large, lightweight reflector

B. are unfurled

C. produce a spot of light

D. can work as a supplementary component

5. It can be inferred from the text that _____.

   A. different methods were used to control the orbit of Cosmos 1

   B. Cosmos 1 was incapable of carrying out a wide-range of functions

   C. US worked alone on the Cosmos 1 project

   D. Cosmos 1 failed

D. Explain the underlined parts.

1. Not quite so long ago, someone stood alone on a sandy shore and <u>gazed longingly up at the seemingly endless expanse of space, suffused softly with sparkling stars, musing</u> "I wonder, what's out there?". Then, <u>they fashioned a spacecraft,</u> rigged it with a large cloth to catch the Sun, and set sail.

2. This observation <u>inspired him to suggest</u> that "<u>ships and sails proper for heavenly air should be fashioned</u>" to glide through space.

3. Halley's Comet was <u>to make its closest approach to Earth</u> in 1986, and NASA <u>conceived the exciting idea of propelling a probe via solar sail to rendezvous with the comet.</u>

4. These sail designs are <u>robust enough for deployment</u> in a one atmosphere, one gravity environment and <u>are scalable to much larger solar sails</u>—perhaps as much as 150 meters on one side. A NASA flight test is possible by the year 2010.

5. If successful, <u>Cosmos 2 and its successors could profoundly affect the future of science and exploration missions.</u>

Unit 16　Mind and Brain

Text A

The Big Similarities and Quirky Differences between Our Left and Right Brains

1. There is nothing more humbling or more perception-changing than holding a human brain in your hands. I discovered this recently at a brain-cutting lesson given by Jean-Paul Vonsattel, a neuropathologist at Columbia University. These lessons take place every month in a cold, windowless room deep within the university's College of Physicians and Surgeons. On the day I visited, there were half a dozen brains sitting on a table. Vonsattel began by passing them around so the medical students could take a closer look. When a brain came my way, I cradled it and found myself puzzling over its mirror symmetry. It was as if someone had glued two smaller brains together to make a bigger one.

2. Vonsattel then showed us just how weak that glue is. He took back one of the brains and used a knife to divide the hemispheres. He sliced quickly through the corpus callosum, the flat bundle of nerve fibers that connects the halves. The hemispheres flopped away from each other, two identical slabs of fleshy neurons.

3. Sometimes surgeons must make an even more extreme kind of slice in the brain of a patient. A child may suffer from epilepsy so severe that the only relief doctors can offer is to open up the skull and cut out the entire hemisphere in which the seizures start. After the surgery, the space soon fills with cerebrospinal fluid. It may take a child a year of physical therapy to recover from losing a hemisphere—but the fact that patients recover at all is stunning when you consider that they have only half a brain. It makes you wonder what good two hemispheres are in the first place.

4. In fact, scientists have spent a lot of time pondering this very question. Their best answer has a lot to do with the form and evolutionary history of our bodies. From early in our development as embryos, humans take on a left-right symmetry that eventually gives rise to our two eyes, our two big toes, and every paired structure in between. All vertebrates are symmetrical in the same way, as are butterflies, scorpions, and a vast number of other invertebrates. This left-right structure is probably inherited from the

common ancestor of all bilaterally symmetric animals, a creature that apparently emerged over 570 million years ago.

5. There were some obvious survival benefits from left-right symmetry. With muscles and limbs on both sides of their bodies, animals could move forward quickly and efficiently. Once established, symmetry had a powerful effect on how new organs evolved. Eyes and antennae tended to develop in left-right pairs, for example. When early fish began to evolve complex brains, those too developed according to left-right rules. The human brain is very different from the brain of a lamprey, but in both species the neocortex—the outer layers of the brain—is divided into two mirror-image hemispheres.

6. Of course, our bodies are not perfectly symmetrical (heart on the left, appendix on the right), and neither are our brains. Some regions are slightly bigger on one side than on the other, and these differences translate into imbalances in how the human brain works. Most people, for example, tend to favor their right hand over their left. In the mid-1800s, the French physician Paul Broca discovered a region on the left side of the brain that is essential for language; damage to Broca's area, as it is called, leaves people unable to talk. The same region on the right side is not so vital. Another area, on the underside of the brain, is important for recognizing people's faces. The right half of this region, known as the facial fusiform area, does most of the work of recognizing. In fact, if people view a face only through their left eye (which is linked to the brain's right hemisphere), they will do a better job of recognizing it than if they use only their right eye.

7. These sorts of findings helped to turn the hemispheres into pop phenoms. People were tagged as "right brains" if they could draw and "left brains" if they were analytical. Academics made some big claims about the hemispheres as well. In the 1990s psychologist Michael Corballis of the University of Auckland in New Zealand argued that the asymmetry of the brain—known as lateralization—was a key step in the evolution of our species, giving us language and additional mental powers that other animals lack.

8. Today Corballis readily admits he was wrong. Lateralized brains are not unique to humans. Parrots prefer picking up things with their left foot. Toads tend to attack other toads from the right but go after prey from the left. Zebra fish are likely to look at new things with their right eye and familiar things with their left. Even invertebrates are biased. Pinar Letzkus, a vision researcher at Australian National University, rewarded bees with sugar whenever they extended their tongue at the sight of a yellow rectangle on a computer screen. He then fashioned tiny eye patches and put them on a new set of subjects. Bees with their left eye covered learned almost as quickly as did bees without a patch. But bees with their right eye covered did far worse.

9. The broken symmetry of the nervous system may thus be as old as the symmetry itself. If so, it is an ancient puzzle. Being biased to one side would seem like a serious handicap: A toad that hopped to the

left whenever it was startled by a predator, for instance, would be easy prey for an attacker that could anticipate which way it would go; the same holds for any other kind of ingrained behavioral imbalance. A number of scientists have run experiments to find the benefits that might offset such costs.

10. One hypothesis is that a lateralized brain is more powerful than one that works like a mirror image. Instead of two matching parts of the brain performing an identical task, one can take charge, leaving the other free to do something else. Lesley Rogers, a biologist at the University of New England in Australia, tested this hypothesis on chickens. The birds use their left hemisphere to peck for seeds and their right hemisphere to detect predators. Some chickens have more lateralized brains than others, and there is a simple way to make any chicken more lateralized: Just shine a light on it while it is still in the egg. Chick embryos usually develop with the left eye tucked inward and the right eye facing out. The stimulation of light on the right eye alters the developing left-brain hemisphere but not the right.

11. Rogers and her colleagues reared 27 chicks that had been exposed to light and 24 that had not. Each day the researchers put the chicks in a special box with grain and pebbles scattered on the floor; at the same time, they distracted the birds by moving a hawk-shaped cutout overhead. They then observed how well the chicks were able to distinguish between pebbles and grain. Light-exposed chicks learned to do a much better job. Rogers concludes that lateralized brains allowed the chicks to multitask more effectively, with each eye handling a separate job.

12. David Stark of Harvard Medical School recently found additional clues about lateralization in his studies of 112 different regions in the brains of volunteers. He and his collaborators discovered that the front portions of the brain are generally less tightly synchronized across the hemispheres than are the ones in the back. It may be no coincidence that the highly synchronized back regions handle basic functions like seeing. To observe the world, it helps to have unified vision. At the front of the hemispheres, in contrast, we weave together streams of thought to produce complex, long-term plans for the future. It makes sense that these areas of the brain would be more free to drift apart from their mirror-image partners.

13. No matter how lateralized the brain can get, though, the two sides still work together. The pop psychology notion of a left brain and a right brain doesn't capture their intimate working relationship. The left hemisphere specializes in picking out the sounds that form words and working out the syntax of the words, for example, but it does not have a monopoly on language processing. The right hemisphere is actually more sensitive to the emotional features of language, tuning in to the slow rhythms of speech that carry intonation and stress.

14. Neuroscientists know that the hemispheres work together and that they do so by communicating through the corpus callosum. But exactly how the hemispheres cooperate is not so clear. Perhaps paired regions take turns being dominant. That is known to happen in some animals. For instance, dolphins use

this strategy to sleep and swim at the same time: One hemisphere remains active for hours, then fades while the other takes over. Bird brains switch as well. In order to sing, a songbird makes the two sides of its lungs open and close. The two hemispheres of the bird's brain take turns controlling the song, each dominating for a hundredth of a second.

15. The intimate cooperation between the two hemispheres makes it all the more remarkable that a person can survive with just one—a sign that the brain is far more malleable than we once thought. After a hemisphere is forced to manage on its own, it can rewire itself to handle all the tasks of a full brain. In fact, two hemispheres can cause more trouble than one if they cannot talk clearly to each other. Neuroscientists have linked some mental disorders, including dyslexia and Alzheimer's, with a breakdown in left-right communication.

16. The two sides of the brain may be a legacy that we inherited from our wormlike ancestors. But their delicate balance of symmetry and specialization is now woven into the very essence of human nature.

(http://discovermagazine.com/2009/may/15-big-similarities-and-quirky-differences-between-our-left-and-right-brains)

Glossary

neuropathologist [ˌnjuərəupə'θɔlədʒist] a specialist who practices neuropathology—the study of disease of nervous system tissue, usually in the form of either small surgical biopsies or whole autopsy brains *n*. 神经病理学家

mirror symmetry ['mirə'simitri] one side looks like the other; bilateral symmetry or reflective symmetry *n*. 镜像对称

hemisphere ['hemisfiə] half of a sphere *n*. 半球

slab [slæb] block consisting of a thick piece of something *n*. 平板,厚的切片

epilepsy ['epilepsi] a disorder of the central nervous system characterized by loss of consciousness and convulsions *n*. 癫痫症

seizure ['si:ʒə] a sudden occurrence (or recurrence) of a disease *n*. 急发症状

cerebrospinal [ˌseribrəu'spainl] of or relating to the brain and spinal cord *adj*. 脑脊髓的

vertebrate ['və:tibrit] animals having a bony or cartilaginous skeleton with a segmented spinal column and a large brain enclosed in a skull or cranium *n*. 脊椎动物

lamprey ['læmpri] primitive eellike freshwater or anadromous cyclostome having round sucking mouth with a rasping tongue *n*. 八目鳗,七鳃鳗

fusiform ['fju:zifɔ:m] tapering at each end; spindle-shaped *adj*. 纺锤状的,两端渐细的

ingrained [in'greind] firmly fixed or held *adj*. 根深蒂固的

lateralized ['lætərəˌlaizd] move or displace to one side so as to make lateral *adj*. [医]单侧性的

collaborator [kə'læbəreitə(r)] an associate who works with others toward a common goal *n*. 合干者,合作者,共同研究者

synchronize ['siŋkrənaiz] operate simultaneously *v*. 使同时,同时发生

coincidence [kəu'insidəns] an event that might have been arranged although it was really accidental *n*. 巧合,同时发生

syntax ['sintæks] the grammatical arrangement of words in sentences *n*. 句法

monopoly [mə'nɔpəli] exclusive control or possession of something *n*. 垄断,独占,控制

hemisphere ['hemisfiə] either half of the cerebrum *n*. 半球

corpus callosum ['kɔːpəs'kæləsəm] a broad transverse nerve tract connecting the two cerebral hemispheres *n*. 胼胝体

malleable ['mæliəbl] easily influenced; capable of being shaped or bent or drawn out *adj*. 可塑的,易改变的

dyslexia [dis'leksiə] impaired ability to learn to read *n*. 阅读障碍

Alzheimer's ['ɔːltshaimərz] a form of dementia where a person's mental capacity decreases as a result of physical changes to the person's brain *n*. 阿尔茨海默病

Exercises

A. Fill in each blank with one of the given words in its correct form.

monopoly	synchronize	seizure	ponder	coincidence
evolution	malleable	capture	hemisphere	ingrained

1. According to the study, ant communities in the northern _____ may have suffered more extinctions as a result of the climate changes that occurred between 53 and 54 million years ago.

2. Approximately 10 percent of affected children have intractable epilepsy, a condition in which medications alone do not control _____ and _____ have a disabling effect on quality of life.

3. "It's really important to intervene early before violent behaviour is too _____," says Jacinthe Guèvremont, who has started a program at the Université de Montréal daycare that aims to prevent developmental problems.

4. Colliding galaxies eventually merge, and become a single galaxy. When the orbit and rotation _____, galaxies merge quickly.

5. Construction of new coal-fired power plants in the United States is in danger of coming to a standstill, partly due to the high cost of the requirement — whether existing or anticipated — to _____ all emissions of carbon dioxide, an important greenhouse gas.

6. By splitting airport "types" into two categories — those with a _____ and those that host multiple airlines — Dr. Ater began to see clear patterns emerge.

7. _____ detection is important when a person associates a smell with a specific memory or assigns importance to an event.
8. Research published in Molecular Psychiatry suggests that those carrying "vulnerability genes" are not only more likely than others to be adversely affected by negative experiences but to also benefit more than others from positive environments, making them more _____ or plastic, not just vulnerable.
9. It is widely believed that Darwinian natural selection is responsible, but research led by a group at Uppsala University, suggests that a separate neutral (nonadaptive) process has made a significant contribution to human _____.
10. Another key finding for Russian policy makers to _____, said Leon, is that the majority of the 271 products purchased were a cheaper source of alcohol than standard Russian vodka.

B. Skim the text and then answer the following questions.
1. What does the author mean by saying, "There is nothing more humbling or more perception-changing than holding a human brain in your hands"?
2. What are some special functions controlled by different region of the two hemispheres?
3. In what way is being biased to one side of the brain a serious handicap?
4. What does the experiment carried out by Rogers and her colleagues indicate?
5. How do the two hemispheres take turns in working for certain species?

C. Read the text and choose the correct answer to each of the following questions.
1. According to the text, which of the following is NOT TRUE concerning a child who may suffer from severe epilepsy? _____.
   A. The only relief for the child could be to open up the skull and cut out one hemisphere
   B. It will take a year for the child to recover from the disease
   C. The child can recover from losing one hemisphere
   D. After the hemisphere is taken out, cerebrospinal fluid will take its place
2. A number of _____ may not be symmetrical in structure.
   A. mammals   B. birds   C. vertebrates   D. invertebrates
3. Which of the following statements is incorrect in respect to the non-perfect symmetrical body of humans? _____.
   A. That the brain is not of a perfect symmetrical structure can account for certain aspects of the way our brain works
   B. People's preference of one hand over the other is a result of the fact that we are not perfectly symmetrical in body
   C. Damage to the left side of the brain will leave a person unable to distinguish between people
   D. To view a face only using the left eye is a more efficient way to recognize people

4. Which of the following creatures is not mentioned as having lateralized brains? _____ .
   A. The parrot	B. The toad	C. The zebra	D. The bee
5. The phrase "tune in" in "The right hemisphere is actually more sensitive to the emotional features of language, tuning in to the slow rhythms of speech that carry intonation and stress" means _____ .
   A. to select a channel	B. to pay attention
   C. to make work as well as possible	D. to adjust

D. Explain the underlined parts.
1. There is nothing <u>more humbling or more perception-changing than holding a human brain in your hands</u>.
2. It may take a child a year of physical therapy to recover from losing a hemisphere—<u>but the fact that patients recover at all is stunning when you consider that they have only half a brain</u>.
3. From early in our development <u>as embryos</u>, humans take on a left-right symmetry that eventually gives rise to our two eyes, our two big toes, and every paired structure in between.
4. Some regions are slightly bigger on one side than on the other, <u>and these differences translate into imbalances in how the human brain works</u>.
5. <u>These sorts of findings helped to turn the hemispheres into pop phenoms. People were tagged as "right brains" if they could draw and "left brains" if they were analytical</u>.
6. <u>The broken symmetry of the nervous system may thus be as old as the symmetry itself</u>. If so, it is an ancient puzzle.
7. <u>Instead of two matching parts of the brain performing an identical task, one can take charge, leaving the other free to do something else</u>.
8. Rogers concludes that <u>lateralized brains allowed the chicks to multitask more effectively, with each eye handling a separate job</u>.
9. At the front of the hemispheres, <u>in contrast</u>, we weave together streams of thought to produce complex, long-term plans for the future. It makes sense that these areas of the brain <u>would be more free to drift apart from their mirror-image partners</u>.
10. <u>The right hemisphere is actually more sensitive to the emotional features of language</u>, tuning in to the slow rhythms of speech that carry intonation and stress.
11. The intimate cooperation between the two hemispheres makes it all the more remarkable that a person can survive with just one—<u>a sign that the brain is far more malleable than we once thought</u>.

E. Read the passages in this section and decide whether each of the following statements is true or false.

Passage One

   Brain games for kids stimulate their restive thinking abilities, which is crucial for success in every field. The competitive world demands extreme levels of preparation to sustain at the top in a chosen area. Whether it is sports, sciences or literature; every field today demands extra special abilities to be acknowledged as a top performer. But it is more important to ensure that children do not get burdened by the competition, rather enjoy their activities. This is very important both for developing their thinking power and long term interest in the process. Brain teasers are one of the best ways to do it, accompanied by lot of fun and enjoyment.

Brain Teasers for Young Kids

The process can begin with easy brain teasers for kids like asking funny one word answers to some tricky questions mentioned below.

What would a tall chimney say to a short chimney? (Ans: You are too young to smoke.)

What clothes does a house wear? (Ans: Address)

What do you need to spot a building 20 miles away? (Ans: Good eyesight)

Which animal sleeps with its shoes on? (Ans: Horse)

What has a horn but does not honk? (Ans: Rhinoceros)

It might sound silly for adults in the first instance, but a careful study will make you realize that these one liners make kids think out-of-the-box and logically. Unknowingly and playfully, these type of questions foster greater understanding of the surroundings. For example, the questions on animals test their knowledge of animals and make them aware of their physical features. Knowledge gained such way is retained for a long time, if not forever.

(http://www.buzzle.com/articles/brain-teasers-for-kids.html)

_____ 1. Every field today demands people to have extra special abilities.

_____ 2. To make sure children enjoy the competition instead of considering it a burden is very important for developing their thinking power.

_____ 3. Children remember what they've learned from brain teasers for a relatively long period of time.

Passage Two

Michael Jackson's brain isn't resting peacefully with the rest of his body-at least not yet. The LA County Coroner is holding a portion of Jackson's brain to run further testing to help determine what brought on the sudden cardiac arrest that killed the King of Pop.

This is likely part of the reason why no burial plans have been announced for Jackson, even though the public memorial service occurred on Tuesday in Los Angeles. The whereabouts of the rest of his body are not known to the public and such details will likely not be released until a decision has been made as to the location of his final resting place.

The tests being performed on the brain are likely focusing on the possibility of sedatives or other prescription drugs playing a role in his death. As the brain hardens after death, it becomes easier for forensic scientists to determine what drugs were active in the brain at the time of death.

Now the speculation is mounting as to where exactly Jackson is going to be buried and whether or not a formal, permanent memorial will be constructed for the public to pay their continued respects. Shortly after his death, many in the media were speculating that Neverland would become a working monument to Jackson, much in the way that Graceland works for Elvis. But with Jackson's estate and assets in such turmoil, it's unlikely that something like that could be done for several years.

(http://www.buzzle.com/articles/michael-jackson-brain-being-held-for-tests.html)

_____ 4. Michael Jackson's brain was examined to help determine the cause of his death.

_____ 5. The tests were conducted to find sedatives or other prescription drugs playing a role in his death.

_____ 6. It's likely that Neverland would become a working monument to Jackson.

Passage Three

Genetic mapping, imaging technology, and psychopharmacology have converged to give us an unprecedented understanding of how the brain works and how we can affect its operation. But what does this mean? Already our brains are working differently than they did just one hundred years ago, as we respond to the barrage of media images, violent and provocative, and attend to the demands of the modern world. "Cosmetic" drugs that work in the brain to prevent us from feeling drowsy, depressed, anxious, or fearful, or that enhance concentration and memory are readily available. Dramatic treatments to repair damage in the brain are becoming common.

In *The New Brain*, Dr. Richard Restak guides you through the frontiers of modern brain science and offers cautionary but also optimistic thoughts on the direction of his work. He says that in the era of the New Brain it will be necessary to tread carefully, lest we imprison ourselves in the concept that diminish, rather than enhance our freedom. The era of the New Brain is upon us. Once a mysterious, hidden organ locked within our skulls, modern brain science now provides us with insights about the brain that only a few decades ago would have been considered the stuff of science fiction. We can now study the brain in "real time", witnessing how it functions while taking a test, practicing a craft, experiencing an emotion, or making a decision. Brain tests can even indicate when we're telling the truth or when we're lying.

Dr. Richard Restak reports from the frontiers of modern brain science and asks the relevant questions such as, is Attention Deficit Disorder the brain syndrome of the future? Is it a "normal" response to the modern world's demand to attend to several things at once? What happens in our brains when the image replaces language as the primary means of communication? How does exposure to violent imagery affect our brains? Are we all capable of "genius" and training our brains to perform at a superior level?

The New Brain is the story of technology and biology converging to influence the evolution of the human brain. Dramatic advances are now possible, as well as the potential for misuse and abuse.

Dr. Restak, author of more than 15 books on the brain, leads you through the latest research and the expanding field of cognitive science, explains its implications, and even offers practical advice such as how to:

—Understand and mitigate the affects of media images and technology on our thoughts and emotions

—Estimate the effects of stress on our brain function and how to predict who is at greatest risk for harm

—Develop the habits that result in peak brain performance

No longer science fiction or fantasy, *The New Brain* recounts what our brains are capable of—today.

(http://www.buzzle.com/editorials/8-29-2003-44780.asp)

_____ 7. Genetic mapping, imaging technology, and psychopharmacology can help with the understanding of how we can affect the operation of our brain.

_____ 8. "Cosmetic" drugs help keep people away from unpleasant feelings.

_____ 9. We still cannot probe the brain when it carries out different activities.

_____ 10. Dr. Restak offers advice on how to estimate the effects of stress on our body in his book.

F. Cloze. Fill in each blank with one suitable word.

The psychology of stress and maintaining emotional hygiene is being increasingly studied by brain and __1__ researchers. One recent confirmation of a long-held belief is that the brain __2__ "neuroplasticity", that is, the malleable ability to "rewire" its neuron synaptic connections to __3__ to extremely challenging intensive external stimuli. This cerebral mechanism is particularly maladaptive to the patterned stimuli so prevalent in repetitive stress situations that can ultimately result in physical anxiety symptoms. In today's active life, whether __4__ businessman, upscaling career woman, harried parent, or worried retiree coping with an uncertain future, the stressors endemic to these lifestyles will, over time, force the brain to adapt __5__ as only it can. However, this same process can be used to heal, as well as harm. Let's look at some of the latest strategies to undo stress' effect on the brain.

We all know the power of distraction; this is a common stress __6__ technique. Distraction is being used to good advantage in the latest computer games with the melding of brain research and the video gaming industry leading to games being developed for "emotional hygiene". One of these innovative games uses an __7__ pattern-recognition computer program for training the user to choose a smiling "approving" face from a changing grid of __8__ "disapproving" ones. As the lag time in choosing the cheerful face decreases through diligent, __9__ effort, the player's brain becomes trained to more rapidly __10__ socially approving stimuli and more effective at ignoring negative input. This practice of downplaying "hostile information" reduces social fear of refection with its heightened stress levels.

1. A. neurological   B. physiological   C. cerebral   D. physical
2. A. shares   B. exhibits   C. is   D. indicates
3. A. adapt   B. turn   C. repel   D. avert
4. A. driving   B. drive   C. driver   D. driven
5. A. negatively   B. positively   C. automatically D. unconscious
6. A. enhancing   B. relief   C. evading   D. challenging
7. A. ingenious   B. impartial   C. indicative   D. interactive
8. A. moving   B. annoying   C. frowning   D. irritating
9. A. focused   B. relaxed   C. continuous   D. strenuous
10. A. receive   B. conceive   C. perceive   D. deceive

G. Translate the following passages into Chinese/English.

1. The fact that some naturally left-handed children are forced into becoming right-handed may even result in levophobia, an irrational fear of the left. Sufferers from this rare condition find their hearts pound as if a heart attack were coming on as a result of their brains releasing adrenalin at the mere prospect of a left-oriented maneuver. They refuse to stand on the left side of an elevator, make left-hand turns when driving, sometimes even to look to the left. Psychologists believe levophobia will only disappear entirely when left-handed children—a minority in all known societies—are fully accepted.

2. 许多麻醉师和心理学家近来报道,在外科手术时,"知觉期"的次数有所增加。为使病人失去知觉而加大使用催眠剂和肌肉松弛剂,以及相应减少使用麻醉药的做法,看来是这种现象的成因。

医生们的报告表明,即使病人在手术过程中失去对事情的有意识的反应,但他们在"熟睡"时可听见手术室的讲话,并能下意识地把听到的信息体现在他们的行为和康复观念中去。

在加州大学戴维斯分校的医疗中心,心理学家亨利·贝内特做了仔细控制的观察研究:让被麻醉的病人在恢复知觉前一刻接受一个建议。被告知在接下来的一次会见中扯自己耳朵的病人大多会照做不误,虽然他们回忆不起曾接受过这样的指令。

Text B

Is Patriotism a Subconscious Way for Humans to Avoid Disease?

1. The long battle between humans and infectious microbes has left its marks all over us.

2. It shows up most obviously in the way our bodies are constructed. The thousands of species of bacteria that swarm over us cannot penetrate our multilayered skin. Entry points, such as the eyes and

nose, are bathed in moisture to help flush out pathogens. The lining of our lungs releases bacteria-killing compounds. Viruses that manage to infect cells are greeted by proteins that attempt to shred them into genetic confetti. Any pathogen that sneaks past all these defenses then faces an army of immune cells, which can devour and destroy the invaders. Immune cells can also manufacture antibodies, which allow them to launch swift attacks if they encounter the same infection elsewhere in the body.

3. This elaborate defense system dates back billions of years. Our single-celled ancestors were infected with viruses; when they got bigger they were infected with bacteria; and after they evolved guts, those guts were infected with worms. Any mutation that offered even a little protection against those pathogens had a chance to be favored by natural selection. Over thousands of generations, mutation upon mutation built up our diversity of immune cells, signals, and weapons. There was never a point at which our defenses stopped evolving, because the pathogens were evolving as well. New generations of invaders slipped past our lines of defense, spurring the evolution of immune upgrades.

4. But it is not just our bodies that have been shaped by this tug-of-war. A number of scientists now argue that the battle against disease has left an indelible imprint on our minds as well.

5. Over the past few years, Mark Schaller, a psychologist at the University of British Columbia, has been developing an intriguing theory that behavior can be just as effective as microbiology at warding off disease. According to this theory, we have what Schaller calls a "behavioral immune system". It's a way of responding to the outside world, and to the people around us, that is so deeply embedded in our minds that we are hardly aware of it.

6. Schaller and his colleagues have been busily running psychological experiments to test his hypothesis. The results so far are preliminary but provocative. If Schaller is right, this behavioral immune system may prove to have a big influence on our day-to-day lives. It might even influence human nature on a global scale, shaping cultures around the world.

7. If the familiar, biological immune system were foolproof, it would be pointless to evolve a behavioral immune system too. In reality, however, our defenses are far from perfect. Some pathogens can disguise themselves well enough to go unnoticed, and others breed so fast that our immune systems cannot keep up. Then again, sometimes our immune system succeeds too well, using such overwhelming force against pathogens that it damages our own tissues in the process.

8. Not getting infected in the first place is a far safer alternative. Scientists have discovered a wide variety of animal species that use behavioral strategies to avoid becoming sick. Some caterpillars blast their droppings like cannons so that parasitic wasps that lay eggs in the droppings won't be able to follow their scent. Sheep instinctively avoid grazing on grass near their own manure, advantageous because many sheep parasites release their eggs in the animals' droppings. A female mouse can smell the difference between a healthy male and one infected with intestinal worms. She will avoid the latter and mate with the

former.

9. Our closest living cousins, the chimpanzees, also display behavioral responses to signs of disease. When the primatologist Jane Goodall observed chimps in the 1960s, one of her subjects was a male she called McGregor, who suffered from polio. He dragged himself around by his arms after his legs became paralyzed, and his loose bladder attracted clouds of flies. Before McGregor got sick, he enjoyed hours of grooming from other chimpanzees, who picked out fleas, mites, and other parasites from his fur. But Goodall watched in amazement as the other chimpanzees stayed away from him once he became ill.

10. None of these animals has a medical degree. None of them has ever read about the germ theory of disease. Instead, they have evolved disease-avoiding behaviors, including specific responses to specific cues from other individuals, that operate on a purely instinctual level. Schaller and his colleagues see strong evidence that humans have evolved these kinds of behaviors as well. Just as in other animals, these human behaviors aren't the result of carefully reasoned decisions. They are driven by overriding feelings that we just cannot explain.

11. Our ancestors evolved strong responses to signs of sickness in others, from strange rashes to loud coughs. In some cases these signs may not actually indicate illness; a person with a dark stain across his face may not have a disfiguring disease but just a harmless port-wine birthmark. Nevertheless, the best strategy for the behavioral immune system is to overreact. Before the age of medicine, ignoring a possible sign of smallpox or plague might have turned out to be fatal.

12. Lesley Duncan, one of Schaller's graduate students at the University of British Columbia, tested this hypothesis by showing a group of test subjects pictures of two men. "Bob" had a port-wine birthmark on his face, but Duncan informed her subjects that it was superficial and that Bob was strong and healthy. "Jake", on the other hand, looked normal, but Duncan told the group that he was sick with drug-resistant tuberculosis.

13. Duncan then had her participants take a test designed to draw out their unconscious associations with the concepts of disease and health. Each subject had to identify a picture of Bob or Jake on a computer screen by pressing a key with either their left or right hand. Between pictures, words like illness and strong would appear on the screen, and subjects had to choose their relation to disease or health by pressing keys, again with the left or right hand. The computer recorded their reaction time on each trial.

14. Duncan found that if subjects became accustomed to identifying disease-connoting words with the left hand and health-connoting words with the right, they had relatively fast reaction times when they were also asked to use their left hand to identify Bob, the healthy man with the birthmark, and their right hand to identify Jake, the truly diseased man. But when subjects were accustomed to identifying disease-relevant words with the right hand and health-connoting words with the left, they responded relatively slowly when they had to use their left hand to identify Bob and their right to identify Jake. This suggests

that, for the majority of subjects, the concept of disease was associated more strongly with Bob than with Jake.

15. Duncan concludes that the behavioral immune system can respond so strongly to superficial facial disfigurement that it often is not overridden by explicit, rational knowledge to the contrary.

16. The behavioral immune system may also produce an instinctive distrust of strangers. Strangers, after all, may carry diseases against which a person has no immune defense. (Just look at what happened to the Aztecs when the Spanish conquistadors showed up with smallpox.) To see if diseases influence how we think of foreigners, Schaller and his colleagues set up another experiment. They had one test group watch a slide show about the health dangers of germs. The researchers then told these subjects that the government would be spending money to attract immigrants to Canada; the participants had to decide how much money ought to be spent to get people to come from certain countries. Another group of participants were asked to do the same thing after watching a slide show on dangers of everyday life that were not related to disease, such as accidental electrocution. Schaller predicted that the slides about germs would trigger a rise in xenophobia. Sure enough, the subjects who watched the germ slides were inclined to spend more money to recruit immigrants from familiar countries and less money to attract people from unfamiliar ones.

17. Another prediction of the behavioral immune system hypothesis is that we are more vigilant against getting sick when we are more vulnerable to disease. Carlos Navarrete, a psychologist at Michigan State University, and his colleagues looked into this issue by studying pregnant women. Infections are especially dangerous during the first trimester. When a woman first gets pregnant, her immune system is suppressed so it does not accidentally attack the fetus. In later months the immune system returns to normal and the fetus develops an immune system of its own.

18. Navarrete and his colleagues had 206 pregnant women read two essays that were written, they were told, by students. One of the essays was by a foreigner who criticized the United States, the other by an American who praised the country. The women then had to rate the essayists for their likability, intelligence, and other qualities. Women in the first trimester were more likely than those in the second or third trimester to give a high score to the American and a low score to the foreigner. The pregnant women's vulnerability to infection, Navarrete concludes, brought with it a heightened disapproval of foreigners.

19. Schaller and his colleagues have performed a number of other experiments that support the idea of a behavioral immune system. At this point the evidence remains circumstantial, and the whole concept is still a fairly speculative hypothesis. But it is one worth tracking, because its implications could be huge. Distrust of strangers or unusual-looking individuals is not something that happens in a vacuum. People share these feelings with other people, and those shared feelings may be powerful enough to shape

an entire culture.

20. Schaller and another of his graduate students, Damian Murray, tested this last possibility by tallying up the prevalence of diseases in 71 regions of the world. The researchers then looked at surveys of personality traits in those regions. In countries like Nigeria and Brazil, which have historically suffered high levels of disease, people were found to have (on average) less promiscuous views of sex and to be less open and extroverted than people in low-disease countries like Sweden and Canada. Their cultures also tend to put a higher premium on collectivism than on individualism. In other words, people who have lived with higher levels of disease tend to develop cultures in which social contact is under more control.

21. Perhaps the culture wars are, to some extent, parasite wars.

Glossary

infectious [in'fekʃəs] caused by infection or capable of causing infection *adj.* 传染的

swarm [swɔːm] move in large numbers *v.* 云集,充满

pathogen ['pæθədʒ(ə)n] any disease-producing agent (especially a virus or bacterium or other microorganism) *n.* 病原体(物)

confetti [kən'feti(ː)] small pieces or streamers of colored paper that are thrown around on festive occasions (as at a wedding) *n.* (婚礼、狂欢节中抛撒的)五彩纸屑

devour [di'vauə] eat greedily *v.* 吞食

antibody ['æntiˌbɔdi] any of a large variety of proteins normally present in the body or produced in response to an antigen which it neutralizes, thus producing an immune response *n.* 抗体

tug-of-war ['tʌɡəv'wɔː] any hard struggle between equally matched groups *n.* 激烈的竞争

indelible [in'delibl] cannot be removed, washed away or erased *adj.* 不能消除的,不能拭除的,难忘的

microbiology [maikrəubai'ɔlədʒi] the branch of biology that studies microorganisms and their effects on humans *n.* 微生物学

preliminary [pri'liminəri] designed to orient or acquaint with a situation before proceeding *adj.* 初步的,开始的,预备的

caterpillar ['kætəpilə] a wormlike and often brightly colored and hairy or spiny larva of a butterfly or moth *n.* 毛虫

parasitic [ˌpærə'sitik] relating or caused by an animal or plant that lives in or on a host (another animal or plant) *adj.* 寄生的

intestinal [in'testinl] of or relating to or inside the part of the alimentary canal between the stomach and the anus *adj.* 肠的

primatologist [ˌpraimə'tɔlədʒist] scientists who study the behavior, biology, ecology, evolution, and anatomy of non-human primates *n*. 灵长类动物学家

polio ['pəuliəu] an acute viral disease marked by inflammation of nerve cells of the brain stem and spinal cord *n*. [医]脊髓灰质炎,小儿麻痹症

paralyze ['pærəlaiz] make powerless and unable to function *v*. 使……瘫痪,使……麻痹

groom [grum] care for one's external appearance *v*. 整饰

mite [mait] any of numerous very small to minute arachnids often infesting animals or plants or stored foods *n*. 小虫

disfigurement [dis'figəmənt] an appearance that has been spoiled or is misshapen *n*. 外貌损伤(损形,瑕疵)

explicit [iks'plisit] precisely and clearly expressed or readily observable; leaving nothing to implication *adj*. 明确的,详述的

conquistador [kɔn'kwistədə:] an adventurer (especially one who led the Spanish conquest of Mexico and Peru in the 16th century) *n*. 征服者

electrocution [i,lektrə'kju:ʃən] killing by electric shock *n*. 电死

xenophobia [,zenə'fəubiə] an irrational fear of foreigners or strangers *n*. 仇外,排外

vigilant ['vidʒilənt] carefully observant or attentive; on the lookout for possible danger *adj*. 警醒的,警戒著的,警惕的

vulnerable ['vʌlnərəb(ə)l] capable of being wounded or hurt *adj*. 易受伤害的

trimester [trai'mestə] a period of three months; especially one of the three three-month periods into which human pregnancy is divided *n*. 三个月

circumstantial [,sə:kəm'stænʃəl] fully detailed and specific about particulars *adj*. 依照情况的

tally ['tæli] determine the sum of *v*. 计算

promiscuous [prə'miskjuəs] casual and unrestrained in sexual behavior *adj*. 杂乱的,混杂的

extroverted ['ekstrəvə:tid] being concerned with the social and physical environment *adj*. 性格外向的

Exercises

A. Fill in each blank with one of the given words in its correct form.

| disfigurement | promiscuous | explicit | vulnerable | circumstantial |
| indelible | parasitic | mutation | extroverted | vigilant |

1. Donald O'Rourke, MD, Associate Professor of Neurosurgery at the University of Pennsylvania School of Medicine and colleagues, were able to accurately predict the specific genetic _____ that caused brain cancer in a group of patients studied using magnetic resonance imaging (MRI).

2. They know that ice ages and glacial retreats are common because these events leave _____ marks on the land.

3. Northern Rwandan inhabitants infected with more than two species of _____ worm are more likely to be underweight than those with just one or with no infection, according to new research published September 15 in the open-access journal PLoS Neglected Tropical Diseases.
4. The first specific genetic mutation which can cause a potentially serious facial _____ has been identified by researchers at Oxford University.
5. These implicit beliefs can affect actions, such as how they vote at the moment it comes time to _____ decide.
6. _____ road users (VRUs) like pedestrians, cyclists and motorcyclists are more difficult to protect because they are hard to see, difficult to track and they often emerge suddenly from unexpected quarters.
7. This test is commonly used in criminal investigations, but as _____ evidence to strengthen the case.
8. A new study challenges long-standing expectations that men are _____ and women tend to be more particular when it comes to choosing a mate.
9. But now researchers have found evidence that supports a stereotype held by many in the United States—that Mexicans are more outgoing, talkative, sociable and _____.
10. Some species are more vigilant in risky areas, while others are less _____, and by being less vigilant, they are able to reduce their exposure to predators because they decrease the amount of time in risky areas.

B. Skim the text and then answer the following questions.
1. Have our defenses against pathogens stopped evolving? Why or why not?
2. What are the methods adopted by certain types of animals to avoid getting infected?
3. What is revealed by Lesley Duncan's experiment?
4. What hypotheses on the behavioral immune system have been tested with experiments?
5. How do you understand "Perhaps the culture wars are, to some extent, parasite wars"?

C. Read the text and choose the correct answer to each of the following questions.
1. Our bodies are constructed in such a way as to fend us against infectious microbes, which can be seen in the following except _____.
   A. the eyes and nose bathed in moisture to help flush out pathogens
   B. the lining of our lungs releasing bacteria-killing compounds
   C. viruses shredding proteins into genetic confetti
   D. immune cells devouring and destroying the invaders
2. According to the text, "behavioral immune system" _____.
   A. concerns how we respond to the interior world of ourselves

B. is something we know so little of

C. proves to influence our day-to-day lives greatly

D. influences human nature on a global scale

3. Which is not the reason why our defenses are not perfect? _____.

   A. Our immune system sometimes fail to notice pathogens under disguise

   B. Our immune system cannot always keep up with the pace of the reproduction of pathogens

   C. Our immune system sometimes damages our own tissues

   D. Our biological immune system and behavioral immune system do not work in harmony

4. The word "connoting" in "Duncan found that if subjects became accustomed to identifying disease-connoting words with the left hand and health-connoting words with the right..." means _____.

   A. predicting   B. showing   C. implying   D. related

5. Which description is incorrect on the characteristics of people who have lived with higher levels of disease? _____.

   A. Their views of sex are relatively conservative

   B. They put a higher premium on collectivism than on individualism

   C. Their social contact is under more control

   D. They are extroverted

D. Explain the underlined parts.

1. Any pathogen that <u>sneaks past all these defenses then faces an army of immune cells,</u> which can devour and destroy the invaders.

2. New generations of invaders <u>slipped past our lines of defense, spurring the evolution of immune upgrades.</u>

3. Duncan concludes that the behavioral immune system can respond so strongly to superficial facial disfigurement that <u>it often is not overridden by explicit, rational knowledge to the contrary.</u>

4. Schaller predicted that the slides about germs would <u>trigger a rise in xenophobia.</u>

5. At this point <u>the evidence remains circumstantial,</u> and the whole concept is <u>still a fairly speculative hypothesis.</u> But it is one <u>worth tracking,</u> because its implications could be huge.

Keys to Exercises

Unit 1

Text A

A.
1. retrieve 2. legitimate 3. consistent 4. insecure 5. fraudulent 6. infrastructure
7. identify 8. token 9. irrevocable 10. decrypt

C.
1. A 2. C 3. A 4. B 5. C

E.
1. F 2. F 3. T 4. T 5. F 6. T 7. F 8. T 9. F 10. F

F.
1. A 2. B 3. A 4. C 5. D 6. A 7. C 8. A 9. B 10. C

G.

1. SearchWiki 的推广有一定难度,因为我们大多数人经过磨练已习惯于快速搜索,飞快地浏览前前后后各个链接,不会花时间对这些搜索结果进行排序或添加评论。更何况它只限于使用谷歌的搜索引擎。如果你喜欢更加个性化的网络搜索,但又希望能用谷歌以外的搜索引擎或是不想做多余的操作,那么你也许会喜欢 Surf Canyon。一旦下载了这个工具,它会在某些搜索结果旁边显示出箭靶图形,表明 Surf Canyon 搜到了一些额外的相关链接。点击这个箭靶图形,那些提示的链接会被从靠后的搜索结果序列中抽出并显示,而且这些链接很可能附带有自己的箭靶图形。随着这一连串资料的持续出现,系统通过相应的算法得知返回的搜索结果中哪些你选择了,哪些你没选择。

2. Surf Canyon recently released an option for users who want long-term personalization, found at my.surfcanyon.com. It lets people select sources from which they prefer to receive news, shopping, research, or sports and entertainment results. Individual sites not listed on this page can also be added to a list of sources to use; likewise, sites can be added to a blacklist so results never come from them. Unlike Google, Surf Canyon doesn't save your history or usage profile. And if you haven't created personalized preferences using the link above, it responds solely using your as-they-happen signals, like when you choose one link over another.

Text B

A.

1. grid 2. infiltrate 3. inspection 4. vulnerability 5. disruptive 6. hysteria 7. grandiose
8. malicious 9. sabotaged 10. divulge

C.

1. A 2. B 3. C 4. C 5. B

Unit 2

Text A

A.

1. flurry 2. meager 3. dislodge 4. vibrate 5. hazy 6. inert 7. fluctuate 8. whack
9. avalanche 10. splattered

C.

1. A 2. C 3. B 4. C 5. B

E.

1. F 2. F 3. F 4. T 5. T 6. F 7. F 8. T 9. T 10. T

F.

1. A 2. B 3. C 4. D 5. A 6. C 7. C 8. B 9. A 10. B

G.

1. 周四,一些科学家说,数百万年后海平面将会下降。现今,人们往往都指责气候的变化导致了目前海平面的上升,而这些科学家却认为,这只是古老地质变迁趋势中一个短暂的插曲。他们说,从8 000万年前恐龙生活的白垩纪开始,海洋就变得越来越深,而海平面也已下降了大约170米(约560英尺)。此前,人们对海平面的下降了解甚少,对海平面下降幅度的估计是40至250米。

基于对地壳大陆结构板块变迁的更新的认识所建立的计算机模型预测出,在未来的8 000万年中,海床将继续沉陷,海平面将继续下降120米。假如海平面真的下降这么多,现在的白令海峡将成为陆地,把俄罗斯和阿拉斯加连接起来,英国将成为欧洲大陆的一部分,而澳大利亚将和巴布亚岛联结成同一个大陆。这项研究可以帮助我们理解,地质状况和冰川时期一样,都对海平面的下降起了重要的作用。在冰川时期,大量的海水可能都被吸附到了陆地上。

2. Rising temperatures raise sea levels because water in the oceans expands as it warms, and many glaciers are melting into the seas. Antarctica and Greenland now contain enough ice to raise sea levels by 50 meters if they all melted, the article said. If all ice on land were gone in 80 million years' time, the net drop in ocean levels would be 70 meters rather than the projected 120. The study challenges past belief that sea levels might have been only 40 meters higher than today in the Cretaceous period by arguing

that measurements from New Jersey in the United States had underestimated the fall. It said that the New Jersey region had itself subsided by 105 to 180 meters in the period, skewing the readings.

Text B

A.
1. idyllic 2. warped 3. buoyancy 4. vortex 5. swerve 6. perch 7. precariously 8. Seismic 9. emanate 10. freak

C.
1. C 2. B 3. B 4. C 5. A

Unit 3

Text A

A.
1. accuracy 2. ubiquitous 3. disruptive 4. pragmatic 5. proliferate 6. consolidate 7. sophisticated 8. intuition 9. burgeon 10. intriguing

C.
1. B 2. C 3. D 4. C 5. A

E.
1. F 2. T 3. F 4. F 5. F 6. T 7. F 8. T 9. T 10. F

F.
1. D 2. C 3. A 4. D 5. B 6. C 7. A 8. C 9. B 10. C

G.

1. 生物统计技术是一种自动化的、依据生理或行为特征来确认或证明一个活着的人的身份的技术。

这一学科分支通过观察和测量活着的个体或群体的有关特点来确认活跃特征或独特特征。独特的生理特性，如：指纹、瞳孔扫描图样、声纹、面孔、签名或手形都可以被使用。所有这些技术都涉及信息的登记与确认。信息登记时，个人需提供生物统计"活样本"，如指纹。它们都被电子化形式储存、加工并作为样本。

2. Scientists have identified the following three biorhythmic cycles: physical, emotional and intellectual. Each cycle lasts approximately 28 days and each is divided into a high energy period and a low energy period of equal length. During the high energy period of a physical biorhythm we are more resistant to illness, better coordinated and more energetic; during the low energy period we are less resistant to illness, less well coordinated and tire more easily. The low period puts energy into our "batteries" for the next high period.

Text B
A.
1. ironclad 2. relate 3. hurdle 4. residue 5. latent 6. invalidate 7. advisory
8. momentum 9. parameter 10. akin
C.
1. D 2. C 3. C 4. B 5. D

Unit 4

Text A
A.
1. accompany 2. replicate 3. underscore 4. debunk 5. downer 6. allege 7. woe 8. Null
9. tilt 10. concoct
C.
1. C 2. C 3. B 4. C 5. A
E.
1. T 2. F 3. T 4. T 5. F 6. F 7. T 8. T 9. T 10. F
F.
1. C 2. D 3. A 4. C 5. D 6. A 7. B 8. C 9. D 10. C
G.

1. 从古至今,让人们对人类行为心理感兴趣的是什么? 可能就是人类行为的复杂性和纷繁各异的本质。以双胞胎为例。尽管他们的基因构成相同,但他们在同一情形下的行为反应却各异。双胞胎的行为区别表明决定人类行为的并不是(至少并不只是)基因。所处环境相似的人表现出相似的行为方式。但是,即使是这样的人也不总是有相同的行为表现。那么,到底是什么因素决定了人类行为心理?

2. We now define "psychology" as the study of human behavior by scientific methods. "Behavior", as used here, refers to more than conduct, department, or manner. It includes all normal and abnormal activities of the whole organism, even those of the mentally retarded and mentally ill. The purpose of this study is to explore the roles of behavior in self-discovery and the varied beneficent behavioral patterns the individual can develop. The aims of applied psychology are the description, prediction, and control of human activities in order that we may understand and intelligently direct our own lives and influence the lives of others.

Text B
A.
1. harassment 2. veterans 3. discreet 4. anecdotal 5. notwithstanding 6. authentic

7. retention 8. downside 9. prick 10. hygiene

C.

1. C 2. C 3. A 4. B 5. C

Unit 5

Text A

A.

1. benign 2. escalate 3. elusive 4. fiction 5. looms 6. vulnerable 7. abundantly
8. viable 9. fusion 10. radioactive 11. rocketed 12. breakthrough 13. insurmountable
14. collapse 15. instability

C.

1. A 2. A 3. B 4. D 5. C

E.

1. F 2. T 3. F 4. F 5. F 6. F 7. T 8. F 9. T 10. T

F.

1. C 2. B 3. B 4. C 5. A 6. D 7. B 8. B 9. A 10. A

G.

1. 现在"核能支持者"的新使命就是消除一代人产生的恐惧和疑虑，他们说核能对人类和地球的危害比燃油和煤还小。而"核能反对者"却说，核能永远不能百分之百地保证人们不受其放射性成分的危害。铀原子在核反应堆中裂变时产生的巨大热能会驱动涡轮机发电。这一过程还同时产生诸如铯-137和锶-90之类的放射性同位素，它们的半衰期约为30年。更高辐射强度的残留物还包括钚-239，它的半衰期是2.4万年。

2. Direct exposure to such highly radioactive material, even for a short period, can be fatal. Indirect exposure, through seepage into groundwater, can lead to life-threatening illness for those living nearby and environmental damage. For now, the best scientific solution for getting rid of the most lethal waste is to shove it deep underground. Yet no country has built a deep geological repository. Governments meet protests each time one is proposed. Another option is recycling. Countries such as France, Russia and Japan reprocess much nuclear waste into new fuel. Recycling, though, produces plutonium that could be used in nuclear weapons—so the United States bans it, fearing proliferation.

Text B

A.

1. projected 2. garnered 3. package 4. parsimony 5. mitigates 6. win-win
7. aggressively 8. conjunction 9. emitted 10. exemplifies 11. amendment 12. multiple

C.
1. A   2. B   3. A   4. A   5. C

Unit 6

Text A

A.
1. habitat   2. notorious   3. extinct   4. ecologically   5. degrade   6. endanger
7. compile   8. deficiency   9. invasive   10. burgeoning   11. conserve   12. rehabilitation   13. terrestrial

C.
1. A   2. C   3. B   4. A   5. B

E.
1. F   2. T   3. T   4. F   5. F   6. T   7. T   8. F   9. F   10. T

F.
1. D   2. B   3. A   4. C   5. A   6. B   7. D   8. A   9. C   10. B

G.
1. 在罗马东南、那不勒斯西北这一带富饶的海滨区域的许多地方，把农场、工厂排出的废物带入地中海的一些河道与渔民和海滩观光者共存。毫无疑问，要使这片地方恢复到污染之前更原始的状态，需要极大的工作量。然而，对于与此处污染程度类似的一些地方，新派景观建筑师建议采用一种根治的解决办法：与其去复原环境，还不如去重新设计环境。设计大自然似乎是一种自相矛盾的说法或者是一种狂妄的行为。但伯格教授并不是简单地建议关闭污染环境的农场和工厂，而是专门研究在被污染严重破坏的环境中创造新的生态系统：改变水的流向，移动山丘，构筑小岛以及种植吸收污染物的新的植物物种，从而创造出一种最终可持续的"人造的"自然环境。

2. He wants the government to buy a tract of nearly 500 acres in a strategic valley through which the most seriously polluted waters now pass. There, he intends to create a wetland that would serve as a natural cleansing station before the waters flowed on to the sea and residential areas. Of course, better regulation is also needed, to curb the dumping of pollutants into the canal. But a careful mix of the right kinds of plants, dirt, stones and drainage channels would filter the water as it slowly passed through, he said. The land would also function as a new park.

Text B

A.
1. sins   2. voracious   3. problematic   4. niche   5. enterprising   6. exotic   7. allegedly
8. explicitly   9. fiddling   10. negligence   11. extirpate   12. preclude

C.
1. C 2. D 3. C 4. C 5. A

Unit 7

Text A
A.
1. abrupt 2. genetic 3. measurably 4. erratic 5. condense 6. breeding 7. projection
8. phenomenal 9. hybrid 10. spike 11. optimism 12. substantially

C.
1. C 2. C 3. B 4. A 5. B

E.
1. F 2. T 3. F 4. F 5. F 6. T 7. T 8. F 9. T 10. T

F.
1. B 2. D 3. A 4. C 5. C 6. B 7. D 8. B 9. A 10. C

G.
1. 但是，即便农作物产量和粮食储备能够恢复，还存在着更多令人担忧的长期的影响，它昭示一个食物价格将永远日趋昂贵的时代的来临。从政治角度上看，最有争议的做法就是从农作物生产转向生物燃料的生产。白宫在促进生物燃料作物方面敢做敢为，但是其他国家的政府或机构，比如欧盟，也为促进该新技术而确定了野心勃勃的目标。美国用玉米生产出的乙醇从2000年的16亿加仑增加到了2006年的50亿加仑。布什总统已经确定了到2017年生产350亿加仑乙醇的中期目标，直到实现政府到2030年生产600亿加仑的最终目标。巴西和印度尼西亚的批评家指责政府为了获得生物乙醇和生物柴油而牺牲了粮食生产和生物多样性。我们是否应该在产量可核实的英格兰东部地区或效率更高的南美洲种植生物燃料作物？

2. Most soils are a mixture of small rock particles and organic plant remains. They were formed by the weathering of solid rock to produce gravel, which was colonized by plants like lichens and mosses. In time, the plants died, with the dead plants producing organic humus. This acts like a sponge to hold water, helps to glue mineral particles together, and releases elements and complex chemicals to provide sustenance for the next generation of plants.

Text B
A.
1. dissolved 2. skeptical 3. decomposes 4. bacterial 5. proliferation 6. uptake 7. stripped
8. domestication 9. fundamentally 10. perennial 11. infiltrates 12. abundance

C.
1. B 2. C 3. A 4. C 5. C

Unit 8

Text A
A.
1. expedition 2. envision 3. preposterous 4. plopped 5. veteran 6. fluids 7. albeit
8. oval 9. logistically 10. terrain 11. microbial 12. resemblance 13. pristine
C.
1. D 2. D 3. D 4. A 5. B
E.
1. F 2. T 3. F 4. T 5. T 6. F 7. T 8. T 9. F 10. F
F.
1. A 2. B 3. C 4. B 5. C 6. A 7. C 8. D 9. B 10. C
G.

1. 上周,北极冰雪消融的速度突破了历史最高纪录,科学界专家警告说,到2013年夏季,北极冰雪将全部消失。

卫星图像表明,阿拉斯加波弗特海域的暴风雪将大量暖空气吹入北极,致使北极冰盖从几天前开始迅速瓦解。

因此,科学家称,北极海上冰雪消失总量已超过去年数值。由于全球变暖在北极影响的加剧,2007年夏季,北极超过一百万平方公里的冰雪已经融化。

2. Total populations of most species run into the millions and some are noticeably increasing, apparently due to sharp reductions in the numbers of Antarctic whales, which compete with penguins for the krill that forms the basis of both animals' diets. Most species of penguins lay two eggs, though the emperor and king penguins lay only one, and incubation is performed by the male and female parent alternately, once the female has returned from some two weeks at sea, where she feeds and recovers from the effort of egg-laying. Here, too, the emperor penguin proves to be an exception to the rule, for the female usually has to walk from 50 to 100 miles to the sea and then walk the same distance back again, by which time incubation is complete.

Text B
A.
1. incentives 2. exacerbate 3. seductive 4. squabbling 5. recklessly 6. ludicrous
7. colossal 8. deter 9. stranded 10. liquidating 11. evaporation 12. severed 13. drooling

C.
1. C   2. A   3. D   4. D   5. B

Unit 9

Text 1
A.
1. devastating   2. newsworthy   3. enthusiastically   4. maximize   5. formalize   6. eschew
7. intervention   8. methodical   9. originally   10. robust   11. catastrophe   12. intuitive

C.
1. A   2. D   3. B   4. A   5. B

E.
1. T   2. T   3. T   4. F   5. F   6. T   7. T   8. F   9. T   10. T

F.
1. C   2. A   3. C   4. D   5. A   6. C   7. B   8. A   9. D   10. B

G.
1. 北极熊并非唯一受到全球变暖危害的北极野生生物。科学家发现北极狐也正因冰面的逐步消失而生存困难,因为它们依赖于海面结冰才能度过严冬。

科学家在阿拉斯加追踪 14 只第一次面对北极寒冬的幼狐的行动,那里 24 小时都是黑夜,气温低至零下 30 摄氏度。其中只有 3 只依靠在结冰的冰面上跋涉几百英里寻觅北极熊吃剩的海豹尸体而存活下来,其余留在大陆上的 11 只无一幸存。

科学家称到冰面上觅食有利于北极狐的存活,因为那里几乎没有它们的天敌,食物也比陆地上容易找到。但是,新的发现引起他们对北极狐在北极逐渐消融的雪盖上生存的关注。

2. However, there is a flaw in the argument that the evolution of wheeled animals was thwarted by the insoluble joint problem. The theory fails to explain why animals have not evolved wheels of dead tissue with no need for arteries and nerves. Countless animals, including us, bear external structures without blood supply or nerves—for example, our hair and fingernails, or the scales, claws, and horns of other animals. Why have rats not evolved bony wheels, similar to roller skates? Paws might be more useful than wheels in some situations, but cats' claws are retractable: why not retractable wheels? We thus arrive at the serious biological paradox flippantly termed the RRR dilmma: nature's failure to produce rats with retractable roller skates.

Text B
A.
1. hypothesis   2. steep   3. simulated   4. highlight   5. accidentally   6. dose   7. maturity
8. infectious   9. oddly   10. wreak   11. midst   12. imminent   13. moderately   14. outspoken

15. reproduction

C.
1. B   2. C   3. D   4. A   5. B

Unit 10

Text A

A.
1. multiplicity   2. Vulnerable   3. nuanced   4. wrest   5. enhanced   6. modification, modification
7. rejuvenation   8. strand   9. steer   10. famed

C.
1. B   2. B   3. C   4. A   5. C

E.
1. F   2. F   3. F   4. F   5. T   6. T   7. F   8. T   9. T   10. T

F.
1. A   2. C   3. B   4. B   5. C   6. D   7. A   8. D   9. A   10. B

G.
1. 项目主持人在报纸上撰文指出，英、美科学家正在培育基因改良猪以期为人类提供移植器官。不孕不育症专家罗伯特·温斯顿在为英国《星期日泰晤士报》所写的评论中表示，伦敦以及加利福尼亚的科学家已经开始进行基因实验，以便为有史以来最长的等候器官移植名单上的病人找出解决办法。仅在英国，正在等候移植器官的患者就大约有 8 000 人。

2. The Sunday Times newspaper reported that the experiments would be moved to the United States following difficulties with funding and regulations in Britain. It said the pigs would be bred in Missouri. "Our US friends will benefit from our technology, and yet another British innovation will be jeopardized; the income we might have generated for Britain will be lost," Winston wrote. Some scientists have previously criticised the idea of using animal organs for human transplant, saying the technique risks spreading animal viruses to humans. Winston said his research project is attempting to breed virus-free pigs.

Text B

A.
1. tamper   2. pinpoint   3. ferocious   4. Coalition   5. statutory   6. retard   7. denominator
8. rein   9. repeal   10. rebut

C.
1. D   2. D   3. A   4. B   5. C

Unit 11

Text A

A.
1. toxic   2. infiltrate   3. surveillance   4. vaccine   5. afflicted   6. incentives   7. lowly
8. Infectious   9. parasite   10. impair

C.
1. C   2. C   3. C   4. B   5. A

E.
1. T   2. T   3. F   4. F   5. F   6. T   7. F   8. F   9. F   10. F

F.
1. C   2. C   3. A   4. C   5. A   6. D   7. B   8. C   9. A   10. B

G.
1. 电惊厥疗法(ECT)：大多数人不愿意接受 ECT。这种疗法只留给严重的抑郁症患者使用，其疗效非常高且比药物疗法见效快。这种疗法需要对病人实施短暂的药物麻醉使之入睡5到10分钟。病人进入睡眠状态时，被注入一种能使肌肉松弛的药物，并让一股微小电流瞬间通过病人脑部。病人醒来后，需要半个小时左右的时间从麻醉剂的作用中恢复过来。ECT 必须在麻醉师、精神科医生及护理人员共同的严密监护下才能实施。最常见的情况是，ECT 每周进行两次，共需大约进行 6 至 10 次，不过经过 1 或 2 次治疗后便可见效。只要 ECT 实施得当，就不会对脑子产生任何方面的损害。

2. We do not fully understand the causes of depression. Genes or early life experiences may make some people easily attacked. Stressful life events, such as losing a job or a relationship ending, may trigger an episode of depression. Depression can be triggered by some physical illnesses, drug treatments and recreational drugs. It is often impossible to identify a "cause" in many people and this can be distressing for people who want to understand the reasons why they are ill. However depression, like any illness, can strike for no apparent reason.

Text B

A.
1. hypnosis   2. alleviate   3. consensus   4. inhibition   5. compliance   6. tantalizing
7. transcendence   8. Confabulation   9. hallucinations   10. cessation

C.
1. B   2. C   3. A   4. C   5. C

Unit 12

Text A

A.
1. breach   2. ferment   3. reign   4. curtail   5. exorbitant   6. wean   7. affiliate   8. viable

9. clamor 10. proliferation

C.
1. C 2. B 3. B 4. C 5. B

E.
1. F 2. T 3. F 4. T 5. F 6. T 7. T 8. F 9. T 10. F

F.
1. A 2. C 3. A 4. C 5. B 6. C 7. A 8. B 9. B 10. A

G.

1. 现今,全世界有435座核反应堆在运行,它们拥有生成370千兆瓦电能的能力并可以提供全球大约17%的电能。许多分析学家乐观地预测这些数据还会激增。例如,麻省理工在2003年进行了一项跨学科研究,概述了即使核能增长缓慢,到2050年其数量仍可达到现在的3倍。发展中国家在此方面的贡献可以增长到整体数量的三分之一,为10千兆瓦到307千兆瓦。但是,达到这些预期量需要在45年的时间保持约8%的年增长量。

2. There are some things about energy that are difficult to understand. The fact that it constantly changes from one form to another makes energy rather like a disguised artist. When you think you know what energy is, suddenly it has changed into a totally different form. But one thing is certain: energy never disappears and, equally, it never appears from nowhere. People used to think that energy and matter were two completely different things. We now know that energy and matter are interchangeable. Tiny amounts of matter can convert into unbelievably huge amounts of nuclear energy. The sun produces nuclear energy from hydrogen gas and, day by day, its mass gets less, as matter is converted to energy.

Text B

A.
1. compel 2. jumbo 3. Geothermal 4. decentralize 5. subsidy 6. corrode 7. lethal
8. environmentally-friendly 9. vessel 10. affordable

C.
1. C 2. C 3. A 4. C 5. A

Unit 13

Text A

A.
1. Signatory 2. disdain 3. en route 4. boggle 5. tangible 6. Quintessential 7. benchmark
8. dissemination 9. vie 10. speck

C.
1. B 2. A 3. C 4. A 5. B

E.
1. F 2. T 3. F 4. F 5. T 6. F 7. F 8. F 9. T 10. F
F.
1. C 2. A 3. C 4. A 5. D 6. A 7. B 8. C 9. D 10. D
G.

1. 寻找供替代的运输燃料已成为国家挑战。一种可帮助国家减少对石油依赖的替代燃料是无水氨,它现在广泛作为肥料使用。由于无水氨的氢含量,它通过小小的改变就能够用在内燃机里,它还能用在直流的氨燃料电池中,也可以给标准氢燃料电池提供氢原料。当汽油单价突破3美元(/加仑)关口时,为了节省花费,用氨作运输燃料就变得切实可行。美国每天大约要消耗2 500万桶石油。

2. Safety and inhalation hazards—although ammonia is not strictly toxic—are major concerns. When compared to gasoline and ethanol, ammonia has a higher ignition energy, higher flash point, and a narrower explosive range when mixed with air, explosion and fire would be less likely with a ruptured ammonia tank than with gasoline or ethanol. The best features of ammonia are those it shares with hydrogen. It can be used both in internal combustion engines and in fuel cells, produces no greenhouse gasses on combustion, and can be produced from a wide variety of fossil and renewable resources.

Text B
A
1. camouflage 2. translucent 3. contraption 4. rigorously 5. mirage 6. crackpot 7. flurry
8. surreal 9. resolve 10. concentric
C
1. D 2. D 3. B 4. D 5. D

Unit 14

Text A
A.
1. catastrophe 2. prudent 3. rover 4. speculative 5. release 6. Herculean 7. abound
8. embark 9. divert 10. etch
C.
1. B 2. A 3. A 4. A 5. A
E.
1. F 2. T 3. F 4. F 5. F 6. T 7. T 8. F 9. T 10. F
F.
1. D 2. B 3. A 4. C 5. A 6. B 7. C 8. C 9. D 10. A

G.

1. 对天文学家来说,纽约市曼哈顿中心区和蒙古乡村地区之间的主要差别就在于夜空的黑暗程度。人口稠密的市区天空要比人口稀疏的地方天空亮25~50倍,所有天空景象除了最亮的以外都被遮住了。然而,杂散光不仅仅是个城市的问题。即使远离时代广场和百老汇大街,一种弥漫的光辉也充斥着星际空间。这种背景光的强度随季节和太阳活动而变化,但是天空本身总是比所有看得见的恒星加在一起都更亮。

2. Part of the sky's optical noise can be eliminated by going to a remote mountaintop, but you cannot escape from scattered sunshine and sprinkled starlight. That radiance is everywhere—including outer space. The Hubble Space Telescope, orbiting 370 miles above the ground, sees a background that is nearly twice as dark as a desert sky. Still, the zodiacal light illuminates the heavens there and obscures faint objects; it is the main diffuse background at visible wavelengths. Hubble must also contend with the dazzling brilliance of Earth below, which fills nearly half the sky.

Text B

A.

1. roam 2. leach 3. precipitation 4. streak 5. preclude 6. discrepancy 7. dilute
8. distribute 9. feast 10. contradict

C.

1. C 2. C 3. B 4. C 5. C

Unit 15

Text A

A.

1. agony 2. enticing 3. proximity 4. foregoing 5. permanent 6. profile 7. swarm
8. Counterintuitive 9. puny 10. eons

C.

1. C 2. C 3. B 4. A 5. B

E.

1. F 2. T 3. F 4. T 5. T 6. F 7. F 8. F 9. T 10. F

F.

1. B 2. B 3. C 4. A 5. A 6. B 7. D 8. B 9. A 10. C

G.

1. 从机器人保姆和水动力轿车,到狗语翻译器和火箭靴,日本的科研工作者已经在化科幻为现实的探索中积累取得了很多近于完美的成果。当前,日本出类拔萃的科学精英们正致力于攻克最伟大的科幻憧憬——太空电梯。迄今为止,人类靠着把自己"喷射"出大气层这种既费力又低效的方法征服了太空。然而,21世纪理应给我们带来一种更加从容地到达这个尚未完全开拓的太空领域的交通工具。对全球的化学家、物理学家、材料学家、航天员和梦想者们来说,太空电梯都代表着最引人入胜的概念:比任何机织纤维都更强更轻的线缆,一端系于地表,另一端消失在大气层外地球同步卫星轨道上的卫星对接站中。

2. Japan is increasingly confident that its sprawling academic and industrial base can solve those issues, and has even put the astonishingly low price tag of a trillion yen (£5 billion) on building the elevator. Japan is renowned as a global leader in the precision engineering and high-quality material production without which the idea could never be possible. The biggest obstacle lies in the cables. To extend the elevator to a stationary satellite from the Earth's surface would require twice that length of cable to reach a counterweight, ensuring that the cable maintains its tension. The cable must be exceptionally light, staggeringly strong and able to withstand all projectiles thrown at it inside and outside the atmosphere. The answer, according to the groups working on designs, will lie in carbon nanotubes—microscopic particles that can be formed into fibres and whose mass production is now a focus of Japan's big textile companies.

Text B

A.

1. configurations 2. wispy 3. robust 4. propulsion 5. torque 6. preliminary 7. deploy 8. bounce 9. rendezvous 10. interplanetary

C.

1. C 2. C 3. A 4. D 5. D

Unit 16

Text A

A.

1. Hemisphere 2. seizures/seizures 3. ingrained 4. synchronize 5. capture 6. monopoly 7. Coincidence 8. malleable 9. evolution 10. ponder

C.

1. B 2. D 3. C 4. C 5. B

E.

1. F 2. T 3. T 4. T 5. F 6. F 7. T 8. T 9. F 10. F

F.

1. A 2. B 3. A 4. D 5. A 6. B 7. D 8. C 9. A 10. C

G.

1. 迫使一些生来就惯用左手做事的孩子改用右手,可能会使他们产生一种"左侧恐怖症",一种对左的不合情理的恐惧。这种少见病的患者发现自己心脏在怦怦跳,好像心脏病在发作,这是他们的大脑一想到左向活动就会释放出一种肾上腺激素的结果。乘电梯时,他们不肯站左边,驾驶车辆时,他们拒绝向左转弯,有时甚至不肯向左看。心理学家们认为只有当惯用左手的儿童——在已知的社会中都是少数——得到充分认可之后,这种左侧恐怖症才会完全消失。

2. Many anesthesiologists and psychologists have reported recent increases in the number of "awareness episodes" occurring during surgery. The greater use of narcotics and muscle relaxants to induce unconsciousness, and the corresponding decrease in the use of anesthetics, seem to be responsible for this phenomenon.

Doctors' reports indicate that even though patients may have no conscious recall of events that occurred during surgery, they can hear operating room conversations while they are "asleep" and can unconsciously incorporated such information into their behavior and attitudes toward recovery.

At the University of California Medical Center at Davis, psychologist Henry Bennett performed a carefully controlled study in which anesthetized patients received a suggestion just before being brought to consciousness. Most patients who were told to pull their ears during a subsequent interview did exactly that, even though they did not recall having received such instructions.

Text B

A.
1. mutation   2. indelible   3. parasitic   4. disfigurement   5. explicitly   6. Vulnerable
7. circumstantial   8. promiscuous   9. extroverted   10. vigilant

C.
1. C   2. B   3. D   4. C   5. D